EDIS, NPLs, Sovereign Debt and Safe Assets

Institute for Law and Finance Series

Edited by
Theodor Baums
Andreas Cahn

Volume 23

EDIS, NPLs, Sovereign Debt and Safe Assets

Edited by
Andreas Dombret
Patrick S. Kenadjian

DE GRUYTER

ISBN 978-3-11-068295-3
e-ISBN (PDF) 978-3-11-068307-3
e-ISBN (EPUB) 978-3-11-068314-1

Library of Congress Control Number: 2019955477

Bibliographic information published by the Deutsche Nationalbibliothek
The Deutsche Nationalbibliothek lists this publication in the Deutsche Nationalbibliografie;
detailed bibliographic data are available on the Internet at: http://dnb.dnb.de.

© 2020 Walter de Gruyter GmbH, Berlin/Boston
Typesetting: jürgen ullrich typosatz, Nördlingen
Printing und binding: CPI books GmbH, Leck
Cover image: Medioimages/Photodisc

www.degruyter.com

Introduction

The European Banking Union was initially conceived of as having three legs, the Single Supervisory Mechanism, the Single Resolution Mechanism and the European Deposit Insurance Scheme ("EDIS"). Each was considered necessary to break the perceived vicious circle or "doom loop" between European banks and their sovereigns which was seen as being at the heart of the Eurozone crisis. However, while the two other legs of the Banking Union are up and running, the Member States of the European Monetary Union have been unable to reach a working agreement on EDIS, despite repeated efforts to do so. In order to examine the reasons for this failure and the prospects for resolving it, on June 14, 2019, the Institute for Law and Finance at the Goethe University, Frankfurt am Main hosted a day-long conference to which it invited senior representatives of all of the major stakeholders involved to discuss the issues and the perceived obstacles to establishing EDIS. The discussion was designed to be "Ergebnisoffen", free from any bias and starting with first principles: why do we think we need EDIS, what do we think it will accomplish and what alternatives to the current proposals as to its form could be contemplated to accomplish these goals, progressing on to the perceived obstacles to its realization and ending up with an analysis of how it might best be structured to fulfill its purpose while meeting the legitimate concerns of some stakeholders. Throughout the day, our priority was on keeping an open mind as to all the issues and focusing on solutions as much as problems. This book contains the reflections of the participants on the issues we discussed.

The consensus of the public sector policy makers was that EDIS was indeed, as originally thought, a necessary condition for the success of the Banking Union, although not a sufficient condition for it, in that it would contribute to the harmonization of protection of depositors across the Monetary Union. Nonetheless, it was recognized that not all of the obstacles initially identified for its implementation had been resolved and that a great deal of political energy had been devoted to what had devolved into a kind of trench warfare on the issue, which needed to be resolved.

The private sector representatives expressed frustration at the ostensible lack of progress since the European Commission's 2015 paper on EDIS and a sense of urgency on the part of a financial sector being asked to operate in a fragmented home market in the Eurozone which hindered the ability to develop financial institutions on a world scale, leading to higher costs for retail customers and an inability to support European industry in their worldwide endeavours. The internationally active bankers were even more unanimous than the

https://doi.org/10.1515/9783110683073-202

policy makers on the need to push forward with a solution, while representatives of local banks expressed continued reservations as to the need for a European-wide mechanism which may amount to little more than a transfer mechanism from solvent banking systems to less solvent systems.

The next two panels examined the principal obstacles most often cited to the implementation of EDIS, the reduction of private sector non-performing assets and the sovereign debt-bank nexus. The NPL problem was identified early on in the process and it was always understood that a degree of risk reduction would have to precede risk sharing. The panel on NPLs acknowledged that the problem was not yet solved, but emphasized that significant progress had been made in recent years, both by supervisors setting stricter rules for dealing with both legacy assets and newly created assets and through the action of the banks and the markets in developing mechanisms for disposing of non-performing assets. As a result, while NPLs are still a focus of supervisory attention, they no longer seem to be a threat to financial stability, thus the issue of whether they should continue to be seen as an obstacle to EDIS appears to be more of a political than a systemic issue.

The panel on sovereign debt wrestled with the issue of whether the over-concentration in EMU bank portfolios of investments in domestic sovereign debt was an obstacle to EDIS and, if so, how to solve it. The two main solutions considered were to restrict the concentration of bank portfolios, either through an upper limit or through a concentration charge, and a change in the rule granting Eurozone sovereign debt a zero risk weight under the capital adequacy rules. The likelihood of introducing risk weights to sovereign bonds on an international level was viewed as slight, so the discussion concentrated on what would happen if Eurozone banks reduced their holdings of domestic sovereign debt, in particular whether this would require or benefit from the creation of "safe assets", made up of Eurozone sovereign debt, especially such as did not require any degree of joint and several liability on the part of the EMU sovereigns. The discussion confirmed that the difficulties in designing safe assets which do not involve mutualization are anything but trivial and revealed that the ratings of such securities could well be considerably lower than the original proponents of such securities had expected, leading to the implicit conclusion that, whatever other attractions safe assets might have, they are probably not the solution to this facet of the EDIS problem and that the solution to the concentration problem lay in limiting it, most probably through a form of concentration charge.

The afternoon concluded with a consideration of how EDIS should be structured, based on the experience of the United States Federal Deposit Insurance Corporation and the political, the economic and legal situation in the European Monetary Union and the legitimate concerns of some concerned stakeholders.

We have added to this book two items published after our conference. The first is an article by a distinguished group of German economists setting forth a proposed structure for EDIS, which we believe complements the work of our conference and articulates an interesting avenue to explore. The second is the "non-paper" of the German Federal Ministry of Finance setting forth its position on the issues surrounding EDIS, which initially raised hopes that progress was possible on the issue. Recently, however, opposition to parts of it have been expressed, leading to the conclusion that agreement may be long in coming.

We nonetheless hope that the day's discussions helped clarify the issues surrounding EDIS and that this book will contribute to pointing the way towards a practical solution which will allow EDIS to be finally adopted.

Andreas Dombret
Patrick Kenadjian   Frankfurt am Main December 2019

Contents

V. Structure of EDIS

The Authors

Roland Boekhout

Roland Boekhout was born in 1963 and studied Business Administration at the Erasmus University in Rotterdam, the Netherlands, before going on to complete CEDEP's General Management Programme at INSEAD in Fontainebleau, France. He began his professional career in 1988 at Unilever in the Netherlands. In 1991, he joined the ING Group as Senior Credit Analyst at ING Bank. After working for the group in New York, Warsaw, Mexico and the Netherlands, 1993–2008, he was appointed CEO of ING Commercial Banking Central and Eastern Europe in 2008. From 2010 until 2017 Roland Boekhout was CEO of ING-DiBa in Germany. Roland Boekhout was appointed as of 8 May 2017 to the Management Board Banking, responsible for ING Bank's retail banking and wholesale banking activities in the Benelux.

In 2019, it was announced that Roland Boekhout would join Commerzbank as Member of the Board responsible for the Corporate Clients segment.

Rebecca Christie

Rebecca Christie is a Visiting Fellow at Bruegel, the Brussels-based European affairs think tank.

She worked in financial journalism from 1999–2016, reporting for the Financial Times, Dow Jones/the Wall Street Journal and Bloomberg News. That time included 13 years in Washington, covering the U. S. Treasury, the Federal Reserve and U. S. bank regulators, as well as five years in Brussels as Bloomberg's senior economics and politics correspondent. Since 2017 she has been an occasional contributor to outlets including the BBC, RTE Irish Broadcasting, the Irish Times and IMF Finance & Development magazine. She also served as expert advisor to the European Economic and Social Committee's working group on corporate taxation.

She served as the lead author on "Safeguarding the Euro: The Inside Story of the ESM in Times of Crisis," the official history of the European Stability Mechanism. She is a graduate of Duke University and holds a master's degree in public policy from the LBJ School of Public Affairs at the University of Texas at Austin.

Anita van den Ende

Anita van den Ende studied Law and Economics at the University of Leiden. Since 1 December 2017 she is the deputy Treasurer General and the director for Financial Markets at the Dutch Ministry of Finance. Before she joined the Ministry of Finance, she was the deputy Director General for International Affairs and the

https://doi.org/10.1515/9783110683073-204

Environment at the Dutch Ministry of Infrastructure and for the Environment (2015–2017). She was director of the (European) Competition and Consumer Policy Directorate (2009–2015) and deputy director (European) Industrial Organization (2006–2009) at the Dutch Ministry of Economic Affairs. From 2002–2006 she was Head of the Financial Stability Division at the Dutch ministry of Finance.

Dr Andreas Dombret

Dr Andreas Dombret was born in the USA to German parents. He studied business management at the Westfälische Wilhelms University in Münster and was awarded his PhD by the Friedrich-Alexander University in Erlangen-Nuremberg.

From 1987 to 1991, he worked at Deutsche Bank's Head Office in Frankfurt, from 1992 to 2002 at JP Morgan in Frankfurt and London, from 2002 to 2005 as the Co-Head of Rothschild Germany located in Frankfurt and London, before serving Bank of America as Vice Chairman for Europe and Head for Germany, Austria and Switzerland between 2005 and 2009.

From May 2010 to May 2018, he has been a member of the Executive Board of the Deutsche Bundesbank with responsibility for Financial Stability, Statistics, Markets, Banking and Financial Supervision, Economic Education, Risk Controlling and the Bundesbank's Representative Offices abroad. He was also responsible for the IMF (Deputy of the Bundesbank), Financial Stability Commission (Member), Supervisory Board of the SSM (Member), Basel Committee on Banking Supervision (BCBS) (Member) and has been a member of the Board of Directors at the Bank for International Settlements (BIS), Basel, until the end of 2018. Since 2009, Andreas holds a professorship at the European Business School in Wiesbaden and teaches, as Adjunct Senior Fellow, at Columbia University in New York since May 2018. He has joined the consultancy Oliver Wyman as Global Senior Advisor.

Colin Ellis

Colin is a Visiting Research Fellow in the Economics Department at Birmingham University in the United Kingdom, and has a broad range of research interests, having published articles on topics ranging from monetary policy, micro-pricing behaviour and investment to private equity, data uncertainty and credit. He regularly speaks at a variety of conferences and has guest lectured at a number of universities. In a professional capacity, Colin has also worked at the Bank of England, Daiwa Capital Markets, the BVCA and Moody's, and is a Fellow of the RSA. He holds degrees from York University, the London School of Economics and Political Science, and Middlesex University.

Andrea Enria
Chair of the Supervisory Board of the European Central Bank
Mr Andrea Enria took office as second Chair of the Supervisory Board of the European Central Bank in January 2019. Before that he was the first Chairman of the European Banking Authority (EBA) since March 2011. He previously served as Head of the Regulation and Supervisory Policy Department at the Bank of Italy, and as Secretary General of the Committee of European Banking Supervisors (CEBS). He also held the position of Head of Financial Supervision Division at the European Central Bank. Before joining the ECB he worked for several years in the Research Department and in the Supervisory Department of the Bank of Italy.

Mr Enria has a BA in Economics from Bocconi University and a M. Phil. in Economics from Cambridge University.

Edouard Fernandez-Bollo
After post-graduate studies in France at the Ecole Normale Supérieure de Saint-Cloud, Section Humanities and Social sciences, and an experience in differents branches of French civil service, Edouard Fernandez-Bollo joined the Banque de France, French central bank, in 1988. He has occupied different posts related to Banking Regulation, lincensing and Supervision. From 2010 to 2013 he was deputy Secretary General, and from 2014 to 2019, Secretary General of the Autorité de contrôle prudential et de resolution, the French integrated supervisory authority for banks, insurance companies and investment firms. In September 2019 he joined the European Central Bank to become a member of its Supervisory Board.

Martin Hellwig
Martin Hellwig is Director Emeritus at the Max Planck Institute for Research on Collective Goods in Bonn, Germany. After completing a doctorate in economics at the Massachusetts Institute of Technology, he held academic positions at Stanford, Princeton, the University of Bonn, the University of Basel, Harvard, and the University of Mannheim. He is a former President of the European Economic Association and the Verein für Socialpolitik, an Honorary Foreign Member of the American Economic Association, and a Fellow of the Econometric Society. He has also been active in policy work, inter alia as president of the German Monopolkommission, as Chair of the Advisory Scientific Committee of the European Systemic Risk Board, and as a member of the European Parliament's Expert Panel on Banking Union – Resolution.

Martin Hellwig has published extensively in many areas of economic theory, banking and finance. His work on financial regulation was honoured with the 2012 Max Planck Research Award. His 1990s publications on systemic risk and financial regulation were the first to expose some of the mechanisms that would be detrimental in the crisis of 2007–2009. His book *The Bankers' New Clothes: What's Wrong with Banking and What to Do About It, co-authored with Anat Admati was published by Princeton University Press in 2013.*

Dr. Levin Holle
Director General
Financial Markets Policy Department
Federal Ministry of Finance, Berlin, Germany

Levin Holle is Director General of the Financial Markets Policy Department of Germany's Federal Ministry of Finance. His responsibilities include the formulation of policies and strategies with respect to federal credit institutions, federal debt management, financial markets as well as anti-money laundering and international financial markets policy. He is also responsible for the supervision of the Federal Financial Supervisory Authority and the Financial Market Stabilisation Authority. Additionally he is supervisory board member of the Deutsche Bahn AG.

Prior to joining the German Finance Ministry he worked 15 years for the management consultancy Boston Consulting Group, his last position being Senior Partner and Managing Director of the Berlin office. In 1996 he earned his Ph.D. at the University of Göttingen.

Georg J. Huber
Head of the Representation to the EU Head of EU Policies
Deutscher Sparkassen- und Giroverband (DSGV)

Georg Huber heads the Representative Office of the German Savings Banks Association in Brussels with 8 employees and is responsible for analyzing and assessing all EU policy matters with relevance for the savings banks organization in Germany.

Georg Huber joined the Association in February 2014 as Head of EU Policies, where he was already based in Brussels. Before, Georg Huber was working within the savings banks organization for more than 12 years when he was employed by Landesbank Baden-Württemberg in Stuttgart and BayernLB in Munich. He headed the international business with financial institutions since July 2009, mainly with a focus on developed markets and Latin America.

Between 2003 and 2009 he was responsible for the client driven asset securitisation activities of BayernLB in Europe. This included the structuring of securitisation transactions for medium sized and large corporates as well as banks.

For more than 25 years, Georg Huber has been in lending and capital markets for corporates and banks. His knowledge in that area is completed with experiences in neighbouring business fields, i.e. credit analysis and restructuring. He is fluent in English and French.

Before working at BayernLB and LBBW, he was with HypoVereinsbank (now Unicredit Germany) in Frankfurt, Munich and Paris.

Georg Huber holds a degree of Diplom-Kaufmann of the University of Passau and an MBA of the Open University Business School, Milton Keynes, UK.

Thomas F. Huertas

Thomas F. Huertas is Adjunct Professor at the Institute for Law and Economics, Senior Fellow at the Center for Financial Studies and Fellow at SAFE (Sustainable Architecture for Finance in Europe), all at the Goethe University in Frankfurt. In addition, he is a non-executive director of Barclays Bank Europe. Formerly, Tom was a partner in EY'S Financial Risk Practice and chaired the firm's Global Regulatory Network. From 2004 to 2011 Tom was an Executive Director of the UK Financial Services Authority as well as Vice Chairman of the Committee of European Bank Supervisors (2009–10), Alternate Chair of the European Banking Authority (2011), Vice Chair of the European Systemic Risk Board (2011), Member of the Basel Committee on Bank Supervision (2009–2011) and Member of the Resolution Steering Committee of the Financial Stability Board (2009–2011). Earlier in his career Tom was Chief Executive and Chair of Orbian plc, an internet-based supply chain finance company. He also held a number of senior positions at Citigroup, including Chief Executive and Chairman of Citibank AG (Germany). He holds a Ph.D. in Economics from the University of Chicago and has published extensively on financial services regulation.

Patrick Kenadjian

Patrick is currently an Adjunct Professor at the Goethe University in Frankfurt am Main, Germany, where he teaches courses on the financial crisis and financial reform and mergers and acquisitions at the Institute for Law and Finance.

Since 2012, Patrick has co-chaired a series of conferences at the University on financial reform, including the need for and design of resolution regimes for banks, insurance companies and CCPs and other potential solutions for "too big to fail", the proposed European Capital Market Union, the importance of culture and ethics in financial institutions, the final agreement on Basel III and collective action clauses in sovereign debt issues. Since 2015 he has served on the Advisory Council to the Salzburg Global Forum on Finance in a Changing World where he served as Program Director in 2013 and 2014.

Patrick is also Senior Counsel at Davis Polk & Wardwell London LLP. He was a partner of the firm from 1984 to 2010, during which time he opened the firm's Tokyo and Frankfurt offices in 1987 and 1991, respectively and spent over 25 years in its European and Asian offices. He speaks French, German and Italian.

Slawek Kozdras
Policy Expert at the European Banking Authority
Slawek Kozdras has been at the EBA since 2015 and is currently leading the EBA's work on topics related to deposit guarantee schemes. He is a co-chair of the EBA's Taskforce on Deposit Guarantee Schemes which is currently developing an assessment of the implementation of the Deposit Guarantee Schemes Directive across the EU. Previously, Slawek worked on DGS and bank resolution topics at the Bank of England, and the UK's HM Treasury. He holds an MSc degree from the London School of Economics and a BA from Utrecht University.

Dominique Laboureix
Director of Resolution Planning and Decisions
Mr Dominique Laboureix as Member of the Board is more particularly in charge of resolution planning and preparations of decisions about banking groups coming from 6 Member States of the Banking Union and 3 GSIBs. He is involved in several policy issues and chairs the Resolution Committee of the European Banking Authority.

Before 2015, he was Deputy Director General in charge of the Directorate of Resolution within the ACPR (Autorité de contrôle prudentiel et de résolution, France) and was notably responsible for the French banking institutions' resolution planning. He has also been involved in several international committees, in particular with the Financial Stability Board and the European Banking Authority. From 2011 to 2013, he was Director of the Finance and Management Control Directorate within the French Central Bank. Previously, between 2007 and 2011, he had been Director of the Research and Policy Directorate of the ACPR, benefiting from over 10 years' experience of banking supervision with the Off-Site Directorate of the prudential authority. Mr Laboureix is a graduate of the Institut d'Études Politiques de Paris and has a masters in commercial law from Paris II University. He has been named Secretary General of the French Autorité de Contrôle Prudentiel et de Résolution as of end of December 2019.

Álvaro Leandro
Álvaro Leandro is an Economist at CaixaBank Research. He was previously a Junior Fellow at the Peterson Institute for International Economics (2017–2019) and a Research Assistant at Bruegel (2014-2016). He holds a masters degree from Barcelona Graduate School of Economics.

Nicoletta Mascher
Nicoletta Mascher is Head of the Banking Division of the European Stability Mechanism.

She previously held managerial positions in the Single Supervisory Mechanism at the European Central Bank and at the Bank of Italy. At the ECB she was Head of Section and Joint Supervisory Team Coordinator overseeing several large banks in Germany, Spain and the Netherlands. At the Bank of Italy she worked as banking supervisor and on-site inspector on a range of financial institutions and led a regional division. Prior to this, Nicoletta Mascher worked in the asset management and insurance sector specialising in fixed income instruments and derivatives.

She is a graduate of Luigi Bocconi University of Milan, where she received a Master's degree in economics. She also studied financial market theory and financial mathematics, engaging in post-graduate and practitioner seminars in international centres for monetary and banking studies. She is a chartered accountant and auditor.

Sylvie Matherat

Former Chief Regulatory Officer and Member of the Management Board, Deutsche Bank AG

Sylvie Matherat was a member of the Management Board and Chief Regulatory Officer of Deutsche Bank AG from November 1, 2015 to July 31, 2019. Most recently she was in charge of Regulation, Compliance, Anti-Financial Crime and the Business Selection and Conflicts Office. In addition to her role at Deutsche Bank, she was Vice Chair (November 2016–November 2018) and subsequently Chair (November 2018–July 2019) of the Global Financial Markets Association.

Before joining Deutsche Bank in 2014 as Global Head of Government & Regulatory Affairs, Sylvie Matherat was Deputy Director General at Banque de France, responsible for regulation and financial stability issues, payment and settlement infrastructures, banking services, and the Target 2 Securities project. She was also a member of the Basel Committee, chair of its liquidity group, member of the BIS Committee on Payment and Settlement Systems (CPSS) and of the ECB Payment and Settlement Systems Committee (PSSC). Previously, she held various positions in the private sector and at the French Banking Supervisory Authority, where she was in charge of Basel 2 implementation and IFRS application.

Sylvie Matherat studied public law and finance at the Institut d'Etudes Politique de Paris, France, and holds a master degree in law and political sciences. She was awarded the Legion d'Honneur in 2014.

Wim Mijs

Wim Mijs (1964) was appointed Chief Executive of the European Banking Federation in September 2014.

Between 2007 and 2014 Wim served as CEO of the Dutch banking association NVB. During this time he transformed the NVB into a modern industry association, positioning it as the key representative of the banking sector in the midst of the financial crisis.

Wim studied law at the University of Leiden in the Netherlands, specialising in European and International law. After his studies he worked for one year at the International Court of Arbitration at the Peace Palace in The Hague. In 1993 he joined ABN AMRO in Amsterdam before moving to Brussels to head up the bank's EU liaison office. Wim moved back to The Hague in 2002 where he became the Head of Government Affairs for ABN AMRO.

Between 2011 and 2015 Wim served as Chairman of the International Banking Federation. From 2012 to 2014 he was Chairman of the Executive Committee of the EBF. From 2013 to 2015 he was Chairman of the Board of Euribor, now known as the European Money Market Institute.

Currently Wim is a member of the Advisory Board of the Leiden Law School and a member of the Advisory Board of the BBVA Center for Financial Education and Capability. Furthermore, Wim chairs the Administrative Committee of the European Parliamentary Financial Services Forum.

Wim is married and has two children.

Arthur J. Murton

Deputy to the Chairperson for Financial Stability
Federal Deposit Insurance Corporation
Arthur J. (Art) Murton is the Deputy to the Chairperson for Financial Stability, responsible for overseeing the deposit insurance, resolution, and research responsibilities of the Federal Deposit Insurance Corporation (FDIC).

Mr. Murton also provides strategic leadership of the FDIC's international outreach regarding the resolution of cross-border financial institutions, including global, systemically important financial institutions.

Through September of 2018, Mr. Murton was the Director of the FDIC's Office of Complex Financial Institutions (OCFI), the unit responsible for resolution planning efforts under Title I and Title II of the Dodd-Frank Act.

Prior to becoming Director of OCFI in July 2013, Mr. Murton was the Director of the Division of Insurance and Research at the FDIC. In that capacity, Mr. Murton was responsible for overseeing the adequacy of the deposit insurance fund, the risk-based pricing of deposit insurance, and the research and statistics function.

During the 2008 financial crisis, Mr. Murton served as the FDIC's acting Chief Operating Officer, led the design and implementation of the Temporary Liquidity Guaranty Program, and led the FDIC's efforts to maintain the liquidity and solvency of the deposit insurance fund.

Mr. Murton received a B. A. in Economics from Duke University and a Ph.D. in Economics from the University of Virginia.

Christian Ossig

Christian Ossig is Chief Executive and Member of the Board of Directors of the Association of German Banks and a former investment banker.

He is, among other mandates, a member of the Board and the Executive Committee of the European Banking Federation (EBF), a member of the Administrative Council and Advisory Board of the German Federal Financial Supervisory Authority (BaFin) and a member of the Administrative Board of the German Accounting Standards Committee (DRSC). He heads the German private banks' deposit insurance scheme and, in this role, serves on the supervisory board of the EIS Einlagensicherungsbank GmbH.

Christian Ossig started his career in investment banking at JPMorgan in London and worked as a financial institutions expert at NM Rothschild. He then became Managing Director and Member of the Management Board at Bank of America and The Royal Bank of Scotland in Frankfurt. Before joining the Association of German Banks, he worked at the Institute of International Finance (IIF) in Washington, DC.

He studied for his undergraduate degree in Business and International Economics at the European Partnership of Business Schools in Germany and France; for his Master's degree and PhD at the College of Europe in Belgium and Cambridge University in the UK.

Fabio Panetta

Fabio Panetta is Senior Deputy Governor of the Bank of Italy and President of the Insurance Supervisory Authority (IVASS). He is Alternate to the Governor on the Board of Directors of the Bank for International Settlements. He is an alternate member of the Group of Seven (G7) and of the Group of Twenty (G20). From 2004 to 2016 he took part in the ECB Governing Council meetings, at first as an Accompanying Person and then as the Governor's alternate. Member of the Supervisory Board of the Single Supervisory Mechanism at the ECB from 2014 to July 2019.

After graduating with honours in Economics from LUISS University (Rome), he obtained an M.Sc. in Economics from the London School of Economics and a Ph.D in Economics and Finance from the London Business School.

Author of books and papers published in international journals such as the American Economic Review, The Journal of Finance, The Journal of Money, Credit and Banking, The European Economic Review, The Journal of Banking and Finance. He has been named to the Governing Council of the European Central Bank starting in 2020.

Dr Karl-Peter Schackmann-Fallis
Executive Member of the Board
Deutscher Sparkassen- und Giroverband

Responsibility for Economy, Policy and Banking Management
Dr Karl-Peter Schackmann-Fallis has been an Executive Member of the Board of the German Savings Banks Association (DSGV) since November 2004, with responsibility for the economics, politics and banking management division. Prior to this, he was Secretary of State for Finance in both Brandenburg and Saxony-Anhalt. After completing his PhD in Economics, he began his career at Germany's Federal Ministry of Economics. As well as his responsibilities on the Board of the DSGV, Dr Schackmann-Fallis holds a number of other posts, including Chairman of the Supervisory Board of S-Rating GmbH, Managing Director of the Savings Banks Protection Scheme and Member of the Board of Administration as well as of the Risk and Credit Committee of the Landesbank Hessen-Thüringen. Since 2004 he has been a Member of the Advisory Board of the German Federal Financial Supervisory Authority (BaFin) and since September 2015 a Member of the European Economic and Social Committee (EESC).

Isabel Schnabel
Isabel Schnabel is Professor of Financial Economics at the University of Bonn. Since 2014, she has been a member of the German Council of Economic Experts, an independent advisory body of the German government. Since 2019, she is also a member of the Franco-German Council of Economic Experts. Moreover, she is spokesperson of the Cluster of Excellence "ECONtribute: Markets & Public Policy", Research Fellow at the Centre for Economic Policy Research (CEPR) in London and at the CESifo in Munich, and Research Affiliate at the Max Planck Institute for Research on Collective Goods in Bonn. She is a member of the Administrative Council and Chair of the Advisory Council of the German Federal Financial Supervisory Authority (BaFin) and Vice Chair of the Advisory Scientific Committee (ASC) of the European Systemic Risk Board (ESRB). Her research focuses on financial stability, banking regulation, international capital flows, and economic history. She has been named to the Governing Council of the European Central Bank starting in 2020.

Nicolas Véron
Senior Fellow, Bruegel and Peterson Institute for International Economics
Nicolas Véron cofounded Bruegel in Brussels in 2002-05, joined the Peterson Institute for International Economics in Washington DC in 2009, and is currently employed on equal terms by both organizations as a Senior Fellow. His research is primarily about financial systems and financial services policies. A graduate of France's Ecole Polytechnique and Ecole des Mines, his earlier experience includes senior positions in the French government and private sector in the 1990s and early 2000s. He is also an independent board member of the global derivatives

trade repository arm of DTCC, a financial infrastructure company that operates on a non-profit basis. In September 2012, Bloomberg Markets included Véron in its yearly global "50 Most Influential" list with reference to his early advocacy of European banking union.

Dr. Klaus Wiedner

Dr. Klaus Wiedner is Director for financial surveillance and crisis management in DG FISMA (Directorate-General for Financial Stability, Financial Services and Capital Markets Union) of the European Commission. His responsibilities include monitoring financial markets and institutions, country surveillance, macro-economic policy, impact assessment of financial sector regulation and bank resolution in close cooperation with the Single Resolution Board.

Klaus Wiedner joined the European Commission in the mid-1990s and held various senior positions since. In particular, he was Head of Unit for Banking Regulation and Supervision, responsible for preparing and negotiating bank prudential regulation, promoting a coherent and integrated European supervision and contributing to the development of Basel standards. Prior to that, he was Head of Unit for Insurance and Pensions, competent for preparing and negotiating prudential and consumer protection regulation and contributing to the development of international standards in the area of insurance, occupational and private pensions. Previously, he was Head of Unit for Procurement, responsible for preparing and negotiating a general reform of the European procurement rules and a new defence procurement framework, and a Member of the European Commission Legal Service on Competition and Internal Market.

Before joining the European Commission Klaus Wiedner was competition expert in the Austrian Ministry for Economic Affairs.

Klaus Wiedner studied Law in Graz/Austria and the College of Europe, Bruges/Belgium.

Prof. Dr. Joachim Wuermeling

Prof. Dr. Joachim Wuermeling took office as a member of the Executive Board of the Deutsche Bundesbank on November 1, 2016. He is responsible for the Directorates General Banking and Financial Supervision, Information Technology and Risk Control. He is a member of the ECB Supervisory Board and represents Deutsche Bundesbank in the Basel Committee for Banking Supervision (BCBS) as well as the German Financial Stability Committee (AFS).

Prior to taking on his current position, Mr. Wuermeling held a variety of executive-level posts in the financial and insurance industries as well as in politics. From 2011 until his departure for the Bundesbank, Mr. Wuermeling was Chairman of the Board of Directors of the Association of Sparda-Banken in

Frankfurt am Main. Prior to that, he was a member of the Executive Board of the German Insurance Association for around three years. From 2005 to 2008, Mr. Wuermeling was State Secretary for European affairs at the Federal Ministry for Economics and Technology, where he was also responsible for coordinating European policy matters. Prior to this, he was a member of the European Parliament (CSU) from 1999 to 2005 and held posts at the European Commission in Brussels, the Bavarian State Chancellery in Munich (1993 to 1999) as well as in the Bavarian representative office in Bonn (1989 to 1993).

He studied law at the Universities of Bayreuth, Erlangen and Dijon, and earned a PhD in European Law from the University of Bayreuth and subsequently a Master of Laws (LL.M.) in Comparative, European and International Laws at the European University Institute, Florence.

Jeromin Zettelmeyer

Jeromin Zettelmeyer is Deputy Director in the Strategy and Policy Review Department at the International Monetary Fund, on leave from the Peterson Institute for International Economics, where he has is the Dennis Weatherstone Senior Fellow. From 2014 until September of 2016, he served as Director-General for Economic Policy at the German Federal Ministry for Economic Affairs and Energy. Previously, he was Director of Research and Deputy Chief Economist at the European Bank for Reconstruction and Development (2008–2014), and a staff member of the International Monetary Fund (1994-2008). He holds degrees from the University of Bonn and MIT (Ph.D. 1994). His research interests include financial crises, sovereign debt and economic growth.

I. The Policy Round: The Arguments For and Against EDIS

Edouard Fernandez-Bollo
EDIS : Unblocking the Banking Union

Edouard Fernandez-Bollo[1], *Secretary general,*
French Prudential Supervision and Resolution Authority

EDIS has been since the launching of the Banking Union in 2012 both a part of its global design and its more contentious item, on which there was no consensus about what could and should be its precise content and, even more important, about the conditions needed to get there.

There was a very broad consensus that the first step should be the single supervisory mechanism and indeed, it was implemented in quite a swift manner, given the importance of this move for European integration : not even two years and a half after the project was launched, on November the 4th, 2014, it was up and running, after completing a comprehensive assessment of more than one hundred banking groups, among them 9 out of the 30 Global Systemically Important Banks identified by the Financial Stability Board.

There was also a broad consensus that it was absolutely necessary to have in place resolution procedures to deal with the difficulties of banks performing critical functions for the financial system, in a way different from simply bailing them out with public money. So, even with the difficult issues surrounding burden sharing, that needed a specific intergovernmental agreement, the Single Resolution Mechanism became operational by January the 1st, 2016.

Concerning EDIS, unfortunately, there has never been such a consensus. So while, following the conclusions of the June 2015 Five Presidents Report on *Completing Europe's Economic and Monetary Union*, (see in particular point 3.1 **Completing the Banking Union**) the Commission issued in November 2015 a proposal to create in three stages a European Deposit Insurance Scheme, to increase resilience against future crisis and diminish fiscal risks, it was unable to go ahead with the project. This has been in particular due to reluctances to the prospect of mutualizing the risk across the different national banking systems, and thus indirectly across different Member States.

After issuing a discussion paper on EDIS in October 2016, and a reflection paper on the deepening of the Economic and Monetary Union in May 2017, the

---

1 The views hereafter expressed are solely those of the author and do not engage nor prejudge of any position of any authority.

https://doi.org/10.1515/9783110683073-001

Commission, in its Communication of 17 October 2017 on **Completing the Banking Union**- which significantly had a foreword from the President of the Commission on the need of compromise for democracy and Europe-, advanced the idea that in a first re-insurance phase, EDIS could provide only liquidity coverage and no loss coverage. It also added that the move to the co-insurance phase would not be automatic but contingent on a set of conditions, to be assessed by a Commission decision. Following this Communication and subsequent Eurogroup discussions on the further efforts to advance on the Banking Union, work is still on going on designing what could be the appropriate Deposit insurance system for a strengthened Banking Union.

To be able to make operational progress on this issue- and indeed on all the other issues relevant to the integration and strengthening of the Banking Union – what seems to be the chief lesson to draw from all these years of discussions on EDIS is that we have to gather enough good will to break the stalemate that is seriously hampering the common goal of a true single market for the European banking sector.

Indeed, progress in the integration of the European banking market has been up to now prevented by the stalemate between those who make EDIS a precondition for lifting regulatory obstacles to further integration of the banking market, and those who think that we need to have a single homogeneous market from the point of view of risk before moving to EDIS, making this integration a precondition for EDIS. We face thus the risk of blocking the progress on both objectives: making sure that the depositor has indeed the same guarantee for its deposits, wherever they are located in the Euro Area, and that the banks can benefit from synergies in the single market. And in this "middle of the way" situation we keep the current difference between the roles of European and national authorities, on the one side in supervision and resolution essentially European, and on the other side for deposit protection, solely national. This situation is clearly detrimental to all: the depositors, the banks and the authorities, both national and European.

To be able to move from this stalemate, we need to have operational ways to build confidence among the different stakeholders : it is indeed because of lack of trust about what can happen in the difficult cases of crisis that the different parties do not want to "get out of their trench", that is, to renounce to what is seen as securing its present situation. And the first precondition to build trust is to show that we hear the concerns of the partners that do not share our point of view, and try honestly to find ways to tackle them, that do foster progress instead of preventing it.

Three main suggestions could be made to this purpose : move to the first stage of EDIS, be completely open about the end result, and try to find an appropriate European/national balance.

The first suggestion is grounded on the observation fact that no one has indeed raised any objection of substance to moving to the first stage, as now reconsidered by the Commission in its 2017 Communication : purely liquidity re-insurance, with no additional public risk sharing and no automatic transition to the second phase.

And indeed thanks to this first phase, leaving losses to be covered nationally and providing liquidity assistance for national schemes if needed, one important objective of EDIS could already be achieved at a low cost: depositors will get the insurance of a uniform protection in case of failure in a very short time (for which liquidity is needed) which is their primary objective, and, on the other hand, there is room to take into account legacy and moral hazard concerns. And this will in no way jeopardize the national specificities currently allowed by the DGS direc-tive, which are fully relevant in some instances.

In fact the only argument against launching this first phase, heard from those who are reluctant to EDIS, is that they do not want to pre-commit to go further, before an agreement is reached on what should be the appropriate final phase. They fear to launch a dynamic that renders inevitable a specific end-situation they mistrust, that is mutualization of losses in one form or another.

This is why, in order to take into account this concern, the second suggestion is to clearly renounce any pre-commitment to go to an end phase. This would mean to make a further step beyond the Commission proposal of 2017, which already states that transition to a form of loss mutualization should not be automatic but subject to conditions : here it will be clearly stated that transition to the first stage only commits the parties to pursue a discussion on what should be the conditions for the transition to a further stage, with a full open spirit, that is even without prejudging that there will be an agreement on the conditions for this eventual transition. Thus the only commitment will be to pursue in good faith the discussions about the possible end-phase.

And in order to pursue these discussions, the third suggestion will be to try to find a better equilibrium in the governance framework of the possible EDIS end-stage, that according to the latest Commission communication could be co-insurance, and not full substitution of the national insurance by a European insurance. It will be consistent with this approach to thus ensure that a national component will remain also in this end stage. This makes room available to tackle some of the concerns expressed. One of them has clearly been the reluctance to completely take away features that have proven useful in the past : specificities like the IPS in Germany for instance, that can have a preventative role in addition to purely pay-box deposit protection capacities.

Another possible way ahead that could be discussed alongside the design of the end-phase could be the improvement of the tools available for liquidation of banks. Indeed improving the liquidation regime applicable to banks in a way that will make it more swift and efficient, is beneficial to all stake holders, and could help lift reluctances on what some may consider as a damaging asymmetry between resolution and liquidation : we have put in place efficient European tools for resolution but not for liquidation; This makes liquidation a more difficult path, jeopardizing in some cases the common goal of completely severing the link between banks and sovereigns as some states will be tempted to intervene also in liquidation. In this field of improving the liquidation framework, we can look for inspiration in Europe, possibly learning from the interesting Italian administrative liquidation regime that allows very swift procedures, but also across the Atlantic, for procedures like the Purchase & Assumption tool of the FDIC, which has an impressive record of efficiency. Clearly such important reforms will need to be coordinated with the other initiatives currently discussed to strengthen the banking Union, for instance by removing the obstacles to the free flow of capital and liquidity that would be no longer justified. But the important point is that going immediately to the first phase will not only deliver a clear message that we are back on the track of reaping the benefits of the Banking Union but also create immediately a space for coordination between national and European authorities that should help building mutual trust and thus be a positive factor for all other possible later developments.

This is why the establishment of the new European Commission and Parliament and the recent adoption of the Banking package, which marks significant progress in terms of risk reduction, should be seen as timely opportunities to build the momentum for an agreement on a "liquidity based-EDIS", that would represent a major step to unblock further progress towards a true single banking market in the Banking Union.

Martin Hellwig

How Important is a European Deposit Insurance Scheme?

1. Discussions about European integration routinely focus on the need for a completion of banking union, in particular, the need to add a European Deposit Insurance Scheme (EDIS) to the Single Supervisory Mechanism and the Single Resolution Mechanism that have been created in 2014. For many proponents of further integration, this is the major item on the agenda. Opponents, in particular from Germany, argue strenuously against EDIS, claiming that it is a mechanism for irresponsible redistribution. I am not convinced that EDIS warrants the political energy that is spent on it. Too much of the discussion on either side is based on a combination of ritual and self-interest, too little on an analysis of what EDIS would actually do. Political energy would be better spent on improving resolution, which so far is not working well and may end up disrupting banking union altogether.

The Discussion about Deposit Insurance as Such

2. In discussions about deposit insurance, one must distinguish between the question of whether a deposit insurance system is desirable at all and the question of who should be in charge. Some of the resistance against EDIS is also a resistance against deposit insurance altogether.

3. On the question of principle, there are two major arguments *for* statutory deposit insurance. First, it helps to prevent bank runs. Second, it protects depositors who may have no other means of protection. On the other side of the debate, there are also two major arguments *against* statutory deposit insurance. First, statutory deposit insurance is a form of government intervention in the market economy. Second, deposit insurance creates moral hazard, as was seen in the US savings and loans saga in the 1980s.

4. In considering these arguments, it is useful to take account of political economy and self-interest. The German resistance against EDIS today is a continuation of previous industry resistance against plans to introduce deposit insurance in the wake of the Herstatt bankruptcy in the 1970s. Whereas the Herstatt bankruptcy had shown a certain need for providing protection to at least some investors, the industry feared that, as in the United States, a government-run deposit insurance scheme would provide a basis for further regulation and

https://doi.org/10.1515/9783110683073-002

government interference with their business. The industry-managed schemes that we have today were introduced to forestall such interference.

5. These schemes have in fact worked moderately well in cases of individual bank failures. In the crisis of 2007–2009, however, they were preempted by the government's announcement of support for the industry. I doubt that without this support, e.g., the private bankers' association's scheme would have been able to deal with the fallout from the possible failures of Hypo Real Estate and Commerzbank/Dresdner Bank. If those two banks had been allowed to fail, Deutsche Bank would have been left to bear the brunt of the burden. I doubt that they would have been able to do so.

6. Still on the subject of political economy: Once the industry is in a crisis, the government may find it impossible to avoid supporting it. Depositors are also voters, and the political implications of their bearing losses can be disastrous. Moreover, when the entire financial system is at risk, it may be cheaper to avert a bank failure by stepping in than to let things go. It is worth remembering that at the end of the Lehman week, the US Treasury thought it better to offer a kind of deposit insurance arrangement to US money market funds because the run on these institutions that followed Reserve Primary's announcement that Lehman had caused them to "break the buck" was threatening to destroy the global financial system. If *ex post* the government cannot help stepping in anyway, it makes sense to have an appropriate scheme *ex ante*.

7. I am not convinced by the moral hazard argument against deposit insurance. The reference to US savings and loans institutions in the 1980s is provincial, in time and space. In time, because there was ample moral hazard in US depository institutions before the introduction of deposit insurance, in space, because the absence of deposit insurance did not prevent moral hazard, e.g., at Herstatt Bank in 1974.[1] In the case of the S&Ls, one must also take account of the fact that a large part of the losses had been incurred before deregulation widened the scope for moral hazard. Kane (1985, 1989) assesses a large part of the industry to have been insolvent as of 1981.

8. Among academics, the view that debt, in particular short-term, runnable debt, serves as a disciplining device, ensuring that bankers are well-behaved, has been important not only in the discussion about deposit insurance but also in the discussion about capital requirements for banks, see, for example, the Squam Lake Report (French et al. 2010), by fifteen US finance specialists. I have rarely

---

1 See Hellwig (1998).

heard this argument from practitioners, indeed one practitioner once asked "Is this an academic thing?"[2]

9. The notion of debt holders' imposing discipline on banks is actually at odds with the observation that banks are by their very nature opaque. To impose discipline, you must observe what is going on and you must be fast enough to take action before "undisciplined" bankers have taken advantage of you. Given the opaqueness of banks, this is hardly realistic. In passing, I note that the most prominent forms of wholesale funding of banks, repo loans and asset-backed commercial paper, provide investors with protection through collateral, so they do not even have to worry about the borrower's solvency.

10. Opaqueness of banks is unavoidable. Bank lending is based on the collection of information that is not freely available; bank debt is viable because diversification across loans contributes to making borrower-specific risks relatively unimportant for the overall earnings of the bank (Diamond 1984, Gorton 2010). Because loan-specific information is not widely available, loans can only be traded at large discounts, if at all. In the absence of market valuations, outsiders are left guessing at what the bank's assets may be worth and what this implies for their liabilities. In this guessing game, the arrival of new information, or even noise, can easily lead to runs and panics as every investor wants to be the first to exit when the news is bad.

11. Whereas the discipline theory of bank funding by deposits and other forms of short-term debt accords with the complaint that deposit insurance is an unwarranted form of government meddling, the opaqueness view actually calls for deposit insurance as a basis for avoiding unwarranted runs (Gorton 2010). I am not convinced that all runs are unwarranted, but I share the view that runs are a costly way to react to negative information (Rochet and Vives 2004). Moreover, the collective-action problems involved in runs and the external effects of bank failures, in particular bank failures from runs, on the rest of the financial system, provide a *prima facie* argument to the effect that market outcomes are not efficient and can be improved upon by government intervention (Diamond and Dybvig 1983). This being said, I also consider it important that the protection of banks, as is provided by deposit insurance, should not end up preventing market exit when banks perform poorly. For individual banks, the risk of being forced to exit provides incentives for proper creditworthiness assessments of loan applicants. For the system as a whole, exit is needed when there is excess capacity in the market and banks cannot earn profits unless they take excessive risks (ASC 2012a, b, Admati and Hellwig 2013a, Ch. 11).

---

2 For an extensive criticism of the underlying theory, see Admati and Hellwig (2013b).

12. Given the developments of the past decade, the discussion about deposit insurance is somewhat anachronistic. In the financial crisis of 2007–2009 and again in the various European crises, we have seen the protection of many holders of debt instruments other than deposits, with amounts far in excess of the €100.000 limit for depositor protection. Even subordinate and hybrid debt instruments, i.e., instruments that had been used as Tier 2 Equity, were fully bailed out. In the case of the German bank Hypo Real Estate, the beneficiaries of the bailout included not only Allianz and Deutsche Bank, but also the established churches, public television organizations, pension institutions, and municipalities.

The Discussion about EDIS

13. The 2012 report "Forbearance, resolution, and deposit insurance" of the Advisory Scientific Committee of the European Systemic Risk Board (ASC 2012a) argued strongly in favour of transferring supervision and resolution from the national to the European level; at the same time, this report suggested that a common deposit insurance scheme was less urgent. As Chair of the ASC and lead author of the report, I thought that a single supervisory mechanism was important in order to end, or at least reduce, the prevailing procrastination of authorities in dealing with problem banks. I also thought that a single resolution mechanism was important because a supervisor who recognizes problems is likely to be at a loss on how to deal with them if there is no viable resolution mechanism.[3] Banking union in supervision and resolution were needed in order to deal with existing, acute problems. In contrast, there seemed to be no acute problem that seemed to require banking union in deposit insurance.

14. Deposit insurance has been on the Commission's agenda for a long time, much longer than supervision and resolution. I have always thought that the arguments given were superficial, some of them even mere rhetorical formulae: The US show that deposit insurance is an integral part of a "modern" banking system. Depositors need to be protected, and, since national governments are unable or unwilling to proceed, Europe must step in. In the currency union, a euro in a Spanish bank ought to be the same as a euro in a German bank, so both must have the same degree of protection. Deposit insurance is needed to break the link between sovereigns and banks. These rhetorical formulae do not address

---

[3] In the subsequent debate about the Commission's proposals, André Sapir, Marco Pagano and I re-emphasized this point; see ASC (2012 b).

the substantive issues involved in considering whether deposit insurance should be introduced at the European or at the national level.

15. A major purpose of deposit insurance is to prevent runs. Does runs prevention require a European deposit insurance? The exodus of depositors from Spanish banks in 2012 and from Greek banks in 2015 (and earlier) might suggest such a need. However, we should keep in mind that both these runs were motivated by fears that the country might leave the currency union or that the currency union might fall apart altogether. I doubt that EDIS would allay such fears of a redenomination risk. Suppose that a country exits the euro and that, as of a certain date, all contracts under national jurisdiction that are denominated in euros will be deemed to be denominated in the new national currency. Suppose also that the national currency is then devalued relative to the euro. Would EDIS protect depositors against this risk? Or would the obligation that EDIS sets for compensating depositors itself be covered by the redenomination? The answer to this question depends on the jurisdiction and on the terms of the contract, but I would expect that redenomination risk will not be covered. In that case, EDIS is incapable of stopping runs that are caused by a fear of redenomination risks.

16. The need to break the nexus between sovereigns and banks is an evergreen in this discussion. It was mentioned in the June 2012 Council decision on banking union, but I have never quite understood what it meant. In the summer of 2012, the problem was one of fiscal capacity. Spain had at last decided to clean up its banking system, which had been badly hit by the burst of the Spanish real-estate bubble. The scope of the crisis seemed to overtax Spain's fiscal capacity, so the Spanish government applied for direct ESM assistance to banks. The Council agreed in principle, but made such assistance conditional on the introduction of the Single Supervisory Mechanism.[4] I have always wondered whether the nexus between sovereigns and banks was a matter of sovereigns' supervisory practices affecting the banks' risks or a matter of banks' risks damaging the sovereigns' fiscal capacities. In the discussion about EDIS of course we also see the interpretation that limits to the sovereigns' fiscal capacities affect the credibility of national deposit insurance and therefore the banks' funding costs and risks of runs.

17. In passing, I note that, as deposit insurance is currently designed, it is not fully suitable for averting runs even if there is no problem of fiscal capacity and credibility. In the summer of 2017, the Spanish bank Banco Popular Español (BPE) was brought down by a run as depositors feared (with reason) that the bank might

---

4 In the end the latter took so long that ESM support for the cleanup did not go directly to the banks after all but through the Spanish government, which had to assume liability.

be insolvent and wanted to get out before resolution was triggered.[5] In this episode, deposit insurance played no role because many deposits exceeded the statutory limit of €100.000. Many local governments had banked with BPE and had deposits above the statutory limit. If we think about protecting the day-to-day management of payments of government institutions or non-financial firms, a statutory limit of €100.000 is too small and leaves ample room for the managers in charge to become nervous and run. The limit of €100.000 is too large if we are concerned about protecting the day-to-day payments management of ordinary people and too small if we are concerned about institutions.

18. If EDIS is intended to avert fears that national fiscal capacities might be insufficient to bail banks out in a crisis, one must ask why intra-euro-area assistance could not take the form of ESM assistance to sovereigns, which would then deal with the banking problems. The Irish or Spanish answer to this question might be that ESM conditionality is disagreeable and perhaps inappropriate in a crisis situation that is not due to fiscal profligacy but to bad banking. The Council's 2012 decision implicitly contains the rebuttal that bad banking is not a force of nature but itself much influenced by national authorities. The Irish and the Spanish banking crises were both preceded by a decade of supervisory inaction in the face of profligate lending for real-estate development. Moral hazard played a role, not just on the side of the bankers who fueled the real-estate bubbles but also on the side of authorities that failed to step in in a timely and effective manner.

19. Given that the Single Supervisory Mechanism is now in place, the moral hazard problem in national supervision might be considered to have disappeared. It might even have been replaced by a moral hazard problem at the level of the supranational supervisor and its parent, the ECB. A central bank that wants commercial banks to engage in lending to the real economy might itself have an interest in delaying cleanups and in getting banks to take risks with new lending. If such risks turn out badly, there is a good case for having the resulting fiscal costs covered at the supranational level.

20. Coming back to the nexus of sovereigns and banks, we should be under no illusion that this nexus can ever be fully broken. Any bank operates under the law of its home country. This involves more than supervision and resolution. Home authorities can also influence the bank's behavior by tax law and labor law, as well as the law on corporate governance. In the summer of 2015, the Greek finance minister even envisioned a nationalization of Greek banks. Such measures need not actually be taken, the mere possibility that they might be taken

---

5 Hellwig (2018b) contains a detailed discussion of the BPE case.

affects the behavior of banks. For example, in many countries, real-estate lending is highly political because (i) builders tend to be politically well connected, at least at the local and regional level, and (ii) existing and aspiring homeowners are an important part of the electorate. The conditions and procedures that banks use in real-estate lending are often designed to avoid negative political fallout.

21. With publicly-owned banks, the nexus is even stronger. Over the decades since the 1970s, when they were created, the German Landesbanken have been a major source of risks in banking. Some of their losses were due to politically motivated lending. BayernLB made losses on its 1990s loans to the Kirch media empire, which the Bavarian government had favoured as a way of turning Munich into a media center. HSH Nordbank made losses on its 2008 acquisition of a share in the Hapag Lloyd shipping company, by which it assisted the Hamburg government in averting a takeover of Hapag Lloyd by a Singapore company. Right now the Landesbanken are strongly exposed in lending for investments in wind energy.[6]

22. I strongly disagree with the proposition that a euro in a Spanish bank ought to the same as a euro in a German bank. A euro that is issued by the Bank of Spain should be treated as the same as a euro that is issued by the Bundesbank. But there is no reason why deposits in different banks should be treated as equivalent if the risks of these banks are different. Homogenization of risks would require more homogenization of sovereign-bank relations than is realistically possible if the European Union does not turn itself into a full-blown supranational state.

23. Given that the moral hazard argument for allocating responsibility no longer cuts one way, some sharing of responsibility for deposit insurance seems appropriate. The issue is to properly calibrate decision making, governance, risk sharing, and ultimate backstops so as to avoid significant abuses. The notion of EDIS as reinsurance for national schemes seems to go in this direction, but the devil will be in the details. Conditionality of risk pricing seems promising but we should remember that such conditionality has not worked well in the past; who is to say that my banks are exceptionally risky? We also need to think about arrangements for ultimate backstops in a systemic crisis where potential losses exceed any previously agreed capacity of the system, ESM or EDIS.

---

6 See Hellwig (2018c).

The Elephant in the Room: Bail-In and the (Non-)Viability of Resolution

24. The discussion about EDIS is somewhat academic, if we do not have a viable resolution regime. In terms of what happens when a bank is in such trouble that it needs to be resolved, deposit insurance only matters if resolution is actually undertaken. The experience so far suggests that we are far from having a viable regime for this purpose.

25. Since the introduction of the Bank Recovery and Resolution Directive (BRRD) and the Single Resolution Mechanism (SRM), we have had one bank that was resolved, BPE. We have also had two years of discussion on what to do about large amounts of non-performing loans on banks' books, and there is a suspicion that, if accounting for non-performance were done properly, we might see many banks in need of recapitalization or resolution. In some instances where the supervisory authorities called for banks to take further write-downs on their loan portfolios and to raise additional capital to fill the gap, the banks in question have found it difficult to do. In the case of Monte dei Paschi di Siena, the government proposed a precautionary recapitalization, which was eventually agreed to by the European Commission, with write-downs of equity and subordinated debt ("Tier 2 Capital") treated as a form of bail-in/investor participation. In the case of the Venetian banks Banca Popolare di Vicenza and Veneto Banca, the government also proposed a precautionary recapitalization, but did not find its way to an agreement with the European Commission and ended up selling parts of the banks to Intesa Sanpaolo, which also agreed to provide interim funding for the other parts, which are being wound down slowly.[7] In other developments, in Germany, in early 2018, the regional governments of Hamburg and Schleswig-Holstein "sold" HSH Nordbank to a consortium of private-equity firms in a transaction involving a side-deal where the bank itself transferred a portfolio of bad loans to the buyers at a price more than one billion below its (already written down) book value. In the political arena, the transaction, which leaves the regional governments exposed to risks of clawbacks from creditors whose positions have been worsened by the transfer, was justified by the need to avoid a winding down of HSH Nordbank under BRRD/SRM rules.

26. In contrast to the case of BPE, in the cases of the Italian banks, there was no question of a run, nor was there a question of limited fiscal capacity. The Italian government wanted to provide the funding needed to keep the banks going and the negotiations with the European Commission were protracted over a

---

7 For critical accounts, see Hellwig (2017, 2018a).

long time. Resistance against having these banks enter the Single Resolution Mechanism seems to have been very strong.

27. In fact, the BRRD and SRM Regulation have substantial weaknesses.[8] First, for institutions like Deutsche Bank or BNP Paribas, which have systemically relevant operations in multiple jurisdictions, the authorities of the different jurisdictions have not accepted the principle of a single-point-of-entry resolution; if such an institution needs to be resolved, different authorities will enter in different jurisdictions and destroy the viability of operations that have been carried out in an integrated manner in different jurisdictions.

Second, the BRRD has no rules for the provision of liquidity/funding in resolution or in a process of winding down. BPE had to be sold overnight to Banco Santander because, with an ongoing run of depositors, the Single Resolution Board would have been unable to forestall a default on the next day. Whereas the BRRD maintains a fiction of a resolution authority carefully choosing between different resolution tools, in fact the authority may not have the time to so because there is no funding.[9] In contrast, in the United States, the Federal Deposit Insurance Corporation maintains payments, possibly with interim funding from the US Treasury, and when the resolution process ends, it imposes clawbacks on uninsured/unsecured creditors and/or a levy on the rest of the industry.[10]

Third, the BRRD has no rules for the case where the exceptions from bail-in are so extensive that existing assets are insufficient. To be sure, the BRRD stipulates minimum requirements for bail-in-able liabilities, but for example in the case of Anglo-Irish Bank, these minimum requirements would not have been sufficient to cover the bank's losses. The BRRD was introduced with a promise that taxpayers would never again be made to pay for banks' losses. At the time, any suggestion that a fiscal backstop might be needed was therefore treated as

---

8 For the following, see Hellwig (2014).

9 See Hellwig (2018b).

10 The funding problem also concerns the winding down of a bank. The standard insolvency law principle that old debt is frozen and new debt is privileged over old debt is problematic because so much of a bank's debt is short-term. If this debt is frozen, there can be strong systemic effects, as in the case of Reserve Primary breaking the buck and triggering a run on money market funds after the Lehman bankruptcy. If the short-term debt is not frozen, funding needs are so large that investors may consider new debt to be too risky. The problem is exacerbated by the fact that the winding down of a loan portfolio takes time, on the order of ten to fifteen years, if further destruction of value is to be avoided. Because of these considerations, the Italian government dealt with the Venetian banks outside of standard insolvency law, with a guarantee to Intesa, which provided the funding. The outcome effectively provides a bailout to the senior unsecured creditors of the banks. See Hellwig (2018a).

politically incorrect. The approach is understandable, but I am afraid that the lack of legislation of the matter will be unhelpful in a major crisis.

28. These "practical" shortcomings of the BRRD and SRM Regulation are very important, but they probably are not the reason why national authorities and banks are trying to avoid resolution under the new rules. On the side of banks, as with all other firms, resistance against resolution is as natural as resistance against bankruptcy: As long as you are in charge, kicking the can down the road is attractive – perhaps something will come up and make the bank viable again. On the side of supervisory authorities and governments, the same reflex might explain why the Spanish and the Italian authorities looked the other way when cajas and banks sold preferred stock and subordinated debt to unsophisticated retail investors; it might also explain why the German authorities procrastinated for so long on the need for HSH Nordbank, BremenLB and NordLB to acknowledge large losses on shipping loans.

29. A key political issue involves the principle of bail-in. With non-financial companies, bail-in, i.e., the participation of creditors in losses that exceed the company's equity, is taken as a matter of course. With banks, bail-in is regarded as politically illegitimate in many polities. The Brussels-imposed bail-ins of subordinated debt in the Italian banks caused public outrage in Italy and contributed to the 2018 election results' causing a change of government. When in 2013 equity and subordinated debt in Slovenian banks were bailed in, not only was the bail-in contested in the courts, but public prosecutors started criminal investigations of the officials in charge. The bail-in of equity and subordinated debt in BPE is also being contested in the courts. Whereas the BRRD stipulates that resolution should not make any creditor worse off than in an insolvency, the overnight sale to Santander has foreclosed any means of verifying this condition; moreover, the sale itself and the bail-in took place on the basis of a valuation that the auditors themselves called "provisional", because the available time had been very short.

30. To some extent, these developments are an example of frictions associated with the introduction of new legal rules. In law, as well as taxation, new rules are often deemed to be bad, and old rules good. From the perspective of traditional insolvency law, the very introduction of bank resolution as a separate procedure is an outrage. Whereas write-downs of equity, junior and senior debt, in reverse order of priority, are treated as natural in bankruptcy, the imposition of such write-downs outside of bankruptcy is criticized as an infringement of private property, a violation of the investors' constitutional rights. As an economist observing such discussions, I have often been amazed at the insolvency lawyers' ability to elevate bankruptcy procedures and bankruptcy rules to the level of fundamental rights and wondered whether the real issue at stake wasn't the

human capital of the specialists.[11] The fact that the constitutional protection of private property does not extend to situations where the owner's use of this property imposes a danger on society is easily glossed over, as is the fact that bank resolution as an alternative to bankruptcy is intended to avert the very substantial damage that a bankruptcy of a systemically important bank can cause.[12]

31. There is more to the unrest, however, than merely the quirks of adjustment to a new set of rules. Resistance from the affected parties and their advocates resonates with the public, locally, regionally, and nationally, which is one reason why member state governments actually prefer bailouts to resolution with bail-ins. I see several reasons for the difference in reactions to creditors' losses in non-financial companies. First, whereas with non-financial companies, creditors tend to be specialists, banks or suppliers, for whom a risk of losses is deemed to be part of the business, with banks, many creditors are ordinary people with whom the public at large finds it easier to sympathize. Second, the effect is reinforced if at least some of the debt is a result of mis-selling, especially with banks selling their own junior debt or preferred stock as perfectly riskless. Third, the outrage is reinforced if the authorities are perceived as being co-responsible for the banks' difficulties. Such a view arises naturally in countries with a tradition of close government-bank relations, with loose supervision and banks' investments attuned to the authorities' wishes. If the authorities have tolerated the mis-selling of risky claims by banks, the outrage will be that much greater.

32. In the context of banking union, the discontent is reinforced by the fact that the rules for bail-in are based on a European directive, and the application of the rules is overseen by the European Commission. If the national government proposes a precautionary recapitalization and the Commission's state aid control insists on some private-sector participation or some bailing in of investors, it is easy to generate populist outrage against the European rules. The fact that, prior to the introduction of the BRRD and the SRM, some countries had enormous bailouts of banking systems with taxpayer money, in the case of Germany more than € 70 billion, adds to the sense of outrage and unfairness.

33. To conclude: I firmly believe that monetary union needs the banking union. Banks are a key part of the monetary transmission mechanism. Unless the resolution mechanism becomes viable, politically as well as technically, I see a danger that banking systems in the euro area will remain unhealthy and that financial stability considerations will continue to impose undue constraints on

---

11 For an example of such a discussion, see Juristentag (2010).

12 In the 2010 discussion mentioned in the preceding footnote, this point was forcefully made by the constitutional-law scholar Wolfram Höfling; he pointed to the fact that, under the German constitution, the substance and limits of private ownership rights are determined by general laws.

monetary policy. Given this concern, I believe that political energy, which is after all a scarce resource, would be much better spent on making resolution viable than on adding deposit insurance to the existing two pillars of banking union. Dreams of completing banking union by adding EDIS will prove to be pipe dreams if, meanwhile, populist revulsion against bail-in and resolution endangers the banking union altogether.

References

Admati, Anat R., and Martin F. Hellwig (2013a), *The Bankers' New Clothes: What's Wrong with Banking and What to Do about It,* Princeton University Press, Princeton, N.J.

Admati, Anat R., and Martin F. Hellwig (2013b), "Does Debt Discipline Bankers? An Academic Myth about Bank Indebtedness", Rock Center for Corporate Governance at Stanford University, Working Paper No. 132.

ASC (2012a), "Forbearance, resolution, and deposit insurance", Report No. 1 of the Advisory Scientific Committee of the European Systemic Risk Board, Frankfurt.

ASC (2012b), "A contribution from the Chair and Vice-Chairs of the Advisory Scientific Committee to the discussion on the European Commission's banking union proposals", Report No. 2 of the Advisory Scientific Committee of the European Systemic Risk Board, Frankfurt.

Diamond, Douglas W., (1984), "Financial Intermediation and Delegated Monitoring," *Review of Economic Studies* 51, 193–414.

Diamond, Douglas W., and Phillip H. Dybvig (1983), "Bank Runs, Deposit Insurance, and Liquidity," *Journal of Political Economy* 91, 401–419.

French, Kenneth, Martin N. Baily, John Y. Campbell, John H. Cochrane, Douglas W. Diamond, Darrell Duffie, Anil K Kashyap, Frederic S. Mishkin, Raghuram G. Rajan, David S. Scharfstein, Robert J. Shiller, Hyun Song Shin, Matthew J. Slaughter, Jeremy C. Stein, and René M. Stulz (2010), *The Squam Lake Report: Fixing the Financial System,* Princeton University Press.

Gorton, Gary B (2010), Slapped by the Invisible Hand: The Panic of 2007, Oxford University Press.

Hellwig, Martin H. (1998), "Banks, Markets, and the Allocation of Risks", *Journal of Institutional and Theoretical Economics* (JITE) 154, 328–351.

Hellwig, Martin F. (2014), Yes Virginia, There is a European Banking Union! But It May Not Make Your Wishes Come True, in: Austrian National Bank, *Towards a European Banking Union: Taking Stock,* 42nd Economics Conference 2014, 156–181.

Hellwig, Martin F. (2017), "Precautionary Recapitalisations: Time for a Review", Report to the European Parliament's Economic and Monetary Affairs Committee, http://www.europarl.europa.eu/RegData/etudes/IDAN/2017/602089/IPOL_IDA(2017)602089_EN.pdf; also available as Preprint 2017/14, Max Planck Institute for Research on Collective Goods, Bonn 2017.

Hellwig, Martin F. (2018a), "Competition Policy and Sector-Specific Regulation in the Financial Sector", Preprint 2018/07, Max Planck Institute for Research on Collective Goods, Bonn 2018.

Hellwig, Martin F. (2018b), "Valuation Reports in the Context of Banking Resolution", Report to the European Parliament's Economic and Monetary Affairs Committee, http://www.

europarl.europa.eu/RegData/etudes/IDAN/2018/624417/IPOL_IDA(2018)624417_EN.pdf, also available as Preprint 2018/06, Max Planck Institute for Research on Collective Goods, Bonn 2018.

Hellwig, Martin F. (2018c), "Germany and the Financial Crises 2007–2017, Case Study on a Past Crisis: The Case of Germany", Paper presented at the fourth Annual Macroprudential Conference of the Swedish Riksbank, June 2018, https://www.riksbank.se/globalassets/media/konferenser/2018/germany-and-financial-crises-2007-2017.pdf

Juristentag (2010), Verhandlungen des 68. Deutschen Juristentags Berlin, Abt. Wirtschaftsrecht: Finanzmarktregulierung – Welche Regelungen empfehlen sich für den deutschen und europäischen Finanzsektor?, Verlag C.H. Beck, München. (Financial Regulation – What Rules for the German and European Financial Sector? Proceedings of the 68th Annual Congress of the German Legal Profession).

Kane, Edward J. (1985), *The Gathering Crisis in Federal Deposit Insurance*, MIT-Press, Cambridge, USA.

Kane, Edward J. (1989), *The S & L Insurance Mass, How Did It Happen?* Urban Institute Press, Washington.

Rochet, J.-C., and X. Vives (2004), "Coordination Failures and the Lender of Last Resort: Was Bagehot Right After All?" Journal of the European Economic Association, 2(6): 1116–1147.

Slawek Kozdras

The EBA's Emerging Proposals to Improve the EU Depositor Protection Framework

1. Introduction and background

The well-documented Northern Rock deposit run of 2007, where within a few months the bank lost half of its £23bn of deposits, cast light on the importance of unequivocal and unconditional depositor protection. The events of the ensuing months, and the spread of the global financial crisis, led the European Council to agree in October 2008 'that it is a priority to restore confidence and proper functioning of the financial sector [and it undertakes to take] all necessary measures to protect the deposits of individual savers'. The Council also 'welcomed the intention of the Commission to bring forward urgently an appropriate proposal to promote convergence of deposit guarantee schemes'[1] (DGSs).

Twelve years later, in 2019, the European Banking Authority (EBA), itself born out of the financial crisis, is reviewing the depositor protection framework introduced as a direct response to the dramatic events of 2007 and 2008, drawing on lessons learned since then. The review will result in three EBA so-called opinions addressed to the European Commission (Commission), the first of which, on eligibility of deposits, coverage level and cooperation between deposit guarantee schemes (DGSs), was published on 8 August 2019. It included 43 proposals, of which 28 recommend an amendment of the Deposit Guarantee Schemes Directive (DGSD) or to related products such as EBA guidelines, or express a need to study a particular topic further, while the other 15 require no such amendments. The other two opinions in this trilogy – on DGS payouts, and DGS funding and uses of DGS funds – were still being prepared at the time this article was going to print. They are likely to include a similar number of proposals and so across all three opinions the EBA will likely propose about 100 amendments to the current EU legal framework.

While this article focuses on EBA's proposals to improve the current DGSD, such proposals may also be indirectly relevant for the ongoing discussions concerning the European Deposit Insurance Scheme (EDIS). The article starts with a short historical background of the EU depositor protection framework, including the genesis of EDIS, showing the role previous reviews of the depositor

---

1 https://eur-lex.europa.eu/legal-content/EN/TXT/PDF/?uri=CELEX:32009L0014&from=EN

https://doi.org/10.1515/9783110683073-003

protection framework done by the Commission have played in shaping the legislative proposals adopted later. It then presents a brief summary of bank and credit union failures since the implementation of the revised DGSD until mid-2019 serving as an important empirical base for the analysis of the implementation and performance of the current framework. Finally, and most importantly, it outlines the results of the first of the three EBA opinions, as well as the key topics to be addressed by the other two opinions.

1.1 Historical background

The section below briefly outlines major milestones in the evolution of the current framework, and thus, the role that reviews of the implementation of previous amendments to the DGSD have played in shaping future reiterations of the framework.

The first EU Deposit Guarantee Schemes framework was introduced in 1994. Its main features included a harmonized coverage level at ECU 20,000 per depositor, a requirement to cover depositors at branches set up by credit institutions in other Member States and a repayment period of maximum three months. The first Directive aimed at ensuring the existence of a DGS in each Member State and a harmonized minimum level of depositor protection, wherever deposits are located in the EU.

Eleven years after the introduction of the first DGS framework, the Commission performed a review of the Directive, assessing whether the existing rules were still fit for purpose given changing market conditions and further integration of the European banking sector[2]. The review was based on a consultation process amongst stakeholders, which revealed substantial differences between Member States' coverage levels per depositor and how DGSs were financed. The review assessed a number of topics, for example the definition of a deposit and the scope of coverage, the introduction of risk-based contributions, how to improve depositor information, the deadline for reimbursement and the idea of a Pan-European/ regional DGS. Although the Commission highlighted in its review a substantial number of areas where there were deficiencies, at the time, in November 2006, and so two years before the crisis, it took the view that many improvements could be achieved in the short run without the need to change the existing Directive,

---

2 See http://www.europarl.europa.eu/RegData/docs_autres_institutions/commission_europee nne/com/2006/0729/COM_COM(2006)0729_EN.pdf

providing some recommendations and interpretative guidance on a number of issues.

When the global financial crisis hit the European banking sector in 2008-2009, the deficiencies revealed by the review three years earlier resurfaced. An amendment to the 1994 Deposit Guarantee Schemes Directive was subsequently adopted in March 2009 and harmonised arguably two most important elements of the depositor protection framework – how much is protected (up to EUR 100,000 per depositor) and how quickly depositors regain access to their money (20 working days). The amendment also required the Commission to analyse and prepare a report on a plethora of related issues, including 'the determination of contributions to the [DGSs], the effectiveness of cross-border cooperation between [DGSs], and emergency payout mechanisms[3] [...] upon the application of the affected depositor, within no more than three days of such application'. It also required further assessment of 'certain temporarily increased account balances' and 'set-offs and counterclaims'.

Consequently, in July 2010, the Commission submitted a report reviewing the amended DGSD[4] to the European Parliament and to the Council confirming that the coverage level of EUR 100,000 is appropriate. It also recommended the extension of coverage to all enterprises (not just SMEs) striving to simplify and harmonise the system to ensure faster payouts. It also recommended that coverage should not be extended to local authorities. Underlining the importance of faster payouts, the Commission hinted at reducing the payout period to seven days and argued against the need for emergency payout mechanisms, as it is 'much more efficient to ensure the necessary conditions to achieve a much faster standard payout'. It also included an assessment of a 'single pan-EU [DGS]' with mutual borrowing facility as 'the first step to establishing a pan-EU scheme in the future'. Shortly thereafter, the Commission issued a proposal for a revised DGSD.

In 2014, the depositor protection framework underwent further, more extensive, but arguably less fundamental amendments, including further shortening of the repayment period (gradually decreasing to 7 working days by 2024) and the introduction of the requirement to set up ex-ante DGS funds, the introduction of risk-based contributions, as well as the introduction of a standardized information sheet and a role for the host DGS in the repayment of depositors at branches (on behalf of the home DGS). The list of deposits excluded from repayment by a DGS was extended and the type of deposits that may be granted higher protection

---

3 The 'emergency payout mechanism' was the term used for what became the cost of living payout in the recast DGSD of 2014.
4 See https://eur-lex.europa.eu/legal-content/EN/TXT/PDF/?uri=CELEX:52010DC0369&from=EN.

levels were further clarified (amongst which temporary high balances resulting from real estate transactions relating to private residential properties). The recast DGSD also included a voluntary mutual borrowing facility between DGSs, previously outlined in the Commission review in 2010 as the first step towards a pan-EU DGS. A fully-fledged EDIS was proposed by the Commission a year later, as one of the three pillars of the banking union.

The recast DGSD, also included an explicit requirement for the Commission, supported by EBA, to 'submit to the European Parliament and to the Council a report on the progress towards the implementation of the DGSD'. The report was to be finalised in 2019 – ten years after the introduction of the harmonised coverage level of EUR 100,000. To support the Commission in meeting its obligation to review the recast DGSD, the EBA committed to drafting three opinions, including this opinion on the deposit guarantee scheme (DGS) payouts with the aim of proposing recommendations for amendments, based on the experience gained by deposit guarantee schemes (DGS) and designated authorities (DGSDA) during the years of application of the DGSD.

1.2 Credit institution and credit union failures since the adoption of the recast DGSD

The EBA has been monitoring credit institution and credit union failures since early 2015. The EBA is aware of 79 credit institution and credit union failures in the European Union (EU) in the period between 2015 to August 2019 (28 in 2015, 21 in 2016, 19 in 2017, 9 in 2018 and 2 in 2019). Within the broader set of failures, the number of liquidation cases has decreased in the last four and a half years (17 in 2015, 21 in 2016, 18 in 2017, 8 in 2018 and 2 in 2019) (see Figure 1). In total, during that period, liquidations of credit institutions and/or credit unions occurred in 20 Member States. In the period from 2015 to August 2019, most failures occurred in the UK (15), Italy (12), Poland (12), Lithuania (6), and Hungary (5).

Figure 1: Number of liquidations and resolutions of credit institutions and credit unions in the EU (2015-Aug 2019)

Three of these countries (UK, Poland and Lithuania) have a large number of credit unions, which failed more often than credit institutions in those jurisdictions during that period. Although credit unions make up a small proportion of total deposit-taking institutions in the EU, of the 65 liquidation in the presented period, 34 were credit unions and 31 were credit institutions. Member States where no failures occurred between 2015 and August 2019 are Bulgaria, Finland, France, the Netherlands, Romania, Slovakia, Slovenia and Sweden.

While payout cases are operationally challenging, in most cases outlined above, they did not create major issues. However, there have been a number of cases that, due to their complexity or specific idiosyncratic circumstances, highlighted important gaps and/or inconsistencies in the current framework. Together with the analysis of the implementation of the DGSD, these real-life cases provided an empirical basis for drawing lessons on the performance of the current depositor protection framework.

2. EBA's work on the review of the implementation of the DGSD

2.1 Subject of the review

The Deposit Guarantee Schemes Directive (DGSD) requires that the Commission, "supported by EBA, shall submit to the European Parliament and to the Council a report on the progress towards the implementation of" the DGSD. That report "should, in particular, address:

a. the ex ante funds target level for deposit guarantee schemes (DGSs) "on the basis of covered deposits, with an assessment of the appropriateness of the percentage set, taking into account the failure of credit institutions in the EU in the past";

b. "the impact of alternative measures used in accordance with Article 11(3) on the protection of the depositors and consistency with the orderly winding up proceedings in the banking sector";

c. the DGSD implementation's "impact on the diversity of banking models";

d. "the adequacy of the current coverage level for depositors";

e. whether or not these matters "have been dealt with in a manner that maintains the protection of depositors."

The EBA committed to fulfilling this mandate by submitting three opinions to the Commission, on:

– eligibility of deposits, coverage level and cooperation between DGSs (published on 8 August 2019),

– DGS payouts (to be published in October 2019), and

– DGS funding and uses of DGS funds to be published later in 2019.

Table 1, below, provides a list of topics analysed in the three EBA opinions.

Table 1: Topics covered by the EBA opinions on the DGSD implementation.

Opinion on eligibility of deposits, coverage level and cooperation between DGSs	Opinion on DGS payouts	Opinion on DGS funding and uses of DGS funds
Home-host cooperation and cooperation agreements:	**Unavailability of deposits:**	**Target level and funding:**
The EBA's role in DGS cooperation agreements	Unavailability of deposits and the institution's 'financial circumstances'	Target level percentage and target level basis
Sharing of data between DGSs	Current prospect of repaying deposits and supervisory moratoria	Raising contributions after reaching the target level
Temporary high balances in cross-border payouts	**DGS payouts and money-laundering/financing of terrorism concerns:**	Raising contributions when available means fall below the target level
Transfer of contributions:	Treatment of cases where there is a suspicion of ML/TF	DGS's control of DGS funds
General considerations in relation to credit institutions changing DGS affiliation	Responsibilities of different authorities in a DGS payout process	Definition of available financial means
Considerations in relation to third country branches	Informing depositors in AML-related cases	**Contributions from third country branches:**
DGSs' cooperation with various stakeholder	Cooperation between relevant AML/CFT and DGS authorities	Approach to third county branches' contributions
Coverage level	**The payout process:**	Method for calculating third country branches' DGS contributions
Current list of exclusions from eligibility, including issues in relation to:	Repayment period	**Payment commitments:**
Financial institutions and investment firms	Payout method	Approach to payment commitments

Opinion on eligibility of deposits, coverage level and cooperation between DGSs	Opinion on DGS payouts	Opinion on DGS funding and uses of DGS funds
Pension schemes and public authorities	Identification of depositors and representatives	Irrevocability of payment commitments
Deposits the holder of which was never identified	Provision of information to depositors during payouts	Accounting and prudential treatment of payment commitments
Coverage of deposits at EU credit institutions' branches in third countries	End of the payout period for a DGS	**Extraordinary contributions and alternative funding arrangements:**
Current provisions on eligibility, including issues in relation to:	**The payout of sums in accounts where the depositor is not absolutely entitled to the sums held in the account:**	Sequence of uses of different funding sources
Definition of deposit	Payout approach	Ways to optimise the use of alternative funding arrangements
Joint accounts	Repayment period	Ways to ensure ex-post contributions and alternative funding arrangements are available
Absolute entitlement to the sums held in an account	**Home DGS reimbursing depositors in the host Member State**	Repayment of previous contributions
Dormant accounts	**Passported services without having established branches**	**Investment strategy:**
Administrative cost threshold	**The approach to temporary high balances:**	Responsibility for investment strategy
Depositor information, including information provided to depositors:	Practical application of THB protection	Requirement to invest funds in low-risk assets and ensure sufficient diversification

Opinion on eligibility of deposits, coverage level and cooperation between DGSs	Opinion on DGS payouts	Opinion on DGS funding and uses of DGS funds
In the standardised information sheet	THB time limit, THB amount and scope of THB protection	**Using failed institution's assets for a DGS payouts:**
When there are certain changes to the credit institution	Informing depositors about THB provisions	**Failure prevention measures:**
Third country branches' DGS membership	Impact of a depositor moving funds into different accounts	Implementation and real-life cases of using such measures
Cooperation between the EBA and the European Systemic Risk Board (ESRB)	The impact of THBs on DGS contributions	Consistency of current provisions in the DGSD with state aid rules
Implications of the European Supervisory Authorities Review and amendments to other EU regulations and EU directives	**The approach to set-off of liabilities fallen due**	**Reporting of data**
	The cost of living payout	**Impact of risk-based method on different business models**

2.2 Data sources and methodology

To provide an assessment and, where appropriate, policy recommendations to the Commission, in October 2018 the EBA collected data from Deposit Guarantee Schemes Designated Authorities (DGSDAs) and DGSs on the implementation and practical application of the DGSD across Member States. These data, together with other information available to the EBA, served as the basis for an extensive analysis of each topic presented in the three opinions.

Furthermore, to be able to take a comprehensive and accurate view across all EU Member States the EBA used a range of data sources and types of information. The EBA used what it deemed to be the most suitable type, scope and depth of analysis for each topic and subtopic, to account for the fact that there are differences in:

- the characteristics of topics (qualitative versus quantitative);
- the materiality of the issues identified;
- the level of real-life experience of applying certain provisions.

In practice, this means that the analysis in relation to some topics is:

- based on numerical data and calculations, while in other cases it is purely qualitative;
- accompanied by detailed assessments, including uses of scenarios and various options, while other topics, particularly if they are less material, are analysed in less detail;
- focused mainly on how provisions have been implemented, while in other cases the focus is more on the practical application of such provisions.

The EBA also used information that it had previously collected for other purposes, such as information on:

i.   covered deposits and available financial means, collected in accordance with Article 10(10) of the DGSD and published on the EBA's website;
ii. approach to third country branches and equivalence assessment, collected in February 2018 as part of work performed in relation to the withdrawal of the United Kingdom from the European Union;
iii. real-life cases collected in the context of EBA's mandate in relation to depositor protection.

2.3 Proposals in the EBA opinion on eligibility of deposits, coverage level and cooperation between DGSs

The EBA opinion on eligibility of deposits, coverage level and cooperation between DGSs, addressed ten broad topics, and eventually presented 43 proposals. These proposals are summarised in this chapter. The topics covered by the EBA opinion could be grouped under the following three headings:
– topics directly relevant to all depositors, such as coverage level and depositor information,
– topics relevant for specific groups of depositors, mainly related to the eligibility and exclusions from eligibility,
– topics which cover important technical aspects of the functioning of the depositor protection framework, but not directly related to coverage, such as DGS membership of third country branches, transfers of DGS contributions between DGSs, and, cooperation between various stakeholders.

2.3.1 Topics directly relevant to all depositors

Coverage level
To assess the current coverage level of EUR 100,000, the EBA asked the DGSDAs and DGS whether they consider current coverage level to be adequate, and also replicated the quantitative assessment previously performed by the Commission in 2010. Based on the quantitative and qualitative analyses, the EBA proposed that the current coverage level is adequate and therefore no changes to the DGSD seem necessary.

The EBA also proposed that the currently applicable options for currency of repayment in relation to the coverage level included in the DGSD seem adequate and there is no need for an amendment of the Directive.

Depositor information
On depositor information, the EBA proposed that the depositor information sheet (in Annex I of the DGSD) outlining the key features of how deposits are protected could be amended in favour of a more flexible approach to how to specify the information that the depositor should receive. Instead, the DGSD could list only the set of essential elements to be included in the information sheet (based on what is currently included, with further amendments also proposed by the EBA below), while another legal instrument, such as EBA guidelines or EBA draft technical standards to be adopted by the Commission,

could further specify that necessary information and the format of that information.

In terms of content of the depositor information sheet, it could be amended to:

– include the details of the credit institution as a first point of contact for information on the content of the information sheet and include its contact details (address, telephone, e-mail, etc.) while retaining the link to the relevant DGS's website in the information sheet;
– abolish the requirement for acknowledgement of receipt by the depositor;
– clearly highlight the purpose of the information sheet,
– include further information relevant to the depositors, such as relevant provisions concerning temporary high balances and the application of set-off, and other relevant information.

The EBA also proposed that the DGSD should not be amended with regard to the frequency at which information about DGS protection should be provided, and the current requirement for an annual update should be retained.

In relation to the application of the current provision on the depositors' right to withdraw or transfer eligible deposits without incurring any penalties in certain circumstances, the EBA proposed that the DGSD should be amended so that such provisions should be limited to changes in the coverage of deposits.

In relation to the information provided to depositors in cases of mergers, conversions of subsidiaries into branches or similar operations, including when there is a change of DGS affiliation, the DGSD should clarify that all depositors in both institutions should be informed of such events, but that the information should be provided in the most efficient and cost-effective manner (i.e. by electronic means and/or by incorporating relevant information about the operation into the regular, active and direct communication that banks have with their customers). The EBA also proposed that the DGSD should be amended to ensure that at least the depositors who will lose coverage for some of their funds because of the merger, conversion of subsidiaries into branches or similar operations should be informed of their right to withdraw their funds without incurring a penalty up to an amount equal to the lost coverage of deposits. This means that, although all depositors should be informed of the abovementioned events, not all depositors in the credit institutions in such scenarios should be informed of the right to withdraw funds without incurring a penalty, as this right will in most cases apply to relatively few depositors.

Finally, in relation to the currently applicable timelines for informing depositors in the abovementioned cases, the EBA notes that respondents to the survey identified some issues. However, the EBA has not discussed this aspect of the current DGSD framework in detail and so proposes that the Commission should take note and revisit this topic in the future.

2.3.2 Topics relevant for specific groups of depositors

List of exclusions from eligibility
In relation to the current list of exclusions from eligibility in the DGSD, the EBA proposed that no change is needed in the Directive with regard to the definition of financial institutions and investment firms, other than those necessary in relation to excluded entities in the context of absolute entitlement to the sums held in an account (as discussed below).

In relation to the current exclusion from coverage of public authorities, an amendment of the DGSD may be appropriate and the amendment could extend DGS coverage to the public authorities with no need to differentiate between them based on their budgets. However, further analysis of the impact of such an extension may be warranted.

In relation to personal pension schemes and occupational pension schemes of small and medium-sized enterprises, at this stage no changes to the DGSD seem necessary. There also seems to be no need to provide any further guidance or advice using other instruments.

In relation to deposits the holder of which was never identified, an amendment of the DGSD is necessary. If depositors have never been identified through no fault of their own, the amendment should introduce the flexibility for DGSs to make those depositors' funds available to them, subject to any necessary checks under the DGSD and Anti-money Laundering Directive (AMLD), to be performed by the insolvency practitioner or the authorities best placed to do such checks. The revised DGSD text should be aligned with other requirements, for example those stemming from the AMLD, and it would need to be accompanied by the necessary safeguards to avoid cases in which anonymous and/or unidentified depositors are repaid.

In relation to the coverage of deposits at EU credit institutions' branches in third countries, an amendment of the DGSD is appropriate. The amendment should ensure that deposits in these branches are not protected by an EU DGS of which the EU credit institution is a member.

Current DGSD provisions on eligibility for coverage
In relation to the current DGSD provisions on eligibility for coverage, the Directive should be amended to remove from the definition of a deposit the word 'normal'

in relation to banking transactions. The EBA also proposed that the Commission should assess further the need to provide clarity in relation to the treatment of structured deposits, including cases where they may yield negative returns, considering the options outlined in the attached report, their pros and cons, and the materiality of structured deposits as outlined in the EBA Report on cost and past performance of structured deposits published on 10 January 2019.

In relation to joint accounts, at this stage no changes to the DGSD seem necessary. There also seems to be no need to provide any further guidance or advice using other instruments.

In relation to absolute entitlement to the sums held in an account, the harmonisation of the approach to the identification of the person absolutely entitled to the sums is not necessary. Also in relation to absolute entitlement to the sums held in an account, there is no immediate need to address the issue of the calculation of contributions for accounts whose holder is not absolutely entitled to the sums, but this topic may be revisited in the next review of the EBA guidelines on methods for calculating contributions to deposit guarantee schemes.

However, the Commission should enhance clarity in the DGSD on how the see-through approach applies to deposits placed with credit institutions by account holders who are excluded from eligibility. The topic of absolute entitlement to the sums held in an account is complex, so further analysis may be needed of how best to formulate the wording in different pieces of EU legislation. In subsequent policy considerations concerning investment firms and financial institutions, it is recommended to take a holistic view regarding the relationship between those institutions and their clients, the related safeguarding requirements and the implications they have for DGS protection.

In relation to the deferral of repayment of dormant accounts provided for in Article 8(5)(c) of the DGSD, there is no need to remove the possibility of deferring the payout of dormant accounts. However, there is merit in amending Article 8(5)(c) of the DGSD to clarify that, if a depositor has multiple accounts and at least one is non-dormant, all the amounts should be aggregated and the aggregated amount should be made available to the depositor before the deadline envisaged in Article 8(1) of the DGSD.

In relation to the administrative cost threshold as per Article 8(9) of the DGSD, the Directive should be amended to allow DGSs to repay depositors irrespective of the amount of funds in their account and the dormancy of the account. The DGSD should also be amended to allow DGSs to set an administrative cost threshold below which they would be allowed not to take active steps to make the amount available to the depositor, but depositors would have the right to receive their funds upon request. Finally, also in relation to the administrative cost threshold, the EBA proposed that the DGSD should be amended to specify that the administrative cost threshold must be sufficiently low and justifiable, and communicated ex ante to the depositors via the information sheet.

2.3.3 Topics which cover important technical aspects of the functioning of the depositor protection framework

Third country branches' DGS membership
On third country branches' DGS membership, the EBA proposed that the DGSD should be amended to stipulate that branches established within the territory of Member States by a credit institution that has its head office outside the Union, if they are licensed by the relevant supervisory authority in the EU to take deposits as defined by the DGSD, must join a DGS in operation within the territory of the relevant Member States. The EBA proposed that it could be considered that, by way of derogation from the above provision, some flexibility could be provided to Member States to exempt branches established within their territory by a credit institution that has its head office outside the Union from the obligation to join a DGS in operation within their territories.

Such a decision could potentially be made on the basis of a voluntary equivalence assessment, and where it is absolutely necessary in order to maintain the level playing field, depositors' confidence and financial stability. If protection is not equivalent, Member States must stipulate that such branches must join a DGS in operation within their territories.

Transfers of DGS contributions
On transfer of previous contributions between DGSs where a credit institution changes its DGS affiliation, there is a need to amend the current provisions in Article 14(3) of the DGSD, in which the amount of contribution transferred is linked to the contributions paid in the 12-month period prior to the institution changing its DGS affiliation or the transfer of some of the activities to another Member State. The EBA proposed that there is a need to develop a different methodology addressing the issues highlighted further in the opinion, taking into account the diversity of current methodologies to calculate risk-based contributions allowed under the EBA Guidelines on methods for calculating contributions from DGSs. Given this topic's technical nature, the EBA, together with its member authorities and schemes, is best placed to develop the new methodology, and so the opinion invites the Commission to consider conferring corresponding mandates to the EBA. To ensure uniform application across Member States, the

methodology should be specified through EBA draft regulatory technical standards to be adopted by the Commission.

In relation to the current provisions on the transfer of contributions for third country branches, the DGSD is sufficiently clear and there is no need to propose changes to the Directive in relation to this matter and/or to provide any further related guidance or advice.

DGSs' cooperation with various stakeholders

On DGSDAs' and DGSs' cooperation with the affiliated credit institutions, competent authorities, resolution authorities and other DGSs, there is no need to propose changes to the DGSD, and there is no need to provide any further guidance or advice using other instruments. However, the EBA proposed that the current lack of engagement between the DGSDAs/DGSs and the anti-money laundering (AML) authorities should be considered further in the EBA Opinion on DGS payouts, which will address issues related to DGS payouts where there are AML concerns.

Home-host cooperation and cooperation agreements

On home-host cooperation between DGSs, including cooperation agreements currently required under the DGSD, the EBA proposes that no changed are needed on the EBA's role in such cooperation agreements. There also seems to be no need to provide any further guidance or advice using other instruments. Furthermore, it is not necessary to amend the DGSD in order to include a more explicit and clearer requirement in the DGSD to share the most important data, because the current text of the Directive does not prohibit the sharing of these data and requires home DGSs to exchange them with the host DGSs. Also, the type of data to be shared is already outlined in the bilateral agreements signed by DGSs. Finally, in relation to the temporary high balances in cross-border payouts, no changes to the DGSD, at this stage, seem necessary. There also seems to be no need to provide any further guidance or advice using other instruments.

Cooperation between the EBA and the European Systemic Risk Board (ESRB)

On cooperation between the EBA and the ESRB on systemic risk analysis concerning DGSs, as currently required by the DGSD, the EBA proposed that there is no need to change the DGSD and/or to provide any further related guidance or advice. The EBA and the ESRB are in a position to agree bilaterally on the content and the timing of the cooperation on such an analysis concerning DGSs.

**Implications of the European Supervisory Authorities Review and amendments
to other EU regulations and EU directives**

Finally, on the implications of the European Supervisory Authorities Review and
amendments to other EU regulations and EU directives, the EBA proposed that to
minimise the risk of possible inconsistencies and to eliminate possible misinterpretation, the DGSD would need to be amended should the term 'peer reviews' be
replaced by a different wording in the mandate of the European Supervisory
Authorities. Similarly, all the cross-references in the DGSD to other EU regulations
and directives should be updated in due course to avoid misinterpretation.

2.4 Topics to be covered by the EBA opinions on DGS payouts, and DGS funding and uses of DGS funds

The other two EBA opinions related to the implementation of the DGSD will focus
on the topics presented earlier in Table X. Similarly to the first opinion, they will
cover a mix of topics directly relevant to all depositors, some relevant for specific
groups of depositors, and important technical issues not directly related to coverage. They will also cover fundamental topics straddling all three groups of topics,
which the EBA has observed in real-life cases. In the EBA opinion on DGS
payouts, such topics will include highlighting current lack of clarity or gaps in the
current framework in relation to the treatment of deposits where depositors
cannot access their funds which are due and payable, but the conditions for
triggering the unavailability of deposits, and thus the DGS payout, have not been
met.

The opinion will also address some gaps and/or lack of clarity in the current
EU framework in relation to DGS payouts where there are money-laundering and/
or terrorism financing concerns. The EBA opinion on DGS funding and uses of
DGS funds will address the fundamental topic of the sequence of using different
sources of DGS funds in a crisis, and the consistency of current DGSD provisions
on failure prevention measures with the EU State Aid framework. The EBA will
invite the Commission to consider the EBA's proposals if and when proposing a
revised DGSD.

Klaus Wiedner

A Common European Deposit Insurance System on the Path Towards a Steady-State Banking Union

Introduction

Financial services play a pivotal role in supporting single market activities. Multiple economic transactions as well as investments rely on bank accounts, and consequently, on confidence in the underlying financial institutions involved. Financial services are large users of the euro as a currency, including in foreign trade and investment. At the scale of consumers, a bank account is the gateway to employment, rented housing, home loans, savings, social services, consumer credit, payment services, including by non-bank providers, and much more. Deposits in a bank usually constitute a constant portion of that bank's liabilities, thereby creating a strong obligation on the credit institution to respect and protect those deposits when carrying out their investment activities. Faced with the prospect of bank insolvency, the first loss experienced by depositors is one of trust. If bank runs materialise as a result, the viability of both the bank and potentially also of related payment systems could be further compromised. Deposit insurance is therefore not a matter of improvisation. The policy and related tools must be properly developed and treated as a crisis management measure in their own right, contributing to financial stability, financial markets and consumer protection.[1]

The financial crisis that started in the US in 2007 and developed into a European sovereign debt crisis in 2009 exposed significant vulnerabilities in the EU financial system and heavily dented depositor confidence. As part of a comprehensive strategy to promote sustainable EU economic recovery, through new institutions at European level for EU financial markets and a Banking Union within a deeper Economic and Monetary Union (EMU), the European Commission sought to further develop the policies supporting depositor confidence. Shortly

---

1 For a broader explanation of the systemic consequences of bank runs, drawing on examples from the 1930s and 2008 banking crisis in the US, see *Forbearance, resolution and deposit insurance*, Report of the Advisory Scientific Committee, European Systemic Risk Board, July 2012. This report comments on the idea of a combined EU resolution and deposit insurance authority, while also considering a scenario in which the authority would not manage the deposit insurance funds directly for transition purposes. It would instead rely initially on national competent deposit insurance institutions.

https://doi.org/10.1515/9783110683073-004

after targeted improvements to national deposit guarantee schemes, the Commission also promoted the idea of a European Deposit Insurance Scheme (EDIS).

On a national level, depositors continue to be protected by means of deposit guarantee schemes (DGSs)[2] administered still today by national authorities whose activities are regulated by the Deposit Guarantee Scheme Directive (DGSD).[3] The coverage of national DGSs has been harmonised at €100,000 per depositor since 31 December 2010. In July 2010, the Commission also proposed new rules introducing faster pay-outs and improved financing, notably through the *ex ante* funding of deposit guarantee schemes paid for by contributions from banks. By 3 July 2024, this funding should reach at least 0.8 % of the amount of the covered deposits of participating banks.

On a European level, a comprehensive system known as the Banking Union was launched in 2012 to implement a substantial financial reform agenda, fulfilling commitments made in the G20 in response to the financial crisis, and to address EMU specificities in the euro area. The aim of these efforts was to make financial institutions and markets more stable, more competitive and more resilient. The choice was made then to introduce dedicated measures and common institutions to tackle the specific risks within the euro area. In a context where pooled monetary responsibilities since 1999 had spurred close economic and financial integration, bank failures in one Member State could have real and tangible cross-border spill-over effects. Moreover, it was also considered crucial to break the link between sovereign debt and bank debt and the vicious circle which had resulted in the use of EU taxpayers' money to rescue banks during the crises.

A common deposit insurance system – early policy ideas

On 25 February 2009, a high-level group on financial supervision in the EU, chaired by Jacques de Larosière, published a report and set of recommendations[4] drawing on lessons learned since the crisis. The report, which led to a fundamental overhaul of macro- and micro-prudential supervision in the EU through new institutions[5] and regulation, argued that crisis prevention, crisis management

---

2 There are 38 DGSs in the EU: 27 in the euro area and 11 in the rest of the EU. (EBA data, 2019)
3 Directive 2014/49/EU.
4 Recommendation 13 in J. De Larosière *et al.*, *Report of the High-level Group on Financial Supervision in the EU*, Brussels, 25 February 2009.
5 For micro-prudential oversight at the EU level: the European Banking Authority (EBA); the European Securities and Markets Authority (ESMA) and the European Insurance and Occupa-

and crisis resolution tools would need to be handled in a *"consistent regulatory framework"*. The Group also called for *"a coherent and workable regulatory framework for crisis management in the EU."*

The De Larosière report, as it came to be known, provided a significant contribution to a broad public and institutional understanding of priority post-crisis reforms and inspired some of the later thinking. Soon, it became clear that the emergence of a new European-level supervisory and crisis management architecture would also help curtail the increasing risk of fragmentation of EU banking markets, which would significantly undermine the single market for financial services and impair the effective transmission of monetary policy to the real economy throughout the euro area. An important lesson from the crises was that coordination between supervisors, however vital, was not sufficient for a single currency area. There was a need for common decision-making and therefore common institutions. In this context, there was a rightful place for a European system for depositor protection.

On 7 July 2010, the European Parliament adopted a report on cross-border crisis management in the banking sector.[6] The report called for the Commission to submit by end-2010 one or more legislative proposals relating to an EU crisis management framework, an EU stability fund and a resolution unit. According to this report, the envisaged European crisis management framework would need to be bound by a common set of rules and ultimately lead to common resolution and bank insolvency legislation applicable to all EU credit institutions. It would need to seek, among others, *"to optimise the position of depositors and guarantee their equal treatment across the Union."*

In the wake of the sovereign debt crisis in the euro area, on 26 June, 2012, the Presidents of the European Council, Commission, Eurogroup and European Central Bank, came forth with a shared vision for a new set of financial reforms. Their report laid out a set of strategic objectives drawing on key lessons learned, for example, the need for an integrated financial framework. According to this vision, a new institutional framework was needed to raise to the European level the responsibility for financial supervision, resolution and depositor protection in the euro area. Back then, the thinking was that the integrated financial framework would build on the single rulebook and that it should have *"two central elements: single European banking supervision and a common deposit insurance and resolu-*

---

tional Pensions Authority (EIOPA). For macro-prudential oversight of the EU financial system: the European Systemic Risk Board (ESRB).

6 European Parliament resolution of 7 July 2010 with recommendations to the Commission on Cross-Border Crisis Management in the Banking Sector (2010/2006(INI)).

tion scheme.[7] This new governance system would in turn ensure an optimal alignment of liability and control in the euro area with positive spill-over effects on the rest of the internal market.

On 12 September 2012, the Commission published a Roadmap towards a Banking Union – a long-term initiative. The initial focus would entail shifting the supervision of significantly important banks to the European level by conferring specific supervisory tasks upon the European Central Bank (ECB), and therefore establishing the Single Supervisory Mechanism (SSM) – the first pillar of the Banking Union. This would subsequently be combined *"with other steps such as a common system for deposit protection, and integrated bank crisis management."* [8]

The reason behind this sequential approach was to progressively build trust between Member States and among depositors. First, by ensuring that high prudential standards would be applied consistently at the European level. Second, by introducing a new system to restructure or close ailing banks while minimising costs for the taxpayer and ensuring that bank shareholders and creditors would bear their full share of bank losses and recapitalisation costs. At the same time, work would be accelerated to deliver outstanding reforms, for example, on capital requirements and national deposit guarantee schemes, thereby contributing further to risk reduction and updating the single rulebook. The latter was to be completed with a single supervisory handbook which would minimise the opportunities for regulatory arbitrage. This approach was being developed on the back of a fundamental overhaul of the EMU's economic governance system the Commission had launched in 2010 to address the weaknesses of its economic surveillance and the creation of sovereign rescue mechanisms and dedicated institutions.[9] It was hoped that trust would increase among Member States, as this was seen to be a pre-condition for the introduction of any common financial arrangements to simultaneously protect depositors and support the orderly resolution of failing banks. The overall vision for the Banking Union in this respect would be delivered through a step-wise approach, taking into account

---

7 https://www.consilium.europa.eu/uedocs/cms_data/docs/pressdata/en/ec/131201.pdf.
8 COM(2012) 510 final.
9 Commission communications of 12 May 2010 (COM (2010) 250 final) and 30 June 2010 (COM (2010) 367 final), and its "six pack" legislative proposals of 29 September 2010 (COM (2010) 522–527 final) comprising: three Regulations strengthening the European budgetary surveillance framework (the SGP), two Regulations introducing a new surveillance procedure for macroeconomic imbalances and a Directive imposing minimum standards for Member States' national budgetary frameworks. These measures were supplemented by the "Two-Pack" Regulations, adopted on 21 May 2013, setting up a tighter monitoring and coordination process of national budgets.

possible new areas for harmonisation, as well as very different fiscal environments, banking sectors and risk concentrations. Given the challenge at hand, some measures were prioritised over others while keeping in sight the long-term goal of a single euro area with a single supervision and crisis management framework.

It took EU Member States and the European Parliament a remarkable seven months to agree on the Commission's legislative proposal to establish the SSM. In the meantime, it was considered more pressing to decouple deposit insurance from resolution in order to pave the way for an earlier delivery of a single resolution framework. In this vein, in the Interim Report of 12 October 2012[10] of the earlier Four Presidents' Report, the definition of the integrated financial frame did not cover common depositor protection: *"An integrated financial framework must comprise a single supervisory authority, a common resolution framework implemented by a common resolution authority, and national deposit guarantee schemes built on common standards."*

On 28 November 2012, the Commission adopted a "Blueprint for a Deep and Genuine EMU".[11] While recalling in a footnote the overall vision for the Banking Union, including common depositor protection, the blueprint called for the establishment of a single resolution mechanism after the conclusion of legislative negotiations on the Bank Recovery and Resolution Directive (BRRD)[12] and on a recast of the 1994 DGSD. Negotiations on the former had started in June 2012, while those on the DGSD had been ongoing since 2010. Both had complementary regulatory objectives: the former, to transfer the responsibility of rescuing failed banks to their shareholders and creditors; the latter, to improve the protection of depositors through existing national DGSs.

At the request of Member States, as of the second half of 2012, BRRD and DGSD issues were discussed in parallel in the Council Financial Services Working Party, with a view to accelerating the pace of negotiations and discuss issues where there were obvious synergies (*e.g.* the use of national DGSs to fund resolution). As negotiations picked up speed, so did the political pressure for them to conclude. Those negotiations continued to shed light on reluctance within both the Council and the European Parliament to consider a European-level depositor protection system, even as a long-term perspective, largely because of moral hazard considerations – in this case, weaker incentives for banks to invest

---

10 https://www.consilium.europa.eu/uedocs/cms_data/docs/pressdata/en/ec/132809.pdf.
11 COM(2012) 777 final.
12 Directive 2014/59/EU.

responsibly, because contributions from other banks would be available to cover their depositor protection needs.

A pragmatic choice was made instead to focus on achieving more harmonisation, especially of *ex ante* funding of national DGSs. This would allow the gradual build-up of the national funds through contributions from credit institutions within the remit of each individual deposit guarantee scheme. In the event of payouts, the DGSs would be participating in the absorption of losses, together with senior creditors and in proportion to the share of covered deposits in the balance sheet of the failing bank. Viewed from this perspective, harmonised *ex ante* funding, improved the ability of Member States to contain bank runs on their own, provided the scale of such events was manageable. During the crisis, moral hazard situations had occurred within Member States, because of market expectations of *ad hoc* national responses such as state guarantees,[13] which led to further systemic repercussions because of the challenge of protecting depositors and the financial system at the same time. Building on the SSM and on the post-crisis rules, other reforms and measures were needed to effectively tackle the root causes of moral hazard behaviour in relation to the provisioning for adequate depositor protection and viable bank balance sheets.

The final DGSD compromise fixed mid-2024 for a critical mass of *ex ante* funds to be set aside. By then, the Banking Union supervision and resolution[14] institutions would be fully operational and evolving further. It was hoped that at some point in the future, political and systemic conditions would end up being more favourable to the achievement of further steps towards a common depositor protection system. Indeed, the DGSD contains a transitional provision whereby, the Commission should *"submit a report, and, if appropriate, a legislative proposal to the European Parliament and the Council setting out how DGSs operating in the Union may cooperate through a European scheme to prevent risks arising from cross-border activities and protect deposits from such risks."*

The 2015 EDIS proposal

At the start of the Juncker Commission, in November 2014, the ECB was due, under the SSM, to take over the supervision of roughly 130 financial institutions

---

13 *Forbearance, resolution and deposit insurance,* Report of the Advisory Scientific Committee, European Systemic Risk Board, July 2012.
14 Ultimately, in July 2013, the Commission proposed the establishment of a Single Resolution Mechanism (SRM). The proposal was agreed by the Council and European Parliament in March 2014 and entered into force in July of the same year.

with holdings of 85 % of the banking assets of the euro area. Separately, preparations were underway to implement the SRM, through creation of the Single Resolution Board (SRB) which would start operations on 1 January 2015. The SRB was to manage the Single European Fund (SRF)[15] which would be gradually built up through bank contributions between 2016-2023. The deadline for reaching a target level of at least 1 % of the amount of covered deposits of eligible Banking Union credit institutions was 31 December 2023 – six months before the DGSD target level deadline.

Through the SRM, the Banking Union acquired a second pillar, lending further credibility to the new common supervision regime. Against this background, the new Juncker Commission found it preferable to frontload a legislative initiative that would establish EDIS as the missing third pillar of the Banking Union. The timing was also justified by the fact that negative sovereign-bank feedback loops were still a major legacy of the successive crises. In this context, it was expected that a unified Banking Union architecture would deliver complementary solutions to solving the problem more durably, failing which, bank insolvencies would continue to endanger public finances and sovereign stress would continue to threaten the viability of exposed banks.

On 22 June 2015, Jean-Claude Juncker, together with his counterparts in the European Council, Eurogroup, ECB and European Parliament, released a report presenting a strategic vision of shorter and longer-term priorities for completing the EMU.[16] The report set the scene not just for EDIS but also for the establishment of a common backstop to the SRF by means of a line of credit from the European Stability Mechanism (ESM) to the SRF. Once activated, funds made available through the backstop would be recovered by means of *ex post* levies to the banking industry. This report argued EDIS was needed because it presented a set of advantages over the national DGS system. It would be better able to handle large shocks by diversifying risks more widely. It would cover the same banks as the SSM (mandatory for the euro area; open to all other Member States) and would need to be designed in a way that avoided moral hazard. The report acknowledged that building EDIS would take time and that it mattered, therefore, to take the first concrete steps towards achieving the long-term vision of a Banking Union

---

15 The SRF is largely regulated by an inter-governmental agreement covering: (i) transfers of the contributions levied by national resolution authorities to the national compartments of the SRF; (ii) mutualisation of the funds of national compartments during an eight-year transition period; (iii) lending between national compartments and (iv) the potential contribution of non-euro area participating Member States to the SRF. See *Agreement on the transfer and mutualisation of contributions to the Single Resolution Fund*, 14 May 2014, Council of the European Union, 8457/14.
16 https://ec.europa.eu/commission/sites/beta-political/files/5-presidents-report_en.pdf.

relying on three fully developed pillars. On that occasion, the possibility of providing a reinsurance system at European level for national DGS was first floated.

EDIS and the common backstop combined, would further strengthen the idea that EU taxpayers would no longer be called upon to rescue banks in need. Along with the new measures introduced by the BRRD as well as a privately-funded SRF, the EU's crisis management toolkit would develop into one where the responsibility for preparedness rested with credit institutions. Moreover, in an extreme crisis scenario, where banks of different sizes would default simultaneously, EDIS and the common backstop would demonstrate their added value over a system already improved by the DGSD and BRRD. A common deposit insurance system would be of particular relevance for those banks that did not pass the public interest assessment[17] – and were therefore subject to national insolvency. EDIS would represent a step forward with respect to the existing national DGS system, by centralising at least the depositor protection aspect of remaining interventions after public interest was not considered justified.[18] Thus, EDIS would also ensure that the level of depositor confidence in a bank would not depend on its location.

On 24 November 2015,[19] the Commission proposed an amending regulation to the Single Resolution Mechanism Regulation (SRMR) to introduce EDIS in incremental steps. As a first measure, EDIS would comprise a reinsurance arrangement. The second phase would upgrade cooperation through the introduction of a co-insurance system. In a final stage, EDIS would be fully mutualised by 2024, in line with other regulatory Banking Union deadlines.

Operationally, the SRB would administer the single deposit insurance fund established for the purpose of implementing EDIS. The Fund would then be in a position to act as a safety net for national DGSs in times of extreme stress. By means of the proposal, the Commission sought to ensure that EDIS would not increase the overall costs for the banking sector in relation to obligations under the DGSD. Contributions by banks to EDIS, would be deducted from their national DGS contributions. Throughout the gradual build-up of the Fund, contributions to national DGSs would be progressively reduced in parallel with increases in their respective EDIS contributions. To take account of the application in July 2015 of the new DGSD rules, efforts were made in different components of the EDIS

---

17 Public interest in relation to resolution action, carried out at the point a bank is deemed "failing or likely to fail", is defined in Articles 18(5) of Regulation (EU) 806/2014 (SRMR) and 32(5) of Directive 2014/59/EU (BRRD).

18 Still today, there is no common procedure to handle bank insolvency in the EU, resulting in different solutions (including state aid) being applied in similar situations.

19 COM(2015) 586 final.

proposal to leverage a rapid and complete transposition of the DGSD and to synchronise the co-existence of a central deposit insurance fund with the continued operation of national DGSs.

Under the 2015 proposal, during the re-insurance phase, a national DGS could resort to EDIS for reinsurance support only once it had first exhausted all its funds and under the condition that all applicable DGSD rules had previously been fully implemented and applied. The national DGS could then receive liquidity assistance and cover excess losses from the Fund of up to 20 % of the shortfall or excess loss it faced, subject to certain capping conditions. These limits on liquidity support were necessary to take into account legacy issues relating to different funding levels among national DGS and to avoid the moral hazard of a national DGS. Safeguards would be included to avoid any possible abuse of the system.

After a period of operation as a reinsurance scheme, EDIS would become a progressively mutualised system ("co-insurance"). In the next occurring co-insurance phase, the national DGS would receive liquidity assistance immediately – *i.e.* from the first euro of pay-out, not simply once the DGS had exhausted its funds – based on a progressively mutualised scale starting at 20 %, and subject to appropriate conditions and safeguards. The share contributed by EDIS would increase over a four-year period until it reached 100 %. By then, EDIS would enter its final phase and fully insure national DGSs as of 2024.

In the two earlier build-up phases, the SRB would manage the Fund by levying *ex ante* contributions to meet the progressively increasing target levels of the Fund. The levies would be based on the deposits of each bank and existing risk adjustment elements to reflect the risk profile of each bank. The national DGSs would calculate and collect the contributions from banks in the Member States on the SRB's behalf, rendering necessary some adjustments to SRB governance arrangements. EDIS would apply to banks in participating Member States on the same terms as in the DGSD. Taking into account cross-border banking activities, a branch located in the Banking Union of a bank headquartered elsewhere in or outside the Banking Union would be covered by the national (home) DGS. Conversely, a subsidiary would be covered by the national (host) DGS.

The communication[20] accompanying the EDIS legislative proposal also announced a full set of measures the Commission should pursue to reduce risk and ensure a level playing field in the Banking Union. These included the timely transposition and implementation of the DGSD and BRRD, ratification of the inter-governmental agreement on the SRF, reducing national options and discretions in the application of prudential rules, legislating to implement by 2019 the

---

20 COM(2015) 587 final.

Financial Stability Board's recommendations on total loss absorbing capacity (TLAC) for banks, greater convergence in insolvency law and initiatives as regards the treatment of banks' exposure to sovereign risk.

2016–2018: Progress in risk reduction

From the outset, the EDIS proposal did not gain sufficient support in the Council to progress further than the technical level, revealing differences of opinion about how to implement the longer-term Banking Union vision. For some Member States, risk sharing and risk reduction had to progress in parallel, together with continued reinforcements to the overall institutional framework, including stronger accountability in the euro area. Other Member States attached priority instead to addressing risk reduction first, starting with decisive measures to tackle legacy issues, including non-performing loans (NPLs). These localised actions would need to be further supplemented with more comprehensive rules at EU level in order to effectively contain other risks to the financial system. This notwithstanding, since its creation in January 2016, the Council Ad Hoc Working Party on the Strengthening of the Banking Union, has undertaken a significant volume of quality technical work on different aspects of EDIS design, its scope and possible interactions with other files in the Banking Union context. Every rotating Council Presidency records the main outcomes of the Working Party's activities during its sixth-month term in a progress report.[21]

In June 2016, the Commission further presented an effect-analysis[22] based on three policy options (reinsurance, mandatory lending between national deposit guarantee schemes and full insurance). The analysis demonstrated that pooling risk under all three approaches delivers, in every circumstance, a significantly stronger deposit guarantee system rather than relying solely on a system of national schemes performing voluntary lending. Overall, the reinsurance and full insurance options yielded stronger results.

Also in June 2016, under the Dutch Presidency of the Council of the European Union, the Council adopted a roadmap,[23] which effectively subordinated the launching of political negotiations on EDIS to the prior achievement of a number of risk reduction measures. The most comprehensive deliverable involved key

---

21 *e.g.* http://data.consilium.europa.eu/doc/document/ST-14452-2018-INIT/en/pdf – Austrian Presidency report of 23 November 2018.
22 https://ec.europa.eu/info/sites/info/files/161011-edis-effect-analysis_en.pdf.
23 https://www.consilium.europa.eu/en/press/press-releases/2016/06/17/conclusions-on-bank ing-union.

amendments before the end of 2016 to the single rulebook's prudential and resolution provisions. First, in order to improve bank resilience, the Council roadmap expected the Commission to propose amendments to the BRRD to implement the internationally agreed TLAC standard and review the minimum requirement for own funds and eligible liabilities (MREL). In this context, the Council also asked the Commission to put forward a proposal on a common approach to the bank creditor hierarchy, to enhance legal certainty in case of resolution. Second, the Council sought amendments to the Capital Requirements Directive (IV) and Regulation[24] to introduce into the EU regulatory framework global standards on the leverage ratio and net stable funding ratio agreed in the Basel Committee on Banking Supervision (Basel III reforms), as well as new EU rules to further reduce market fragmentation. The Commission delivered a proposal known as the "Banking Package" on 23 November 2016[25] addressing these and other risk-reducing measures. It took just over two years for the package to be finalised by the Council and European Parliament and it is today being implemented.

The June 2016 Council roadmap also sought to achieve progress on the common backstop and on the development of a common EU insolvency framework in the context of the Capital Markets Union. Due to ongoing work at the time in the Basel Committee on the regulatory treatment of sovereign exposures, the Council agreed to consider possible next steps in the European context once the outcomes of international efforts were known. As for EDIS, negotiations would start as soon as *"sufficient further progress"* had been made in delivering the risk reduction measures contained in the roadmap *"in the appropriate sequence"*.

To further support the inter-institutional legislative process, in its Communication on completing the Banking Union of 11 October 2017,[26] the Commission suggested ideas to introduce EDIS in a more gradual manner, commensurate with progress achieved in relation to risk reduction and the tackling of legacy issues, starting with a more limited reinsurance phase (this time, providing only liquidity support based on a gradually increasing scale) and moving thereafter to co-insurance. In order to recognise concerns about legacy issues and moral hazard, the Commission suggested that progress from the first phase to the second would be conditional on the performance of an asset quality review on participating banks to address NPLs and Level III assets. Banks not meeting a set threshold would be required by supervisory authorities to prepare appropriate strategies on these issues. Once conditions were met, the co-insurance phase would start, this

---

24 Regulation (EU) 575/2013.
25 COM(2016) 850-854 final.
26 COM(2017) 592 final.

time with a 30 % EDIS contribution following a key which would develop progressively.

For its part, the European Parliament had earlier delivered a draft report on 4 November 2016 calling for a more cautious and conditional approach. In this spirit, it suggested only two stages of implementation (reinsurance and co-insurance) and extended the timeline of the Commission's proposal (2024 at earliest for full insurance), subject to a range of risk reduction conditions similar to the June 2016 Council Roadmap. With the Council not in a position to engage politically, legislative follow-up in both institutions was confined to technical discussions.

Meanwhile, work has progressed further as regards risk reduction. Different EU institutions are deploying a series of measures aimed at ensuring that banks would be sufficiently robust on a standalone basis. The ECB in its supervisory capacity, the Single Supervisory Mechanism, national competent authorities and the European Banking Authority (EBA) are playing an important role in enhancing the supervision and reporting of NPLs in Europe. On 11 July 2017, the Council agreed an action plan to address the problem of non-performing loans in the banking sector.[27] In addition to the preparation of regular NPL progress reports, the Commission proposed on 14 March 2018, a package of measures to address remaining stocks of NPLs and prevent their possible build-up in the future. The package included proposals to introduce common minimum coverage levels (a prudential backstop) for newly originated loans that become underperforming,[28] a directive on credit servicers, credit purchasers and the recovery of collateral,[29] as well as a blueprint for Member States choosing to set up national asset management companies.[30] In December 2018, the Council and European Parliament agreed the prudential backstop regulation, which introduces minimum levels of coverage for future NPLs arising from newly originated loans.[31] The actions by the Commission, the ECB, the EBA and the European Systemic Risk Board will create important synergies. The proposed statutory minimum coverage requirements should provide strong incentives for banks' management to prevent the accumulation of future NPLs through better NPL management and stronger loan origination practices. This will reinforce the expected effects of the ongoing work by the ECB and the EBA on banks' loan origination, NPL management, monitoring and internal governance practices. Work on NPL information and

---

27 https://www.consilium.europa.eu/en/press/press-releases/2017/07/11/conclusions-non-perf orming-loans/.
28 COM(2018) 134 final.
29 COM(2018) 135 final.
30 SWD(2018) 72 final.
31 Regulation (EU) 2019/630.

market infrastructure should further enhance the functioning of secondary markets for NPLs.

The bi-annual NPL progress reports from the Commission to the ECOFIN Council indicate that measures taken by banks, supervisors as well as national and European policy-makers, supported by economic recovery, are delivering results. The latest report of 12 June 2019[32] shows that the ratio of NPLs in EU banks decreased to 3.3 % in the third quarter of 2018 (compared with 6.7 % since the end of 2014) and is down by 1.1 percentage points year-on-year, marking a further decline towards pre-crisis levels (See Figure 1). Separately, the application of the International Financial Reporting Standard (IFRS) 9 in the EU, starting 1 January 2018, should improve the accounting treatment and valuation of financial assets and liabilities, relevant both for greater convergence in national insolvency proceedings and for banks' non-performing exposures. IFRS 9 includes rules applicable to the impairment of financial assets.

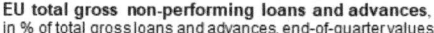

EU total gross **non-performing loans and advances**,
in % of total gross loans and advances, end-of-quarter values

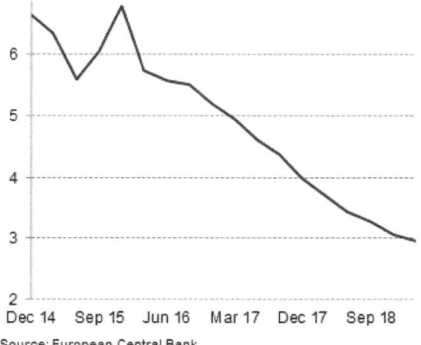

Source: European Central Bank

Figures 1: Non-performing loans ratio in the Union

These results are matched by progress on other risk reduction indicators monitored by the Commission, the ECB and the ERB at the request of the President of the Eurogroup since 2017. These joint monitoring reports are intended to help develop a common understanding of state-of-play towards the completion of the Banking Union. Overall, banks are better capitalised and less leveraged since end-2014, making them better prepared to fend off fears of economic shocks. Liquidity positions, a key element of past crises, have also improved materially,

---

32 COM(2019) 278 final.

and the reliance on short-term, volatile sources of funding has decreased significantly (See Figure 2). In parallel, MREL buffers have continued to improve thanks to the application of the 2018 SRB guidance. Overall, almost 93 % of the MREL build-up has already been achieved across the Banking Union. In addition, substantial progress has been made with the adoption of several legislative and non-legislative risk-reduction measures at EU and national level. A special issue of the Joint Monitoring Report is due in 2020.

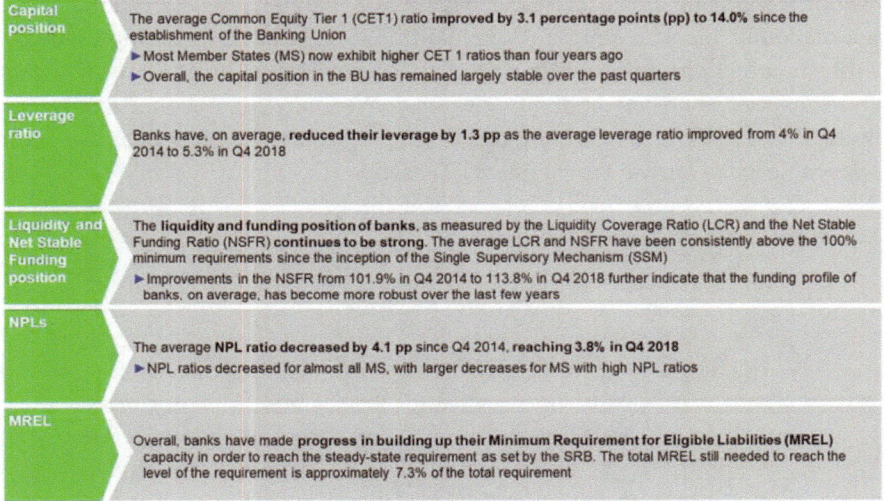

Figure 2: Overall developments (Fourth Joint Monitoring Report, May 2019)[33]

On 25 May 2018, the Council agreed its institutional position on the Banking Package, setting the scene for negotiations with the European Parliament and, beyond that, adoption of an agreed text. In this light, the June 2018 Euro Summit agreed that *"adhering to all elements of the 2016 roadmap in the appropriate sequence, work should start on a roadmap for beginning political negotiations on the European Deposit Insurance Scheme"*. Some momentum was created for the activities of the Ad Hoc Working Party under the Austrian Presidency. Discussions focussed on EDIS design, in particular, options for liquidity support and appropriate conditionality aspects, with no agreement. Political guidance on key para-

---

33 https://www.consilium.europa.eu/media/39688/joint-risk-reduction-monitoring-report-may-2019-_vfinal.pdf. NPL figures are based on the latest available NPL Progress Report at the time of publication.

meters was not forthcoming. Up to the end of the Austrian Presidency, the three main options discussed were mandatory lending, reinsurance and a hybrid model aimed at reflecting Member State diverging interests. Difficulties in breaking out of the risk reduction vs. risk sharing dialectic started to become difficult to comprehend. Remaining issues that could conceivably be put forward as new risk reduction objectives each had their own set of challenges (*e.g.* new prudential requirements for sovereign exposures, a common safe asset or a harmonised bank insolvency framework).

From the Commission's perspective, the time spent on technical exploration between 2016-2018 until sufficient progress was achieved on risk reduction has been both rich and useful. Whenever it had to make its case on EDIS, the Commission has often argued that the cost of waiting for the next crisis before finding the collective resolve to complete the EMU reforms is unaffordable.[34] That logic still stands today and could be well served by fresh perspectives on EDIS that could help explain better why a common deposit insurance system constitutes a positive agenda.

Towards a steady-state Banking Union – the role of common deposit insurance

Since the beginning of 2019, the narrative on EDIS is starting to cover other dimensions. This has been largely the result of an inter-governmental High-level Working Group on EDIS established, further to the inclusive Euro Summit of 14 December 2018, at the level of the inclusive Eurogroup Working Group. The Group has been mandated to work on next steps and is considering not just EDIS but the rest of the Banking Union as well. If successful, the Group's discussions could pave the way for the roadmap on beginning political negotiations on EDIS envisaged in the June 2018 Euro Summit. Much of the Group's work this year has sought to develop a common understanding on what the steady state of the Banking Union could look like and preferable transition paths to that end. Although there continue to be differences of opinion, the Group has fostered a better understanding of the role of EDIS as part of the Banking Union architecture.

Seen from this perspective, the original Banking Union long-term vision finds some resonance in the Group's discussions. In a report dated June 2019, elements of a steady-state vision are described as follows: *"In the steady state, a uniform*

---

34 https://ec.europa.eu/commission/sites/beta-political/files/reflection-paper-emu_en.pdf.

and effective level of protection of covered depositors across the entire Banking Union, regardless of their geographic location, is ensured. This significantly reduces the negative link between banks and their home sovereign. The implementation of EDIS should fully preserve the alignment of liability and control in the Banking Union (SSM, SRM and depositor protection). EDIS should be fully funded through risk-based contributions raised from the banking sector. In line with the Deposit Guarantee Schemes Directive (DGSD), national deposit guarantee schemes are fully built up to their target level."[35]

The Banking Union ultimately needs a transparent and credible common deposit insurance system. When fully built up, a common deposit insurance fund would operate more efficiently if it were based clear definitions of situations where EDIS interventions are needed and where they are not. For this to happen, the resolution and insolvency part of the Banking Union needs to be further developed.[36] At the same time, the Banking Union safety net would be greatly enhanced by the timely completion of ongoing work on a common backstop to the SRF and on liquidity in resolution. In this "bigger picture" scenario, roles would be clearly assigned across the whole institutional part of the financial system: common Banking Union institutions, European-level and Euro area supervisors, the SRB, the institution in charge of common deposit insurance, national competent authorities and, ultimately, banks themselves. Depositor confidence should increase in such a scenario and the incentives for moral hazard[37] should diminish. In this context, a common deposit insurance system would help improve both the robustness and the resilience of the EU financial system because of better coherence across the different component parts of the Banking Union architecture. In this long-term perspective, an integrated crisis management system could become more feasible and a common backstop provided through the European Stability Mechanism more desirable.

---

35 https://www.consilium.europa.eu/media/39768/190606-hlwg-chair-report.pdf.

36 On 30 April 2019, the Commission has adopted a report (COM (2019) 213 final) reviewing the application of the BRRD and SRMR. In its assessment, the Commission takes stock of the implementation of the resolution legislation and its application to concrete banking cases. Given that the legislation has been applied only in a very limited number of cases – a number of which concern "legacy issues", which had accumulated before and during the financial crisis – the Report concludes that more time is needed to fully assess the implications of the legislation. In addition, essential provisions in the two legislative instruments amended as part of the Banking Package (such as MREL) still need to be fully applied.

37 See De Larosière Report, Paragraph 127 on the ambivalent potential of "constructive ambiguity" regarding decisions about using public sector support in banking crisis management situations. Ten years since the report, the progression towards more clearly delineated roles in crisis management is part of the ongoing debate on how to complete the Banking Union.

One relatively new argument in favour of EDIS[38] is emerging in the home-host context, where a new delicate balance has been found as a result of concluding the Banking Package. Conceptually, the existence of a common deposit insurance scheme would support cross-border banking. In particular through its loss-making component, EDIS could constitute a harmonised safety net to cater for an adequate settlement of claims in the event of deposit pay-outs. This could be of particular relevance for large cross-border banking groups in parallel, of course, with further harmonisation and streamlining of resolution and bank insolvency tools. So far, the EU's regulatory approach to the continued use of capital and liquidity waivers by national authorities has been to encourage their phase-out through proposed amendments to CRR/CRD. Often, Member States have justified the continued use of ring-fencing because of the need to preserve the essential functions of national DGSs[39] while resorting to national insolvency remedies in case of failure of the foreign parent company supervised by a home supervisor. Perhaps a solution could involve the reverse regulatory approach, namely to promote a common deposit insurance system as a safeguard for host jurisdictions combined with a further revision of the bank resolution and liquidation toolkit.

By way of reminder, the 23 November 2016 legislative proposal of the European Commission for the Banking Package included a possibility to substitute, fully or partially, pre-positioned internal MREL instruments with cross-border collateralised guarantees provided by the parent entity. Such an approach would have reduced market fragmentation and delivered lower levels of prepositioning and, more importantly, greater flexibility to employ the loss absorption and recapitalisation capacity anywhere within the group, when needed. In its report from June 2018,[40] the European Parliament also supported the free circulation of capital, liquidity and loss absorption and recapitalisation capacity within the single market and notably within the Banking Union. However, upon the insistence of a large number of host Member States, the Council general approach of

---

38 In June 2009, a high-level committee set up in Belgium to provide feedback to the De Larosière Report argued that a European deposit insurance scheme could have been implemented as a first step towards burden sharing in crisis management. Taking the perspective of a jurisdiction hosting the subsidiaries of what would later be designated as systemically important banks, the Belgian report advocated common deposit insurance as an important safeguard in the home-host context. Belgium and other EU Member States whose GDPs were significantly exposed to large banks outside their jurisdiction, had been hit hard during the financial crisis: https://finances.belgium.be/sites/default/files/downloads/High_level_committee_on_a_new_financial_architecture_final_report_20090616 %20(1).pdf.
39 I. Schnabel, N. Véron, *Breaking the stalemate on European deposit* insurance, 07 April 2018. https://voxeu.org/article/breaking-stalemate-european-deposit-insurance.
40 A8-0243/2018.

25 May 2018, required a 100 % prepositioning of internal MREL capacity with the subsidiary, without any possibility of cross-border collateralised guarantees or cross-border waivers. This view prevailed in the negotiations on this matter with the European Parliament. Progress in the home–host relationship will require the material legal or practical barriers to the use of financial resources among banking groups to be identified and addressed. Restoring trust between home and host authorities necessarily goes through the development of workable mechanisms and arrangements that would provide certainty to host jurisdictions that the TLAC/MREL that has not been pre-positioned would be available in due time to recapitalise a subsidiary.

Still today, despite the establishment of Banking Union institutions, host jurisdictions continue to favour "self-preservation" over trust in a so far untested framework. At the same time, the crises have left the banking sector more fragmented than before. As a consequence of the crises, banks have retreated to their domestic markets[41] and reduced lending to non-domestic banks (See Figures 3 and 4). Inter-bank flows across borders are however key to bolster the shock absorption capacity and resilience of the sector to asymmetric shocks. For ten years, there have been no large-scale cross-border bank mergers within the euro area. In the near future, consolidation of smaller banks within countries appears more probable than cross-border expansion. At the same time, banks still hold sizeable domestic sovereign bond portfolios, which maintain the link between sovereigns and banks.[42] The sector is also facing a challenging environment of low profitability, against the background of an extended period of low interest rates, and several structural adjustments. The post-crisis regulatory framework has introduced additional costs for banks and requires business model adjustment. For example, the requirement to raise capital reduces returns, and MREL and TLAC raise funding costs. The technological landscape (digitalisation, Big-tech and shadow banking) is changing fast, imposes heavy adjustment costs and enhances competitive pressures.

---

41 L. Emter, *et al.*, *Cross-border banking in the EU since the crisis: what is driving the great retrenchment?* ECB Working Paper No. 2130, February 2018.
42 Forthcoming in 2019: *Quarterly Report on the Euro Area*, Volume 2, European Commission.

Source: ECB.

Note: A higher indicator signals greater financial integration as measured by the dispersion of financial prices, ranging from zero (full fragmentation) to one (full integration).

Figure 3: Financial integration in the euro area as measured by the ECB price-based indicator

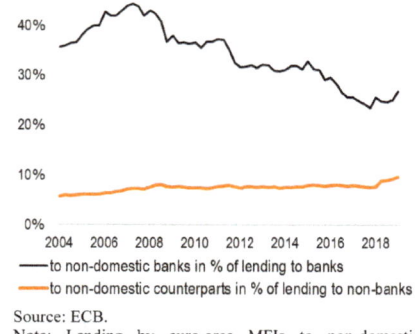

Source: ECB.

Note: Lending by euro-area MFIs to non-domestic residents (other euro area and other EU Member States) in % of lending to EU residents (including domestic residents).

Figure 4: Bank lending to non-domestic counterparts, euro area

In terms of immediate policy follow-up, the High-level Working Group is continuing its work on possible transition paths towards the steady-state and is expected to report back to the Eurogroup in December 2019. There is no clear vision today of a likely outcome. On a positive note, these comprehensive discussions could provide a basis for a feasible and carefully weighted step-by-step approach to a fully mutualised EDIS, however long it will take and however small the first few steps. In the interest of establishing common ground, some Member States might prefer a system limited to liquidity support only or based on hybrid solutions floated earlier by the Austrian Presidency. Others might find that prospect acceptable only if firmly grounded in an end-state involving full loss coverage and other Banking Union improvements. In either scenario, it would help to find ways to reflect as many interests as possible to improve the quality of the resulting solutions.

Conclusion

In the thick of the crisis, tensions over rescue packages showed that risk-sharing cannot be envisaged without the control-sharing that comes with common governance. Banking Union institutions have now reached a mature stage of development and the single market is further supported by centralised micro-prudential oversight under three European supervisory agencies. In addition, a serious and comprehensive risk reduction programme has been steadfastly put together and is being implemented and updated. The crisis has laid bare the paradox that banks operate on a European scale, in the internal market, with the corollary risk of contagion should they default. Despite significant institutional reforms, as long as that lack of alignment continues, the Banking Union is still unable to deliver a fully robust and coherent financial system which in turn would greatly strengthen the resilience of EU economies to future bank crises and better cross-border integration of financial services.

With this in mind, and also taking into account the steady-state perspective of the Banking Union, a common deposit insurance scheme would substantially increase the firepower of the European Union to protect depositors in times of crisis. A fully mutualised system would properly align liability and control in the Banking Union in the longer term. It may take time to build up such a system, and there will necessarily need to be a confidence-building period which, as suggested by the Commission in October 2017, could rely on liquidity support channelled incrementally through a central fund until the appropriate conditions are met for loss-sharing.

The European Commission remains committed to completing the Banking Union, by means of a common deposit insurance system. Efforts should also be intensified to add a common backstop to the Single Resolution Fund and agreed liquidity in resolution options to the EU's crisis management toolkit.

Joachim Wuermeling

A Single Deposit Insurance Scheme as a Component of a Stable Banking Union?

There is much debate about whether a common deposit insurance scheme is needed to complete the European banking union, with extensive discussions centring on who will pay more and who less, who has done their homework and who hasn't. Yet the more heated the debate, the more apparent it becomes that some of the arguments put forward are intended to serve vested interests and thus lose sight of the overarching objective: the stability of the euro area and its resilience to future financial crises.

The banking union as a stabiliser in the euro area: good, but not good enough

What is the status quo? With the banking union and reformed regulatory framework, we are much better prepared for crises than we were five years ago, but still not well enough. More measures need to be taken to reduce the likelihood and magnitude of a future banking – and hence euro – crisis.

But is a European deposit insurance scheme the right weapon of choice? Launched in 2014, the European banking union has already achieved a great deal. A Single Supervisory Mechanism under the aegis of the ECB and a Single Resolution Mechanism have been created. Banks are now subject to stricter and more consistent supervision, and ailing institutions can no longer count on being bailed out by taxpayers, instead having to face resolution. And the harmonisation of national deposit insurance schemes in all EU Member States means that deposits of up to €100,000 already receive an equal level of protection today. Isn't this enough to shield the euro area from banking crises and their repercussions?

The counterargument is certainly plausible. We cannot yet rule out the possibility of banking crises leading to a bank run and/or a sovereign insolvency, nor of a sovereign insolvency resulting in a banking crisis and a run on banks.

The reason for this is the close linkage between sovereigns and their banks, commonly known as the sovereign-bank nexus. This situation has arisen chiefly because banks are by far the largest creditors of sovereigns. Doubts about sovereign solvency can therefore quickly undermine the soundness of those financial institutions.

https://doi.org/10.1515/9783110683073-005

The reverse situation, in which a struggling banking system fuels uncertainty about sovereign solvency, is similarly dicey. In extreme cases, these kinds of crisis can raise concerns about the stability of monetary union as a whole – as shown by events in Greece and Cyprus.

To effectively limit these risks, we still need to comprehensively reform the institutional architecture of monetary union. A European system could kick in precisely when the purely national systems are under too much strain. This solution is also in Germany's interest: the sovereign debt crisis, in particular, showed how closely the member states of a monetary union are connected and how quickly crises can cross from one euro area country to the next, and indeed how quickly doubts about a member state's stability spread to the entire monetary union. A European deposit insurance scheme can thus strengthen financial stability in the euro area as a whole for the benefit of all member states.

How far along is the political process at present? More than four years ago, on 22 June 2015, the European Commission published a plan for the future of the Economic and Monetary Union, calling for the swift creation of a single deposit insurance scheme as a third pillar in the banking union and the EU.

On 24 November 2015, this was specified in more detail in a draft regulation for the creation of a European Deposit Insurance System (EDIS). The European Commission's plans, which had already set out fixed implementation phases and their timeframes, were stalled at the political level on the basis of key points of criticism. The Commission subsequently presented a new proposal for EDIS in October 2017, which envisaged that it would initially begin with liquidity coverage in the first phase and then be developed into a co-insurance scheme in the second phase. According to the proposal, the first phase would have begun on 1 January 2019 and the second phase would have been implemented depending on an evaluation of the risk situation rather than based on a fixed timeframe.

Since the collapse of negotiations, the European Commission has not yet put forward a new timetable. No political negotiations regarding EDIS are currently taking place, and a new proposal from the new Commission is expected by the end of 2019.

A European deposit insurance scheme, but which one?

While the need for a European solution to the issue of deposit insurance appears clear, it is unclear which approach would be best suited to curbing risks as effectively and efficiently as possible. And here, the special nature of the EU has to be factored in: it is a union formed of sovereign states, not a federation.

Since 2015 at the very latest, when the European Commission proposed replacing all national deposit insurance schemes with a European one, the idea of a fully integrated EU insurance scheme has had a prominent role in the debate. Its merits are likely to lie in its clear and centralised structure, which can alleviate doubts about its ability to function during a crisis. Nonetheless, a purely supranational pot of funds is not necessarily the most efficient way to mitigate risk in the EU.

When it comes to crises that a national system can overcome on its own, there is no need for a supranational pot. In this context, the alternative of an EU reinsurance scheme is currently being discussed, in various shapes and forms, by the European Parliament and by economists, for example. The idea is for a European system of national deposit insurance schemes as a first line of defence. When the national funds are exhausted, the EU reinsurance system would kick in. This approach also has its strengths and weaknesses. A key advantage is that distorted incentives for national economic policy, which could result in high levels of risk in domestic bank balance sheets, would be better restricted, allowing established national insurance schemes to continue performing their stabilising function.

One disadvantage would be the greater institutional complexity which, in a crisis, could spread uncertainty among market participants about whether the system can function.

This means that a workable safety net for the financial sector does not necessarily need to be European. A safety net is workable if it makes full use of every single robust instrument to prevent a bank run from being triggered.

In some respects, the existing deposit insurance schemes in Germany and Europe go far beyond the mere payout function that the Commission is lining up for EDIS. Indeed, the institutional protection schemes in the savings bank and credit cooperative sectors with their key objective to protect the member institutions and to avert emerging or existing financial difficulties by fully protecting the business relationships and thus avoiding having to use the deposit guarantee scheme – reinforce the safety net if one of their members is on the brink of insolvency. Similarly, the voluntary deposit insurance offered by the private commercial banks makes a payout under the deposit insurance scheme a less likely scenario. In any case, new models of deposit insurance must contribute to financial stability to at least the same extent as the tried and tested national systems, like the one in Germany.

No joint risk liability without joint risk reduction

Irrespective of the decision for a supranational approach or a reinsurance system, deposit insurance can only be reformed if key conditions for a sound foundation are created. I would like to highlight three of these conditions.

1. **First**, the legacy risks lurking on European banks' balance sheets need to be contained. We need to further reduce existing non-performing loans (NPLs) and restrict new NPLs.

   While the average non-performing loans ratio in Europe has fallen considerably since 2014, the problem largely concerns individual, hard-hit countries.

   In some cases, the NPL stocks in the national banking systems are distributed in a highly heterogeneous way. While Bundesbank appreciates the work already done regarding NPLs, further action needs to be taken to reduce what are still, in some cases, large holdings of NPLs which accumulated on banks' balance sheets due to national developments.

2. **Second**, looking at government bonds, the situation is not much better.

   In this regard, government bonds need to lose their preferential treatment and the sovereign-bank nexus needs to be dissolved. Many banks in the EU have significant sovereign exposures on their balance sheets, particularly against their respective home countries. Of course, this is linked to corresponding credit and concentration risks. However, as long as the holding of government bonds continues to receive preferential regulatory treatment, banks have no incentive to reduce these risks on their balance sheets and, as a result, remain dependent on the economic situation of their home country. A single deposit insurance scheme should not mutualise sovereign debt via a European deposit insurance scheme.

3. The **third** necessary course of action is to establish minimum standards for insolvency regimes – for example, more efficient collateral management.

   In the EU, national economic policy still has a major bearing on domestic banks' financial situations. The same is true of the legal framework. As a result, insolvency law, for example, still differs to a very large degree at national level, meaning that the timing (insolvency duration) and amount of collateral recovery (insolvency ratio) can vary considerably. However, uniform legal bases in the field of insolvency are a vital prerequisite for a European deposit insurance scheme.

The first two pillars of the banking union have already greatly reduced the risks for euro area banks and sovereigns. But a number of gaps still have to be plugged, not to mention establishing the final major pillar. However, before we can tackle the issue of a deposit insurance scheme, we have to continue dismantling risks in bank balance sheets, further reduce the banks' susceptibility to crises, and break up the tight sovereign-bank nexus – taking this as our motto: first a solid foundation, then a sturdy house.

II. The Bankers' Round: What EDIS Does For Us and Our Customers

Roland Boekhout

Completing Banking Union: Time to Meet the Challenges

The European banking sector's regulatory and supervisory framework has changed fundamentally in recent years. As a consequence, banks have become much better capitalised and risk profiles much more moderate. In addition, thanks to recovery and resolution measures and the introduction of the bail-in principle, according to which investors in bank debt instruments will be charged if a bank fails, it has become much less likely that deposit insurance schemes will ever have to be called upon again.

In particular, the decision taken in response to the financial crisis of 2008 and 2009 to establish a European Banking Union has been an important step to strengthen financial stability and ensure a proper functioning of European financial markets. Thanks to the introduction of single supervision in 2014 and the setup of a single resolution fund, vital progress has been made in reducing the likelihood and possible impact of future banking crises.

Progress in establishing the third pillar of the Banking Union, the European Deposit Insurance Scheme (EDIS), however, remains slow. This is particularly due to the fact that a number of Member States insist that risk sharing via EDIS is to be made conditional on further risk reduction in terms of reducing non-performing loans (NPLs) and sovereign exposures of banks, especially in Southern Europe. Although there are good arguments to reduce these risks even further, as will be pointed out below, it should also be acknowledged that NPLs have come down significantly in the past few years and a very substantial degree of risk sharing in Europe has already taken place via monetary policy instruments (e.g. Target 2, OMT, ESF) and cross border exposures of banks and other financial institutions.

Notwithstanding, it is clear that further steps are needed to prevent bank failures in case of systemic crises, eliminate contagion risks and really break the bank-sovereign nexus in Europe. In the view of ING, the following issues in particular need to be prioritised:

- Reduction of ringfencing and ensuring a free flow of funds
- Reduction of home biases in sovereign risk exposures
- Harmonisation of insolvency laws
- Harmonised application of macroprudential policies
- Deepening secondary markets: establishing Capital Markets Union

https://doi.org/10.1515/9783110683073-006

Reduction of ringfencing and ensuring a free flow of funds

In order to ensure that cross-border banking groups in the Eurozone can effectively manage their risks, and to foster financial stability and the efficient allocation of funds across the Eurozone, cross-border banking groups should be able to centrally manage their capital, liquidity and loss absorbency requirements without fragmentation across Eurozone borders.

However, to date, cross-border banking groups continue to face a number of important impediments in transferring assets across borders. This is because in the current situation, the liquidity backstop ensuring the national deposit guarantees schemes' (DGS) ability to provide bridge financing also in times of great stress, is still to be provided by the national sovereign. As a result, national authorities continue to feel responsible for domestic financial stability and play a role in the oversight of banks that are active within their borders. This practice even continues under the existing Capital Requirements Regulation (CRR) 2 regulation, as a result of which individual member states still have significant discretion in setting local large exposure limits and preventing the provision of waivers for liquidity, solvency and large exposures for cross-border banking groups.

As long as national authorities remain focused on their national interests and preferences, given that national resources remain at stake, there is a clear incentive to hamper free movement of liquidity and deposits across member states. This effectively limits cross-border banking groups to efficiently allocate internal capital and liquidity, as they face limitations that block resources from flowing to where they are most in demand from businesses and households. This, in turn, leaves them unable to compete with bigger and more efficient global peers and (at least partly) explains the absence of major European bank mergers in the last decade, as well as the increasingly excessive exposure of European banks to home countries. For instance, interbank loans in the Eurozone exhibit a domestic share of approximately 60% (see ECB 2017, statistical annex). Cross-border private risk sharing thus remains limited too, which effectively lowers the whole system's loss absorption capacity.

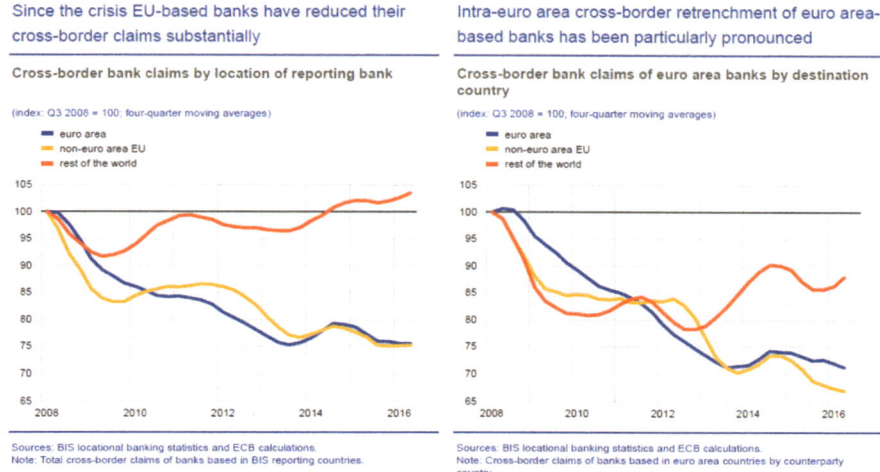

Since the crisis EU-based banks have reduced their cross-border claims substantially

Intra-euro area cross-border retrenchment of euro area-based banks has been particularly pronounced

Cross-border bank claims by location of reporting bank

Cross-border bank claims of euro area banks by destination country

(index: Q3 2008 = 100; four-quarter moving averages)

Sources: BIS locational banking statistics and ECB calculations.
Note: Total cross-border claims of banks based in BIS reporting countries.

Sources: BIS locational banking statistics and ECB calculations.
Note: Cross-border claims of banks based in euro area countries by counterparty country.

In sum, what this boils down to very much looks like a classical prisoner's dilemma: efforts to achieve local (domestic) financial stability in the end worsen financial stability in the international system. In turn, this means that financial stability is worse in all jurisdictions, an issue eloquently described by the Bank for International Settlements. [1]

Therefore, it is fundamental to establish a European deposit insurance scheme (EDIS) at the same (European) level where the competence and authority for banking supervision and resolution lie, including a liquidity backstop at the European level (e.g. in conjunction with the ESM), with a strict liquidity only character to prevent permanent fiscal transfers via the backdoor, ensuring that any shortfall in EDIS will eventually be funded by banks. Hence, it is good news that European leaders recently agreed to put a liquidity backstop in place, but unfortunately its credibility remains questionable, as it only will be a limited backstop.

Reducing home biases in sovereign risk exposures

Another important element in addressing contagion risks relates to sovereign risks. For as long as banks have significant exposure to their home sovereign in their government bond portfolio ("home bias"), contagion may occur from gov-

---

1 Gambacorta, Leonardo and Rixtel, Adrian Van and Schiaffi, Stefano, Changing Business Models in International Bank Funding (March 2017). BIS Working Paper No. 614. Av

ernments to banks, in case of economic or financial trouble. Investors will anticipate this, and the "sovereign bank doom loop" remains intact. Therefore, next to EDIS, the home bias of European bank sovereign bond portfolios should be removed.

The optimal solution would be the introduction of a Europe-wide "safe asset", since the past 10 years have clearly shown that national sovereign bonds cannot fulfil this role in all circumstances. Providing Eurozone governments with stable access to finance, joint issuance would provide the financial system with a new top-rated asset, which could help to reduce home bias in bank sovereign bond portfolios.

Yet, as this kind of solution is politically controversial at present, and thus not easily implemented in the short to medium run, it is important to also think about alternatives.

It could be worthwhile considering an approach first developed by Mario Monti in 2010 – called the "E-bond" approach, which basically attempts to strike a balance between creating a liquid safe asset and incentivising prudent fiscal behaviour. As outlined in a Peterson Institute policy brief by Jeromin Zettelmeyer and Álvaro Leandro[2], the main characteristics of the E-Bond approach include common issuance through the European Stability Mechanism (ESM), no joint but several liability (meaning each participating member state would be responsible for its commensurate share of the liability), and a senior-junior structure ensuring the Member State's liability to the ESM would be senior to the rest category of domestically issued debt of all Eurozone government (safeguarding that the ESM issued bond is senior to MS issued bonds, to ensure liquidity and remove any risk of a sovereign default).

Another next-best solution could be to treat sovereign bond exposures as a concentration risk from a prudential perspective. Concentration charges could be applied at consolidated group level, rising with exposure to bonds issued by individual sovereigns. This would incentivise banks to invest in a basket of different (Euro) sovereign bonds for their liquidity portfolio.

Harmonisation of insolvency laws

Another important obstacle in completing the banking union relates to the divergence of national insolvency. Fragmented insolvency laws across national

---

2 Zettelmeyer, Jeromin and Leandro, Alvaro, The Search for a Euro Area Safe Asset (March 8, 2018). Peterson Institute for International Economics Working Paper No. 18-3.

borders add to concerns of host countries and thus motivate ring-fencing. E.g. in Italy banks tend to keep NPLs longer on their books, because writing them off could mean that their chance of seizing collateral diminishes in court (as taking provisions/writing off is likely to be interpreted such that "the bank considered it already lost anyway").

In the absence of 'public interest', failing banks continue to be liquidated under national law. In other words, when a bank in failure does not endanger financial stability, it is to be resolved like any other business in the market. Yet, recent evidence of failing banks indicates that the term 'public interest' is defined differently in the EU framework and across member states. This obviously fuels uncertainty about the outcomes of the liquidation procedures.

In addition, the implementation of a resolution action also remains rooted in national insolvency law for the purposes of protecting creditors and applying resolution tools at legal entity level. The SRB is tasked with assessing whether shareholders and creditors would have received a better treatment under insolvency proceedings than in resolution (so called "no creditor worse off", or NCWO). The insolvency law of the member state where the resolution takes place is to be used for the purpose of carrying out the NCWO assessment (e.g. ranking of claims). Yet, in the absence of a harmonised regime for banks' insolvency law, the NCWO principle would not result in similar outcomes across the banking union in the case of the resolution of a cross-border group.

At the same time, it is important to put concerns around NPL portfolios of southern European banks into perspective. As the graph below illustrates, NPLs as a percentage of total loans in southern Europe have already come down significantly since the crisis, to reach pre-crisis levels.

Non-performing loans (% of all loans)

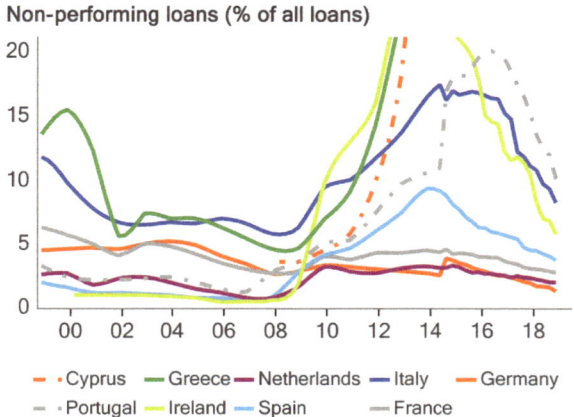

Source: ING calculations based on ECB, 2018, statistical annex

Harmonised application of macroprudential policies

With the establishment of the Single Supervisory Mechanism (SSM) and the Single Resolution Board (SRB), significant steps have been taken to establish microprudential supervision and resolution in the hands of Banking Union institutions. Yet, a deeper harmonisation of how macroprudential policy is set at Eurozone level remains necessary. Admittedly, since there can be circumstances warranting country-specific actions, national authorities should remain primarily in charge of executing such policies. But the European Central Bank (ECB) setting out consistent methodologies, supplemented with the local knowledge of national supervisors about emerging risks, would institutionalise a common rationale for applying macro-prudential policy consistently in the Banking Union.

For non-harmonised macro-prudential rules, be it on setting the buffers or the portfolio specific instruments, can lead to banks with similar risk profiles experiencing significantly different regulatory requirements in the markets in which they operate. E.g. increasing capital requirements are not neutral in terms of funding costs. Banks would need to compensate by repricing their products, notably by increasing loan margins or lowering interest rates on deposits. Therefore, if macroprudential policies are not applied consistently, it is possible that banks with identical risk profiles face significantly different product pricing conditions, thereby creating an undue distortion of the level playing field.

More broadly, the Banking Union would benefit from more clarity, predictability and transparency regarding this crucial banking regulation. Harmonised methods that make macroprudential policy more predictable can facilitate adequate pricing of risks by bank investors and avoid unwarranted uncertainty in financial markets.

Deepening secondary markets: establishing Capital Markets Union

Another important step to be taken is to increase opportunities for banks to offload risk-carrying exposures, by increasing their broker role in markets without eroding their capital ratios. For as a result of the introduction of bail-in capital as well as stricter capital and liquidity requirements (e.g. Basel IV, MREL/ TLAC), the financing costs for banks have increased significantly over the past few years.

Yet, apart from financial stability, creating a more diverse mix of financing sources would also strengthen economic stability. Banks in Europe currently finance two thirds of all debt by households and businesses, compared to one third in the US. For SMEs and MidCorps in particular, banks remain the dominant financing channel. And even despite the low interest rates and spreads in recent years, the share of market-based financing of companies has only seen marginal increases.

In turn, banks too will benefit from a deepening of the investor base, as they currently issue loans against too low margins to be sustainable. And securitising these loans and distributing them to market participants, generally requires a fair return, so that's why strengthening secondary markets is so important, as this will discipline banks to originate assets at market clearing price.

On top of that, the EU also needs to act, because after Brexit, its most important capital market will sit outside of the EU. So to ensure that European banks will continue to play their intermediating role in the real economy successfully, e.g. in activities like syndicated lending and long term finance, it is even more crucial to establish a functioning capital markets union (CMU) on the continent.

Conclusion

The development of the SSM, SRM, SRB and EU recovery and resolution framework have made national arguments for ring-fencing capital and liquidity less valid than they were before and during the crisis. Moreover, it is noted that risk-sharing via monetary policy instruments has been significant in the past few years and a lot of progress has been made in reducing NPLs. Nonetheless, many host countries still seek to protect shareholders, creditors and taxpayers by ring-fencing capital and liquidity, using measures that exceed and / or differ from the prudential standards that were agreed upon at the global level. As long as the national sovereign will continue to provide the liquidity backstop ensuring the existing national deposit guarantees schemes' (DGS) ability to provide bridge financing also in times of great stress, national authorities continue to feel responsible for domestic financial stability and play a role in the oversight of banks that are active within their borders.

As a consequence, the post-crisis European banking landscape remains fragmented across national borders. Cross-border banking groups are not able to efficiently allocate internal capital and liquidity as they face limitations that block resources from flowing to where they are most in demand from businesses and households. This leaves them unable to compete with bigger and more efficient global peers. It could also help explain the absence of major European bank mergers in the last decade, as well as the increasingly excessive exposure of European banks to home countries.

Therefore, establishing a European deposit insurance scheme (EDIS) at the same (European) level where the competence and authority for banking supervision and resolution lie, is absolutely essential. Enhancing the ability of cross-border EU bank to operate across the Internal Market will not only promote competition, but also the penetration of new and improved services across national borders. This is because, due to e.g. technological progress and innovation, banks are increasingly able to offer remote services, optimised allocation of resources across border. So at the end of the day, it is the customer who will benefit most from a free flow funds across border, as this will reduce costs and improve conditions and the level of services banks offer to their clients.

Bank M&As – number of transactions (y-axis) in the Euro Area (ECB 2017)

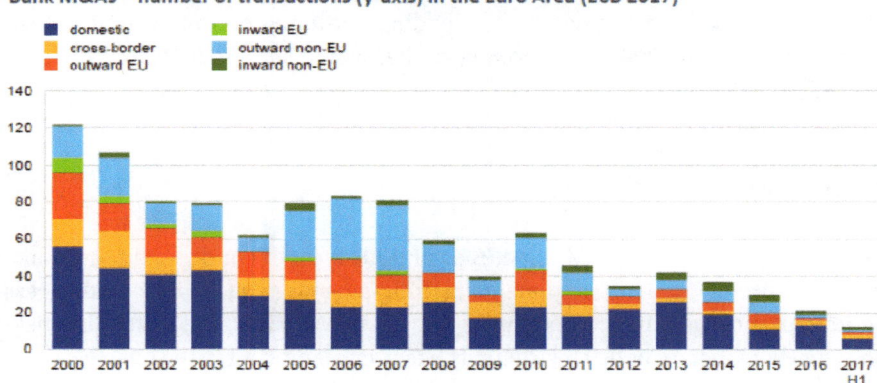

Sylvie Matherat
"EDIS Might Not Revolutionise European Banking – But it can Liberate Europe from Regulatory Fragmentation"

Introduction

The European Deposit Insurance Scheme (EDIS) is the missing pillar of the Banking Union, designed to provide the same level of confidence in deposit protection arrangements across all Member States. EDIS does not increase or expand the level of protection enjoyed by depositors across the Union. But EDIS is important, because it provides a solution to the "sovereign-bank nexus", which underpins concerns about sovereign solvency when countries have to step in for bank failures. The unsolved nexus and the lack of trust between home and host authorities is a key reason behind the regulatory and market fragmentation in EU and in particular Eurozone financial markets. EDIS has the potential to solve the nexus by offering a common protection of all deposits of any failing bank, removing the risk that host Member States could be liable for failings of local entities headquartered elsewhere in Europe. This is then expected to improve trust between authorities and facilitate the development of a truly harmonised single supervision area within the Banking Union, avoiding the costs of trapped liquidity and capital.

It is these benefits that make EDIS important for banks, especially cross-border ones, and their customers. There will be potential direct costs (for large banks) and benefits (enhanced depositor confidence in some jurisdictions) from moves towards mutualisation of deposit insurance in the EU. Whether or not the outcome of this initiative justifies its costs and the political effort put into it will depend on whether it manages to unlock the potential of the Banking Union and delivers the "...deeper financial integration [that is] key for a wider choice of services at lower prices".[1]

---

1 *European Commission Communication to the European Parliament, the Council and the European Central Bank, the European Economic and Social Committee and the Committee of the Regions on completing the Banking Union*, 11 October 2017.

https://doi.org/10.1515/9783110683073-007

The role of deposit insurance in Europe

In Europe, where household deposits[2] constitute c.50 % of bank funding and corporate deposits make up another 15 %, depositor confidence is absolutely fundamental to financial stability. The 2008 financial crisis highlighted shortcomings in deposit protection within the EU and there were even incidents of bank runs, illustrating a lack of such confidence. Inconsistent coverage, low covered amounts and a lack of clarity for depositors about availability of funds to support individual Deposit Guarantee Schemes (DGS) were prevailing. It was clear Europe needed a more credible deposit guarantee framework to support resilience and stability in the financial system.

Over the subsequent years, deposit insurance have been substantially enhanced in Europe. The Deposit Guarantee Scheme Directive (DGSD), agreed in 2014,[3] brought a number of important enhancements to deposit insurance in Europe. There has also been a concentrated effort to raise awareness and increase transparency in the existence and capacity of DGS, through the work of the European Banking Authority (EBA). This has translated into improved deposit protection in all European Member States, albeit mostly in relation to retail customers and bank business lines. Corporate deposits are typically above the covered amount and therefore do not benefit from DGS protection. Other liabilities are also not covered.

BOX 1. *Overview of DGSD features*

- Significant increase in the resources available and harmonisation of funding – Banks across the EU have to pay an annual levy into the (often new) national DGS. In principle a DGS should have funds equal to at least 0.8 % of covered deposits (deposits that are eligible for protection by a DGS) by 3 July 2024.
- Increase in the amount of deposits covered from EUR 20,000 to EUR 100,000. For liabilities arising from securities transactions, 90 % cover limited to the equivalent of EUR 20,000. Under "temporary high balances", the coverage level for deposits increases to a total of up to EUR 500,000 for a period of six months after the amount has been credited and was caused by lifetime event, e.g. real estate transactions relating to private residential, marriage, divorce, retirement, dismissal, redundancy, birth, sickness, care dependency, invalidity, disability or death.
- All types of deposits are covered, i.e. demand, term, savings deposits and registered savings certificates. Deposits are protected irrespective of currency held in. Coverage also

---

2 *Report on Funding plans*, EBA, September 2018: https://eba.europa.eu/documents/10180/235 7155/EBA+Report+on+Funding+Plans.pdf
3 Directive 2014/49/EU

for deposits in a dependent branch of a DGS member bank in another European Economic Area (EEA) country.
- Reduction of the pay-out time to 7 days.
- All private individuals, partnerships and corporations are entitled to protection and compensation. Not protected are deposits by banks, institutional investors such as financial service providers, or insurance undertakings or deposits by public authorities.

Main characteristics of German IPS and DGS schemes

Germany has two parallel statutory schemes for deposit protection: Institution Protection Schemes (IPS) for public-sector savings banks (Sparkassen), State banks (Landesbanken), State building and loan associations (Landesbausparkassen) and co-operative banks (Genossenschaftsbanken), and DGS for all other banks. This dual arrangement is covered by the DGSD.
- Banks are only required to be members and contribute to either an IPS or the DGS and their customers are only covered by the respective scheme.
- A key difference is that IPS have the objective to preserve the member banks from insolvency and liquidation. Like that their customers are also protected from losing of their deposits.

In addition to the statutory deposit schemes, German banks have set up voluntary deposits protection to offer further protection, such as the one for private banks, administered by the Association of German Banks (Bundesverband deutscher Banken).

The impact of the financial crisis

The financial crisis impacted European banks in multiple ways, however, one of the critical drivers was the insufficient level and scattered landscape of financial supervision and the lack of crisis preparation, which created risk loopholes. The global financial system faced similar challenges at different degrees.

The post-crisis years have seen a coordinated effort to enhance the regulatory framework both globally and in Europe, in order to improve the quality of financial supervision, the resilience of the banking sector and support the economy overall. Global coordination was carried out under the auspices of the Financial Stability Board (FSB), through the Basel Committee on Banking Supervision (BCBS), the Committee on Payments and Market Infrastructures (CPMI) and the International Organization of Securities Commissions (IOSCO).

The reforms of prudential requirements for banks and other financial firms, including the creation of a new discipline for resolution in case of gone concern situations, were ambitious and extensive. The changes captured all areas of regulation, with enhancement of conduct standards and more resilience, openness and transparency for financial markets. In Europe in particular these reforms were accompanied by an institutional overhaul and the creation of the three European Supervisory Authorities (ESAs), aiming to harmonise the financial regulatory rulebooks and reduce divergence that created an uneven playing field across the Union.

The close interdependency of the economies using the euro required an even more fundamental overhaul of financial supervision, in order to break the vicious circle between weak banks and their sovereigns, which at one point threatened the zone's viability. EU leaders decided to establish the Banking Union with a single source of authority for the going and gone concern oversight of the Eurozone banks and any other Member States that wished to participate.

BOX 2. *Overview post crisis regulatory and institutional reforms in the EU*

Prudential regulation
- Enhance capital and introducing new liquidity requirements through an overhaul of the prudential requirements and implementation of globally-agreed Basel standards (Capital Requirements Directive and Regulation – CRD/R[4]).
- Introduction of a resolution regime for failing banks (Bank Recovery and Resolution Directive – BRRD[5]) alternative to national bankruptcy proceeding, which included earmarked loss-absorbing debt, the possibility for authorities to use the bail-in tool to absorb losses and recapitalise the bank, in order to avoid taxpayer-funded bail-outs, as well as the requirement for advance resolution planning.

Markets regulation
- The 2008 crisis evidenced the need for further information on risks and more transparency in financial markets. The Commission responded with a review of the Markets in Financial Instruments Directive (MiFID) to increase pre and post-trade transparency in equities and fixed income markets and reinforce investor protection requirements. For Over-The-Counter (OTC) derivatives, the European Markets Infrastructure Regulation (EMIR) implemented the G20 agenda, mandating reporting of all transactions, directing more derivatives to clearing houses and guaranteeing that OTC transactions are sufficiently collateralised.
- In order to broaden the sources of financing in Europe and deepen the single market for financial services, the Commission launched the Capital Markets Union (CMU) initiative with a set of regulatory measures, which included:
  1. A revamped securitisation regime with preferential prudential treatment to re-start the market safely following the financial crisis.
  2. Further harmonisation of prospectus regulatory requirements, to facilitate issuance and distribution across borders.
  3. Reducing divergence in the supervisory requirements for asset managers.

---

4 Directive 2013/36, Regulation 575/2013.
5 Directive 2014/59.

Institutional reforms
- Establishment of the European Systemic Risk Board (ESRB) to provide macroprudential oversight of the EU financial system and the prevention and mitigation of systemic risk.
- Establishment of the three ESA for the creation of a single rulebook in financial supervision for banks (EBA), financial markets (European Securities and Markets Authority – ESMA) and insurers (European Insurance and Occupational Pensions Authority – EIOPA).
- Setting up of the Banking Union for consolidated oversight of the Eurozone financial sector – participation open to non-Eurozone Member States:
  1. Creation of the two pillars of Single Supervisory and Resolution Mechanisms (SSM/SRM) to ensure consistent supervision for the Eurozone's most systemically important banks and their resolution in case of failure. SSM was coupled with the Single Resolution Fund (SRF), so that bank failures can use arrangements pre-funded by banks, should their own resources not suffice, instead of government resources.
  2. SSM functions assumed by the European Central Bank, SRM assumed by the new Single Resolution Board (SRB).

These interventions were necessary, but did not come without cost, not only for banks but for the economy overall. Since 2010, banks have deleveraged substantially and have reduced their overall balance sheets, while capital markets' return on equity (ROE) have been reduced by a factor of 5.[6] Although the observation period is still short, these reforms appear to have been successful, inasmuch as banks did see a material improvement of their resilience with their high-quality capital ratios almost double, and a substantial clean-up of their balance sheets.[7] The wider economic impact of the reforms and their performance in a crisis is still under debate.

The Banking Union and EDIS

Since its inception, the Banking Union was envisaged to be based on three pillars, in order to ensure full equality for all the participating banks and their customers: common supervision, resolution and deposit insurance. As the post-crisis regulatory framework was being updated almost in parallel, for all three areas the aim was not so much to increase the standards, but rather to improve the integration into one coherent economic system without weak links, a prerequisite for a stable

---

6 *Impact of Regulation on Banks' Capital Markets Activities – An ex-post assessment*, AFME, PwC, April 2018.
7 *The post-crisis regulatory agenda: What is missing?* Speech by Fernando Restoy, 19 February 2018.

monetary union. For the case of deposit protection in particular, DGSD should offer sufficient confidence about the safety of bank deposits, at least up to EUR 100,000. There was no compelling case for additional deposit protection.

The 2015 so-called Five Presidents report by the leaders of the main EU institutions on the completion of the Economic and Monetary Union (EMU) explained that "the current set-up with national DGSs remains vulnerable to large local shocks."[8] That is because national DGSs are underwritten and supported only by the banks they cover and behind those banks, stand respective national governments, should their resources become insufficient. That dependency between the so-called "sovereign-bank nexus", the intrinsic link between national government finances and the banks in a given country, was in the route of much of the Eurozone crisis experience.

One of the key aims of the Banking Union was to break that nexus by integrating supervision and resolution and, as a third pillar, by ensuring there was a deeper pool of resources to cater for bank failure. This is why the Five EU Presidents considered that a common deposit insurance would increase the resilience of the Banking Union against future crises. Indeed, simulations have shown that, depending on the structure, EDIS can lead to a near elimination of aggregate uncovered losses for the fund in a crisis scenario even in extreme scenarios at a confidence of more than 99.9 % of cases.[9] That led to the European Commission proposal for EDIS in November 2015. However, negotiations stalled due to Member States' insistence of the need for more risk reduction. Technical discussions on the establishment of EDIS have nonetheless progressed. Following renewed efforts to overcome the contentious points, this proposal is under debate in both the Council and the European Parliament.

BOX 3. *Overview of EDIS proposal and status*

Original European Commission proposal (November 2015)
- Mutualisation of all deposit liabilities across the Banking Union into a single DGS in three phases:
  1. Re-insurance phase – First 3 years: Creation of a new Deposit Insurance Fund (DIF), funded by national DGS. Limited risk-sharing, DIF to provide liquidity assistance (mostly repayable loans) to national DGS if their own funds were exhausted by a bank failure within their national remit.

---

8 *Completing Europe's Economic and Monetary Union*, 22 June 2015
9 *Effects analysis on the European Deposit Insurance Scheme (EDIS)* (non-paper), European Commission, 11 October 2016

2. Co-insurance phase – Following 4 years: Higher degree of risk-sharing, as DIF can offer National DGS access liquidity support before they exhausted their own funds. DIF to share a progressively larger proportion of any losses, but never the full amount.
3. Full mutualisation phase – End goal: National DGS fully insured through the DIF, which can fully cover losses in the event of a resolution procedure or pay-out if a covered bank were to fail.
- National DGS to benefit from EDIS only when their funds are fully built up
- Contributions into the DIF by banks directly using a risk-based methodology, Member States to reduce contributions to their national DGS accordingly.

Discussion progress and status in June 2019

In view of the impasse, the European Commission suggested in October 2017 that the proposal could be modified to avoid full mutualisation of national DGS.

1. Re-insurance phase: DIF will only provide liquidity to national DGS and no direct loss coverage for depositors of failing banks. At the end of this phase and before 2022, an Asset Quality Review (AQR) would assess issues to be addressed, e.g. excessive Non-Performing Loan levels.
2. Co-insurance phase: Would only start after this AQR. Following the model of Resolution Funds, there would be progressive sharing of losses between national DGS and DIF. In parallel some Member States have suggested alternative or hybrid structures in the form of liquidity support that would qualify as "alternative funding arrangements", already envisaged by DGSD. According to such alternatives: National DGS would first exhaust their funds before they could rely on liquidity support provided by other national DGS pro-rata to the total amount of their covered deposits. Alternatively, lending would be provided or shared by DIF (the re-insurance phase of the original Commission proposal). No consensus proposal has emerged.

In the meantime, despite progress of the post-crisis reforms on a micro level, the European financial market cannot yet reap all the benefits from the enhanced resilience and integration provided by the Banking Union setup. That is demonstrated by the trapping of economic activity, credit exposure and funding along national borders, which is an indicator that banks and capital markets assign a foreign jurisdiction risk factor within the EU. Consumers also do not seem to reach out beyond their borders for banking services. Indeed, there is evidence that the market views bank credit risk on the basis of their location, with banks headquartered in peripheral countries paying higher rates in the interbank liquidity market than non-peripheral banks.[10] The ECB found that the provision of cross-

---

[10] Euro area interbank market fragmentation: New evidence on the roles of bad banks versus bad sovereigns, S. Gabrieli, C. Labonne, 2 November 2018, https://voxeu.org/article/euro-area-interbank-market-fragmentation

border bank loans declined in 2017, reaching a share of 8.6 % of total loans to firms and a negligible 0.9 % share of loans to households. The share of cross-border bank deposits held by firms and households also stood at similarly low levels and has been declining since the crisis.[11] The limited holdings of non-domestic assets, the low level of banking integration and the increased market concentration along national borders since the crisis are signs of fragmentation of the Single Market.

There are many drivers of market fragmentation, but the regulatory environment is a key factor. Regulatory fragmentation refers to a situation where rules do not afford an overarching treatment to cross border activities, but instead impose requirements on a limited scope, typically along jurisdictions or legal entities, also known as ring-fencing. The root for this fragmentation can be found in the level fiscal responsibility linked to failing banks, which remains national. That includes in particular deposit insurance. As long as elements of the sovereign-bank nexus remain unchanged, such as the dependency of DGS on their national systems, the supervision and resolution of banks cannot be fully transferred to a supranational level. There are many examples of regulatory fragmentation currently in the EU.

Box 4. *Examples of regulatory fragmentation in EU prudential regulation*

- Ring-fencing of capital, liquidity and loss absorption: Although the revised Basel III standards set a consolidated level of application, in the EU the CRR sets an entity (solo) level of application for prudential standards. This is further aggravated by the requirement for Minimum Requirements for Own Funds and Eligible Liabilities (MREL) for loss-absorption purposes in resolution, which applies not only at the level of the resolution entity (external MREL) but also at the individual entity (internal/individual MREL) without any cap or range. These approaches result from a mistrust between home and host authorities on capital and liquidity transfer in times of crisis. They encourage host authorities to increase entity-level requirements, in order to ensure there is sufficient resilience in case of a crisis. As a result, banks with comprehensive global business models need to trap liquidity and capital at local level, which is an inefficient resource management.
- National score buckets for D-SIB capital surcharge: While the methodology for calculating the Domestic Systemically Important Bank (D-SIB) score is harmonised across the EU through EBA Guidelines, there are inconsistent methodologies for assigning D-SIB scores to capital surcharge buckets across Member States. Because the highest of the Global or the D-SIB score applies, this creates an uneven playing field, as banks with comparable D-SIB scores could receive different D-SIB capital surcharge, thus reducing the domestic constraint.

---

11 *Financial integration in Europe*, ECB, May 2017 and May 2018

The real value of EDIS for Europe

Regulatory and market fragmentation will continue, as home and host authorities aim to control the banking systems they are liable for, while the sovereign-bank nexus persists. That means the post-crisis reforms have left important pieces incomplete, which results in limited benefits from the entire structure. Europe still needs to complete the journey to a single market for financial services.

It is here that the real value of EDIS lies for banks and their customers. Delivering the final pillar of the Banking Union should remove the final vestige of the sovereign-bank nexus and increase trust between authorities. That would allow authorities to encourage further regulatory integration, at least within the Banking Union, by allowing banks to deploy capital and liquidity freely across border and legal entities. That in turn will aid capital efficiency and should lead to greater choice and better pricing for banking products across the Union.

Fragmentation can have significant economic costs, as it limits the capacity of banks to efficiently link uses and sources of capital. It has been estimated that removing regulatory fragmentation would allow better allocation of about EUR 21 billion of CET1 capital and EUR 59 billion of liquidity, now trapped in various banking entities.[12]

A complete Banking Union would not only be more efficient for banking services, it would also be more resilient, as it would allow the entire system to benefit from the post-crisis enhancements. Indeed, many economists consider that risk sharing, which would be an effect of EDIS, allows for a smoother risk management and loss absorption across more diversified markets and deeper pools of capital. The case for systemic resilience has been made by the most senior EU stakeholders, including Mario Draghi, president of the European Central Bank (ECB).[13]

Regulatory authorities have also called for EDIS and made the connection with the currently observed fragmentation.

- Andrea Enria, as EBA Chair at the time, argued that, in order to restore integration in the European banking market and to reverse the ring-fencing measures used in the Euro crisis, a more comprehensive safety net was

---

12 *Momentum for further European banking integration – French case*, Oliver Wyman, 2017.
13 *Risk-reducing and risk-sharing in our Monetary Union*, Speech at the European University Institute, Florence, 11 May 2018, https://www.ecb.europa.eu/press/key/date/2018/html/ecb.sp18 0511.en.html

needed, in order to increase trust and decrease fragmentation. That net included EDIS.[14]

- Danièle Nouy, as SSM Chair at the time, observed that "In a Banking Union, there is much less need to ring-fence national banking markets. And there will be even less need to do so once we have a European back-up for the Single Resolution Fund as well as [EDIS]. [...] Introducing EDIS would restore that balance by placing both control and liability at the European level."[15]

Regulatory fragmentation and its risks have also been identified at a global stage, and addressing them is one of the priorities of the Japanese Presidency of the G20. With the conclusion of the Banking Union, Europe has the opportunity to address fragmentation domestically and thus join the global debate, where the challenges of trust among authorities and cooperation for cross-border financial services supervision persist.

It is imperative that Europe joins this debate with a constructive attitude that does not prolong fragmentation either internally or globally.

'Keep it simple' – how to deliver EDIS

The final structure of EDIS may be a subject for national governments, and many alternatives can deliver on the same or similar economic outcome, while taking into account national sensitivities. For banks, especially those operating across borders, it is the cost concentration that is key, and whether it may outweigh the benefits deriving from the system in terms of financial market integration and efficiency. Given the profitability of the Eurozone banking sector and other capital headwinds, adding further costs would not help short term resilience of the system.

EDIS must therefore have an efficient structure and avoid adding new costs into the banking system – the objective must be credible deployment of existing resources, not ever greater expansion of contingent liabilities related to potential bank failures. Rather than a new mechanism, EDIS is an improvement on the system's efficient deployment of existing resilience arrangements, i.e. national DGS, and comes on top of other existing pre-funded arrangements, such as loss-

---

14 SRB conference 2018: https://srb.europa.eu/sites/srbsite/files/fp0418900enn.pdf

15 *Risk reduction and risk sharing – two sides of the same coin*, Speech at the Financial Stability Conference 2018, Berlin, 31 October 2018 https://www.bankingsupervision.europa.eu/press/spee ches/date/2018/html/ssm.sp181031.en.html

absorbing debt and the SRF. It should therefore not create a duplicative over-lapping structure. Instead, it should either integrate existing structures, as was the long-term objective of the Commission's proposal, or establish back-up support arrangements without additional pre-funding, as some of the ideas around a liquidity scheme suggest. Its structure should be future proof and allow it to be quickly deployed and sustain pay-outs in a crisis, in order to have the necessary credibility.

Banks are agnostic on the specific structure or arrangement, but simplicity is key.

Most Member States supported the principle need for EDIS, but many asked that before any next steps in risk sharing, there should be further risk reduction. Their main argument is that there are still many areas where banks had excessive exposures and insufficient resilience. In such a situation, setting up EDIS first would endanger the pooled resources. That was the premise of the Risk Reduction Package, with the amendments to the CRD/R, the BRRD and the Single Resolution Mechanism Regulation,[16] implementing the first part of the Basel III and FSB standards. After three years of negotiation, this Package is now adopted and implementation is starting. Parallel regulatory changes came with the various measures on Non-Performing Loans, including EBA requirements for reporting and transparency, amendments to the CRR ("Prudential Backstop") for all EU banks to hold additional loss-coverage for Non-Performing Exposures in the form of extra capital and similar measures by the ECB for Banking Union banks.

Other reforms and further risk reduction have also been proposed, for instance in relation to sovereign exposures. Many other risk areas can emerge, as it is anyway the nature of finance. One of the key functions of banks is to manage risk while intermediating between capital sources and uses. Banks have always faced risks and there will always be new areas of risk that need better understanding and management, for instance through technological innovations. Other areas of risk, like sovereign exposures, may at the same time serve multiple purposes in an economy, making their risk reform a complex task that requires thorough impact assessment and global coordination.

The adoption of the Risk Reduction Package and the change of EU priorities away from the post-crisis repair make it a compelling case that the EU concludes both the Banking and the Capital Markets Union. That will allow the economy to reap the benefits of the reforms launched under the Juncker Commission and repeatedly supported by European Council conclusions. Government and banks will then have a more solid basis and the necessary capacity to shift their

---

16 Regulation 806/2014

attention to future challenges, including those stemming from new technologies, geopolitical risks and the economic cycle.

It is therefore essential that EDIS is delivered as part of a political package, ensuring that its benefits are not postponed to a distant future but are realised simultaneously with its implementation. To do that, Member States should acknowledge that EDIS sufficiently addresses the "sovereign-bank nexus" and thus the underlying reason for the lack of trust between home and host authorities. With EDIS, they should therefore also eliminate regulatory fragmentation at least within the Banking Union. That would ensure the conclusion of the Banking Union and a complete Single Market. Otherwise, the Eurozone financial markets will remain fragmented, and thus mistrust will infect every new area of regulation, prolonging this vicious circle.

Supervisory and regulatory authorities should continue to monitor exposures, require banks to understand and manage them appropriately, and where needed adopt rules for a more effective treatment. Nevertheless, the need for appropriate risk management and adequate protection should not stop the Banking Union from reaching completion. Such dependencies would add further complexity to the project and the constant addition of preconditions would give the impression of a moving goalpost by Member States.

Since an integrated Banking Union is considered a boost to trust and resilience, progress would support risk management, while further delay could leave room for pockets of new risks to develop.

Conclusion

EDIS aims to offer a common protection of all deposits of any failing bank in the Banking Union, and improves the level of confidence. Through that, EDIS can solve the "sovereign-bank nexus", removing the risk that host Member States could be liable for failings of local entities headquartered elsewhere in Europe. That nexus prevents Member States from fully entrusting bank oversight to the supranational level and encourages them to continue with the current regulatory fragmentation along national borders and legal entities.

Addressing the nexus can unlock trust between authorities, allowing the integration of the Banking Union. Member States should be able to remove regulatory barriers and liberate the Single Market in financial services. That can open the flow of the economic advantages pursued by the original proposals and enable a more efficient allocation of resources.

EDIS is therefore a means to an end, not an end in itself: Although it does not increase or expand the level of deposit protection, it is the most effective way to achieve Banking Union integration, that would benefit banks and their customers. Its finalisation should therefore be prioritised and kept as simple as possible, through a political agreement. The final structure should respect the sensitivities of all participating Member States, but avoid excessive additional cost to the industry or the economy. The Banking Union should not be held back any longer.

Wim Mijs
EDIS: Groundhog Day or Back to the Future

Introduction

Whenever the discussion turns to the possible introduction of the European Deposit Insurance Scheme (EDIS), it seems like we have somehow ended up in the movie Groundhog Day. Unlike Bill Murray's character, we are not reliving the same day over and over again, but we are reliving the discussions that we have been having for the past four years over and over again. Despite all those years of deliberation, it feels like there has not been any progress. We have not found a concrete solution that would solve the sovereign-bank nexus, we are still discussing the issue of moral hazard and who would win and who would lose if an EDIS was to be introduced, and despite all the progress made in reducing the levels of NPLs and the introduction of new legislation for the provisioning of NPLs, the topic of NPLs is still a highly contentious topic for a number of member states (Council of the European Union, 2019b).

In the wake of the global financial crisis, EU member states have been quite active and successful in pursuing further European integration. Aside from setting up temporary and permanent support facilities like the European Financial Stability Facility (EFSF) and the European Stability Mechanism (ESM), EU leaders have also embarked on the creation of a Banking Union, which was supposed to be put on three pillars: the Single Supervisory Mechanism (SSM), the Single Resolution Mechanism (SRM), and the European Deposit Insurance Scheme (EDIS). The work on the first two pillars has been quite successful, the work on the third pillar not so much.

By now it is commonly accepted that we have reached a political stalemate with regard to the work on the third pillar, the EDIS. There is little prospect or ideas of how this stalemate could be overcome. The Council's High-level Working Group (HLWG) has also failed to deliver tangible results (Council of the European Union, 2019b). As Mário Centeno, the President of the Eurogroup, has remarked, there is "broad convergence [within the HLWG] on the principles that should guide the further strengthening of the Banking Union" (Council of the European

Note: Disclaimer: The views expressed are those of the author and do not necessarily reflect those of the European Banking Federation. I would like to extend my gratitude to Lukas Bornemann, who is the specialist on EDIS in the EBF, for his patience and help in preparing my contribution. The discussion with Lukas sharpened my thinking and added valuable insights into the EDIS debate.

https://doi.org/10.1515/9783110683073-008

Union, 2019a), but there is no agreement on the next steps. This lack of concrete results, which is the result of a complex constellation of interests, is fatal.

A fully fledged EDIS, or at least more European cooperation, would have important benefits, which would outweigh short-term disadvantages faced by individual member states. An EDIS could establish additional safeguards and increase confidence in our crisis management framework, which, in the long term, would be to the benefit of everyone. Therefore, the creation of EDIS could be a positive sum game as opposed to the general depiction as a zero sum game. The article will thereby answer the following two questions:

1. What is the burden that needs to be shared?
2. How can EDIS help in sharing the burden?

The purpose of this article is to highlight two benefits of EDIS, which are indispensable for a well-functioning banking system that should also have the ability to withstand severe negative shocks. The two benefits, or rather motives, which will guide the article, are safety and confidence. The safety would come from the actual EDIS whose resources can be called upon in case of a crisis. The confidence would come from the fact that an EDIS would represent a credible commitment by the Eurozone member states to support each other's banks in a situation of crisis. Both of those motives are interlinked and cannot be viewed in isolation. We would like to start the article by taking stock and to give an overview of where we have arrived. We will then discuss the current crisis management and prudential framework and highlight the advantages and disadvantages of those. We will then discuss the benefits of EDIS. The article will close by reflecting on the current state of the debate and what could be done to solve the deadlock we are finding ourselves in.

Completing the Banking Union and reducing risks

The three pillars of the Banking Union

In late summer 2008, when the global financial crisis started, the world was very different. There was supervisory cooperation within the Committee of European Banking Supervisors (CEBS), which was the precursor of the European Banking Authority (EBA), but supervision was largely at the national level. The European Central Bank (ECB) dealt exclusively with monetary policy and the SSM was still far away. Only a short while later, European decision-makers learned that much more effort was needed and that the design of the Economic Monetary Union had serious shortcomings. Ten years later, there is a Single Supervisor and a Single

Resolution Mechanism. Those accomplishments made the Euro much safer and the Banking Union represents the most significant integrationist project since the introduction of the common currency. Yet, the Banking Union remains incomplete, because EU member states failed to reach agreement on a design for the European Deposit Insurance (cf. Howarth & Quaglia, 2018; Council of the European Union, 2019b).

The Single Supervisor has an important role in making sure that banks are managed properly and that they do not take excessive risks. The role of the ECB as the Single Supervisor is to challenge banks and the ECB is eager to leave no doubt that it is willing to exercise this role seriously, as can be seen in the case of Banca Carige, when the ECB decided to take measures of early intervention (ECB, 2019a). Although, naturally, there are occasionally disagreements about the right policies between the banking sector and the SSM, the contribution of the ECB to a safer banking sector is undisputed. The single supervisor makes sense, because the quality of supervision across countries was different before the crisis and banking failures tend to produce huge externalities (cf. Beck et al., 2018; cf. Gren et al. 2015), which affect other institutions as well as the broader economy. It also helps to address problems of national forbearance.

The Single Resolution Mechanism addresses another problem. The problem that the SRM is supposed to solve is that of cross-border resolution. When banks like Fortis found themselves in financial stress, supervisors realized that the existing framework had serious limitations.

The financial crisis revealed what is called a "financial trilemma" (Schoenmaker 2009; 2011). With regard to national financial systems, policy makers can pursue three objectives: financial stability, financial integration, and national financial policies. The trilemma demonstrates that from those three objectives only two can be accomplished, but not all three at the same time. Because of the common currency, there is financial integration among the EU member states. Due to the importance of financial stability, it makes little sense to choose national financial policies as the second objective. That is why there is an SRM.

Lastly, one of the drawbacks that is inherent in the design of the Economic and Monetary Union (EMU) is that there are very few options for members of the Euro to absorb shocks (De Grauwe & Ji, 2015), whereas in countries that have monetary sovereignty, the central bank can jump in as a lender of last resort (ibid.), should the sovereign be unable to raise new funds and run the risk of insolvency. This absence of shock absorbers proved fatal for some member states in the crisis. In the Eurozone, the ECB is forbidden to finance the debt of members, which means that it cannot exercise the role of the lender of last resort to member states. Therefore, the shocks which affect a sovereign need to be absorbed through the sovereign's budget. However, once the capacity of the budget is exhausted, there is not much else that can be done. The credibility of a national deposit guarantee scheme (DGS) depends on the sovereign that stands behind it and that provides the backstop. Thus, if a DGS should be overwhelmed, because the shock to the banking sector is too big, the sovereign will need to support the DGS and make up the missing amount. As it became evident in the crisis, in some cases the capacity to absorb those shocks can be very limited. Although an EDIS cannot fill the role of a lender of last resort, it can put in place an additional safety net that at least protects deposits in case of a systemic crisis.

In sum, what becomes evident is that the crisis reforms undertaken by the EU member states have addressed several problems in the architecture of the EMU. They have established a Single Supervisor that ensures that supervision is of high quality across the Eurozone. The Single Resolution Mechanism can help in cross-border resolution and prevent disruptions. The EU developed solutions for several problems in the EMU design, yet the envisioned third pillar was never completed.

Risk reduction

Aside from the discussion as to whether or not an EDIS provides a clear added value, the need for reducing risks before the introduction of EDIS has also taken an important place in the public discourse. One of the most prominent issues of those debates on risk reduction was the topic of non-performing loans (NPLs). NPLs have soared from an already high level of 5.4 % of total loans in 2010 to 7.5 % in 2012 (EBF 2018). Since then NPL ratios have been decreasing to 3.7 % in 2017, which is below world average and represents a substantial achievement (EBF, 2018). In August 2019, the ECB even reported that – in March 2019 – the NPL ratio decreased to 3.1 % for the EU (ECB 2019b). Overall banks have made strong progress and significantly reduced their NPL ratios. Nevertheless, it also needs to be recognised that NPLs are much more concentrated in the southern member states than in the so-called northern member states (EBA, 2019), which explains the north-south divide on EDIS. Furthermore, NPLs remain a top priority for regulators and supervisors and the pressure on banks remains high. This is demonstrated by the Council's NPL action plan (Council of the European Union, 2017) and other regulatory initiatives, such as a recently adopted regulation on minimum loss coverage for non-performing exposures (European Parliament and Council of the European Union, 2019). Although those regulations are sometimes excessively restrictive, there is no denying that the authorities are taking the issue of NPLs seriously and working hard to come up with relevant solutions. This attentiveness of public institutions also represents a credible reassurance to member states that supervisors and regulators will continue to push banks to further reduce their NPLs. Despite the substantial progress regarding the reduction of NPL ratios and the strong regulatory focus on NPLs, non-performing loans remain a roadblock for the completion of the Banking Union.

In addition to NPLs, it is criticised that banks do not have sufficiently high minimum requirements for own funds and eligible liabilities (MREL) ratios (Huertas, 2019). MREL is an important part of the new crisis management framework designed to reduce the risk to the deposit guarantee scheme and to impose losses on investors. It is an important complement to the global total loss absorbing capacity (TLAC) requirement, which is only applicable to to global systemically important banks (G-SIBs). One might argue that all the safeguards such as the MREL requirement would make an EDIS obsolete as a bank could be put into resolution at the right time and the risk that the DGS would have to pay would be effectively zero (ibid.). On the contrary, an insufficient build-up of MREL, as it is claimed by Huertas (2019), would be a good reason not to introduce EDIS. Although it is debatable whether or not a proper functioning of the MREL makes an EDIS irrelevant, part of the truth of low MREL ratios is also that there is a reason why this requirement is particularly challenging for some banks.

In late 2017, the ECB was perceptive enough to realise that the MREL would be a particularly burdensome requirement for banks that cannot place debt with international investors (ECB, 2017). What seems to transpire from the experience to date is that the "middle class" of the banking sector pursues a "business model [that] appears to be incompatible with the satisfaction of stringent MREL requirements, as imposed by the resolution framework" (Restoy, 2018). Those banks are rather small and therefore not interesting for investors who would invest in MREL. Therefore, what becomes obvious is that the MREL requirement simply does not match the business reality of a certain type of bank. Consequently, it would make sense to at least discuss if the introduction of EDIS should be dependent on the MREL issue or if there can be alternative solutions.

In sum, the current framework has several weaknesses and remains incomplete in many ways. The much hoped for third pillar of the Banking Union is still out of reach and the north-south divide within the Eurozone makes it difficult to reach a common solution.

The benefits of EDIS

Safety

EDIS, if introduced, would deliver one key benefit: a common deposit insurance on a European level that derives its strength from the fact that all Eurozone members commit themselves to guarantee the safety of insured deposits. In that regard, an EDIS would greatly enhance the safety of the financial system. From a customer's perspective, the system is already fully arranged. The Deposit Guarantee Schemes Directive (DGSD) ensures that deposits up to certain amounts are guaranteed and will be paid out within a clearly defined timeframe. However, as this section will explain, under certain circumstances the current system of national DGSs may not be enough. Thus, the question of how the national systems are funded becomes relevant and this is what justifies expending further political resources on it.

The initial proposal of the European Commission envisioned the introduction of EDIS as a three-stage process (European Commission, 2015c). At first there would be a reinsurance system, then a co-insurance system, and at the very end a full mutualization of the national schemes. The discussion about moral hazard that surrounds the public EDIS debate within a potential EDIS among member states points to one thing: the high level of distrust among Euro area members. Therefore, it is impossible to predict what EDIS will look like in the end. Regardless of the form and shape that more European cooperation within the domain of deposit insurance will take in the end, what is important is that EDIS provides at least an extra layer of security for national schemes.

Currently, the national DGSs are highly susceptible to idiosyncratic shocks, which could quickly lead to a depletion of the national deposit insurance fund. There are at least two scenarios that can lead to a DGS being overwhelmed. The first scenario would be the failure of a bank that holds more insured deposits than are available in the deposit guarantee fund. This was the case in Latvia where ABLV Bank failed after a money laundering scandal. ABLV bank held 6.7 % of insured deposits (SRB, 2018), whereas the deposit guarantee fund only covered 1.6 %. Indeed, in those cases where the bank holds such large amounts of insured deposits, it is crucial that it also has sufficient bail-in-able liabilities and be put into resolution at the point of non-viability (PONV). An exercise of forbearance which delays resolution beyond the PONV or a bail-out would be disastrous for the crisis management framework. What becomes obvious here is that the proper functioning of the resolution framework and the impact on the respective DGS, hinges on one factor: the crisis management framework needs to work as expected. However, that is quite a strong assumption and the reality may look very different. Especially the SRM with multiple actors and veto points is a very complex and for the most time "untried" (Mayes, 2018) system. It will take time to see how it really works in practice (cf. Mayes, 2018). As already outlined above, the regulatory framework may impact the banking sector in various ways and produce unintended consequences, as for example the case with MREL.

The second scenario that can be envisioned is not the failure of a large or even globally systemic institution, but a situation where a large number of institutions that are members to the same national DGS come under pressure. Although, for example, the institutional protection schemes (IPS) of savings and cooperative banks have a good track-record, it is doubtful if their IPSs could handle a crisis that simultaneously affects a critical number of institutions at the same time. One might think that a collective of banks that is made up of many, but rather small banks, may not pose a great risk to the financial system. In case any of those banks became insolvent, they would undergo insolvency procedures and leave the market. However, it is important to note that some of those collectives follow a very similar business model and are made up of a large number of banks, whose assets collectively amount to a quite a substantial amount. This high degree of similarity increases the probability that multiple banks are affected at the same time, therefore we can quickly end up in a situation not of "too big to fail", but "too many to fail". This is another example of where a deposit guarantee scheme would not be able to handle the stress. In this case it also would be important to have a European layer of security that can compensate for the shock. The argument that individual events can overwhelm national DGSs is recognized by academics, practitioners and industry representatives alike (cf. Schackmann-Fallis, 2018; cf. Bénnassy-Quéré et al. 2018; cf. European Commission, 2015b). In short, the risk of asymmetric or idiosyncratic shocks is severe and supports the case for the introduction of at least a reinsurance system, which could later be developed into a fully mutualized system.

In addition to the scenarios outlined in this section, EDIS can also have an important function as a safeguard in case there is a financial crisis. In 2018, the ECB published a paper which discussed the introduction of an EDIS and simulated several stress scenarios (Carmassi et al., 2018). The conclusion was that an EDIS, in combination with safeguards like MREL, would be able to weather a storm much more severe than the one in 2008 that ultimately contributed to the sovereign debt crisis. Although it could be argued that this makes the case for EDIS a lot less urgent, the experience from the 2008 crisis should make us wary of those arguments. In principle, the case for EDIS is still valid, because it is difficult to say how severe the next crisis will be. Given that the EU has taken ten years to deal with the fallout of the global financial crisis, it is of utmost importance to complete the Banking Union and thereby increase the resilience of the banking sector.

In conclusion, even though the design of national DGSs may be sound and the risk quite small, EDIS would contribute a great deal to the resilience of the banking sector and thereby help to handle to future crises. In addition to the physical safety measures that EDIS represents, there is another feature of EDIS that would be highly desirable: confidence.

Confidence

When the financial crisis started in the US, the German minister of finance remarked that this was a purely American problem (Reuters, 2008). Only a short while later, Chancellor Merkel and her finance minister went in front of the cameras to declare that the government would guarantee all German deposits. The Germans were not alone in providing a government guarantee to depositors, the Irish and other governments did the same. Unlike in the Irish case, the guarantee of the German government worked and prevented bank runs by depositors. This little anecdote illustrates two things: first, that it is easy to misjudge the impact of crises on one's banking sector, and, second, that those government guarantees are very fragile.

Those government guarantees are emergency plans that are hastily put together, but it is highly questionable if those guarantees work once they are called upon. While being practically useless as an actual guarantee, the purpose of those government promises is that they can create confidence. They can make consumers believe that their money will be safe and therefore prevent them from starting a bank run, provided that depositors trust their government to live up on that promise. Consequently, the limits of those guarantees as a crisis management tool are quite strict. In a monetary union, such as the Euro, there are even other drawbacks. Aside from the fact that in the worst case, those guarantees might not be enough, they can actually worsen the crisis (cf. Quaglia et al. 2009). In a monetary union, where capital can move freely between jurisdictions, those guarantees might attract deposits from other member states, thereby increasing the deposits that have to be guaranteed and potentially exacerbating the problem. The key benefit of EDIS would be that those guarantees will no longer need to be given, as members commit themselves to support each other. Ultimately this would also lead to an equal treatment of depositors across the EDIS members and therefore remove any incentive of depositors to move their money to EDIS members that are perceived as safe havens.

In other contexts, we have seen what happens when such a credible commitment is absent with quite dramatic consequences. In the euro crisis member states failed to credibly reassure financial markets that countries like Greece or Italy would remain in the Euro and not be pushed out of the monetary union. Ultimately, it was up to ECB president Mario Draghi to save the Euro by promising to do "whatever it takes" to save the Euro.

Another thing the Euro crisis has demonstrated is that progress and institutional innovations will only happen when member states are under severe pressure to act. Applying this experience to EDIS, it is fair to conclude that there is a need for a credible crisis management framework. Once a bank run happens, there is little that can be done, and can even push the most prudently managed bank into insolvency. Therefore, providing a credible reassurance makes a lot of economic sense and not doing this in a period where the situation is relatively benign, is simply a lost opportunity.

Another reason why the confidence enhancing function of EDIS is so important is the complexity of the system. Even if MREL would always be sufficient to protect deposits, having those physical safety measures in place is just one part of the story. The best designed crisis management system for banks is useless if people do not believe in it and start panicking. The whole resolution and bail-in process is so complicated that it is difficult for the average customer to understand. They are probably not even aware that all those safety measures exist and that they protect their deposits. For the consumers it is simply very difficult to wrap their head around concepts like bail-in, MREL, TLAC etc. However, the general concept of EDIS is something that they can easily understand. What needs to be made clear beyond any doubt is that if a national DGS runs out of money, this DGS will be supported by its peers from the Euro area. Thus, if, for example, the Belgian or Austrian DGS runs out of money, customers need to be reassured that their deposits are safe and that there is at least a reinsurance system in place. If push comes to shove, the Belgian or Austrian government may not be able to backstop the DGS for reasons explained above. The argument that EDIS has a positive impact on the confidence in the deposit insurance is not a new one. It has been around since the beginning of the discussion on EDIS. Some argue that this argument is based on a dogmatic argumentation (DSGV, 2018). However, it cannot be emphasized enough that this argument is not based on dogmas, but hard facts.

There are multiple cases where banks have come under stress, because depositors either did not believe in the system or were worried that they might lose their savings. This was the case in the UK where there was a bank-run on Northern Rock and the coverage for insured deposits was later expanded as a result of that. Another example can be taken from Germany where depositors moved their savings across different DGSs when the crisis started (Fecht & Weber, 2019). In the German system cooperatives and savings banks operate their IPSs, which are recognized as DGSs under the DGS Directive. The peculiar feature of those IPSs is that they are built on the principles of solidarity and joint liability. The purpose of those schemes is that banks can support each other before they end up in trouble, thus, preventing contagion effects. Thus, those IPSs de facto provide unlimited deposit protection. In principle the level of protection for a deposit at a cooperative and a savings bank should be identical. However, because German local governments are shareholders of the savings banks, the savings banks, at least in the eyes of the depositors, enjoy an implicit government guarantee. As Fecht and Weber (2019) demonstrate, depositors moved their deposits from cooperatives to savings banks when the financial crisis started to take up speed. This only stopped after the German government provided its government guarantee for all depositors. This German episode demonstrates how actual deposit protection measures can increase confidence and in the case of the savings banks this protection was only perceived and not real. The depositors would not have been able to derive any legal right from that.

Therefore, those two episodes of the financial crisis demonstrate that if depositors on the other hand know that the scheme that protects their deposits has sufficient firepower, they have no reason to start a bank run. Since an EDIS, regardless of the form or shape, would already be an improvement over the current situation, it is reasonable to conclude that we will less often see people lining up at their local bank to desperately protect their life savings.

Lastly, in the context of resolution policies, Mario Draghi pointed out that "policies that reduce risks for the banking system as a whole will also lead to larger risk-reduction for individual banks." (Draghi, 2018) and that confidence is indispensable. Therefore, EDIS itself has the potential to create a positive feedback loop, which would mean that simply the existence already has a positive impact on the overall risk of individual banks.

This demonstrates that all of those benefits that are conferred on the banking sector are equally enjoyed by customers as well. Looking at the benefits of an EDIS, one thing becomes clear: EDIS does a whole lot for customers and banks equally. Customers indirectly benefit from a higher resilience in the banking system as this will reduce the risk that the DGS needs to be called upon, which could potentially imply a loss of the uninsured deposits, and banks will be able to benefit from it directly, because it can help in avoiding bank runs and foster confidence in the system.

The way forward

There are two reasons why EDIS should be introduced: first it enhances stability by improving the shock absorption capacity of the Eurozone and, second, by establishing much needed confidence in the Eurozone's crisis management system. Although there seems to be broad agreement among academics and policymakers that an EDIS, in one form or another, would be desirable, there is little progress and political negotiations have reached a stalemate. However, what member states disagree on is how to arrive at an EDIS, meaning which steps need to be taken. Part of this may be owed to the uncertainty and lack of consensus on what the optimal design for EDIS would be. For example, some suggest that EDIS can be built on top of national compartments, which would be used to absorb the losses until their funds are depleted, then the European funds would be mobilized (Carmassi et al., 2018; Bénassy-Quéré et al. 2018). Others claim that having national compartments could be counterproductive and actually destabilizing (Schoenmaker, 2018). This disagreement about a seemingly straightforward question already illustrates how complex the whole discussion is and how, consequently, it may be even more difficult to find agreement on the more detailed and less straightforward aspects of EDIS.

The usual recipe for those situations to break up the stalemate would be to try to agree on small, concrete steps. Instead of focusing on the end product, a fully-fledged EDIS, it would be necessary to try to find agreement on small individual proposals. Ultimately, an agreement on the full EDIS would be possible. However, the deliberations of the High-Level Working Group on EDIS do not inspire much confidence that we will be able to see substantial progress anytime soon. The limited results demonstrate how entrenched the differences of opinions among the member states are. In general, it is highly understandable why some Euro members are more willing to create EDIS than others. NPLs are just one of many issues.

Nevertheless, despite all the justified concerns, one cannot escape the thought that there is something substantially wrong with the current debate. What is obvious is that the debate is very much phrased as a zero-sum game. Of course, burden sharing per definition means that some members will have to carry more weight than before. However, in the eyes of the public it must seem that there are clear winners and losers under an EDIS. The debate on "moral hazard" demonstrates this problem most effectively. Since Southern member states tend to have banks with higher NPL ratios and higher amounts of debt from their respective sovereign, those banks would be assumed to be the first to rely on an EDIS if the Eurozone was going to enter into a full-blown recession. Therefore, it would seem that they gain more from an EDIS in comparison to countries where those problems are less pronounced. The more stable countries would therefore be net contributors to the scheme. Aside from the fact that this narrative makes it incredibly difficult for politicians from those more stable countries to sell anything EDIS-related at home to their constituents, it is also a very narrow perspective on the EDIS discussion that reveals how much the current discussion led by policy makers is dominated by a mindset based on solely national issues. It is true that in the short-term Southern countries would likely benefit more from the EDIS than their Northern peers. This is undisputed and for the sake of honesty should also be acknowledged, yet this national mindset eclipses the bigger picture in which EDIS could provide a real added value to the banking sector, but also to society at large.

However, what this perspective on the current debate completely neglects are the long-term benefits for everyone involved in EDIS. If one considers the long term, EDIS turns from a zero-sum game to a positive sum game. The previous sections outlined the positive impact of EDIS on financial stability through its various transmission mechanisms. This is one aspect of those long-term benefits. In addition, it should maybe be recalled what the purpose of an insurance is. An insurance is a scheme to which members sign up in order to protect themselves financially against future adverse events. The key factor is that no one knows what kind of events they may have to deal with. If everyone knew what life holds for them, the net contributors would opt out of an insurance (or never join in the first place) and the net beneficiaries would opt in. This type of insurance would not work, as it would be impossible to fund the insurance. There would be a market failure and the whole scheme would break down.

In the case of EDIS this example has particular relevance. Individual governments may be able to improve their own economic situation. It should be kept in mind that at the end of the 90's many pundits considered Germany to be the "sick man of the Euro" (Economist, 1999, June, 3). Ten years later, during the sovereign debt crisis, Germany had become the "economic powerhouse of the Eurozone" (Financial Times, 2019). While some countries can improve their economies and thereby their capacity to backstop their respective DGS, it can obviously work the other way around. A previously stable country can be hit by an exogenous shock and may find itself in a bad place, economically speaking.

Another reason how countries can benefit from EDIS is the interdependency of individual Eurozone members. When countries are in a monetary union as it is the case with the Euro, their own economic policies can create substantial externalities. Exit from the Euro is for example expected to be very costly for everyone who is in the Euro. This explains the motivation of Euro member states to bail-out countries like Greece (Schimmelfennig, 2015). In other words, once someone has joined the Eurozone, turning back and rolling back European integration is possible, but extremely expensive. Hence it means that Eurozone members will have to support each other when one member runs into trouble. This is true with or without an EDIS. Thus, member states have two opportunities:

1. Devise a framework with clear enforcement rules that reduce moral hazard to a minimum, for example, through making sure that national DGS have sufficient amounts of funds to make sure that EDIS really is the last resort when it comes to reimbursing depositors, or
2. Come up with a hastily developed emergency plans for ailing member states once the crisis is there as it happened in the sovereign debt crisis.

Moving from more general reflections about the EDIS discussion to the more detailed question as to how this deadlock can be solved, particular attention should be given to the NPL issue, because this is one of major impediments to a European Deposit Insurance.

It is important to assign a high priority to this topic and that NPLs as a source of risk are being taken seriously, however, it seems that the current approach has lost the balance. The current supervisory and regulatory initiatives are focussed on tightening requirements and imposing ever more restrictions on banks. Even though it is true that one part of the story is about credit underwriting standards (Enria, 2019), the many initiatives on NPLs are focusing too much on the treatment of symptoms. It is difficult to expect banks to shed NPLs at the same pace as they have done so far just by tightening restrictions, when the proper environment for disposing the NPLs is not there. The banking sector's experience shows that banks manage to rid themselves of those NPLs that are relatively easy to sell off, the ones that are not as attractive to investors stay on banks' balance sheets the longest (cf. ILF, 2019). From a supervisory perspective this is understandable, because the supervisor only uses the means at his disposal to do what they consider the best way to keep banks safe. Establishing those preconditions would need to be a project for the legislator. There are two initiatives that could be taken that would represent a sustainable solution: the harmonization of insolvency laws as a long term objective and the creation of NPL trading platforms as a short term objective.

There are several reasons why those solutions would be more preferable to those that simply impose more onerous requirements on banks. The first reason is that they are more sustainable. For example, harmonizing insolvency laws can help in reducing the time that cases spend in insolvency proceedings, thus helping banks to shed NPLs much sooner and helping purchasers to bid higher prices based on expected higher rates of recovery. Another reason is that those onerous requirements put additional strain on banks. Forcing stricter provisioning on banks can also lead to a situation where banks will dispose of those NPLs at a price that is below the amount that can reasonably be expected to be recovered if banks were given more time. Those price depressing fire sales would then come at a time at which banks are already under pressure due to a low interest rate environment and low profitability. In this sense, pursuing solutions, such as a harmonization of insolvency laws and the creation of NPL trading platforms would create huge efficiency gains, without the excessive negative impact for the industry. The idea for an NPL trading platform has also been floated by the ECB and would therefore enjoy the support from the banking supervisor (ECB, 2018). Also, those proposals would most likely have very little, if any, redistributive consequences. Therefore, this could be a step forward.

Conclusion

So, coming back to our friend Bill and the groundhog: what would be needed to move forward? Bill Murray finally manages to escape from the time loop he has been caught up in, by changing himself. Bill Murray turns from a bitter cynic into an optimist, professes love to his crush and thereby manages to get on with his life.

The steps that need to be taken in order to help create an EDIS would not need to be quite as radical. However, a few things need to be done and those are as follows. We need to attempt small steps instead of already defining the end product of European deposit insurance. Moreover, we need to change the way we think about EDIS. Instead of seeing it as a zero-sum game, we should highlight the long-term benefits, which would be enjoyed by everyone, making this in fact a positive sum game. With regard to concrete policy proposals, Euro members can attempt the following: creating NPL trading platforms as a short-term objective and harmonising insolvency laws as a long-term objective. Both would significantly enhance the efficiency of the NPL market and the NPL disposal process in general with little redistributive effects.

Those two proposals would contribute to further risk-reduction and thereby help solve the NPL problem, which is one of the reasons for the lack of progress on EDIS. The benefits of EDIS are then increased safety and confidence. The safety comes from the increased resilience of the banking sector and a strengthening of the crisis management system and the confidence derives from having a credible commitment among Euro member states to support each other in times of crisis. This idea of mutual support in turn should provide the necessary comfort to the depositors that their deposits will be safe even if the funds of their own DGS will be exhausted.

Thus, there are two potential future scenarios for the discussion on deposit guarantee schemes. We can exchange the same arguments over and over again and remain stuck in our time-loop, like Bill Murray, or we can try an alternative path similar to the one we took during the crisis. To progress, member states would need to gather the necessary political will similar to what happened with the first two pillars and introduce an EDIS. Going back to this situation where there was sufficient political momentum to attempt ambitious projects, is where the future lies for the EMU. Hence, it up to us to decide if we want to remain stuck in debates of the past or if we want to go back to the future.

References

Beck, T., Silva-Buston, C., & Wagner, W. (2018). *The economics of supranational bank supervision*. https://voxeu.org/article/economics-supranational-bank-supervision

Bénassy-Quéré, A., Brunnermeier, M., Enderlein, H., Farhi, E., Fratzscher, M., Fuest, C., Gourinchas, P., Martin, P., Pisani-Ferry, J., Rey, H., Schnabel, I., Véron, N., Weder di Mauro, B., & Zettelmeyer, J. (2018). Reconciling Risk Sharing with Market Discipline: A Constructive Approach to Euro Area Reform. *CEPR Policy Insight, No 91*. Retrieved August 14, 2019 from https://cepr.org/sites/default/files/policy_insights/PolicyInsight91.pdf

Carmassi, J., Dobkowitz, S., Evrard, J., Parisi, L., Silva, A., & Wedow, M. 2018. *Completing the Banking Union with a European Deposit Insurance Scheme: who is afraid of cross-subsidisation?* European Central Bank Occasional Paper Series 208. Retrieved August 14, 2019 from https://www.ecb.europa.eu/pub/pdf/scpops/ecb.op208.en.pdf

Council of the European Union (2017). *Council conclusions on Action plan to tackle non-performing loans in Europe*. Retrieved August 14, 2019 from https://www.consilium.europa.eu/en/press/press-releases/2017/07/11/conclusions-non-performing-loans/

Council of the European Union (2019a). Remarks by Mário Centeno following the Eurogroup meeting of 13 June 2019. Retrieved August 14, 2019 from https://www.consilium.europa.eu/en/press/press-releases/2019/06/14/remarks-by-mario-centeno-following-the-euro group-meeting-of-13-june-2019/

Council of the European Union (2019b). Considerations on the further strengthening of the Banking Union, including a common deposit insurance system. Report of the HLWG chair. Retrieved August 14, 2019 from https://www.consilium.europa.eu/media/39768/190606-hlwg-chair-report.pdf

Draghi, M. (2018). *Risk-reducing and risk-sharing in our Monetary Union*. Speech by Mario Draghi, President of the ECB, at the European University Institute, Florence, 11 May 2018. Retrieved August 14, 2019 from https://www.ecb.europa.eu/press/key/date/2018/html/ecb.sp180511.en.html

De Grauwe, P. & Ji, Y. (2015). Correcting for the Eurozone Design Failures: The Role of the ECB. *Journal of European Integration*, 37 (7), 739-754.

DSGV (2018). *Zentrale EU-Einlagensicherung: DSGV warnt vor Ansteckungsgefahren*. Retrieved August 14, 2019 from https://www.dsgv.de/newsroom/blog/edis-kritik.html

EBA (2018). *2018 EU-wide transparency exercise*. Retrieved August 14, 2019 from https://eba.europa.eu/risk-analysis-and-data/eu-wide-transparency-exercise/2018

EBF (2018). *Facts and Figures 2018*. Retrieved August 14, 2019 from https://www.ebf.eu/wp-content/uploads/2018/09/Banking-in-Europe-2018-EBF-Facts-and-Figures.pdf

ECB (2017). *Macroprudential Bulletin. Issue 4. December 2017*. Retrieved August 14, 2019 from https://www.ecb.europa.eu/pub/pdf/mpbu/ecb.mpbu201712.en.pdf?51c43803f43 bfaa3085e53856e5270e6

ECB (2018). *Financial Stability Review. November 2018*. Retrieved August 14, 2019 from https://www.ecb.europa.eu/pub/pdf/fsr/ecb.fsr201811.en.pdf?d2951e7f82f867e0f22497d3865 ef306

ECB (2019a). *ECB appoints temporary administrators for Banca Carige*. Retrieved August 14, 2019 from https://www.bankingsupervision.europa.eu/press/pr/date/2019/html/ssm.pr190102.en.html

ECB (2019b). *ECB publishes Consolidated Banking Data for end-March 2019.* Retrieved August 14, 2019 from https://www.ecb.europa.eu/press/pr/date/2019/html/ecb.pr190807~b9baa29 c5a.en.html

Economist (1999, June, 3). The sick man of the Euro. *Economist.* Retrieved August 14, 2019 from https://www.economist.com/special/1999/06/03/the-sick-man-of-the-euro

Enria, A. (2019). *Non-performing loans in the euro area – where do we stand?* Speech by Andrea Enria, Chair of the Supervisory Board of the ECB, at the Conference "EDIS, NPLs, Sovereign Debt and Safe Assets" organised by the Institute for Law and Finance, Frankfurt, 14 June 2019. Retrieved August 14, 2019 from https://www.bankingsupervision.europa.eu/press/ speeches/date/2019/html/ssm.sp190614~bee1d0f29c.en.html

European Commission (2015a). *The Five Presidents' Report: Completing Europe's Economic and Monetary Union.* Retrieved August 14, 2019 from https://ec.europa.eu/commission/sites/ beta-political/files/5-presidents-report_en.pdf

European Commission (2015b). Communication from the Commission to the European Parliament, the Council, the European Central Bank, the European Economic and Social Committee and the Committee of the Regions. "Towards the completion of the Banking Union". COM(2015), 587 final. Retrieved August 14, 2019 from https://eur-lex.europa.eu/legal-content/EN/TXT/?uri=CELEX:52015DC0587

European Commission (2015c). Proposal for a REGULATION OF THE EUROPEAN PARLIAMENT AND OF THE COUNCIL amending Regulation (EU) 806/2014 in order to establish a European Deposit Insurance Scheme. COM/2015/0586 final – 2015/0270 (COD). Retrieved August 14, 2019 from https://eur-lex.europa.eu/legal-content/EN/TXT/?uri=CELEX:52015PC0586

European Parliament and Council of the European Union (2019). REGULATION (EU) 2019/630 OF THE EUROPEAN PARLIAMENT AND OF THE COUNCIL of 17 April 2019 amending Regulation (EU) No 575/2013 as regards minimum loss coverage for non-performing exposures. Retrieved August 14, 2019 from https://eur-lex.europa.eu/legal-content/EN/TXT/PDF/?uri= CELEX:32019R0630&from=EN

Fecht, F. & Weber, P. (2019). What We Can Learn from the Introduction of Blanket Deposit Guarantees in Germany 2008 about the Benefits of EDIS. *Ifo DICE REPORT,* 17 (1), 26–29.

Financial Times (2019). *Germany confronts growing risk of economic slowdown.* Retrieved August 14, 2019 from https://www.ft.com/content/994a9ec4-bac7-11e9-96bd-8e884d3ea203

Gren, J., Howarth, D. & Quaglia, L. (2015). Supranational Banking Supervision in Europe: The Construction of a Credible Watchdog. *Journal of Common Market Studies,* 53, 181–199.

Howarth, D. & Quaglia, L. (2016). *The Political Economy of European Banking Union.* Oxford: Oxford University Press.

Howarth, D. & Quaglia, L. (2018). The difficult construction of a European Deposit Insurance Scheme: a step too far in Banking Union? *Journal of Economic Policy Reform,* 21 (3), 190–209.

Huertas, T. (2019). Completing Banking Union, forthcoming in: Andreas Dombret and Patrick S. Kenadjian, editors), *EDIS, NPLs, Sovereign Debt and Safe Assets, ILF Series,* De Gruyter (2019).

ILF (2019). ILF Conference on 14 June 2019: "EDIS, NPLs, Sovereign Debt and Safe Assets" – part 2. https://video.uni-frankfurt.de/Mediasite/Play/08fd4be4795b4d18b9ed4c26ca03ffde1d

Mayes, D. G. (2018). Banking union: the problem of untried systems. *Journal of Economic Policy Reform,* 21 (3), 178-189.

Quaglia, L., Eastwood, R. & Holmes, P. (2009). The Financial Turmoil and EU Policy Co-operation in 2008. *Journal of Common Market Studies,* 47 (1), 63–87.

Restoy, F. (2018). *Bail-in in the new bank resolution framework: is there an issue with the middle class?* Speech at the IADI-ERC international conference on Resolution and deposit guarantee schemes in Europe: incomplete processes and uncertain outcomes, Naples, Italy, 23 March 2018. Retrieved August 14, 2019 from https://www.bis.org/speeches/sp180323.htm

Reuters (2008). *U. S. will lose financial superpower status: Germany.* Retrieved August 14, 2019 from https://www.reuters.com/article/us-financial-germany-steinbruecknews1/u-s-will-lose-financial-superpower-status-germany-idUSTRE48O2L020080925

Schackmann-Fallis, K.-P. (2018). EDIS: why the diversity of the EU banking system is at stake. *Views. The EUROFI Magazine*, September 2018, 39–40.

Schimmelfennig, F. (2015). Liberal intergovernmentalism and the euro area crisis. *Journal of European Public Policy,* 22 (2), 177–195.

Schoenmaker, D. (2009). *The financial crisis: Financial trilemma in Europe.* Retrieved August 14, 2019 from https://voxeu.org/article/financial-crisis-and-europe-s-financial-trilemma

Schoenmaker, D. (2011). The financial trilemma. *Economics Letters,* 111, 57–59.

Schoenmaker, D. (2018). *Building a stable deposit insurance scheme.* Retrieved August 14, 2019 from https://bruegel.org/2018/04/building-a-stable-european-deposit-insurance-scheme/

SRB (2018). DECISION OF THE SINGLE RESOLUTION BOARD of 23 February 2018 concerning the assessment of the conditions for resolution in respect of ABLV Bank, AS (SRB/EES/2018/09). Retrieved August 14, 2019 from https://srb.europa.eu/sites/srbsite/files/decision_srb-ees-2018-09_ablv_lv_non_confidential_version_final_0.pdf

Karl-Peter Schackmann-Fallis and Georg Huber

EDIS: Why the Diversity of the EU Banking System Is at Stake

I. Overall Architecture of a Well-Functioning Banking Union

I.1. The third Pillar of the banking union has already been completed by the revision of the EU Deposit Guarantee Scheme Directive

The 2014 revision of the EU Deposit Guarantee Scheme Directive 2014/49/EU (DGSD) imposes ex ante funding arrangements on all deposit guarantee schemes in the EU amounting to 0.8 % of covered deposits (exception: 0.5 % for highly concentrated banking markets [France]). In addition, each scheme can levy extraordinary annual contributions of up to 0.5 % of the covered deposits and borrow from third parties in order to bridge temporary liquidity shortfalls until funds can be returned from the insolvency assets. Furthermore, the Directive requires proof of eligibility for compensation within seven working days and, with an amount of EUR 100,000, provides comprehensive protection for a very wide range of eligible depositors.

The revised DGSD means that each and every euro that is deposited is secured to the same extent in every EU country and everywhere within the euro area. There is no divergence in the level of protection. The "Third Pillar" of the banking union has therefore already been completed with the revision of the EU Deposit Guarantee Scheme Directive and the creation of harmonised standards, in particular the sound financial resources of the guarantee schemes.

I.2. Full mutualisation weakens financial stability due to an increase in interconnectedness and potentially forces the ECB to neglect its focus on price stability

As a general principle, a centralised deposit guarantee scheme in line with the European Commission's 2015 draft will lack credibility. The changes proposed in the October 2017 communication of the European Commission do not alter this. This is due in particular to two reasons:

(i) the lack of any country-specific "firewall" means that depositors will be unsettled on a cross-border scale even in the case of regional banking crises

https://doi.org/10.1515/9783110683073-009

due to the fact that all contributions are going into one fund and not to separated national funds;

(ii) there is no effective and credible (fiscal) lender of last resort at the European level (to bridge the liquidity requirements of the deposit insurance scheme until the return of funds from the insolvency assets of liquidated institutions).

The combination of an increase in cross-border contagion or interconnectedness and the lack of an effective lender of last resort will, in an emergency, lead to a centralised European deposit guarantee scheme being dysfunctional.

Nor can any comparison be made in this respect with the US Federal Deposit Insurance Corporation (FDIC) since the US has a central fiscal level that is capable of acting within the framework of its governmental structure. For example, the FDIC has a permanent USD 100 billion credit line granted by the US Department of Treasury, which, if required and with the approval of the Board of Governors of the Federal Reserve System and the US President, can even grow to as much as USD 500 billion. This enables the centralised FDIC system to take action and makes it credible.

By contrast, the European Commission is not itself in a position to act as a backstop for a centralised European deposit guarantee scheme, drawing attention to its lack of powers to levy taxes. The European Stability Mechanism (ESM) could theoretically serve as a backstop (lender of last resort). However, the structure of the ESM means that there has to be a unanimous decision by its Board of Governors, and in some cases the approval of national parliaments. It would not therefore be possible to calm the deposit markets quickly in a situation of pronounced uncertainty.

This would leave the European Central Bank (ECB) as the only lender of last resort at the European level. However, it is still unclear whether this would contradict its intended sovereign mandate of safeguarding price stability, or would induce excessive inflation. As a result, the ECB is not unequivocally capable of performing the function of a lender of last resort for an EDIS.

It would therefore be a matter of the Member States to grant short-term credit to a centralised European deposit guarantee scheme, at least to bridge any liquidity shortfall. However, it is foreseeable that Member States will only be willing to do this for their own jurisdictions. A centralised European deposit guarantee scheme will therefore tend to hinder the integration of the single financial market or make it impossible.

I.3. Misguided incentive effects for national economic policy (moral hazard), lack of a European legal basis and encouraging distributional conflicts between Member States

The mutualised liability aspect of a European deposit guarantee scheme creates distorted incentives (moral hazard) because national economic policy actions no longer have to take sufficient account of their impact on banking market stability. Added to this is the danger of offsetting financial risks between banking systems with different stability (cultures).

Article 114 of the TFEU (harmonisation of laws in the internal market) is not sufficient as a legal basis. This view is held by the German Federal Government and has been confirmed in an expert opinion prepared by Professor Herdegen, Director of the Institute for Public Law and the Institute for International Law at the University of Bonn: the required minimum legal basis would be Article 352 of the TFEU (unanimous treaty amendment), an international treaty or an amendment to the TFEU itself.

Apart from that, an EDIS would represent a redistribution channel between Member States. There would be a clear sense of there being winners and losers. Additional centralisation measures and transfers between Member States would accelerate the permanent loss of acceptance of the EU. It would give rise to a strong feeling of external control.

I.4. It is foreseeable that a risk-based contribution structure will not work

In its 2015 draft, the European Commission proposed levying risk-based contributions for EDIS. Although this makes sense at a theoretical level, it is predictable that it will be impossible to implement it in practice or in political decision-making, as the detailed definition of the contribution structure will lead to a direct conflict of distribution if the overall funding target is fixed.

Political conflicts of distribution like this already emerged when the system of contributions to the banking levy, i.e. the contributions to the Single Resolution Fund (SRF), was being developed, and they prevented an economically appropriate structure that would have had a steering effect regarding systemic importance and risk profile. A similar outcome is to be feared for the system of contributions to a European deposit insurance scheme.

I.5. Solving the so-called "home-host issue" does not need an EDIS

There are two sides to the home-host issue:

- A group parent company operating in several European countries is (potentially) restricted with regard to its subsidiaries (not its branches) by national ring-fencing requirements in an overall liquidity management system. There are complaints that this impedes the cross-border operations of transnational banking groups – to the extent they are organised in the form of subsidiaries – and thus results in a restriction of the single financial market.
- Conversely, individual countries (e.g. Portugal) whose banking market is dominated by subsidiaries of foreign financial groups fear a withdrawal of liquidity by the group parent companies in the event of a crisis and a subsequent restrictive lending policy by the subsidiaries to the real economy, or recourse to the deposit guarantee schemes in their own country. They are therefore calling for the retention of national ring-fencing options for liquidity management at subsidiaries of foreign banks.

Both sides argue that EDIS would render the need for a national ring-fencing option obsolete and hence promote cross-border activity in the single financial market.

From an objective perspective, however, EDIS is not necessary for dispensing with the national ring-fencing option: this could also be solved more easily and more efficiently by the equal regulatory treatment of parent/subsidiary-structures and parent/branch-structures in deposit insurance:

- In the case of parent/branch-structures, the deposit insurance obligation already has to be covered by the parent company's guarantee scheme under current law. This means that, on the one hand, no national liquidity ring-fencing is necessary relating to branches and, on the other, there is no room for threats to the host country's deposit insurance scheme (and thus potentially the national fiscal budget) being burdened.
- If an equivalent scenario – meaning a responsibility of the parent company's guarantee scheme – were to be established in the case of parent/subsidiary-structures, the concerns outlined above could be resolved.
- From a consumer protection perspective, responsibility for deposit insurance in the parent company's home country in principle would be unproblematic. First, the deposit insurance standards have been largely harmonised by the DGSD. Second, the host country deposit guarantee scheme already makes advance payments for payout events, including in the case of a branch structure, and subsequently claims the repayments back from the home country guarantee system (Article 14(2) of the DGSD). This system could also

by way of changes to the legal framework be extended to subsidiaries of foreign EU banks without compromising consumer protection interests.

II. Design of a DGS for the Banking Union

II.1. Diversity in the DGSD: Pay-Box and Institutional protection approach

Article 1 (2) of Directive 2014/49/EU (the DGSD) specifies three permissible approaches or systems safeguarding the special protection of deposits:
a. statutory deposit guarantee schemes (DGSs)
b. contractual DGSs that are officially recognised as DGSs in accordance with Article 4(2)
c. institutional protection schemes (IPSs) that are officially recognised as DGSs in accordance with Article 4(2).

From a factual perspective, the systems specified are to be distinguished into two categories:
– "pay boxes", offering pure compensation for deposits in the event of insolvency, and
– institutional protection schemes (IPS).

Sparkassen and cooperative banks in Germany use the possibility under current EU law to fulfil the deposit protection obligation by an IPS (Article 4(2) of the Deposit Guarantee Scheme Directive 2014/49/EU).

Institutional protection works like a form of early restructuring: the focus is on the institution in question continuing as a going concern through liquidity loans, equity injections, and potentially transfers of assets or a merger. The primary objective is not to compensate depositors, but to ensure continuity of customer relationships and to prevent insolvency.

The institutional protection schemes recognised as statutory deposit guarantee schemes therefore have a single fund – with a target level of 0.8 % of covered deposits – from which measures primarily intended to protect institutions, i.e. to avoid insolvency, are financed (Article 11(3) of the Deposit Guarantee Scheme Directive 2014/49/EU). As a fall-back position, an institutional protection scheme recognised as a statutory deposit protection scheme must retain at least 25 % of the target level for payout events and must not use it for institutional protection measures (Article 11(5) of the Deposit Guarantee Schemes Directive 2014/49/EU).

II.2. Functioning of the IPSs in the Sparkassen and cooperative banking sector in Germany

The IPS protects Sparkassen and their affiliates in the case of financial problems. It is operated by Sparkassen associations and fully funded by the Sparkassen themselves. The IPS intervenes in the event of liquidity or solvency problems; via bridge loans, asset purchases, capital injections or by imposing a merger with another Sparkasse. The aim of institutional protection is the continuation of the business activity by giving financial support or by merger.

The institutional guarantee System is officially acknowledged as deposit protection (Art. 4 (2) DGSD). The DGS target level is exclusively reserved for this purpose. Although institutional protection precludes insolvency and thus compensation necessity — and in the past, compensation has never occurred — the legal framework requires this emergency backup, in the unlikely case the institutional protection measures fail.

To avoid moral hazard or too risky business behaviour, the IPS has an ongoing monitoring system and early intervention rights. Through a set of qualitative and quantitative indicators, institutions are classified into different risk categories (in a four-coloured traffic light scheme, i.e. green, amber, red, dark red). Depending on the classification, the IPS has powers of intervention vis-à-vis the institution.

The IPS gives a special promise to customers on the one hand. On the other hand, the continuation of business activities ensures the credit relationships for small and medium-sized enterprises (SMEs) in the region, many of which are Sparkassen customers. Overall, the IPS provides a noticeable contribution to financial stability, because liquidity and solvency problems are handled noiselessly and without triggering market uncertainties.

The IPS is a core structural element of the Sparkassen network in Germany and of crucial importance for its functioning. So, both Sparkassen and cooperative banks in Germany are deeply concerned about EDIS. The reason for this is that — according to the Commission proposal — institutional protection schemes are effectively abolished. We believe this to be wrong and unjustified. Thus, we are opposed to the Commission project as it is currently discussed.

II.3. Potential conflict between institutional protection schemes and EDIS

In November 2015, the European Commission adopted a proposal for a regulation to create a centralised deposit insurance scheme (European Deposit Insurance Scheme [EDIS]). According to this proposal all financial resources of national guarantee funds would be combined into a single fund at European level (Deposit Insurance Fund [DIF]). The proposed European deposit insurance scheme will only provide for depositor compensation in the event of insolvency or payout events, and not provide institutional protection measures.

The mechanics of EDIS will also force the institutional protection schemes of the Sparkassen and cooperative banks to transfer their funds to a centralised system. In order to maintain the existing standard of customer protection, and in particular institutional protection, the Sparkassen would then have to save an additional amount of approximately EUR 5 billion in an additional scheme. This is simply impossible in light of the current low interest rate environment, the considerable increase due to contributions to the SRF over the last years and the additional burdens from banking regulation. As a result, EDIS will effectively abolish the institutional protection schemes and destroy a core element of the network structure of Sparkassen and cooperative banks in Germany.

Without their own institutional protection scheme, the only options available to Sparkassen in the event of financial problems will be insolvency, support by their responsible bodies (district or municipal authority, etc.) or a (private) capital increase by third parties. Alternatively, insolvency could be avoided if Sparkassen form a corporate group. EDIS thus constitutes an assault on the fundamental structure of the Sparkassen network and ultimately would result in an integration of Sparkassen into a banking group. At any rate, the regional element of the network structures and their benefits to the real economy is up for discussion as a result of such legislative interventions.

The loss of decentralised analysis and decision-making elements in lending to the real economy would have an adverse effect on the stability of SME financing in the German banking market. Empirical evidence shows that large banks and multinational banking groups retreat into their home regions in the event of a macroeconomic crisis and cut back their exposure to structurally weak and peripheral business areas.[1]

A decentralised banking system is crucial for stable, reliable SME financing in Germany. In this respect, it is in the Federal Republic of Germany's vital interest to agree on a deposit guarantee mechanism that preserves the network structures and their institutional protection schemes within the framework of a European solution.

---

1 Cf. Schackmann-Fallis, K.-P./M. Weiß 2018, "Post-Financial Crisis Times: Only a Short Phase of Re-Intermediation and Re-Direction to Boring Banking Business Models? – Regulatory Burden, Fintech Competition, Concentration Processes", *DIW Vierteljahrshefte zur Wirtschaftsforschung*, vol. 87(4), 87–117.

II.4. Requirements for a design that integrates the IPS into a European deposit insurance scheme

If the political process – despite all objectively justified concerns – decides for a European deposit insurance scheme, the stabilising elements in the functioning of an IPS must be taken into account. The following are required in particular to safeguard the ability of the IPS to function properly:

- unrestricted operational decision-making power at the level of the IPS in the design of institutional protection measures on a case-by-case basis and the use of funds,
- unrestricted, independent power to design and define the contribution system (in line with EBA/GL/2015/10) that allows the specific characteristics of the IPS, and
- unrestricted access by the IPS to the target level for use in institutional protection measures.

In order to fulfil these requirements, the institutional protection schemes under Article 113(7) CRR that are recognised as statutory deposit guarantee schemes should be excluded from the scope of a European deposit guarantee scheme.

II.5. Subsidiarity principle: Mandatory lending as an alternative

The European Union's subsidiarity principle, under which tasks and problems must be resolved at the lowest adequate level of government, is violated by EDIS because full mutualisation is not necessary to create greater financial stability and greater integration of the single financial market. A structure that, on the one hand, enables the definitive decoupling of financial risks attributable to the banking sector from national fiscal budgets – i.e. further loosens the sovereign-bank nexus – and, on the other hand, ensures the functionality of institutional protection schemes, would constitute a system of mandatory lending between the national deposit guarantee schemes.

Mandatory lending was envisaged by the European Commission itself in its proposal to revise the Deposit Guarantee Scheme Directive in 2010. However, there was no majority support in the subsequent legislative process. During the debate on EDIS, this approach was revitalised by the French banks under the name of EDRIS (European Deposit Re-Insurance Scheme). Under this proposal, a crisis lending scheme would maintain the sovereignty of the national schemes, while at the same time creating a backstop mechanism in case of need.

Restricted participation of IPS-systems: Another possible option could be that the IPS-participation in the DIF is limited to a certain amount. Thus, the DIF would be the fall-back for the unlikely case institutional protection measures fail, equivalent to the existing allegation under Article 11(5)(b) of the DGSD 2014/49/EU.

III. Conditionality for Next Steps

However, before pursuing considerations of mandatory lending, there must be convergence towards a comparable level of risk in the different national banking systems. This applies, for example, to the highly diverse levels of non-performing exposures (NPEs) and the TARGET II-balances. These divergences are due in part to the heterogeneous economic growth in recent years. However, structural causes such as different insolvency regimes also play an important role.

If there is another asset quality review (AQR) that covers all credit institutions, the experience gained from the pre-SSM asset quality review should be taken into account. The analyses must be robust and must not be subject to any political influence. An AQR means high costs and an intensive workload for the credit institutions, so special attention must be paid to the benefits for financial stability. In addition, numerous stress tests and stability analyses are already ongoing and do not need to be duplicated.

Equally, there is also a need for limits on credit institutions' sovereign exposures. If these are not implemented, sovereign risk would be mutualised via deposit guarantee schemes. This would be contrary both to the requirements of the TFEU and to the principle of "unity of liability and control".

In the interests of political credibility, the sustainable objective of a European deposit insurance scheme must be clearly communicated by the lawmakers and the European Commission. Mandatory lending or other constructions must therefore be seen as "completing the third pillar of the Banking Union", and not merely as a springboard to full mutualisation, which is actually the case with the Commission's October 2017 communication.

IV. A critical view on EDIS in more detail

IV.1. Does the Banking Union really need EDIS?

There is no need for EDIS in order to ensure the functioning of the Banking Union. One can argue that the Banking Union is already completed due to the harmonized European landscape of deposit insurance under the DGSD of 16 April 2014.

According to the EU Commission, today there is full transposition in the Member States[2]. So the questions we should ask are:

- Who benefits most from a European deposit scheme and who loses out on it? The answers to that question give a lot of insight into the hidden agenda behind EDIS, especially the issue of entering into a transfer union through the backdoor.
- What is the reason for the European Commission to move control over national systems from the Member States' level to the European level via the extinction of the national systems?
- Would it ever be possible to exercise this control and effectively stabilize any crisis without any collaboration of national stakeholders? The answer is no. There are simply too many details that have to be taken care of and there is a strong need for respecting national discretions – different insolvency laws being only one of them.

Therefore, there is no strong case in favour of a European scheme since the other two pillars of the banking union also have strong national elements or have proven not to be workable on the European level alone. In contrast, EDIS is threatening stability within the Banking Union:

- The separation of risk and liability – that is inherent to any centralization – cannot and will not make savers' deposits any safer in the long term, but will rather strain the existing basis of trust between customers and their banks. Trust could even be damaged irreparably.
- Moreover, the aspect of a higher cross-border contagion risk is very important and clearly underrepresented in the general discussion.

---

2 https://ec.europa.eu/info/publications/deposit-guarantee-schemes-directive-transposition-status_en

IV.2. EDIS would negatively affect the structures of the European banking market and would weaken financial stability: Banks operating at a local level and their clients might suffer the most disadvantages from EDIS.

One thing needs to be remembered: According to the EDIS proposal, all national schemes will cease to exist after a certain time. You cannot imagine much more of an "impact" on a well-functioning deposit guarantee scheme. And let's be clear: The October 2017 communication of the European Commission has not changed this ultimate result.

The centralization of deposit insurance on the European level would undermine core features of financial networks. Centralization at the European level and thus the removal of the ability to deal with problems in the appropriate way – meaning not just providing a pay-box function – represents an existential threat to the proven capability of these networks to operate effectively.

According to the Commission's EDIS proposal, the IPSs in these networks would have to transfer 0.8 % of their covered deposits – a figure in the order of around EUR 9 billion. The national schemes would have to replenish any withdrawals and would also have to save the same amount again. This is simply impossible in light of the current low interest rate environment and in particular the considerably stiffer regulatory capital requirements now in place.

The European Commission is therefore factually incorrect when it claims that EDIS will not lead to any further costs for the banks. This may be the case for simple compensation systems ('pay boxes'), but it is demonstrably incorrect for institutional protection schemes.

When EDIS is implemented, having rendered national schemes obsolete, it will become very hard to have a close cooperation in financial networks. For example, sharing the same brand (i.e. the red "S") is a symbol of the core values of the Sparkassen and can only be used if an institution belongs to the network and follows its principles. One of these is the support by an IPS. Additional measures generating considerable additional costs would have to be implemented in order not to damage the brand.

German Sparkassen are embedded in their local communities. Their IPS is legally acknowledged under the DGSD and as such accepted by the European Commission. Both citizens and small and medium-sized enterprises in each region benefit from this set-up. So instead of eroding Sparkassen and local banking by abolishing their IPS, the way forward has to be to look at what is really needed in terms of mutualisation and what is the logical order of steps to be taken.

There is a high probability that the multinational banking groups benefit most from EDIS, because – given their size – their potentially destabilizing power in a crisis scenario is the biggest and would have widespread consequences for depositors. But politics must be very careful not to cross the border where measures of centralization have a detrimental effect on competition, risk diversification and also capital allocation.

Banks operating at a local level and their clients might suffer the most disadvantages from EDIS. In an EDIS-world, these banks could be as prudent and well managed as possible, but still they would have to bear the costs and the potential losses from the most risky bank in a European scheme – especially when there are no individual national schemes any more. Their capital allocation function – which in Germany is so important for the rural areas and the local economy – would simply become too costly.

IV.3. The Banking Union is already safe, with the SRF and a backstop

It makes sense to provide the SRF with a backstop, as decided by the Euro Summit in December 2018. In a systemic crisis, caps quickly lead to speculation or panicky fire sales. A backstop in the sense of a lender of last resort rebalances this and creates a stabilizing effect. Even an enlarged SRF would have a fixed limit. The problem with fixed ceilings however is that in times of crisis, some market participants speculate against it. Generally, speculators are less likely to test systems without caps – which ultimately has a stabilizing effect.

Apart from that, the Sparkassen already pay EUR 140 million to the SRF each year; the German banking industry a total of 1.7 billion. At the end of the replenishment phase, this adds up to around EUR 15 billion of German contributions. To consider even higher contributions is economically impossible in times of low interest rates.

The backstop function could have been the European Stability Mechanism (ESM), but theoretically also the European Central Bank (ECB). Priority has rightly been given to the ESM to avoid potential conflicts with price stability and the monetary policy agenda. Thus it is the ESM's task to act more strongly than before as a lender of last resort in case of a financial market crisis and as a backstop for the SRF.

By doing so, the ESM would evolve towards a European version of the IMF, as the IMF is not only a lender in cases of sovereign debt crises – or in the case of fixed-rate exchange rate crises – but also safeguarding financial stability through the analysis of the causes and market intervention. The SRF combined with an extended ESM can also serve as a backstop for national deposit guarantee schemes. Due to depositors' preferred creditor status, a bridging liquidity facility is the only instrument that is needed in the context of EDIS anyway.

The extension of the ESM and its conjunction with the SRF bring real value added in terms of financial stability and are therefore very important for the further development of the monetary union. Political forces should therefore be invested in this project instead of getting bogged down in other details, such as EDIS.

V. Summary

The EU Deposit Guarantee Scheme Directive (DGSD, 2014/49/EU), which was to be transposed into national law by the beginning of July 2015, has legally enshrined the rights of depositors of up to EUR 100,000 in all Member States of the European Union (EU) as well as strict quality standards within the various systems. The current EU legal framework for deposit insurance, harmonised through the DGSD, ensures the same level of protection all over Europe.

The DGSD forms the third pillar of the Banking Union and, alongside the Single Supervisory Mechanism (SSM) and the Single Resolution Mechanism (SRM), completes it. Depositors in all Member States are protected up to EUR 100,000. Hence, we face a harmonized European Deposit Guarantee Scheme (DGS)-landscape.

Not untypical for political discussions, the Banking Union is subject to widely different interpretations. A widespread perception is that the Banking Union needs to be "completed" and that its current state is only a partial solution. This view appears to be rarely checked for accuracy as the Banking Union is indeed complete from an economic perspective. Its third pillar is built upon the DGSD, which ensures a common depositor protection in every Member State according to the very same, harmonized requirements.

In order to achieve the alleged goal of increasing depositors' trust in the stability of the financial system, it is not necessary to mutualise the funds into one deposit guarantee scheme. It is even better not to put all eggs in one basket to avoid contagion, if mistrust were to come back again.

The additional European Deposit Insurance Scheme (EDIS), as proposed by the EU Commission in November 2015 (COM(2015) 586 final) is not a tool of harmonization but of centralization. In sharp contrast to the DGSD, EDIS eliminates diversity and aspires unification through centralization without regard to costs.

Unlike EDIS, the DGSD allows for different approaches: in the DGSD, European legislators have recognised the different approaches pursued by pay boxes and institutional protection schemes (IPSs), Article 4(2) DGSD. IPSs are designed to avoid institutions going into insolvency and ensure that all business relationships with customers of a covered institution can be continued, thereby providing a much higher level of stability.

EDIS is not the right way forward. It does not provide for the integration of well-functioning systems and will consequently leave an important part of European depositors worse off.

Rendering IPSs economically unworkable seriously impedes regional banking. In fact, with EDIS, the very diversity of the EU banking sector is at stake

The DGSD explicitly allows DGSs to use their funds for alternative measures in certain cases. EDIS (indirectly) eliminates this option without justification. This is not trivial, as it could mean the end for institutional protection schemes that are officially recognized as deposit guarantee schemes in accordance with the DGSD. Under EDIS, they will have to transfer all funds to a European fund. It is very doubtful if they will be able to raise lost funds a second time through additional contributions from their member institutions.

A defining quality of the EU banking sector is its profound diversity. Concerning regional banks, this diversity relies in a large part on institutional protection schemes and network constructions. In contrast, the EDIS does not take into account these differences.

It has been argued that EDIS has no negative effect on IPSs as they could be set up as a voluntary scheme next to the European DGS. Consequently, members of an IPS would be faced with a double burden, extinguishing IPSs in the end.

Proponents of the European Commission's EDIS proposal argue that IPS membership could be "rewarded" by a reduced DGS contribution, thus leaving funds available for voluntary support. This, however, would only work for DGSs and IPSs that are separated. But a number of IPSs, such as the one of the German Sparkassen (and the German cooperative banks as well), are indeed recognized under current legislation as a DGS at the same time. Transferring their existing funds to a mutualized system would eliminate the funds necessary to maintain a functioning IPS. Therefore IPSs, and in particular IPSs recognized as DGS, would become economically unviable under the EDIS proposal.

In the end, EDIS would eliminate existing IPSs and would have far-reaching consequences for financial stability as well as for local banking and banking market structures. It is, therefore, imperative to ensure the workability of IPSs recognized as DGSs into any form of discussions about a European deposit protection system.

Pushing for a centralized European deposit insurance with a mutualized fund breaks the bond between risk and liability. It introduces the danger of moral hazard

Apart from its irrevocably damaging effects on diversity, EDIS would have negative systemic impacts as well. An obvious one is the occurrence of moral hazard for policymakers in ignoring the effects of national economic policy on banking stability by mutualizing the resulting financial consequences. But EDIS would also give rise to contagion risk as depositors become aware of the interconnectedness that is inherent to EDIS, ultimately leading to destabilising spillover effects.

A fully fledged EDIS would uncouple risk and accountability. Since higher-risk banking sectors will be backed by EDIS, they would be prone to favour riskier business models altogether. Banking sectors with lower-risk business models would implicitly support their competitors in other Member States.

Another word of caution, when looking at the discussion of a (statistical) reduction of non-performing exposures (NPEs): This should not mislead us to rushing into EDIS. Legacy risks are not restricted to NPEs. We lack a harmonized insolvency law within the EU. Moreover, a coerced European centralization could very well be the missing link that will allow risks to leap from one Member Sate to the other, endangering financial stability and trust.

Apart from the potentially severe implications of EDIS for diversity and for networks of regionally focused credit institutions, the issue of risk imbalances remains largely unaccounted for. It is of crucial importance to address the sovereign-bank nexus as reflected in the persisting home-bias present in banks' sovereign risk portfolios. Deteriorations of sovereign debt have the potential to exercise severe pressure on banks' capital positions, particularly when they are already faced with a high NPE ratio.

A fully mutualized EDIS will not prevent bank crises. This can only be achieved via sound and sustainable business models and a clear path to dealing with the risk weighting of sovereign exposures. A fully mutualized EDIS will create cross-border liability obligations without offering adequate possibilities of (risk) control.

Alternative: Mandatory Lending

Harmonized standards of depositor protection, level playing field, prevention of regulatory arbitrage, and enhanced stability of the banking system, all these objectives are already explicitly addressed by the DGSD. The question remains if there is any net benefit to be expected from EDIS. The intended backstop mechanism for national shocks can also be reached by a system of mandatory lending. This is a much less invasive way to address this link between deposit insurance and national fiscal budget. Such a construction would permit a DGS in a stressed liquidity situation to borrow from all other schemes. A system of mandatory lending could be implemented under the DGSD review which was due in 2019.

The European banking landscape is extremely rich and diverse, reflecting the EU's motto "United in Diversity". If this diversity of bank business models – ultimately leading to a more resilient overall financial system – is to be preserved, regulators need to take care not to overburden small and medium-sized locally focussed credit institutions with their legislation. The principle of proportionality is key in this respect. Another element is network building to maintain economies of scale. Institutional protection schemes provide locally active credit institutions an overarching element for networks of independently governed credit institutions.

Enhancing trust and depositor protection within the framework of the Banking Union needs a well-conceived construction. A pure centralization of DGSs is not the adequate approach. Instead, mandatory lending or construction of a restricted participation of IPS-systems in EDIS should be taken into consideration. Small and regional credit institutions, such as the German Sparkassen, have been making use of institutional protection for decades. Their IPS has more than 40 years of experience protecting depositors. To promote financial stability and to encourage local banking, EDIS must not eliminate existing IPSs.

Thomas F. Huertas
Completing banking union

To complete banking union, there should be a single European deposit insurance scheme (EDIS) alongside the single supervisor and the single resolution authority. This would ensure uniformity across the Eurozone and facilitate the removal of barriers to the mobility of liquidity and capital within the single market. That in turn would promote efficiency in the banking sector and in the economy at large — just at the time that the EU needs to boost growth in order to remain competitive with the US and China.

If the "E" in EDIS is to be meaningful to the depositor EDIS is meant to protect, "E" can only mean one thing: that the holder of an insured deposit in a Eurozone bank will promptly receive 100 cents on the euro in euro, if the bank in which s/he holds the deposit fails. This promise should be unconditional. As far as insured deposits in the Eurozone are concerned, a euro should be a euro, regardless of the Member State in which the deposit is placed, and regardless of how much money there may be in the deposit guarantee scheme.

In national schemes, such a promise effectively comes from the government. The government stands behind the guarantee given to insured deposits. That is appropriate, for the risk given resolution to insured deposits where insured deposits have preference comes predominantly from the possibility that the central bank and/or other authorities exercise forbearance and allow the bank to operate beyond the point of non-viability.

But who will stand behind the commitment that EDIS would make to depositors across the Eurozone? Who is the "E" in EDIS? Is its promise credible, even in a crisis? If a deposit guarantee scheme fails to deliver what people expect, panic would very likely erupt. Instead of strengthening financial stability, deposit insurance could destroy it.

Yet this is the risk that current proposals pose. They create the impression that there will be a single deposit guarantee scheme. There will not. Instead, there will be a complex set of liquidity and reinsurance arrangements among Member State schemes. Nor do the proposals designate the "E" that will backstop EDIS.

These defects need to be remedied. To do so, we propose creating a European Deposit Insurance Corporation (EDIC) alongside national schemes. For banks that meet EDIC's strict entry criteria and decide to become members, EDIC will promise to reimburse promptly — in the event the member bank fails — 100 cents on the euro in euro for each euro of insured deposits, regardless of the Eurozone Member State in which the bank is headquartered. In effect, the single deposit guarantee

https://doi.org/10.1515/9783110683073-010

scheme would be created via migration to EDIC rather than mutualisation of existing schemes. This would increase the mobility of capital and liquidity and lead to a convergence of interest rates across the Eurozone. That in turn will improve the effectiveness of monetary policy, foster integration and promote growth.

Deposit insurance in a single national jurisdiction

A deposit guarantee scheme ("DGS") protects insured deposits from loss in the event that a bank fails.[1] If the resolution of the failed bank results in loss to deposits covered by the DGS, the DGS bears such loss, not the holder of the covered deposits. Moreover, deposit guarantee schemes undertake to reimburse covered deposits promptly, so that the depositors can continue to access such funds to meet their own obligations.

A DGS therefore curtails the contagion that could possibly arise, if unsophisticated depositors were to conclude from the failure of one bank that all banks were in trouble. With credible deposit insurance depositors have no incentive to withdraw deposits covered by the scheme. As far as the depositor is concerned, covered deposits are safe. The DGS bears any risk attributable to covered deposits and the DGS has the responsibility to monitor the bank holding such deposits.

Whether deposit insurance promotes or weakens financial stability depends on the design and execution of the guarantee scheme as well as on the interaction of deposit insurance with other aspects of bank regulation and supervision, including the access of troubled banks to lender of last resort facilities.[2] On its own, deposit insurance creates moral hazard: if its deposits are insured, a bank may take more risk and therefore increase the probability that it will fail.[3] To counteract this possibility, there should be restrictions on the ability of the bank to take risk, similar to the covenants that a private guarantor or creditor would impose.[4]

---

1 The core principles for effective deposit insurance schemes (IADI 2014) emphasise the importance of (a) making individuals and small-to-medium sized businesses eligible to receive deposit insurance, (b) ensuring 100 % coverage of all deposits below a certain threshold (in the EU this is €100,000), (c) delivering on the commitment to reimburse covered deposits promptly, and (d) funding the DGS via premiums from banks, backstopped by a guarantee and/or line of credit from the government.
2 Demirgüç-Kunt and Detragiache (2002); Cerrone (2018).
3 Anginer and Demirgüç-Kunt (2018).
4 Dewatripont and Tirole (1994: xxx).

Super preference for insured deposits reduces risk to deposit guarantee scheme

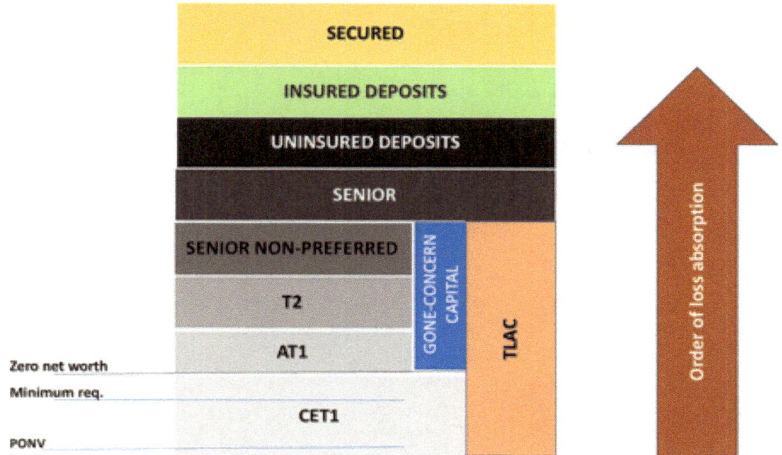

In banking, these restrictions take the form of regulation. The bank's license limits the activities in which the bank may engage.[5] Various rules restrict the risk the bank may take in connection with permitted activities, whilst other requirements stipulate the capital and liquidity that the bank must maintain in order to conduct such permitted activities. Banks must regularly report their compliance with these restrictions and open themselves to official supervision. Finally, the resolution regime provides the remedies open to the deposit guarantor as well as to other creditors, if the bank does not meet regulatory requirements.

Thus, the risk to the DGS is a product of two factors: the probability that the bank will enter resolution, and the loss to DGS given that the bank has entered resolution. The latter depends critically on the point at which the authorities put the bank into resolution as well as on the position of covered deposits in the creditor hierarchy. The risk to the scheme is less, if the authorities put the bank into resolution at or before the bank reaches the point of non-viability (PONV). In such cases, the failed bank is likely to have positive net worth, so that there will be no loss attributable to covered deposits and accordingly no loss to the DGS. The risk to the scheme is also less, if insured deposits enjoy preference and there is a significant amount of uninsured liabilities (such as uninsured depos-

---

5 Note. However, that such restrictions limit only the types of risk the bank may take, not the amount of risk the bank actually takes. For further discussion see Huertas 2016b.

its) junior to covered deposits but senior to the instruments counting toward the bank's TLAC requirement (see Figure 1). In such cases, losses would have to exceed not only the entire amount of CET1 capital, but also all of the bank's gone-concern capital (Additional Tier 1 and Tier 2 capital, senior non-preferred debt) as well as all of the bank's senior obligations and uninsured deposits before any losses would accrue to the bank's covered deposits. Thus, if authorities promptly put banks into resolution as soon as they reach the PONV, there should be little or no risk of loss to the DGS, and therefore only a limited burden for the DGS to bear.

Forbearance increases risk to deposit guarantee scheme
Secured borrowing from central bank pushes inured deposits down the credit hierarchy

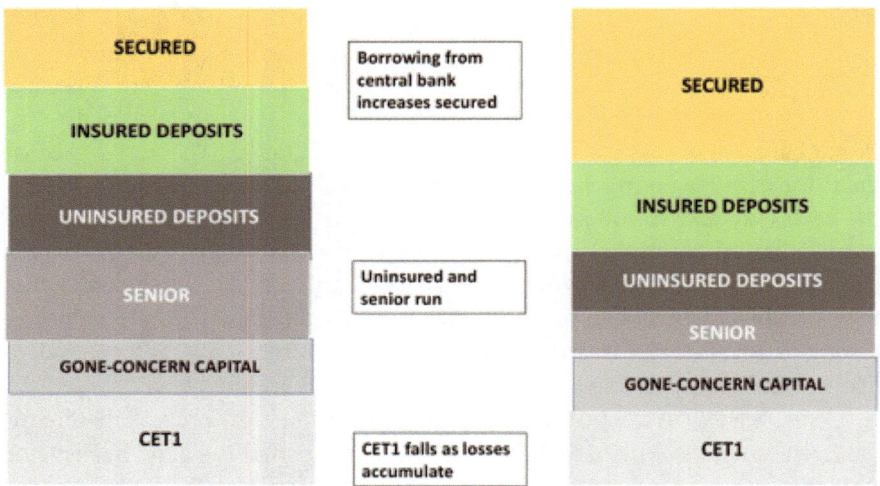

In contrast, the DGS may have a significant burden to bear, if the authorities exercise forbearance. In particular, emergency liquidity assistance (ELA) from the central bank may allow the bank to continue to operate beyond the PONV. If so, such secured lending raises the risk to the deposit guarantee scheme, for it pushes insured deposits down in the creditor hierarchy. Essentially, liabilities junior to insured deposits decline, and liabilities senior to insured deposits increase. This raises the likelihood that the DGS will incur a loss, if the authorities do eventually place the bank into resolution.

Accordingly, it is appropriate that the government backstop the commitment that the DGS makes to holders of insured deposits to reimburse covered deposits promptly, in the event that the bank holding the deposit fails. Indeed, it is this government backstop that makes the deposit guarantee scheme credible, that curtails contagion and promotes financial stability.[6]

Deposit insurance in the Eurozone

The Eurozone differs from other jurisdictions. The 19 Member States of the Eurozone are embedded in the EU (28 Member States [prospectively 27 after the exit of the UK]). The EU has established the European Banking Authority (EBA) as the single banking regulator in the EU,[7] and the EBA has created a single rule book to which all institutions in the EU must adhere.[8] Via the Banking Recovery and Resolution Directive (BRRD) the EU has established the framework by which Member States must resolve credit institutions that are failing or likely to fail.[9] And, via the Deposit Guarantee Schemes Directive (DSGD) the EU has established standards that each Member State's deposit guarantee schemes must meet.[10]

The Member States of the Eurozone have adopted the Euro as their common currency and delegated the management of that currency to the European Central Bank (ECB).[11] In addition, the Eurozone Member States have created the Single Supervisory Mechanism (SSM) to conduct bank supervision within the Eurozone under the aegis of the ECB. The ECB directly supervises significant institutions in

---

6 Bonfim and Santos 2017.

7 Under Regulation EU 2010/1093, the European Banking Authority (EBA) is the single regulator for credit institutions in the EU.

8 The European Banking Authority (EBA) has developed the Single Rulebook applicable to all credit institutions in the EU. It "provides a comprehensive compendium of the level 1 text for the Capital Requirements Regulation (CRR) and the Capital Requirements Directive (CRD IV); Bank Recovery and Resolution Directive (BRRD); the Deposit Guarantee Schemes Directive (DGSD); the Payment Services Directive (PSD2); the Mortgage Credit Directive (MCD) and the corresponding technical standards developed by the European Banking Authority (EBA) and adopted by the European Commission (RTS and ITS), as well as the EBA Guidelines and related Q&As." The interactive version may be accessed at www.eba.europa.eu.

9 EU 2014a.

10 Under the Deposit Guarantee Schemes Directive (EU 2014c) the EU required Member States to have at least one deposit guarantee scheme and to ensure that each bank headquartered within its jurisdiction belonged to a deposit guarantee scheme. Such schemes must protect the deposits of individuals and SMEs up to a limit of €100,000 per depositor per bank and must reimburse promptly insured depositors at a failed bank. In addition, the DGSD harmonized funding according to the ex ante principle as well as set a minimum target funding ratio for deposit guarantee schemes in the EU (see Funding below).

11 ECB 2014b provides details of the legal framework under which the ECB and the Eurosystem of national central banks operate.

the Eurozone and sets the standards by which national competent authorities supervise the remaining institutions.[12] Member States have also established the Single Resolution Mechanism to implement the tasks assigned to the resolution authority under the BRRD under the direction of the Single Resolution Board (SRB).[13]

However, emergency liquidity assistance (ELA) and deposit insurance remain the responsibility of each Member State. National central banks can provide ELA to troubled banks, subject to no objection from the ECB. The ECB can only object to ELA on the grounds that ELA could compromise monetary policy.[14]

Currently, deposit insurance is the responsibility of each Member State, and its government effectively stands behind its deposit guarantee scheme(s). But this backstop has limits. A Member State cannot simply create euros. It has to collect them in taxes or borrow them in the market. Hence, bank failures may not only exhaust the capacity of the DGS, but also the capability of the government to support it. Such was the case in Cyprus.[15] And, if the government itself had to reschedule its debts, the backstop would vanish, just at the time it might be most needed (since the debt rescheduling could push banks to or beyond the point of non-viability). Such was the case in Greece.[16]

---

12 For Member States in the Eurozone the Single Supervisory Mechanism subjects the prudential supervisory activities of national competent authorities to the oversight and direction of the ECB, specifically to the Single Supervisory Board. For details of the Regulation see ECB 2014a.

13 For member states in the Eurozone the Single Resolution Mechanism establishes the Single Resolution Board as the resolution authority responsible for the resolution of credit institutions headquartered in such Member States. The SRB has the responsibilities and powers assigned to and required for a resolution authority under the terms of the BRRD. It delegates the implementation of its decisions to national resolution authorities. For details see EU 2014b.

14 ECB 2017.

15 In 2012 banks in Cyprus failed as a result of losses incurred on their holdings of Greek government bonds as a result of the write-off and rescheduling of such debt held by private creditors ("private sector involvement"). The loss to insured deposits far exceeded the capacity of the Cypriot scheme to reimburse such deposits. In the overall restructuring program for the country, insurance coverage was ex post restricted to EU residents and access of such residents to their funds was restricted. For details see Michaelides and Orphanides (2016) and Theodore and Theodore (2016).

16 Banks in Greece also suffered large losses as a consequence of "private sector involvement" and the subsequent recession. However, Greek banks generally continued in operation, thanks to liquidity from the ECB (via normal lending facilities under softer collateral requirements) and from the Bank of Greece (via ELA) pending recapitalisation of the banks in the context of the overall restructuring programme for Greece. For details, see Mourmouras (2017) and Götz et al. (2018).

In both cases, the Eurozone Member States collectively developed an ad hoc solution for insured deposits as part of the overall restructuring program for the country. Although insured deposits up to the coverage limit were protected from loss, depositors faced strict limits on the amounts that they could withdraw, especially in cash. That restricted their ability to transact and hindered economic recovery.

Would insured depositors in Cyprus and Greece fared better, if EDIS had been in place? In the popular imagination, yes. They would have promptly received 100 cents on the euro in euro for each euro of their covered deposits with no restrictions on their ability to access such funds. In other words, as far as the insured deposits were concerned, EDIS would have operated much the way that the FDIC operates in the United States.[17]

What stands in the way of EDIS?

In theory, there should be little that stands in the way of EDIS. The single regulator's single rule book requires that banks keep capital in relation to the risks that banks run. The single supervisor determines (on the basis of the bank's individual capital adequacy assessment process [ICAAP],[18] the supervisory review and evaluation process [SREP][19] and system-wide stress tests[20]) the amount of "going concern" capital (common equity tier 1 [CET1] capital) that the bank must maintain. This lowers the probability that the bank will fail and enter resolution.

---

17 The FDIC has an outstanding record of consistently and promptly reimbursing insured deposits of failed banks. In part this is due to its ability to prop up the failing bank until it has completed its preparations and is ready to push to push the failing bank over into resolution. As a result, depositors in the US have come to expect that their deposits covered by the FDIC will be immune from loss and practically exempt from suspension.

18 In its ICAAP the bank must estimate the capital it will require to meet not only the risks it is currently running but also the risks it is likely to incur over the next twelve months, including risks for which regulatory capital is currently not required. For details see ECB 2018. The bank must also conduct a similar exercise for liquidity, the Individual Liquidity Adequacy Assessment Process (ILAAP). For details see ECB 2018c.

19 Under the SREP the ECB will determine for each significant institution in the Eurozone the Pillar 2 capital requirement for the bank according to guidelines established by the EBA (2018c).

20 In conjunction with the European Systemic Risk Board (ESRB) the EBA periodically conducts a system-wide stress test to determine the resiliency of the EU banking system to various shocks under scenarios developed by the ECB. For credit institutions in the Eurozone the ECB administers the test. For the methodology of the test see EBA 2018a and for the results see EBA 2018b.

Under the Single Resolution Mechanism the Single Resolution Board (SRB) mandates that significant institutions in the Eurozone create resolution plans and meet an institution-specific minimum requirement for own funds and eligible liabilities (MREL) so that they will have gone-concern capital sufficient to recapitalise the bank in the event that the bank fails.[21] This "pre-pack" resolution process ensures that investors bear the cost of bank failures, and it creates the basis for the bank-in-resolution to continue to perform its critical economic functions.

"Gone concern" capital (additional Tier 1 capital, Tier 2 capital and qualifying senior non-preferred debt)[22] lowers the likelihood that insured deposits will be subject to bail-in and the DGS exposed to loss. Under the BRRD this gone-concern capital is junior to other liabilities of the bank (see Figure 1 above). It can be bailed-in (written down or converted into CET1 capital) in the event the authorities determine that the bank is failing or likely to fail.[23] If the authorities do in fact intervene in this prompt fashion, the bank is likely to still have positive net worth, and the bail-in of gone concern capital is likely to recapitalise the failed bank.

Thus, if supervision and resolution work as outlined above, insured deposits are practically immune from loss. If authorities intervene promptly and the bail-in of "gone-concern" capital recapitalises the failed bank, the bank-in-resolution can resume operations the next business day with depositors retaining unrestricted access to their funds. In other words, under a pre-pack resolution insured deposits are not only immune from loss, but exempt from suspension.[24]

In effect, each bank has self-insured its covered deposits via the issue of gone concern capital. Provided authorities do not exercise forbearance, the risk from the bank to the DGS should be zero. There is no burden for the DGS to bear, and consequently no burden to share.

---

21 The SRB determines the amount of MREL an institution should hold on the basis of a "default formula, made up of two components: (i) a default loss-absorbing amount (LAA), which reflects the losses that the bank will incur in resolution, and (ii) a recapitalisation amount (RCA), which reflects the capital needed to meet ongoing prudential requirements after resolution. The latter component is complemented by a market confidence charge (MCC), necessary to ensure market confidence post-resolution." (SRB 2018, p. 6).

22 For details see SRB (2018:10-14).

23 The EBA has developed Regulatory Technical Standards for the key elements in the BRRD including the criteria for failure (EBA 2015) and bail-in (EBA 2017).

24 Huertas (2018). Note that resolution authorities may only use the bail-in tool, if it is in the public interest to do so. Unless the failing bank passes this test, it will be liquidated under the terms of the national insolvency procedures of the Member State in which the bank is headquartered.

However, theory alone cannot provide the basis for EDIS. Supervision and resolution do not yet work as outlined above. Forbearance persists. Sufficient MREL does not yet exist. Bank balance sheets contain current risks (e.g. non-performing loans) and prospective risks (e.g. sovereign exposures) against which they may maintain insufficient capital. Finally, EDIS lacks funding and EDIS lacks a credible backstop. Consequently, Eurozone Member States have, with varying degrees of enthusiasm, agreed that risk reduction should precede risk mutualisation.[25]

Forbearance persists. Since the crisis central banks have funded troubled banks. Thanks to "eligibility easing" by the ECB troubled Eurozone banks have been able to pledge worse and worse rated assets as collateral for normal lending facilities, including long-term lending facilities.[26] In addition, national central banks have tended to transform emergency liquidity assistance into extended liquidity assistance. Indeed, in Greece, Cyprus, Ireland and Portugal ELA has remained outstanding for months, and in some cases years.[27]

As outlined above, such assistance may constitute forbearance. If so, claims on the DGS could be significant, as and when troubled banks are put into resolution — claims that many national deposit guarantee schemes are neither financially nor operationally able to bear (see funding below).[28]

Sufficient MREL does not yet exist. Banks have not yet met requirements for gone-concern capital. At the end of 2018 the principal components of gone-concern capital (AT1 and T2 capital) at significant institutions in the Eurozone amounted to only 3.6 % of risk-weighted assets, clearly an amount insufficient to recapitalise the bank, if it were to fail, much less to restore market confidence in the bank-in-resolution. It would also be an amount insufficient to allow the SRB to have recourse to the Single Resolution Fund.[29] So banks do not yet have in

---

25 For an economic analysis of this trade-off see Bénassy-Quéré et al. (2018).

26 Huertas (2017).

27 Mourmouras (2017), Praet (2016).

28 Deposit guarantee schemes are moving toward a uniform ex ante funding model (see EBA 2019) with a target fund level in 2024 equal to 0.8 % of covered deposits. According to the DGSD (EU 2014) deposit guarantee schemes in the EU should be able to reimburse insured depositors within 7 days of the bank's failure. To do so the DGS must meet various operational challenges, including without limitation determining (a) to whom money should be paid; (b) the amount that each such person should receive; and (c) how and where such funds should be paid (for details see IADI 2012 and IADI 2014: 56). For a discussion of the operational challenges facing a DGS see Ognjenovic, 2017.

29 The amount of AT1 and T2 capital is estimated as difference between total capital ratio and CET1 capital ratio in ECB (2019: 32). Under the BRRD the resolution authority may only have recourse to the Single Resolution Fund, if 8 % of the liabilities of the bank have been bailed in.

place the gone-concern capital buffer that would protect operating liabilities in general and insured deposits in particular. This raises the risk to the DGS, for it increases the likelihood that bail-in could extend to insured deposits, if the bank were to fail.

It may take some time for banks to issue sufficient MREL. During 2019 the Single Resolution Board will finalise the requirements for gone-concern capital within the broader process of setting levels for minimum requirement for own funds and eligible liabilities (MREL) for each significant institution in the Euro-zone. Banks will then have a period of time to issue the instruments necessary to meet these requirements.

Deposit guarantee schemes may already face significant claims. Supervisors have allowed (or, in the case of the SSB, been forced to allow) banks to continue to carry non-performing loans at historic cost even though the level of provisions for such loans is unlikely to cover fully the loss that the bank may incur on such loans over time.[30] Thus, the economic value of the bank's capital may be substantially below its book value, perhaps even below minimum requirements.

Table 1: NPEs may pose risk to deposit guarantee schemes in the Eurozone.
Capital, non-performing and forborne exposures at significant institutions in the Eurozone, year-end 2018

	CET1 capital		Non-performing Exposures		Forborne exposures Performing		Non-performing		Adjusted CET1 ratio	
	Amount €bns	Ratio	Amount €bns	Coverage ratio	Amount €bns	Coverage ratio	Amount €bns	Coverage ratio	100% of NPEs	Forborne exposures
Belgium	38.1	19.1%	11.4	41.6%	2.1	2.4%	3.5	24.6%	15.7%	17.3%
Germany	185.7	15.4%	40.1	40.8%	10.0	3.8%	21.3	42.4%	13.4%	14.0%
Estonia	C	C	C	C	C	C	C	C	C	C
Ireland	31.1	18.6%	17.0	26.5%	6.8	4.2%	13.0	24.2%	11.2%	10.9%
Greece	26.0	15.3%	88.3	48.1%	16.0	7.9%	35.3	38.3%	-11.7%	-1.5%
Spain	169.9	11.9%	96.9	42.6%	43.5	8.5%	52.9	40.8%	8.0%	8.5%
France	347.9	14.2%	138.8	48.0%	14.1	7.1%	31.2	41.6%	11.3%	13.2%
Italy	123.6	12.7%	156.2	51.1%	25.1	5.2%	47.4	42.4%	4.8%	8.7%
Cyprus	3.1	13.9%	10.0	46.7%	1.7	3.0%	4.9	36.8%	-10.2%	-3.6%

30 The ECB (2018) modified its original guidelines on NPLs (ECB 2017) in response to concerns expressed by the European Parliament.

Table 1: (continued)

	CET1 capital		Non-performing Exposures		Forborne exposures Performing		Forborne exposures Non-performing		Adjusted CET1 ratio	
	Amount €bns	*Ratio*	Amount €bns	Coverage ratio	Amount €bns	Coverage ratio	Amount €bns	Coverage ratio	100 % of NPEs	Forborne exposures
Latvia	C	C	C	C	C	C	C	C	C	C
Lithuania	2.9	*18.6 %*	0.9	25.4 %	0.1	2.1 %	0.3	31.4 %	14.4 %	16.9 %
Luxem-bourg	9.6	*25.5 %*	1.1	31.5 %	0.3	0.9 %	0.3	24.2 %	23.5 %	24.5 %
Malta	1.5	*15.5 %*	0.5	27.7 %	0.1	3.9 %	0.3	28.8 %	11.5 %	13.0 %
Nether-lands	105.8	*16.4 %*	37.8	24.8 %	14.0	1.7 %	16.8	22.9 %	12.0 %	13.4 %
Austria	35.0	*13.6 %*	11.8	51.6 %	2.5	3.8 %	4.4	47.2 %	11.4 %	12.3 %
Portugal	15.3	*12.7 %*	20.2	51.4 %	4.0	2.0 %	9.4	55.2 %	4.6 %	7.7 %
Slovenia	2.5	*18.6 %*	1.2	58.2 %	0.2	8.2 %	0.6	53.5 %	15.0 %	16.1 %
Slovakia	–	–	–	–	–	–	–	–	–	–
Finland	35.9	17.1 %	8.5	25.8 %	3.6	0.9 %	C	C	14.1 %	C
Total	**1137.2**	***14.3 %***	640.8	45.3 %	144.2	5.9 %	244.3	39.1 %	9.9 %	11.7 %

Source: ECB 2019.

Although the overall level of non-performing exposures (NPEs) has been declining in the Eurozone, NPEs remain a substantial problem at significant institutions (SIs) in several Member States. For example, at year end 2018 SIs headquartered in Italy stated a CET1 capital ratio of 12.7 % and CET1 capital of €124 billion. However, Italian SIs had €156 billion in NPEs, 51.1 % of which were covered by provisions. In absolute terms provisions against NPEs amounted to €79 billion, leaving €77 billion in NPEs net of provisions. This amounts to 62 % of Italian SIs' outstanding CET1 capital. Consequently, if expected losses exceed the amount of provisions taken, the CET1 capital ratio at Italian SIs would fall from the stated level of 12.7 % of RWAs to a lower level. Indeed, if all NPEs were to default and if the loss given default were 100 %, the CET1 capital would be reduced by €77 billion (the amount of un-provisioned NPEs) and the CET1 ratio at Italian SIs would fall to 4.8 % (see Table 1). Alternatively (and perhaps more plausibly), if the need for additional provisions is restricted to forborne exposures, the CET1 ratio would fall to 8.7 % of RWAs, a level close to, if not already at the PONV.

Similar issues arise in connection with SIs headquartered in Cyprus, Greece, Ireland, Portugal and Spain (see Table 1).

Deposit guarantee schemes face significant potential risk. Currently, banks may hold an unlimited amount of government bonds issued by Member States in the banking book at historic cost, free from capital requirements (as such bonds carry a zero risk weight).[31] That reflects the view that such bonds are immune from rescheduling or default. They are not. There is a risk that a government's bonds will decline in price, either because the ECB raises rates generally and/or the fiscal outlook for the sovereign in question deteriorates. Indeed, if the sovereign reschedules or defaults on its debt fails, the banks that have invested heavily in its bonds may fail as well.[32]

Table 2: Applying Basel Accord treatment of sovereigns to Eurozone Member States would raise capital requirements

	CET1 Ratio	Claims on home govt	Rating	Risk weight Basel accord	Risk weight EU	Capital required under Basel	Adjusted CET1 ratio	
							Current Rating	One-grade Downgrade
Belgium	18.8 %	71	AA	0 %	0 %	0	18.8 %	18.2 %
Germany	15.4 %	450	AAA	0 %	0 %	0	15.4 %	15.4 %
Estonia	C	1	AA-	0 %	0 %	0	C	C
Ireland	18.7 %	18	A+	20 %	0 %	0.3	18.3 %	17.7 %
Greece	15.8 %	17	B+	100 %	0 %	1.3	14.4 %	13.7 %
Spain	11.5 %	273	A-	20 %	0 %	4.4	11.1 %	10.5 %
France	13.9 %	352	AA	0 %	0 %	0.0	13.9 %	13.7 %
Italy	12.7 %	383	BBB	50 %	0 %	15.3	10.7 %	8.7 %
Cyprus	13.2 %	7	BBB-	50 %	0 %	0.3	11.9 %	9.3 %

---

31 For an overview of the capital requirements applicable to exposures to sovereigns see BCBS 2017.

32 This confluence poses significant challenges for monetary policy. If the ECB decides to raise euro interest rates, this would increase the fiscal deficit in heavily indebted Member States and therefore tend to increase the risk premium that their governments would have to pay in order to raise funds. For both reasons the price of outstanding issues would fall, especially for long-dated fixed rate bonds. That would deplete the economic value of the bank's capital and push the banks holding such bonds toward default, especially in Member States where the market for such bonds is thin. The general rise in rates would also weaken further the position of creditors, making recovery of non-performing loans more difficult and in some cases impossible.

Table 2: (continued)

	CET1 Ratio	Claims on home govt	Rating	Risk weight Basel accord	Risk weight EU	Capital required under Basel	Adjusted CET1 ratio	
							Current Rating	One-grade Downgrade
Latvia	22.4 %	1	A-	20 %	0 %	0.0	21.9 %	21.1 %
Lithuania	19.0 %	2	A	20 %	0 %	0.0	18.5 %	17.7 %
Luxemburg	21.9 %	3	AAA	0 %	0 %	0.0	21.9 %	21.9 %
Malta	15.4 %	2	A-	20 %	0 %	0.0	14.9 %	14.1 %
Netherlands	16.1 %	82	AAA	0 %	0 %	0.0	16.1 %	16.1 %
Austria	13.1 %	51	AA+	0 %	0 %	0.0	13.1 %	12.8 %
Portugal	12.9 %	44	BBB-	50 %	0 %	1.8	11.0 %	9.1 %
Slovenia	19.9 %	5	A+	20 %	0 %	0.1	18.4 %	16.2 %
Slovakia	*	9	A+	20 %	0 %	0.1	C	
Finland	C	18	AA+	0 %	0 %	0.0	C	

This risk is higher, the lower the credit rating of the sovereign in question. For sovereigns rated A+ or lower, the Basel accord requires banks to set aside capital to offset the risk that the sovereign could default. It assigns a risk weight of 20 % to exposures rated "A", 50 % to exposures rated BBB and 100 % or more to exposures with a non-investment grade rating. Accordingly, the EU decision to accord all banking book exposures to Member States a zero risk weight allows banks to save significant amounts of capital. If EU banks had to keep capital with respect to sovereign exposures in line with the Basel standards, capital ratios at such banks would be up to two percentage points lower (this would be the case for Italian banks).

Although this would in itself not be enough to push the banks to the point of non-viability, further downgrades in the credit rating of the sovereign might well do so, especially if that downgrade pushed the risk weighting over the cliff from single A- to BBB+ or from BBB- to BB+.[33] A one full-grade downgrade in the

---

[33] Indeed, in such an environment banks with high exposures to low-rated sovereigns are more likely to fail, since such banks also have high levels of un-provisioned NPLs relative to CET1 capital (see above).

sovereign's rating would be especially onerous for banks in Italy, Cyprus and Portugal (see Table 2).

Deposit guarantee schemes lack funding. Although deposit guarantee schemes in Eurozone Member States are rapidly accumulating the funds that they might require, in aggregate such funds only amount to 0.45 % of covered deposits, barely more than half of the 0.8 % target ratio established under the DGSD (see Table 3). Under the DGSD banks have until 2024 to reach the target ratio level.

Table 3: Funding at deposit guarantee schemes in the Eurozone. Year-end 2018

	Covered deposits. € billions	DGS fund. € billions	Coverage ratio	Shortfall to target. € billions
Belgium	292.8	3.70	1.25 %	0.0
Germany	1815.3	8.20	0.45 %	-6.3
Estonia	9.4	0.20	2.37 %	0.0
Ireland	106.1	0.30	0.30 %	-0.5
Greece	104.3	1.50	1.43 %	0.0
Spain	726.3	2.00	0.28 %	-3.8
France	1168.1	4.10	0.35 %	-5.2
Italy	698.9	1.70	0.24 %	-3.9
Cyprus	9.4	0.02	0.24 %	-0.1
Latvia	8.5	0.20	2.14 %	0.0
Lithuania	14.4	0.06	0.43 %	-0.1
Luxembourg	31.7	0.20	0.76 %	-0.1
Malta	12.0	0.10	0.97 %	0.0
Netherlands	498.8	1.40	0.28 %	-2.6
Austria	218.7	0.60	0.30 %	-1.1
Portugal	144.0	1.80	1.25 %	0.0
Slovakia	32.4	0.20	0.63 %	-0.1
Slovenia	18.9	0.05	0.28 %	-0.1
Finland	129.4	1.10	0.89 %	0.0
Total	6039.4	27.43	0.45 %	-23.9

The aggregate shortfall is nearly €24 billion. Larger Member States account for over 90 % of this shortfall. The five largest Member States (Germany, France, Spain, Italy and the Netherlands) hold over 80 % of covered deposits in the Eurozone: In these Member States the coverage ratio ranges from 0.24 % (Italy) to 0.45 % (Germany). In absolute terms Germany and France face the largest shortfalls.[34]

Current proposals could be counterproductive

In current proposals for EDIS the "E" is missing, both from the guarantee and the guarantor. EDIS would not guarantee to insured depositors across the Eurozone that they would promptly receive 100 cents on the euro in euro, if the bank holding that deposit failed. Nor would an "EDIC" be immediately created. Instead, the Commission is proposing that EDIS should essentially function as a reinsurance scheme for national plans. The Commission is proposing to introduce EDIS gradually, first restricting it to provision of liquidity to national schemes, then introducing EDIS as a co-insurer alongside national schemes before finally shifting to full mutualisation of risk under EDIS.[35]

This liquidity/reinsurance scheme carries three risks. First, it may weaken the protection that depositors currently have. De facto, insured depositors already have recourse to a European backstop. If a bank failure results in losses to insured deposits, the current chain of responsibility starts with the deposit guarantee scheme that covered the deposit, proceeds to the government of the Member State in which the scheme is located, and then to the European Stability Mechanism, either within the broader context of restructuring programs, or the narrower context of lending to support indirect or direct bank recapitalisation. Effectively, Commission proposals threaten to interject the deposit guarantee schemes of other Member States between the "exhausted" scheme and the government of the Member State in which it is located, or between the scheme's Member State and other Member States (in other words, a Member State could have access to deposit guarantee schemes in other Member States without necessarily having to subject itself to the conditionality that would otherwise be imposed by the ESM.[36]

---

34 For Member States with more than one scheme (e.g. Germany, Austria), the coverage ratios for the respective Member States in the text and in Table 3 represent the aggregate ratio for the country (sum of funds available to DG schemes/total covered deposits).
35 EC 2017 summarises the proposals and the positions of various stakeholders. Carmassi et al. (2018) provide an analysis. Howath and Quaglia (2017) detail political background.
36 For details of the support that the ESM may currently provide to banks see ESM 2014.

Second, current proposals increase the correlation risk facing banks in the Eurozone, and it is not inconceivable that supervisors will demand in the context of stress testing that banks hold higher capital against the possibility that they will be called upon to make higher contributions to their own national DGS so that the DGS can meet demands for support coming from another Member State's scheme.[37]

The third and potentially most significant risk arises from a possible discrepancy between what the public believes EDIS to be and what EDIS actually delivers. Politically, EDIS is being sold as a guarantee that the insured depositor at a failed bank will promptly receive 100 cents on the euro in euro with no restrictions on access. In practice, s/he may not, and, if s/he does not, public confidence in deposit insurance could diminish, if not vanish entirely. This could cause a flight to quality (especially cash) and a run on banks perceived to be weak or headquartered in fiscally weak Member States. Instead of strengthening financial stability, EDIS as currently proposed could weaken it.

The path(s) to EDIS

Fortunately, perhaps, debate on EDIS has stalled. This creates space for alternative ways forward. One is to extend and expand risk reduction. Another is to create EDIC directly as a 28th regime alongside the 27 national schemes.[38]

Continue to reduce risk

This should not only encompass further efforts to reduce NPLs, but also include measures to reduce the risk posed by exposures to sovereigns as well as measures designed to reduce the likelihood of forbearance.

---

37 The risk posed by banks in Member State A to the deposit guarantee schemes (and therefore to the banks) in other Member States would be a product of three factors:
- the likelihood that banks in State A reach the PONV;
- the loss that the national deposit guarantee scheme would suffer, if such banks were put into resolution; and
- the ability of the national DGS to bear such losses. This in turn will depend on the ability of the national scheme to retain its assessment base.

38 This numeration presumes that the UK will exit the EU. Restoy 2019 also proposes to create an EDIC, but this would result from the harmonisation of national schemes, rather than as a "28th" regime as proposed here. See also EP 2019.

Reduce the risk posed by NPLs. This remains a high priority for the SSB, and it intends to use the supervisory methods at its disposal to induce banks to meet the standards set out in relevant regulatory guidelines.[39] In addition, the introduction of the IFRS9 accounting standard will accelerate provisioning for non-performing exposures, at least for significant institutions (who are more likely to use IFRS).[40]

Reduce the risk posed by exposures to sovereigns. Although the creation of a risk-free asset may be desirable from the standpoint of monetary policy and capital market efficiency,[41] it is not a necessary precondition for EDIS. Here the problem is that banks carry risks against which they do not hold capital. From an economic standpoint the solution is simple: require the banks to hold the appropriate amount of capital. However, from a political standpoint the solution is complex. It needs to avoid making explicit and apparent to all that Member States differ with respect to creditworthiness as well as avoid implying that governments of third countries, such as the United States, could ever default on their full faith and credit obligations. That rules out imposing capital requirements on exposures to sovereigns held in the banking book.

However, it does not rule out imposing capital on exposures to sovereigns in the trading book. Indeed, such exposures are already subject to capital requirements.[42] Thus, one could reduce the risk from exposures to sovereigns by requiring that all such exposures be held in the trading book. This would ensure that such exposures are marked to market (and therefore reduce the possibility that capital is overstated) as well as require capital against possible future losses without having to opine officially on the creditworthiness of any Member State.

To minimise the possible disruption that such a measure might unleash, it could be restricted, at least at first, to significant institutions within the Eurozone. For such institutions the SSM could introduce this requirement gradually, starting first with longer-dated bonds (see Table 4) and requiring from end 2020 forward

---

39 Enria 2019.

40 Effective 2018 banks using the IFRS standard shifted to the expected loss method of provisioning (IFRS 9). Non-performing loans are likely to be classified as category 2 so that banks will be required to take provisions for losses that may arise over the life of the loan. This will tend to increase provisions and reduce "hidden" losses. Although there is a transition period during which banks may defer taking such additional provisions into account for the purposes of calculating capital requirements, banks that do so must disclose any benefit that they realise. For details see EBA 2018d.

41 On the desirability and practicality of developing a safe euro asset (as well as proposals for how to do so) see Bénassy-Quéré et al. (2018).

42 BCBS 2019

the disclosure of any capital benefit the bank may receive from continuing to hold exposures in the banking book.[43]

Table 4: Transition schedule for shifting exposures to sovereigns to trading book at significant institutions in the Eurozone

Remaining maturity	If included in HQLA toward LCR requirement	Other exposures in banking book
Greater than 10 years	2019	2020
Greater than 5 years	2020	2021
Greater than 2 years	2021	2022
Greater than 1 year	2022	2023
Greater than zero	2023	2024

Note: all dates refer to year end

Limit forbearance. In addition to reducing NPLs and ensuring that banks hold capital against their exposures to sovereigns, Eurozone Member States should take steps to limit forbearance, at least for significant institutions.

Here two measures are advisable. The first is to shift responsibility for ELA from national central banks to the ECB. This puts the ELA decision in the same overall entity that has to determine whether an SI is failing or likely to fail. It also puts the LoLR decision at the same Eurozone level at which any EDIS is likely to operate. This removes any temptation that individual Member States could have to defer resolution/exercise forbearance in the expectation that the Member State could shift any additional cost that such a delay might cause to EDIS (and therefore to other Member States).

The second measure is to require SIs in the Eurozone to keep current the valuations that the SRB would require to trigger bail-in. This facilitates the ability of the authorities to intervene promptly and to put the bank into resolution as soon as it reaches the PONV.[44]

---

43 Arguably, given the decline in government bond yields, such a shift to the trading book at this time (July 2019) would potentially result in a capital gain for some or all of the bonds held in the banking book. Any such gain would add to the bank's regulatory capital.

44 In particular, banks would need to keep current the valuation required to determine whether the bank is failing or likely to fail as well as the valuation(s) required to determine whether it would be in the public interest to employ the resolution tool (bail-in). For details see EBA 2019a.

Go directly to EDIS: create EDIC

In addition to reducing risk, Eurozone Member States should consider establishing EDIS directly via the creation of a European Deposit Insurance Corporation (EDIC). This entity would promise to reimburse promptly holders of covered deposits at a failed member bank 100 cents on the euro in euro. EDIC would exercise for its member banks the functions assigned to national resolution authorities in the Eurozone under the BRRD, including the implementation of any resolution plan.

Membership in EDIC would be open to any bank incorporated in a Eurozone Member State that fulfils upon admission all capital requirements, including those pertaining to MREL. In addition, EDIC member banks would be required, both initially and on an ongoing basis, to

- provision for non-performing exposures in accordance with IFRS 9 and SSB policy;
- hold all government bonds and derivative exposures to sovereigns in the trading book;
- keep current the valuations that the SRB would require for bail-in; and
- maintain accurate data regarding the holders of insured deposits and the amount due to each such depositor (single-customer view).[45]

For such bank members of EDIC, the ECB, not the national central bank, would be the lender of last resort prior to resolution. This would place the responsibility for both supervision and emergency liquidity assistance at the ECB and therefore reduce the likelihood of forbearance. The ECB would also provide liquidity facilities to an EDIC member bank, if it were to enter resolution, taking as collateral the unencumbered assets of the failed bank. This would facilitate either the liquidation of the failed bank or resolution via bail-in. However, the ECB would not be responsible for any losses that EDIC might incur in connection with the liquidation or resolution of the failed bank. If EDIC incurs losses in excess of the fund accrued from premiums, EDIC may draw on a backstop to be provided by the

---

45 In addition, EDIC should give consideration to measures that would facilitate payout and/or insured deposit transfer. These could include the establishment of a special purpose bank to which the bank's insured deposits and an equivalent amount of good assets might be transferred immediately upon the determination that the bank is failing or likely to fail. In addition, consideration might be given to requiring member banks to organise themselves as an SE. This would make it easier for EDIC to transfer the headquarters of the bank in resolution from one Member State to another and so provide EDIC with additional flexibility.

European Stability Mechanism (ESM), pending subsequent recovery of such losses from additional premiums on EDIC member banks.

EDIC would charge its member banks a premium based on the risk to covered deposits at the member bank. This would be inversely scaled to the amount of gone-concern capital outstanding at the bank. For member banks that maintained gone-concern capital sufficient to recapitalise the bank, deposit insurance premiums would be minimal (e.g. 3 basis points per euro of covered deposits). They would be nominal in amount (e.g. 0.5 basis point per euro of covered deposits), if the bank's uninsured deposits and other unsecured operating liabilities were greater than the bank's TLAC requirement. In other words, EDIC member banks would not be charged premiums against the possibility that the authorities may wish to exercise forbearance.

Banks that are members of EDIC would not be members of national schemes and would not be required to pay premiums to national schemes. Although this would potentially undermine the viability of national schemes, it would also accelerate the shift to EDIC, so that banking union is achieved, not through the federation of national regimes, but through the creation and growth of a single euro regime.[46] Finally and perhaps most importantly, EDIC member banks would face no restrictions on the movement of capital and liquidity across the offices of the bank in the Eurozone.[47]

Such a regime would have several favourable features. It ensures that an insured deposit in euros at a member bank is worth 100 cents on the euro in euros in the event the bank fails, regardless of the Eurozone Member State in which the bank is located. It would therefore remove the distinction between deposits in different Member States, at least for banks that are members of EDIC. EDIC would also weaken the doom loop. It would open the door to greater freedom of movement for capital and liquidity within the Eurozone. Together these effects would lead to a convergence of interest rates across the Eurozone. That in turn will improve the effectiveness of monetary policy, foster integration and promote growth.

---

46 The withdrawal of a credit institution from a national scheme will reduce ongoing premium income for the scheme, but raise the ratio of the deposit insurance fund to the (now lower) amount of covered deposits.

47 In particular, there would be no restrictions on EDIC member banks establishing branches in other Member States, or on using deposits in one Member State to fund assets originated in a branch in another Member State.

References

Anginer, Deniz and Asli Demirgüç-Kunt (2018). *Bank Runs and Moral Hazard: A Review of Deposit Insurance*, World Bank Working Paper 8589.

Bénassy-Quéré, A, M Brunnermeier, H Enderlein, E Farhi, M Fratzscher, C Fuest, P Gourinchas, P Martin, J Pisani-Ferry, H Rey, I Schnabel, N Véron, B Weder di Mauro, and J Zettelmeyer (2018), "Reconciling Risk Sharing with Market Discipline: A Constructive Approach to Euro Area Reform" CEPR Policy Insight No 91.

BCBS 2017. Basel Committee on Banking Supervision. *The regulatory treatment of sovereign exposures.* DP 425.

BCBS 2019. Basel Committee on Banking Supervision. *Minimum capital requirements for market risk.* DP 457.

Bonfim, D. and J. A. C. Santos (2017), "The importance of deposit insurance credibility", mimeo.

Carmassi, J., S. Dobkowitz, J. Evrard, L. Parisi, A. Silva, M. Wedow. 2018. *Completing the Banking Union with a European Deposit Insurance Scheme: who is afraid of cross-subsidisation?* European Central Bank Occasional Paper 208.

Cerrone, R. (2018) Deposit guarantee reform in Europe: does European deposit insurance scheme increase banking stability?, **Journal of Economic Policy Reform**, 21:3,224–239.

Demirgüç-Kunt, A. and E. Detragiache (2002), "Does deposit insurance increase banking system stability? An empirical investigation", **Journal of Monetary Economics**, 49(7), 1373–1406.

Dewatripont, M. and J. Tirole 1994. *The Prudential Regulation of Banks* (Cambridge, MA: M.I.T. Press).

EBA 2015. European Banking Authority. Guidelines on the interpretation of the different circumstances when an institution shall be considered as failing or likely to fail under Article 32(6) of Directive 2014/59/EU.

EBA 2017. European Banking Authority. Final Guidelines concerning the interrelationship between the BRRD sequence of writedown and conversion and CRR/CRD.

EBA 2018a. European Banking Authority. *2018 EU-Wide Stress Test: Methodological Note.* Available at:

EBA 2018b. European Banking Authority. *2018 EU-Wide Stress Test: Results.* 2 November. Available at

EBA 2018c. European Banking Authority. Guidelines on common procedures and methodologies for the supervisory review and evaluation process (SREP) and supervisory stress testing. Consolidated version

EBA 2018d. European Banking Authority. Final report. Guidelines on uniform disclosures under Article 473a of Regulation (EU) No 575/2013 as regards the transitional period for mitigating the impact of the introduction of IFRS 9 on own funds.

EBA 2019a. European Banking Authority. Handbook on valuation for the purposes of resolution. (22 February).

EBA 2019. European Banking Authority. *Deposit Guarantee Schemes data.* Available at:

EC 2017. European Commission. Communication to the European Parliament, The Council, the European Central Bank, the European Economic and Social Committee and the Committee of the Regions on completing the Banking Union. COM(2017) 592 final. Brussels, 11.10.2017

ECB 2014a. European Central Bank. Regulation (EU) No 468/2014 of the European Central Bank of 16

April 2014 establishing the framework for cooperation within the Single Supervisory Mechanism between the European Central Bank and national competent authorities and with national designated authorities. (SSM Framework Regulation) (ECB/2014/17). Available at: http://data.europa.eu/eli/reg/2014/468/oj.

ECB 2014b. European Central Bank. Legal Framework of the Eurosystem and the European System of Central Banks. July.

ECB 2017. European Central Bank. Banking Supervision. *Guidance to banks on non-performing loans*. March.

ECB 2017. European Central Bank. *Agreement on emergency liquidity assistance*. 17 May 2017.

ECB 2018a. European Central Bank. Banking Supervision. Addendum to the ECB Guidance to banks on non- performing loans: supervisory expectations for prudential provisioning of non-performing exposures. March.

ECB 2018b. European Central Bank. Banking Supervision. *ECB Guide to the internal capital adequacy assessment process (ICAAP)*. November. Available at

ECB 2018c. European Central Bank. Banking Supervision. ECB Guide to the internal liquidity adequacy assessment process (ILAAP). November.

ECB 2019. European Central Bank. Banking Supervision. *Supervisory Banking Statistics*. Fourth Quarter 2018. (April 2019).

Enria, A. 2019. *Non-performing loans in the euro area – where do we stand?* Speech at the Conference "EDIS, NPLs, Sovereign Debt and Safe Assets" organised by the Institute for Law and Finance, Frankfurt, 14 June.

EP 2019. European Parliament. Economic Governance Support Unit. *"Liquidation of Banks: Towards an 'FDIC' for the Banking Union?"* (Authors: J. Deslandes, C. Dias and M. Magnus).

ESM 2014. European Stability Mechanism. Guideline on Financial Assistance for the Direct Recapitalisation of Institutions.

EU 2010. European Union. Regulation (EU) No 1093/2010 of the European Parliament and of the Council of 24 November 2010 establishing a European Supervisory Authority (European Banking Authority), amending Decision No 716/2009/EC and repealing Commission Decision 2009/78/EC. Available at http://data.europa.eu/eli/reg/2010/1093/oj.

EU 2014a. European Union. Directive 2014/59/EU of the European Parliament and of the Council of 15 May 2014 establishing a framework for the recovery and resolution of credit institutions and investment firms and amending Council Directive 82/891/EEC, and Directives 2001/24/EC, 2002/47/EC, 2004/25/EC, 2005/56/EC, 2007/36/EC, 2011/35/EU, 2012/30/EU and 2013/36/EU, and Regulations (EU) No 1093/2010 and (EU) No 648/2012, of the European Parliament and of the Council.

EU 2014b. European Union. Regulation (EU) No 806/2014 of the European Parliament and of the Council of 15 July 2014 establishing uniform rules and a uniform procedure for the resolution of credit institutions and certain investment firms in the framework of a Single Resolution Mechanism and a Single Resolution Fund and amending Regulation (EU) No 1093/2010. Available at: http://data.europa.eu/eli/reg/2014/806/oj.

EU 2014c. European Union. Directive 2014/49/EU of the European Parliament and of the Council of 16 April 2014 on deposit guarantee schemes (recast).

Götz, M.R.; R. Haselmann, J. Krahnen and S. Steffen (2015) : *Did emergency liquidity assistance (ELA) of the ECB delay the bankruptcy of Greek banks?*, SAFE Policy Letter, No. 46, Goethe University Frankfurt, SAFE – Sustainable Architecture for Finance in Europe, Frankfurt a. M. Available at: http://hdl.handle.net/10419/118645.

Howarth, D. and L. Quaglia. 2017. *"The difficult construction of a European Deposit Insurance Scheme: a step too far in Banking Union?,"* **Journal of Economic Policy Reform**, DOI: 10.1080/17487870.2017.1402682.

Huertas, T.F. 2016a. *European Bank Resolution: Making it Work!* (January 26, 2016). CEPS Task Force Report, 2016. Available at SSRN: https://ssrn.com/abstract=2723220.

Huertas, T.F. 2016b. "Six structures in search of stability." in Patricia Jackson, ed. **Banking Reform** *(SUERF Conference Proceedings 2016/2: 73–88). Available at http://papers.ssrn. com/sol3/papers.cfm?abstract_id=2662251.*

Huertas, T.F. 2017. *"Eligibility easing and the lender of last resort."* Vox CEPR Policy Portal. 21 April

Huertas, T.F. 2018. *"Calibrating Capital: When Will Banks Have Enough?"* (January 31, 2018). Available at http://dx.doi.org/10.2139/ssrn.3036925

IADI 2012. International Association of Deposit Insurers. Enhanced Guidance for Effective Deposit Insurance Systems: Reimbursement Systems and Processes. Available at:

IADI 2014. International Association of Deposit Insurers. IADI Core Principles for Effective Deposit Insurance Systems.

Michaelides, A. and Orphanides, A. 2016. **The Cyprus Bail-in: Policy Lessons from the Cyprus Economic Crisis.** *(London: World Scientific).*

Mourmouras, I. 2017. *"On Emergency Liquidity Assistance: theory and evidence".* Speech delivered at Oxford University's The Political Economy of Financial Markets (PEFM) programme. 27 February.

Ognjenovic, D. 2017. Deposit Insurance Schemes: Funding, Policy and Operational Challenges. (London: Palgrave Macmillan).

Praet, P. 2016. *"The European Central Bank and its role as lender of last resort during the crisis".* Speech at "The Lender of Last Resort: An International Perspective", a conference sponsored by the Committee on Capital Markets Regulation, Washington DC, 10 February.

Restoy, F. 2019. "How to improve crisis management in the banking union: a European FDIC?" Speech before Centro de Investigação sobre Regulação e Supervisão Financeira Annual International Conference 2019 on "Financial supervision and financial stability 10 years after the crisis: achievements and next steps," Lisbon, Portugal (4 July). Available at: http://www.bis.org./speeches/sp190715.pdf.

SRB 2018. Single Resolution Board. Minimum Requirement for Own Funds and Eligible Liabilities (MREL): 2018 SRB Policy for the first wave of resolution plans.

Theodore, J. and J. Theodore. 2016. Cyprus and the financial crisis: the controversial bailout and what it means for the Eurozone. (London: Palgrave Macmillan).

**III. How and When Do We Solve the Problem,
   or is it Solving Itself?**

Andrea Enria

Non-Performing Loans in the Euro Area – Where do we Stand?

By 2014, non-performing loans (NPLs) amounting to almost €1 trillion had piled up on the balance sheets of large banks in the euro area. That was a big problem. Since then, this amount has almost halved, and now stands at €580 billion. In the same period, the ratio of gross NPLs to total loans dropped from around 8 % to 3.8 %, falling below the 5 % attention threshold defined by the EBA. Still, the ratio is above pre-crisis levels and significantly higher than in other major industrialised economies.

So, is the problem solving itself? No, it is not. Policy initiatives have played, and will continue to play, a key role in pushing banks to clean up their balance sheets.

The European Central Bank has launched a few initiatives targeting NPLs, which have been fairly successful. We started with some general guidance to banks[1] on how to deal with NPLs. Then we issued an addendum to this guidance[2] which set out what we expect in terms of provisioning for new NPLs. And we later clarified what we expect in terms of provisioning for the stock of NPLs.[3]

All these initiatives have taken a bank-by-bank approach, of course. Our expectations are bank-specific and strictly supervisory; they are not legally binding. They rather serve as a starting point for supervisory dialogue with each bank. Based on this dialogue, we might then adjust our expectations. All this happens within the second pillar of the Basel framework, our supervisory review and evaluation process (SREP).

In a sense, our initiatives have led the way. European legislation has recently been amended to include rules on minimum loss coverage for NPLs.[4] These rules

---

1 ECB Guidance to banks on non-performing loans: https://www.bankingsupervision.europa.eu/ecb/pub/pdf/guidance_on_npl.en.pdf
2 Addendum to the ECB Guidance to banks on nonperforming loans: supervisory expectations for prudential provisioning of non-performing exposures: https://www.bankingsupervision.europa.eu/ecb/pub/pdf/ssm.npl_addendum_201803.en.pdf
3 See *ECB announces further steps in supervisory approach to stock of NPLs*: https://www.bankingsupervision.europa.eu/press/pr/date/2018/html/ssm.pr180711.en.html
4 Proposal for a regulation of the European Parliament and of the Council on amending Regulation (EU) No 575/2013 as regards minimum loss coverage for nonperforming exposures. New text: Regulation (EU) 2017/2401 of the European Parliament and of the Council of 12 December 2017

https://doi.org/10.1515/9783110683073-011

are legally binding and apply to banks across the board. So our initiatives are working well and have now been mirrored in minimum requirements embodied in actual law – Pillar 1. This makes the overall framework even more robust. We will now have to adjust our guidance to make sure that it is consistent and aligned with the new minimum requirements on NPLs, and that is what we are working on.[5] But after these minor tweaks, I would say that the rules and supervisory policies to deal with NPLs are in place.

The problem of NPLs is not solving itself – and it has not yet been resolved. While it is true that the amount of NPLs in the euro area has fallen significantly – by almost 50 % since 2014 – the stock of NPLs is still very high. It is also very old. Many of the NPLs that we see on banks' balance sheets have been there for years. For those banks with the highest levels of NPLs, more than half of their NPLs are older than two years and more than a quarter are older than five years.

At the same time, it seems that inflows of new NPLs are still on the high side – not least when one considers where we are in the business cycle. It also seems that some banks with high NPLs are still reporting increasing default rates. We find this somewhat worrying, and we urge banks to stem this inflow by rethinking their underwriting standards and engaging with distressed debtors.

So we have to continue our work in this area. When I write "we", I am including the banks, of course. There are many ways to reduce NPLs. Banks can restructure viable borrowers, write off unrecoverable loans or sell them, for instance.

Originally, many authorities and banks were concerned that markets for selling NPLs might be shallow and illiquid, and dominated by just a few players. It seems, though, that supply has spurred demand and that the market for NPLs is now less of a buyer's market than many had feared. NPL markets have become more active and have spread across the euro area. Between 2016 and 2018, we saw more and more transactions, sellers and buyers. In 2018 alone, banks from across the euro area sold or securitised around €150 billion of NPLs. Over the same period, they sold around €30 billion of foreclosed assets. For those banks that are directly supervised by the ECB and have high levels of NPLs, sales and securitisations amounted to around one-third of NPL outflows in 2018.

So, more liquid and efficient markets do play a very important role in solving the problem of NPLs. But, in general, the very first thing banks should do is

---

amending Regulation (EU) No 575/2013 on prudential requirements for credit institutions and investment firms

5 Since the time of writing, the adjustment has been made and published on the ECB Banking Supervision Website: https://www.bankingsupervision.europa.eu/press/pr/date/2019/html/ssm.pr190822~f3dd1be8a4.en.html

engage early with borrowers in trouble; they need to identify those borrowers who can be sustainably restructured. These are their customers and they are their responsibility. The earlier banks contact borrowers, understand their financial situation and deal with the issues head on, the better. The problem will not go away if banks turn a blind eye to it, do not invest adequate resources in resolving it or fail to develop the frameworks needed to manage customers.

We have to get a handle on this problem. We have to solve the issue of NPLs now. If banks have to sail into the next storm with too many NPLs on their balance sheets, they will be less able to weather it and come out safely on the other side.

Those banks with high levels of NPLs do understand this, and are acting accordingly. In 2018, many of them reduced NPLs by more than they had planned to. And looking at the most recent NPL strategies, their plans for the future are also quite ambitious. Most importantly, they are particularly aggressive in dealing with the older vintages of NPLs. These strategies, by the way, are a formal part of the SREP, and our supervisory teams closely monitor and challenge the progress banks make. In 2018, many banks overshot the targets by more than 25 %. The problem of NPLs will not solve itself, but the banks can solve it – with our help.

Fabio Panetta
EDIS, NPLs, Sovereign Debt and Safe Assets
NPLs are Not the Only Problem

The NPL issue

In recent years European authorities have done much to tackle the non-performing loans (NPL) issue and a number of different measures have been taken. The
EU action plan (and in particular the new Pillar 1 prudential backstop for banks'
provisioning) has integrated the existing framework at the legislative level[1]. On
the supervisory side, the Single Supervisory Mechanism (SSM) action has been
very intensive. It has issued guidelines for significant institutions on the management of NPLs and has defined its quantitative supervisory expectations on both
flows and stock of NPLs[2]. In such a context, banks have been working hard for
some years now – closely monitored by supervisors – to reduce NPLs in their
balance-sheets and, at the same time, to adopt more prudent and sound policies
for new lending.

The Bank of Italy has been active in the drive to reduce NPLs; for instance, to
my knowledge it has been the first National Competent Authority (NCA) to extend
the SSM guidance to domestic Less Significant Institutions (LSI) and to ask them
to enact ambitious and credible reduction plans. At the same time, it has strongly
argued in favor of a balanced approach. Indeed, while we have aimed for the
maximum speed in NPL reduction which was affordable for banks, we've also
been aware that exceeding the speed limit would have entailed tensions on
several banks at once. Optimal reduction speed is needed for various reasons:
- the Italian NPL market was (and partly still is) a buyers' market, with prices
  deeply influenced by market power and extremely high internal rate of
  returns (IRRs). Despite the extremely high amount of NPL sales in the recent
  years, the wedge between the prices that investors are prepared to pay for

---

1 Regulation (EU) 2019/630 of the European Parliament and of the Council of 17 April 2019
amending Regulation (EU) No 575/2013 as regards minimum loss coverage for non-performing
exposures.
2 Guidance to banks on non-performing loans (ECB, March 2017), Addendum to the ECB
Guidance to banks on non-performing loans: supervisory expectations for prudential provisioning of non-performing exposures (ECB, March 2018), "ECB announces further steps in supervisory
approach to stock of NPLs" (ECB press release, July 2018).

https://doi.org/10.1515/9783110683073-012

NPLs and the prices that banks are prepared to sell them remains still wide, and the new regulatory and supervisory measures on calendar provisioning will decrease banks' bargaining power;

– pressure on NPL reduction (and the related capital hit for banks) has come at a time when banks were (and still are) dealing with additional challenging issues, the most prominent being the need to build substantial Minimum Requirement for own funds and Eligible Liabilities (MREL) buffers.

Actions taken have been very effective: NPLs have quickly declined in the Eurozone as a whole and in Italy in particular, both in gross and net terms. The latest data, which refer to end-2018, show that Italian banks' gross NPL ratio was 8.7 per cent, against 16.5 per cent at end-2015 (when they reached a peak); the corresponding ratios net of provisions were 4.3 and 9.8 per cent, respectively. NPL securitizations and sales have contributed substantially to reducing NPLs (€55 billion in gross terms in 2018 only; around €25 billion expected this year).

While we cannot yet say that the NPL problem is solved, we can safely state that NPLs no longer represent a risk to financial stability. We need anyway to keep our guard up and continue to monitor banks' NPL reduction strategies and loan origination standards. We should also take into account any potential procyclical effect: as GDP growth forecasts (in Europe as well as in Italy) are revised downward, supervisory expectations on NPL reduction plan may have to be re-assessed in order to avoid repercussions to the flow of credit to the economy.

Now that the NPL issue has been largely addressed, we should pause and take stock of the work done. A number of possible unintended consequences need to be properly taken into account.

First, the new measures (Pillar 1 prudential backstop and ECB quantitative addendum) may encourage banks to withhold financial support from firms that, if provided with adequate support, have actually a chance at recovering. Indeed, incentives to abandon these companies may emerge, even in the presence of significant 'signs of life', in order to recover the maximum amount in the shortest possible time (for example, by recovering collateral). The potential negative consequences would not be limited to banks' balance sheets; they would extend to economic growth and employment.

Second, the measures will ask banks to reach very high prudential coverage ratios within pre-established times regardless of the credit recovery times. Therefore, they will presumably have a greater impact on banks in those countries, such as Italy, where recovery procedures are on average (much) longer. In other words, a fundamental level playing field issue is at stake here. While this may not be a supervisor's business, it is a business that needs to be taken serious care of, if Europe is to make progress.

Third, the supervisory approach has been (too) aggressive. Coupled with the Pillar 1 and Pillar 2 requirements against credit risk, the actual content of the new measures (Pillar 1 prudential backstop and ECB quantitative addendum) can bring to the paradoxical outcome of a prudential coverage higher than the foreseen 100 %! In addition, the focus of the supervisory evaluations is still largely based on figures gross of provisions, while it should be adapted to take into consideration the effect of the prudential backstop (that, in practice, sets to zero the "open risk" of the outstanding NPLs).

Summing up, the EU has devoted a lot of attention to NPLs. I argue that NPLs are not the only game in town. Specific risks are posed by other instruments in banks' balance sheet. Market risks, operational and AML risks have been given relatively little attention, as we now realize. Let me focus on market risks, and particularly on instruments classified as Level 2 or Level 3 under the IFRS fair value measurement standards (L2/L3 instruments).

Let me recap why markets and supervisors worry about high volumes of NPLs in banks balance sheets. NPLs (i) do not have a certain yield; in some cases interest continues to accrue, in others it does not; (ii) they are opaque, illiquid and difficult to value for an external investor; (iii) as a consequence, their valuation is uncertain; experience shows that due to the factors just mentioned they tend to be overvalued in banks' balance sheets: the illiquidity premium is not always fully priced in; in addition, banks have the discretion and the incentive to bias valuations upwards.

This very same description, point by point, applies to Level 2 and Level 3 instruments. I could elaborate on this, but for the sake of time I refer you to a December 2017 discussion paper published by Bank of Italy staff (see footnote 4 below). L2 – L3 are to varying degrees bespoke and difficult to value. This entails that their markets are illiquid, i.e. these instruments are not easily transferable without a substantial discount to their book values. Furthermore, banks have incentives to bias their valuations upwards using the discretion allowed by accounting rules to avoid recognizing losses. Proper valuation cannot be ascertained by the supervisor without accurate on-site investigations.

Furthermore, <u>potential</u> risks stemming from L2 and L3 instruments are material. This is gradually being acknowledged also in the international debate. Holdings of L2 and L3 across SSM banks amount to more than €5 trillion (assets and liabilities)[3], representing several times the total amount of net NPLs (€310 billions); they are mostly held by a limited number of large banks. In (hypotheti-

---

3 Updated amounts, based on the Bank of Italy discussion paper cited in footnote 4 below (which refers to amounts as of end-2016).

cal) particularly severe market conditions, under conservative assumptions (asset risks moving in a correlated fashion and hedging turning to be ineffective), simulations show that even moderate changes in the valuations of these instruments might have non-negligible impacts on capital positions of banks with major L2/L3 holdings[4].

Against this backdrop, supervisors need to enhance their intervention also on these instruments: something has been done, but there is still a long way to go. In this regard, the SSM is currently in the process of defining a structured framework to properly investigate L2 and L3 books.

The very fact that NPLs are the only risk (together with sovereign exposures) that is constantly, relentlessly mentioned in the ongoing discussion about risk sharing and risk reduction clearly shows that the debate on EDIS and Banking Union is skewed; it is no longer a debate on economics, but rather on politics, driven by an issue of trust within Europe.

I think that a fair discussion about EDIS should take all risks into account. If we are not ready to do this, for political reasons or for lack of trust, maybe we should focus on other avenues to make progress towards the completion of the Banking Union. Other equally important issues remain unaddressed, and could be tackled.

Risks, EDIS and Banking Union

Indeed, a proper consideration of these other risks is also crucial for the current debate related to the completion of the Banking Union.

While we continue to genuinely support the creation of an EDIS and the completion of the Banking Union, we think it's important to define a framework establishing specific measures to assess, control and contain all relevant risks, including those arising from illiquid and opaque instruments. Hedging of market

---

4 In the occasional paper of Banca d'Italia No. 417 – Risks and challenges of complex financial instruments: an analysis of SSM banks, Roca and Potente (Coordinators), December 2017, a simulation carried out under particularly conservative assumptions (correlated risks in the asset side, no netting and no diversification benefits) showed that, for banks with the largest holding of L2 and L3 assets, as at December 2016, a 5 % decline in the value of L2 and L3 assets would have caused the CET1 ratio to drop by about 350 basis points, on average. Moreover, in its October 2018 Global Financial Stability Report the IMF carried out a simulation similar to that performed in the Bank of Italy's paper, in order to assess potential risks stemming from these instruments. According to the IMF estimates, for the G-SIBs with the largest holdings of Level 2 and Level 3 assets a decline of less than 5 percent in the value of these portfolios would reduce their leverage ratio (i.e. the ratio between capital and non-risk weighted assets) by 100 basis points.

risk for L2/L3 can be an essential tool to reduce the actual exposures (and therefore decreasing capital needs); however, perfect hedge is hardly achievable when dealing with complex instruments with bespoke features and an upsurge of residual risk (basis risk) is not infrequent. Therefore, capital requirements should be set in order to take into consideration imperfect hedging.

As for the second pillar of the Banking Union, i.e. the crisis management framework, the big unresolved issue is how to manage the possible crises of non-systemic banks. Indeed, at the European level it was *de facto* established that only the crises of systemically important intermediaries (about fifty) can be tackled with the resolution tool, while all other banks would remain subject to national insolvency procedures (in Italy, liquidation).

Therefore, for 'all other banks' in case of a crisis (and in the absence of interested buyers) the only option is a piecemeal liquidation approach: the company in crisis would be dismantled and sold in pieces, typically at prices much lower than those obtainable from a sale on the market, putting the repayment of unprotected liabilities at serious risk. The destruction of value linked to fire sales would actually be passed on to the bank's creditors, including uninsured deposit holders. Moreover, the disruption of credit relationships would entail a loss of information on customers' credit history that may well cause a tightening of credit supply, with probable negative consequences for the local economy.

The current two-tiered system ends up by segmenting the banking system and could trigger inefficient customer reallocation processes penalizing small and medium-sized banks. All in all the piecemeal liquidation approach may constitute a recipe for financial instability and potential disruption to the credit market. Therefore, more must be done in this field, and from this perspective the experience of the United States is especially important. The US Federal Deposit Insurance Corporation – a government entity whose reserves are made up of private funds, but which can activate a large line of credit with the US Treasury – has successfully managed the crisis of almost 500 financial intermediaries since 2007, minimising the harm for the economy at large. It is a lesson that merits careful consideration.

Risk reduction in the euro area banking system is pivotal in the debate about EDIS, and thus for the completion of the Banking Union. Much of the attention is on credit risk, which, as I have noted above, is being scaled down quite quickly. However, NPLs are not the only risk that affects banks' balance sheets, and action should be also taken on risks posed from illiquid/opaque/hard-to-value instruments such as L2/L3 instruments, securitizations, leveraged loans.

Christian Ossig
Advancing the European Financial Market
Further Reducing Risk in the EU and Simultaneously Strengthening the Financial Market

Introduction

Since the 2008 financial crisis, much progress has been made on stabilising the global banking market. European banks in particular now hold more and better-quality capital[1], have drawn up recovery plans (outlining the measures they would take to restore their viability in a timely manner during periods of financial distress) and are subject to tighter supervision. Despite all this progress, it should not be forgotten that banks have to remain competitive. Stable and, at the same time, profitable banks finance economic growth and provide European citizens with essential services. Stable and profitable banks are not an end in itself but vital for a prosperous Europe.

The banking sector itself is currently making great efforts to enable it to continue operating as a strong partner for customers and businesses. The challenges are manifold: banks have to cope with the extremely low or even negative interest rates, face fragmented markets and need to undergo a comprehensive digital transformation. Yet banks are rising to these challenges; they are adapting their business models, cooperating with fintechs and expanding their range of products and services. They are also dealing with their legacy non-performing loans (NPLs), which the decrease in NPL ratios shows.[2]

However, there is no denying that some banks' and some European countries' NPL stocks are still very high. Creating a single financial market, with a harmo-

---

1 For German banks see page 37 ff, BaFin Journal, June 2019, https://www.bafin.de/SharedDocs/
Downloads/DE/BaFinJournal/2019/bj_1906.pdf?__blob=publicationFile&v=7
2 Compare EBA Risk Dashboard Q4/2018 and World Bank – Worlddevelopment indicators (EU) –
Bank nonperforming loans to total gross loans (%), retrieved on 24.6.2019.

Note: Disclaimer: the positions expressed in this article are those of the author and do not necessarily reflect the position of the Association of German Banks (Bundesverband deutscher Banken). I would like to thank my colleagues Dr. Jan T. Böttcher, Felix Krohne and Ingmar Wulfert for their valuable contribution to this paper.

https://doi.org/10.1515/9783110683073-013

nised insolvency regime and a functioning Capital Markets Union, would help to further reduce these NPLs. A reduction in NPLs is, in my view, essential and one of the key conditions without which the idea of a common European deposit insurance scheme (EDIS), which represents the third pillar of banking Union, should on no account be tackled. Also EDIS should not be tackled until there is a level playing field between individual member state markets. This again requires a harmonised and functioning single European financial market. Such a single European financial market helps to spread risks better across national borders.

A completed single European financial market will also allow European banks to benefit from economies of scale and thus to increase profitability, which will help them to stay competitive. However, banks that are pursuing the goal of opening up the European market to a greater extent are, quite literally, coming up against boundaries – boundaries that have long since been overcome in other business sectors.[3] The reality for the financial sector is that these boundaries still exist[4], since there is as yet no real single European financial market.

The absence of a functioning single European financial market has even further unmistakable consequences: banks are unable to supply customers in other member states efficiently with financial products; customers, for their part, are denied access to financial services from other member states.[5] This handicap imposed by fragmented markets needs to be eliminated – for the sake of both customers and banks alike. Creating a fully integrated European financial market in which it goes without saying that a customer from Spain can buy products from a bank in France, a customer from Italy can deposit funds with a German bank and an investor from the Netherlands can order securities from a bank in Luxembourg will, however, take some time and require a great deal of harmonisation.

To create a single financial market we don't just need harmonisation of rules in classic banking-related areas, such as those covered by banking union and capital markets union, but harmonisation of a much more far-reaching kind. General provisions of private law must also be harmonised, for example. And in new fields, such as digitalisation or the market for sustainable products, we need to ensure from the outset that we do not end up with a patchwork regime.

---

3 See for example trading in goods (Intra-EU trading): https://ec.europa.eu/commission/press corner/api/files/attachment/855659/Commission_Factsheet_25_years_Single_Market.pdf.pdf
4 See statement by Sabine Lautenschläger, Member of the Executive Board of the ECB, at the 10 Years Vienna Initiative – Anniversary Conference 2019, in Vienna, Austria, 27 March 2019 https://www.ecb.europa.eu/press/key/date/2019/html/ecb.sp190327_2~f288a94261.en.html
5 Only around 1% of household loans and deposits in the euro-area are cross-border. See page 37, ECB Financial Integration Report 2018, https://www.ecb.europa.eu/pub/pdf/fie/ecb.financia lintegrationineurope201805.en.pdf

Such a harmonised market would greatly support the Banking Union and could thus be seen as a fourth pillar of the Banking Union, as state secretary Dr. Jörg Kukies called it.[6]

The following section outlines the progress that has been made in the area of NPLs, identifies continuing problems with NPLs and explains why they currently do not support the introduction of a joint deposit protection scheme. In addition to the question of risk reduction and a common deposit insurance, the question of a single European financial market is crucial for the EU financial market, which is why ideas for its promotion are presented below.

Non-performing loans overall reduced – local issues remain

Non-performing loans (NPLs) have been an issue of considerable concern to both policymakers and supervisors for some time.[7] This is probably mainly due to the very high number of non-performing loans. According to a report by the European Council's Financial Services Committee (FSC) Subgroup on Non-Performing Loans, NPLs in the EU at the end of 2016 amounted to just under one trillion euros (gross, i.e. without provisioning; the net figure, i.e. with provisioning taken into account, was "only" 550 billion euros). This is equivalent to approximately 6.7 % of GDP in the EU or an average NPL ratio of 5.1 %.[8] In 2009, at the beginning of the financial crisis, the NPL ratio was approximately 5.2 %, peaking at just under 7.5 % in 2012.[9] It currently stands at just under 3.2 %, which is close to the pre-crisis level of 2.81 % in 2007.[10] So does this mean there is no cause for concern or are additional measures needed to further reduce NPLs? A closer look at the distribution of NPLs across the countries of Europe throws up some interesting facts. While Greece (41.2 %), Cyprus (34 %), Portugal (10.1 %), Italy (8.3 %) and Bulgaria (8 %) currently have the highest NPL ratios, the lowest are in Great

---

6 Cf. Jörg Kukies in Börsen-Zeitung, 24.05.2019, Dietegen Müller, Frankfurt, number 99, page 4, https://www.boersen-zeitung.de/index.php?li=1&artid=2019099022&titel=Vierte-Saeule-der-Ba nkenunion, data retrieved on 26.06.2019 (Paywall/German).

7 For a definition of "non-performing", see ECB (2018): "What are non-performing loans (NPLs)?" (available at https://www.bankingsupervision.europa.eu/about/ssmexplained/html/npl.en. html).

8 Cf. Report of the FSC Subgroup on Non-Performing Loans, 31 May 2017, page 8. The NPL ratio in the US was 1.7 % at this time, cf. ibid.

9 Cf. World Bank – World development indicators (EU): Bank nonperforming loans to total gross loans (%), data retrieved on 24 June 2019.

10 Cf. EBA Risk Dashboard Q4/2018 and World Bank – World development indicators (EU): Bank nonperforming loans to total gross loans (%), data retrieved on 24 June 2019.

Britain (1.3 %), Germany (1.3 %), Luxembourg (0.9 %), Estonia (0.8 %) and Sweden (0.5 %).[11] There is thus a clear gap in the EU when it comes to the level of NPLs on banks' balance sheets. In principle, therefore, additional regulatory measures aimed at achieving further improvement are both understandable and sensible. Supervisors take a similar view and have responded with a number of proposals. In July 2017, the European Council agreed an action plan to reduce NPLs in Europe.[12] The plan is made up of a total of 14 European initiatives, including proposals for out-of-court procedures to speed up the realisation of collateral, guidelines on the management of NPLs, enhancing the secondary market for trading NPLs and introducing a minimum level of provisioning for loans ("backstop").[13]

March 2017 saw the European Central Bank (ECB) publish its Guidance to banks on non-performing loans, which was supplemented in March 2018 by an addendum to the guidance.[14] In addition, the ECB issued a press release in July 2018 announcing further steps to tackle existing stocks of NPLs at banks.[15]

Among the reasons cited by both the European Council and the ECB for their measures is that persistently high levels of NPLs have an adverse effect on banks' profitability (due, for instance, to the high administrative costs of managing and monitoring NPLs), that the need for provisioning depletes their capital base and unnecessarily ties up capital, which in turn undermines the transmission of monetary policy and the financing of businesses. In addition, a reduction in NPLs could help reduce the fragmentation of the financial markets and facilitate capital flows in the internal market.[16]

---

11 Cf. EBA Risk Dashboard Q4/2018; for Cyprus, the most recent official figures are for Q2/2018, cf. EBA Risk Dashboard Q2/2018.
12 Cf. Banking: Council sets out action plan for non-performing loans – press release of 11 July 2017 (https://www.consilium.europa.eu/en/press/press-releases/2017/07/11/banking-action-plan-non-performing-loans); retrieved on 24 June 2019.
13 Cf. Council conclusions of 11 July 2017on Action plan to tackle non-performing loans in Europe (https://www.consilium.europa.eu/en/press/press-releases/2017/07/11/conclusions-non-performing-loans/); retrieved on 24 June 2019.
14 ECB: Guidance to banks on non-performing loans, March 2017; Addendum to the ECB Guidance to banks on non-performing loans: supervisory expectations for prudential provisioning of non-performing exposures, March 2018.
15 Cf. ECB press release of 11 July 2018: ECB announces further steps in supervisory approach to stock of NPLs.
16 Cf. Banking: Council sets out action plan for non-performing loans – press release of 11 July 2017 (https://www.consilium.europa.eu/en/press/press-releases/2017/07/11/banking-action-plan-non-performing-loans), retrieved on 24 June 2019; Report of the FSC Subgroup on Non-Performing Loans, 31 May 2017, page 18 ff.; ECB: Guidance to banks on non-performing loans, March 2017, page 4.

The various measures put in place by the EU and the ECB are intended to ensure that banks both continue to reduce their stocks of NPLs and avoid accumulating large-scale NPL stocks in the future.[17] The European Council's explicit wish that the action plan should lead to a reduction in existing NPL stocks is somewhat surprising if one takes a closer look at some individual measures. Arguably the most substantive component of the action plan, the so-called "backstop", only applies to loans granted after 25 April 2019 and subsequently classified as non-performing.[18] The same goes for the EBA guidelines on managing NPLs,[19] for example, which apply from 30 June 2019, or its guidelines on disclosing NPLs, which will apply from 31 December 2019.[20] In my opinion, the primary objective of the action plan is to prevent any excessive future build-up of NPLs – an objective which is naturally to be supported. The European Commission, however, considers the success in reducing NPLs to date to be primarily due to the EU action plan.[21] Based purely on the dates when measures were adopted and the dates of their entry into force, however, only the ECB – if anyone – can probably lay claim to a certain success in the reducing NPLs. Its guidelines to banks for dealing with NPLs entered into force on publication in March 2017 and, among other things, require banks to set NPL reduction targets.[22] But since this guidance only applies to significant institutions (SSM banks), a robust measurement of its quantitative effect is not possible.

One of the main reasons for the sharp reduction in NPLs to date may certainly be the pressure on banks resulting from the long-standing discussion of prudential measures. At the same time, however, Europe has recently been enjoying a favourable economic climate overall.[23] The latter explanation is backed up by

---

17 Cf. Banking: Council sets out action plan for non-performing loans – press release of 11 July 2017 (https://www.consilium.europa.eu/en/press/press-releases/2017/07/11/banking-action-plan-non-performing-loans), retrieved on 24 June 2019; ECB press release of 11 July 2018: ECB announces further steps in supervisory approach to stock of NPLs.
18 Cf. Regulation (EU) 2019/630 of the European Parliament and of the Council of 17 April 2019 amending Regulation (EU) No 575/2013 as regards minimum loss coverage for non-performing exposures, L 111/11.
19 Cf. EBA/GL/2018/06, page 5.
20 Cf. EBA/GL/2018/10, page 3.
21 Cf. Fourth Progress Report on the reduction of non-performing loans and further risk reduction in the Banking Union of 12 June 2019, COM(2019) 278 final, page 1.
22 Cf. ECB: Guidance to banks on non-performing loans, March 2017, page 7 f. The NPL ratio in the EU fell from 4 % at the end of 2017 to 3.2 % at the end of 2018, cf. EBA Risk Dashboard Q4/2017 and Q4/2018.
23 Cf., for example, growth in real GDP from Q4/2016 to Q4/2018 (https://de.statista.com/statistik/daten/studie/38319/umfrage/veraenderung-des-bip-in-eu27-und-er17-gegenueber-vor-quartal/) – in German only, retrieved on 25 June 2019; Fourth Progress Report on the reduction of

analysis at EU level identifying real GDP growth and other economic factors (such as local shocks and bubbles on property markets, for example) as the key drivers of high NPL levels.[24] A look at the above-mentioned countries with the highest NPL ratios confirms this. Real GDP growth from 2009 to 2017 was lowest in Greece (-21.7 %), Italy (1.3 %), Cyprus (2.3 %) and Portugal (2.3 %).[25] NPL levels are also influenced by structural factors, such as the lending and monitoring practices of banks, as well as the legal regimes within which banks operate.[26] Average foreclosure proceedings are longest in Greece, Cyprus and Italy, for example.[27]

This all raises the question as to whether the various prudential measures mentioned above are sufficiently targeted to achieve the desired effect. It would have made better sense, in my view, to apply more tailored or flexible rules. For key measures such as the Commission's backstop, for example, I would have liked to see a threshold NPL ratio of 5 % below which the rules did not apply, similar to the arrangement in the EBA's guidelines on managing and disclosing NPLs. This would have avoided placing further administrative burdens on banks where levels of NPLs are low. In our opinion, the one-size-fits-all requirements also create undesirable incentives for banks to remove NPLs from their balance sheets as quickly as possible and sell them to specialised liquidating agents or other investors (e.g. hedge funds) instead of seeking an amicable solution with the borrower.[28] For banks that have adequately hedged their risks, at any rate, the question of whether and to what extent to reduce NPLs should continue to be strategically driven rather than being primarily based on prudential considerations.[29]

---

non-performing loans and further risk reduction in the Banking Union of 12 June 2019, COM(2019) 278 final, page 5.

24 Cf. Report of the FSC Subgroup on Non-Performing Loans, 31 May 2017, page 13.

25 Cf. German Federal Agency for Civic Education: Development of real GDP (http://www.bpb. de/nachschlagen/zahlen-und-fakten/europa/70549/entwicklung-des-bip) – in German only; retrieved on 25 June 2019. Bulgaria's GDP growth of 17.7 % lay significantly above these levels, however.

26 Cf. Report of the FSC Subgroup on Non-Performing Loans, 31 May 2017, page 14 f.

27 Cf. Report of the FSC Subgroup on Non-Performing Loans, 31 May 2017, page 44.

28 Cf. GBIC comment letter on the European Commission's proposal for a Regulation of the European Parliament and the Council on amending Regulation (EU) No 575/2013 as regards minimum loss coverage for non-performing exposures (https://die-dk.de/en/topics/article/comments-european-commissions-proposal-regulation-european-parliament-and-council-amending-regulation-eu-no-5752013-regards-minimum-loss-coverage-non-performing-exposures/), retrieved on 25 June 2019.

29 Cf. cep: cepInput – Vertiefung der Wirtschafts- und Währungsunion – Teil I: Finanzunion, 04/2017, page 14 (https://www.cep.eu/fileadmin/user_upload/cep.eu/Studien/cepInput_WWU_Teil_1/Input_WWU_-_Finanzunion.pdf) – in German only, retrieved on 25 June 2019.

It is beyond dispute that the level of NPLs held by banks in some countries remains very high and needs to be reduced as a matter of urgency. It is also true that it is important to avoid a similarly high build-up of NPLs in Europe in the future. The precise extent to which the prudential measures described above will help achieve these objectives remains to be seen. I believe – not least in the interests of a harmonised single financial market and a uniform European deposit insurance system (EDIS) – that a harmonised insolvency regime in Europe would be more successful in remedying the NPL problem.[30] In turn, a reduction in NPLs could then make a positive contribution to reducing financial market fragmentation in Europe and promoting a single market.[31]

Benefits of a completed single financial market – basis for stable European banks

Particularly when compared with the US, the EU lacks a single, competitive financial market: the European market is still fragmented into many different smaller national markets, so that banks cannot automatically offer and organise their products and services across borders.

A larger single home market for the financial industry could eliminate the substantial inefficiency caused by many small national markets. The resulting cost-cutting potential through economies of scale would make banks more competitive. A thriving, competitive financial sector strengthens the growth process and plays a major part in ensuring prosperity in Europe.[32]

Banks' ability to contribute to economic growth in the EU should not simply be taken for granted, however. The crucial condition for this is their ability to operate profitably. In times of zero and negative interest rates, steadily increasing regulation-related costs and offensively-operating new market players, this is anything but a given.

---

30 Cf. cep: cepInput – Vertiefung der Wirtschafts- und Währungsunion – Teil I: Finanzunion, 04/2017, page 14 (https://www.cep.eu/fileadmin/user_upload/cep.eu/Studien/cepInput_W-WU_Teil_1/Input_WWU_-_Finanzunion.pdf) – in German only, retrieved on 25 June 2019; Fourth Progress Report on the reduction of non-performing loans and further risk reduction in the Banking Union of 12 June 2019, COM(2019) 278 final, page 5.

31 Cf. Banking: Council sets out action plan for non-performing loans – press release of 11 July 2017 (https://www.consilium.europa.eu/en/press/press-releases/2017/07/11/banking-action-plan-non-performing-loans), retrieved on 24 June 2019; Report of the FSC Subgroup on Non-Performing Loans, 31 May 2017, page 26.

32 See page 85, ECB Financial Integration Report 2018, https://www.ecb.europa.eu/pub/pdf/fie/ecb.financialintegrationineurope201805.en.pdf

Particularly in Europe, it is noticeable that the financial sector's share of value added has been declining for years – unlike in the US, for example.[33] A marginalisation of the European banking sector cannot be in Europe's interest, however. European banks that can hold their own against international competitors remain important for the European economy. European banks know what their European customers need; they are able to assess risks adequately and provide competent advice. Over the years, stable customer-bank relationships that are geared not to quick contract closure but to long-term partnership have evolved.

On top of this, a set of shared standards links banks and clients. Take data protection, for example: data is handled completely differently in the EU than in Asia or the US. This makes it all the more important that European banks can continue to offer their customers European solutions.

So that European banks can do all this, so that they can operate profitably and compete internationally, they need a single home market that is big enough to allow economies of scale. In a bigger home market, banks could regain their lost profitability and become the engine of the EU internal market. What is more, a single European financial market would improve what is on offer to European citizens, as attractive financial products would be more quickly available in all member states.

A single European financial market also makes sense from a stability perspective. It would enable banks and financial markets to assess risks consistently across the EU and to hedge these as widely as possible, i.e. across borders.[34] Thanks to the size of a single European financial market, risks and regional imbalances could also be moderated better and contagion effects thus prevented. A single European financial market therefore also supports, not least, the creation of a stable, functioning monetary union. What is clear is: Europe needs a competitive financial market of its own with strong banks that reflects its economic standing and is on a par with other markets. The single European financial market can only remain competitive internationally, however, if the EU speaks with one voice when it comes to establishing and implementing international rules, as in the case of Basel IV, for example. Only as a united community does the EU have enough clout to ensure that the specificities of the European market are taken into account in global rules. It will be much easier for the EU to speak with one voice if it has a single market with a single rulebook. Just as important is that European regulators take global standards as their guide when implementing international

---

33 See https://www.bundestag.de/resource/blob/435538/ca2270cff215d24263472be11615fa43/WD-5-054-16-pdf-data.pdf (German)

34 See page 8, Financial market integration in the EU: A practical inventory of benefits and hurdles in the Single Market https://www.bertelsmann-stiftung.de/fileadmin/files/BSt/Publikationen/GrauePublikationen/EZ_Financial_Market_Integration_2019_ENG.pdf

rules. They should refrain from going it alone here, since doing so – take the repeatedly discussed introduction of a financial transaction tax, for example – would be harmful to European competitiveness.

Creating a single financial market

To create a single financial market, EU rules need to be harmonised further. A single financial market requires not only harmonisation of classical banking rules, such as those on banking union and capital markets union, but much broader harmonisation. For example, general private law also needs to be harmonised. Where new issues like digitalisation and the sustainable products market are concerned, non-uniform rules should be avoided from the outset.

Advancing the single financial market by harmonising the supervisory framework

Europe has, it is true, already come a long way along the difficult road towards a single market in the financial sector, steadily advancing it through numerous initiatives to harmonise regulation and supervisory practice. But the status quo is by no means satisfactory yet. Despite a Single Supervisory Mechanism (SSM) and various harmonisation projects, European banks still face considerable national differences. These differences keep them from offering their services more EU-wide and especially in those member states which have a less diverse banking landscape and rely on lending from abroad. Big banks in particular, which are subject to common cross-border supervision within the banking union, should therefore also be enabled to do business across borders. To allow this, it is vital that harmonisation of regulation is driven forward and that the rules are applied uniformly by supervisors. Better harmonisation could for example be achieved by more use of regulations instead of directives, which require transposition into national law. Some existing directives could also be converted into regulations. Take the CRD: as a result of differing implementation of the CRD, the term "lending business" (Kreditgeschäft) used in Germany, for example, differs from definitions in other member states.[35] Variance of this kind could be minimised by

---

[35] Also the term credit institution used in CRR and KWG differs, see Boos/Fischer/Schulte-Mattler/Vahldiek, 5. Aufl. 2016, KWG § 53b Rn. 13 (German) and Boos/Fischer/Schulte-Mattler/Dürselen, 5. Aufl. 2016, VO (EU) 575/2013 Art. 4 Rn. 3-5 (German).

more use of regulations. In areas where national specificities currently necessitate different treatment, national options and discretions could be exercised on an interim basis. These should be used sparingly, however, and regularly reviewed to see whether they remain necessary. Since they tend to result in a patchwork of rules that makes it more difficult for banks to set up centrally managed units for the entire EU and exploit synergy effects, the number of national options and discretions should be brought down in the long term.

Without any further progress on harmonisation, banks will be forced to continue thoroughly familiarising themselves with the different national rules and supervisory practices before they can, for example, engage in cross-border lending to small and medium-sized businesses. Furthermore, they will have to continuously monitor changes at national level and implement these, both at considerable cost, if they want to carry on doing business. This high barrier to cross-border business, which artificially limits product diversity for European customers, can only be overcome by gradually harmonising the regulatory and supervisory framework.

In order to progress towards a single financial market, cross-border banking groups should also be able to handle their capital and associated regulatory requirements, such as those for large exposures, centrally at group level (cross-border capital and liquidity waivers).[36] Currently, banks have to manage requirements both at European level and, for their subsidiaries, at various national levels as well. This ties up capital and liquidity and prevents these resources from being used efficiently.[37] With the help of waivers, banks could deploy additional billions of capital in Europe where it is needed to generate economic growth. In a Europe that wants to create a single financial market and in which banking groups are already subject to single supervision and resolution mechanisms, there is no reason to withhold cross-border waivers.

Existing rules should also be reviewed prudently. It is not a question here of deregulating the market; after all, the regulation over the past few years has undoubtedly made the European banking market more robust. Many legislative initiatives were, however, launched parallel to each other in an uncoordinated fashion. As a result, banks today are required to report innumerable data points that differ only slightly to various supervisors. At some banks, the number of staff handling reporting has doubled during the past ten years. This is no surprise,

---

36 See statement by Sabine Lautenschläger, Member of the Executive Board of the ECB, at the 10 Years Vienna Initiative – Anniversary Conference 2019, in Vienna, Austria, 27 March 2019
37 See page 18 MOMENTUM FOR FURTHER EUROPEAN BANKING INTEGRATION by Oliver Wyman, 2017 https://www.oliverwyman.com/content/dam/oliver-wyman/v2/publications/2017/dec/EuropeanBankingIntegration_FrenchCase_OliverWyman_ENG.pdf

given that FINREP reporting alone has created a catalogue of around 60,000 data points that can be requested from banks.[38] All this generates high and unnecessary administrative costs that impose an additional burden on banks particularly in times of low or even negative interest margins, ultimately hitting savers and investors as well. Regulation should therefore be made more efficient by utilising synergy effects without lowering the level of security. New solutions are needed to reduce overlaps when drawing up and applying reporting requirements. Ideally, a central, EU-wide data repository should be established. Before issuing new requests for data, supervisory authorities could check to see whether the desired data already existed. This would allow authorities to access existing data more quickly and banks would not need to complete new data fields unnecessarily. The result would be significant administrative relief for banks and customers. When setting up a central repository of this kind, however, it will be essential to ensure that data requests from other sources are simultaneously dropped. Otherwise, we will merely end up adding a further layer to an even more expensive and convoluted regime. Therefore it is to be welcomed, that the European Banking Authority (EBA) is drafting a feasibility report on a possible integrated reporting system which should help to reduce the reporting burden.[39]

Banks also face the problem of having to constantly make adjustments in response to new reporting requirements, thus tying up a large part of their IT budget. Even small changes can be time-consuming and costly, as they have to be thoroughly tested to see how they interact with the rest of the system. These resources could be better invested in developing digital innovations. For this reason, I recommend that more long-term planning should go into reporting requirements.

Fresh impetus to capital markets union

A stable single financial market requires both a functioning banking market and further integration of the European capital market.[40] This is the only way to ensure that risks are spread evenly and appropriately among a number of market

---

38 See EU Implementing Regulation on supervisory reporting (Commission Implementing Regulation (EU) 680/2014 of 16 April 2014)
39 See Art. 430c and Art. 430 (8) CRR II (Regulation (EU) 2019/876 of the European Parliament and of the Council of 20 May 2019 amending Regulation (EU) No 575/2013).
40 See page 85, ECB Financial Integration Report 2018, https://www.ecb.europa.eu/pub/pdf/fie/ecb.financialintegrationineurope201805.en.pdf

participants. Both markets unfold their effect together, i.e. they do not operate side-by-side in isolation. They have to complement each other in what they do.

As part of its efforts to drive forward capital markets union, the European Union has undertaken various measures that – taken individually or as a whole – are unfortunately unlikely to strengthen the European capital market and consolidate its integration in the long term. The EU has, in particular, failed to fully live up to its promise to focus on and foster the market: not only the example of securitisation shows that there is the danger of regulation ignoring market needs being adopted.[41] For this reason, fresh impetus is needed to create a capital markets union.[42]

A continuing obstacle to cross-border transactions in the capital market is the different and complex processes and forms in member states for obtaining refunds of withholding tax on income from securities. This hurdle on the road to capital markets union is also a worldwide obstacle to investment. In the medium term, it would benefit customers if these processes were simplified and harmonised. In the long term, refund processes and forms could be replaced by the application under double taxation treaties of relief from withholding tax for the final beneficiary at the time of payment (relief at source).

Another means of achieving capital markets union is to build on existing projects that have not yet been realised or have not been realised adequately. The proposals of the European Post-Trade Forum (EPTF), for example, still make good sense and should be implemented.[43] Among other things, the report highlights a need for action in the areas of private international law, company law (corporate actions), insolvency law and reporting to improve the cross-border trading of financial products on the secondary market. Work should also proceed on the EU regulation of securitisation, which should be designed in such a way that it can really lead to a responsible revival of the market – securitisations are a key instrument for linking financing by banks with the capital markets.

For the capital market sector, it is vital that there are uniform rules that allow development of the EU market in its entirety. To achieve this, the rules need to be not only uniform but also transparent and reliable. Yet special national rules continue to hinder the cross-border provision of financial products and services.

---

41 See https://www2.deloitte.com/uk/en/pages/financial-services/articles/sts-easy-as-stc.html
42 See also: https://www.ebf.eu/market-securities/markets4europe-to-push-for-reforms-of-eu-financial-markets-for-the-benefit-of-companies-and-investors/
43 See Report of the European Post Trade Forum (EPTF) https://ec.europa.eu/info/publications/170515-eptf-report_en.

Harmonising general private law

The harmonisation of national private law regimes would make cross-border banking considerably easier. However, harmonising nationally-oriented private law poses a particular challenge. Established areas of law such as consumer protection, as well as company law and insolvency law, have evolved over time and affect many other areas of national law going well beyond the banking sector. Harmonisation should be steadily driven forward here. This would greatly facilitate not only cross-border banking business but also other cross-border activities. Unless private law is harmonised, it will be difficult for banks to develop their financial services for a European market, as adapting products to various national rules and running internal processes to monitor national regulation threaten to cancel out the benefits of cross-border business. Conversely, fragmented regulatory regimes mean uncertainty for customers as well: particularly uncertainty about what rights they enjoy in other member states often keeps them from making cross-border transactions. As a result, whole parts of the single market – in the area of both goods and services – effectively remain closed to them. This is illustrated by the fact that to date only 7 % of EU citizens have actually obtained a financial service in another member state.[44]

At present, it is for example very difficult for banks – as well as businesses and retail customers – to know whether they will be able if necessary to enforce contracts they have concluded in other member states. In some countries, it can take more than ten years to realise collateral in the form of real estate. This uncertainty is a major reason why banks do not engage in cross-border business.

It is also difficult for banks to check the creditworthiness of a customer from another member state. The result: these customers are denied access to interesting offers of credit. The EU wants to remedy this with the help of its Consumer Financial Services Action Plan. The plan intends to specify a minimum set of data to be exchanged between credit bureaus for cross-border creditworthiness assessments.[45]

In addition, the EU will investigate to what extent national lawmakers add unnecessary consumer protection rules on top of the European provisions. National "go-it-alone" action leading to a patchwork of rules hampers cross-border

---

44 See Factsheet Consumer Financial Services Action Plan from 23.03.2017 https://ec.europa.eu/info/sites/info/files/factsheet-consumer-financial-services-action-plan-23032017_en.pdf
45 See page 10, Consumer Financial Services Action Plan: Better Products, More Choice, COM (2017) 139 final, https://eur-lex.europa.eu/resource.html?uri=cellar:055353bd-0fba-11e7-8a35-01aa75ed71a1.0003.02/DOC_1&format=PDF

business. I therefore welcome both proposals in the Consumer Financial Services Action Plan.

Attempts by national regulators to outdo each other (gold-plating) make it difficult in general for banks to develop a standard sales strategy for the EU as a whole. Diverging requirements generate higher costs as a result of unnecessary administrative effort and lead to customers from different member states receiving different treatment. Examples in Germany include the implementation of parts of MiFiD II and the Consumer Credit Directive (written form requirement), and the specification of a higher IRB coverage ratio in the German Solvency Regulation. The consistency of implementation should be investigated and national implementing legislation should be pared back to a sensible number of rules and regulations.

Deposit Insurance on a European Level

In light of the aforementioned lack of a truly integrated financial market, still unsolved legacy risks related to, among others things, a high level of NPLs in the banks' balance sheets and a need to further harmonise general private law, in particular insolvency law, the time for a European Deposit Protection Scheme has not yet come.

Irrespective of the specific EDIS proposal of the European Commission[46], which shows substantial legal and technical deficits[47], establishing a European deposit protection scheme requires a high degree of sensitivity. When it comes to EDIS, discussions are – to a surprising extent – emotionally driven. In particular, any form of a European deposit protection scheme is by some Member States automatically regarded as "good for stability". However, whether a European Deposit Protection Scheme would in fact result in a higher degree of financial stability depends significantly on the specific design and the prerequisites that ensure a level playing field and sufficient and ongoing risk reduction.

Even if EDIS were to be restricted to a temporary liquidity assistance between national Deposit Guarantee Schemes (DGS), it still entails a sharing of risk. If funds are centralised or if DGSs would face cross-liability with other DGSs any depletion of such funds bears a contagion risk. A significant crises or bank failure

---

46 "Proposal for a Regulation Of The European Parliament and of the Council amending Regulation (EU) 806/2014 in order to establish a European Deposit Insurance Scheme" of 24 November 2015, COM(2015) 586 final.
47 See EFDI Report, "Technical Considerations for the Design of EDIS", dated 19 November 2018; publically available on the website of EFDI: https://www.efdi.eu.

in one Member State would drain liquidity from all DGSs and credit institutions due to ex-post contributions. In the EDIS proposal the maximum amount of ex-post contributions to be paid by credit institutions is not stipulated. Thus, credit institutions and DGSs alike could be struck by a sudden and significant liquidity outflow. Under the current EDIS proposal any potential depletion of funds related to a crisis in one Member State would mean that even small compensation cases in any other Member State could trigger bank runs and weaken financial stability. Under the current framework of the Deposit Guarantee Scheme Directive (DGSD) this contagion risk does not exist as funds are decentralised with a target level of 0.8 % of the covered deposits.

Therefore, it can only be welcomed that in December 2018 the Eurogroup agreed to set up a high-level working group (HLWG) to undertake technical preparation of a roadmap for starting political negotiations on a European Deposit Insurance Scheme (EDIS) and report to the European Council heads of state and government on its work. The HLWG focusses not only on possible designs of an EDIS but also on the Banking Union in general. Before a full assessment of the status quo and a clear common understanding of the Banking Union in its steady state is achieved, it will be impossible to establish any kind of EDIS, including a liquidity assistance system.

It is of utmost importance never to forget that EDIS should increase depositors' confidence in the protection of their deposits. Once this confidence is lost because of a premature introduction of EDIS, it will be extremely difficult to get back to today's level of trust.

Helping to shape global digitalisation

The banking sector undoubtedly faces sweeping transformation. To avoid being left further behind in future by other economic regions and the global technology providers at home there, Europe needs to sharpen its profile significantly as a digital banking location. With this in mind, care should be taken when developing rules and standards to ensure that these do not fragment the European market but, on the contrary, strengthen it and make it competitive and fit for the future. This is all the more important, given that digital applications and ideas know no national boundaries and are virtually destined to be made available equally to customers throughout Europe.

Existing legally sound rules in force in the analogue world should, in addition, be examined promptly to see whether they can be used in the digital age and adapted where necessary. An example of this is the question of how digital products are, among other things, to be assessed legally – take, for example, stable token offerings (STOs), where digital tokens are issued. Are such tokens securities, currencies or something else entirely? Views differ across Europe about how to classify STOs and their digital tokens. There is little or no consensus on whether, or under what circumstances, these should be regarded as securities or as currency. This point should be clarified at European level by law or, at the very least, supervisory practices should be harmonised by the ESAs. Great uncertainty also exists concerning the extent to which **digital correspondence** can be used in a way that ensures legal certainty. There should be uniform rules throughout Europe determining when a document can be regarded as delivered if it is sent to the postbox of an online banking portal, for instance. Nor is it clear how long digital documents need to be retained. Broadly speaking, it should be possible for an ever-growing number of documents to be legally delivered by digital means. Customers will increasingly expect their banks to communicate with them electronically. They cannot understand why they receive documents sometimes in digital and sometimes in paper form. It should also be made possible to conclude contracts throughout Europe using modern communication channels. Written form requirements should be revised in a uniform manner across the EU in the light of digitalisation.

As digitalisation does not come to a halt at the EU's external borders, the EU must also call internationally for uniform rules that establish a minimum standard for banks and competitors when handling new technologies. Only if the EU speaks as a community pursuing the interests of a single market will it be able to influence the new rules to a sufficient extent.

Big international online platforms have dominated the communications and social media markets in Europe for many years. They manage huge amounts of data and are now also pushing on to the financial market. This makes it all the more important to keep an eye on their business models and ensure compliance with European standards for European consumers in a timely manner. At the same time, legislators must prevent any distortion of competition. As in all areas, the "same business, same risk, same rules" principle should apply here. Negative example: banks are required under PSD2 to make their customer data accessible to third-party providers via an online interface; big data companies can benefit from this without having to provide access to their ever-larger volumes of data in return. Competitors of banks should not be allowed to benefit from access to banks' customer data without themselves having to meet the same requirements as banks in this respect.

For **next-generation technologies** such as artificial intelligence (AI), big data, quantum computing, robotics, blockchain or cloud computing, we need **standards at** European or, even better, **international level** that will facilitate global value chains. Otherwise, European banks may be left behind by these developments. It is surely in the interests of the EU to retain the ability to influence how these technologies are used, especially when fundamental social values such as the right to personal data are affected. This can only be achieved if the EU becomes a leading location for digital technologies. With respect to **artificial intelligence**, the German government unveiled the initial outline of a strategy to promote this technology.[48] This strategy now needs to be fleshed out further and implemented without delay. I hope to see further similar initiatives at European level.

There should be further harmonisation and concretisation across the EU in respect of outsourcing. This concerns both the definition of outsourcing as well as how banks and service providers (such as FinTechs) are to go about fulfilling the associated regulatory requirements.

In particular in the era of digitalisation it is essential that banks can make efficient use of Cloud Services, both as the infrastructure behind their own digitalisation projects and when collaborating with FinTechs. The flexibility and scalability that Cloud Services offer must not be hindered by excessive regulatory requirements that deny banks a level playing field with technology companies. A possible approach to ease the implementation of Cloud Services could be the certification or direct supervision of Cloud Service Providers at European level.[49] To minimise concentration risks, standards must ensure that switching between Cloud Service Providers is as smooth as possible.

The uneven implementation of **anti-money laundering rules** makes it difficult to acquire and onboard new customers throughout Europe. Not only do the identity documents accepted for verification purposes vary from one member state to another, but the security features of identity documents differ too. Different member states require the collection of different know-your-customer (**KYC**) **data**, some of which not all consumers in the EU even have at their disposal. On top of that, the data collected not only differs from one country to another, but also depends on the product involved (e.g. current account vs. securities account). As a result, the "passporting" of verification methods, meaning their cross-border use across the internal market, is only possible to a very limited extent.

We should therefore establish user-friendly, innovative and **uniform KYC processes** for the EU internal market. This will require a common decision on

---

48 See "Strategie Künstliche Intelligenz der Bundesregierung", November 2018, https://www. bmbf.de/files/Nationale_KI-Strategie.pdf (German)
49 See ESA Joint Advice JC 2019 26 from 10.04.19 here which stated that " the Commission could consider a legislative solution for an appropriate oversight framework for monitoring the activities of third party providers when they are critical service providers to relevant entities"

what KYC data should be collected, the standardisation of identity documents which can be used for verification purposes (including their security features), and the specification of a uniform EU identification feature (number or certificate). Ideally, this will enable a digital means of identifying citizens to be created (digital identity). We need to be open to new verification procedures that have been approved in another member state and can therefore be deemed sufficiently secure (principle of "most favourable treatment"): there should be uniform criteria for allowing KYC processes that have been carried out in accordance with EU law to be reused elsewhere.[50]

In addition, these measures should be supported by uniform supervision of anti-money laundering practices. A central authority should ensure that the same criteria are applied throughout Europe.

Sustainable finance

Banks play a key role in financing an economy geared to sustainability principles. The private banks and their subsidiaries have been closely involved in a number of sustainable finance issues for many years. Thanks, not least, to the European Commission's "Financing Sustainable Growth" action plan[51] and presentation of its first legislative proposals, the debate has quickly picked up momentum. When tackling this increasingly important topic, any fragmentation of the single EU market again needs to be avoided from the outset. A framework at European level should foster sustainable finance approaches appropriately but not hamper market dynamics through flawed or excessive regulation.

Conclusion: a single European financial market is paramount for the Banking Union

In respect of still unsolved legacy risks related to, among others things, a high level of NPLs in the banks' balance sheets the time for a European Deposit Protection Scheme (EDIS) has not yet come. EDIS should also not be tackled until there is a level playing field between individual member state markets, that allows for well-functioning cross-border business, which will in itself help to

---

50 For further information see also: https://bankenverband.de/media/files/position_paper_KYC.pdf

51 See "Commission action plan on financing sustainable growth" https://ec.europa.eu/info/publications/180308-action-plan-sustainable-growth_en

better spread risks across borders. However, this requires a harmonised and functioning single European financial market. The key to a single financial market is unquestionably further harmonisation of the rules at European level. While this should be the starting point, capital markets union needs fresh impetus at the same time. What is clear is: a single market is not only a prerequisite for EDIS, but it will also allow us to be competitive today and in the future. A functioning single market will allow banks to harness their potential more fully and help strengthen European growth.

Rebecca Christie

Non-Performing Loans: Stumbling Block or Scapegoat?

NPLs and how they stand between European Banks and better Deposit insurance

Whenever deposit insurance rises to the top of the European policymaking agenda, one topic always highjacks the discussion from the start: bad loans. How can governments responsibly sign on to any new system that includes responsibility for risky transactions of the past? To what extent must those legacy assets be cleaned up before any new risk-sharing system can be justified?

Non-performing loans (NPLs)[1] are a problem, but they're also a shield for politicians reluctant to move forward with banking union. Any conversation of how to clean up bank balance sheets needs to take place in the broader context of the political environment and economic outlook.

As the twin crises of the U.S. subprime mortgage market and euro area sovereign debt recede further into history, the European financial sector has been working through its troubled assets at a respectable pace. Policymakers have set up bad banks, tightened regulatory standards and put new frameworks in place to encourage banks to tackle their NPLs head-on. The financial sector, in turn, has strengthened its secondary market for non performing assets and developed new protocols for valuing, servicing and otherwise working out. As a result, the situation has improved alongside the overall economic outlook.

The European Union's May 2019 risk reduction report[2] confirmed that banks have improved steadily and decreased leverage since 2014, with capital and liquidity positions remaining stable over the past year. NPLs have continued to

---

[1] The catchall term NPLs is often used to refer to broader categories of non-performing assets, even though they may be technically separated into NPLs, non-performing exposures (NPEs) or other categories. For the purposes of this broad discussion I have generally used NPLs, as is common practice. See European Parliament (2018).

[2] EU Commission, ECB, SRB (2019)

Note: The author is a visiting fellow at Bruegel, the Brussels-based European policy think tank. Previously she wrote about economics and financial regulation for Bloomberg News and Dow Jones/The Wall Street Journal. Views here are personal.

https://doi.org/10.1515/9783110683073-014

decline, and Europe has made "susbstantial progress" on risk reduction measures at EU and national levels. According to the European Banking Authority (EBA)[3], the weighted average NPL ratio for European banks had fallen to 3.6 % in June 2018, from 6.5 % in December 2014. This near-halving seems to have held across the sample of banks included in the data for that period: For banks in the third quartile, the worst category of performers given, the NPL ratio peaked at 15.4 % in March 2015 and had fallen to 7.0 % by June 2018. For the first quartile, the ratio moved from 2.1 % to 1.2 %, and the median peaked at 5.8 % before dropping to 2.7 %.

This is the same period in which the euro area has moved toward banking union, entering Single Supervisory Mechanism (SSM) supervision under the European Central Bank (ECB), and the euro area progress has followed the trend. Andrea Enria, the former EBA chair who was appointed in 2018 to lead the ECB's supervisory board, cites[4] three areas of particular importance: giving guidance to banks to manage their NPLs actively; providing supervisory expectations on how banks should cover their loans and write them off over time; and bilateral targets that are defined and set for banks on how to deal with the stock of existing non-performing assets. In addition, the EU adopted an Action Plan[5] for dealing with NPLs in 2017 that set out a strategy for dealing with existing stocks of bad loans as well as future policy.

Enria notes that it is important to distinguish between the measures that Europe has taken on the existing stock of loans and the more recent measures put in place to reduce the risk that we pile up a huge stock of non performing loans going forward. In this second category we see the EU's legislative banking package of 2019, which codified standards for dealing with NPLs and also introduced the concept of a "prudential backstop" of reserves set aside to deal with troubled assets[6].

A brief aside: the "prudential backstop" is an example of an EU policy construction that is both progressive and confusing at the same time. On the one hand, it makes good sense for banks to set aside loss reserves for loans that could become non-performing in the future. On the other hand, "backstop" has traditionally been used to mean public facilities that stand behind the banking system – such as central bank lending lines, deposit insurance funds, or aid programs from international financial institutions. "Prudential," referring specifically to regulatory oversight rather than generalized carefulness, is a more gen-

---

3 EBA (2018a)
4 Enria et al. (2019)
5 Council of the EU (2017a)
6 Council of the EU (2019) and related legislative text

eral term but when combined with "backstop", it could be construed, incorrectly, to mean "provided by the authorities" instead of its actual meaning of "required by regulators". Further referring to the way banks will need to manage their balance sheet as "common minimum loss coverage"[7], as the EU did in its April 2019 explanation of the amount of money banks will need to set aside under the "prudential backstop", is a needlessly blurry way to define regulatory minimum standards for loss reserves.

This is the latest iteration of what has become a recurring feature in the move to banking union. I would argue that European action to redefine English language terms to mean different things from their historic financial-market contexts reflects the EU's ambivalence toward standardizing its regulatory regimes. In some cases, like the "leverage ratio," it is merely a case of getting used to the new math. In others, like bank "resolution", it will mean coming to terms with a European definition that is at odds with long-established U. S. usage[8]. In a report to the European Parliament, Anna Gelpern and Nicolas Véron note that in assessing the state of banking regulation, "Semantics is a particular pitfall. The same words are used in different ways on the two sides of the Atlantic and occasionally also in different contexts inside the EU. This can easily lead to misunderstandings, or to misleading characterisations. This observation applies with special force to key terms, such as resolution, liquidation, and insolvency."

Redefining terms in this manner may be seen as giving the EU an extra measure of control, but there is a cost. By creating new common standards, but using terms that are in some cases the opposite of their earlier contexts, the EU effectively ringfences its supervisory framework. I believe this will have peripheral repercussions for years to come and could contribute to a future financial crisis by increasing uncertainty and the potential for shock-causing miscommunications in times of global market turmoil.

Awkward name aside, the prudential backstop and its accompanying supervisory rules do have the potential to rein in banks from piling up bad loans to the extent they did in the past. The hope is that banks will keep a better eye on their credit risk, so that when the general economy deteriorates, banks can protect themselves from getting dragged down alongside.

All of these measures show that the EU has devoted considerable attention to the question of non-performing assets, both historic and prospective. Nonetheless, these loans continue to be singled out by policymakers as one of the key obstacles toward moving forward with comprehensive euro-area deposit insur-

---

7 ibid.
8 Gelpern and Véron (2019), p. 10

ance, the missing "third pillar" of the banking union concept first put forward in the EU's landmark 2012 declaration[9]. This has led to very little progress since the Single Resolution Board was established[10].

"Legacy risks" are a chief concern in the mid-2019 report of the High Level Working Group on Risk Reduction, a panel put together by euro area finance ministers to study the backdrop for expanding the cross-border safety nets available to financial institutions within the monetary union. The report, presented to the Eurogroup in June, calls for "gradual implementation" of the European Deposit Insurance Scheme (EDIS) in conjunction with movement on "other parts" of banking union architecture and, of course, progress made on legacy assets.

This is the perennial rallying cry of countries that are reluctant to move toward a true euro area deposit insurance scheme, where a euro in any bank in the currency area would be as safe as any other regardless of the state of national finances. As seen in the working group report: "A number of members are of the view that further risk reduction in the European banking sector based on certain benchmarks or targets and an Asset Quality Review (AQR) or comprehensive assessment, is needed before moving forward with (parts of) EDIS." Which benchmarks is another area of disagreement: some countries prefer quantitative targets, while others – who are presumably more interested in moving forward – would recommend qualitative assessments. In any event, the report concludes that more technical work is needed "in parallel" to "preparation of the roadmap for beginning political negotiations on EDIS." That is to say, they see a need for preparatory technical work to go with the preparatory work needed to produce a preparatory document for preparing the start – just the start – of political EDIS talks.

Perhaps in the interest of moving beyond talk of preparations for the preparations, the report floats the prospect of "a first liquidity phase that does not entail loss coverage." This would seem to be a bureaucratic reference to proposals[11] for national deposit insurance systems to offer reinsurance to each other, presumably to be repaid later by the member state where the deposit insurance was used. As Véron and Isabel Schnabel wrote[12] in 2018, this raises the possibility that depositors in some countries would not be treated equally to depositors in others. While

---

9 See the Euro Summit statement of June 2012. The other two pillars are common supervision and a common resolution mechanism, both now in place.
10 Macchiarelli, C., Giacon, R., Georgosouli, A. and Monti, M. (2019)
11 See the first stage of the European Commission proposal of 2015, as well as Gros (2015)
12 "We fear that the deposit re-insurance concept in Gros 2015, which perpetuates autonomous policy decision making on deposit insurance by national authorities, could lead to uncertainty as to the automaticity of payouts, especially in cases where a country's politics or policies are controversial in the rest of the euro area—a possibility that was illustrated in March 2013 in

the European Commission proposal would reduce these national disparities over time, there remains a possibility that, should this first stage of EDIS ever be introduced, the follow-on stages never materialize. Certainly forward progress has so far been slow: in 2016, the European Council said the plan could move forward once there was progress on risk reduction, and policy updates[13] since then suggest that technical work is moving forward with "limited political progress."

For big cross-border banks, who would benefit from a standardized deposit insurance system across the euro area, this stalemate is frustrating. Christian Ossig, chief executive of the Association of German Banks, warns that the euro area risks falling into the trap of piling up and even searching out further preconditions for EDIS to move ahead. He also cautions that the pace of NPL reduction may not be sustainable, since banks will clear out loans that are easier to restructure before turning to the most difficult section of their balance sheet. That said, Enria notes that banks have set out ambitious plans to work through older vintages of NPLs, and suggesting that the industry continues to move in the right direction.

The current political debate has been focussed on NPLs and sovereign debt risk, two forms of banking risk that happen to be bigger problems for countries like Italy that have faced economic pressures in recent times. Those countries, in turn, as why "risk reduction" debates have not tackled other forms of risk that might face geographic outbreaks in other areas. Operational risk and anti-money laundering risk, two banking threats that have cropped up in countries outside those most affected by the euro crisis, were not mentioned in the euro area's December 2018 summit statement calling for risk reduction as a precursor to strengthening the banking union.

Fabio Panetta, senior deputy governor of the Bank of Italy through 2019, says his country in particular has outpaced perceptions that it has lagged in addressing its backlog of bad loans. He argues that there should not be a fixed speed for reducing bad loans, but rather a strategy that takes into account the overall economic situation. For one thing, he says, private secondary markets have needed time to develop, and that pushing banks to deleverage any faster than they have would have put the economy at the mercy of a handful of buyers who could squeeze down valuations and then reap outsize profits. This sort of policy could be procyclical and therefore counterproductive. In any case, Italy has followed the trend of cutting its stocks of bad loans in half: at the end of 2018, the Italian NPL gross ratio was 8.7 %, compared to 16.5 percent in 2015. While weak spots remain, it is no

---

Cyprus. Thus, the operation of the system from the insured depositor's perspective must be fully insulated from national political vagaries[.]" Schnabel and Véron (2018).

13 E.g., the European Commission's 2017 communication on banking union

longer fair to say that Italy is swimming in bad loans, Panetta said[14]: "If you want to go to Italy and want to swim, then you better go to a beach rather than to a bank."

Going forward, he cites three factors that should be driving the conversation about NPLs: accounting standards, timetables, and impact on the general economy. He views[15] the cumulative effect of the EU's prudential backstop, the ECB's "quantitative addendum" on handling troubled loans[16], and other changes as raising the possibility that banks could be asked to set aside more than 100 % of the value of a bad loan if they cannot sell it quickly enough.

This then connects to the question of timing. All banks under ECB supervision are subject to the same standards under the new rules. While this creates a level playing field in some ways, it also can exacerbate differences among national legal frameworks. In some cases, even if a bank wants to restructure a loan and dispose of its collateral, national credit recovery procedures can drag the process out. Bank supervisors cannot control civil justice frameworks but might have reason to consider them in context.

National court systems have certainly been identified as roadblocks for banks and secondary-market NPL investors. In some cases, where contract enforcement and collateral reposession take a long time to work out, there can be a direct impact on NPL pricing. In addition, as a European Council technical committee noted[17], "very lengthy foreclosure and legal resolution timelines could lead to an increasing number of strategic defaults as borrowers do not see any immediate consequences from failing to pay." Some countries also face straightforward capacity problems, as judicial systems strain to work through rising numbers of bankruptcy and restructuring cases.

These two factors create a timing tension for banks looking to clean up their balance sheets. Wait too long, and accounting rules could push a financial institution into worse shape. Move fast, and risk getting bogged down in a legal backlog by not giving judicial systems enough time to catch up to their new caseloads. This, too, could hurt banks and increase the threat to the overall economy.

General economic conditions also are used to make the case for loan forebearance, in which borrowers are given more lenient repayment terms on the grounds that it will lead to fewer systemic losses over time. Under this strategy, rather than foreclose on a bad loan or sell it off at rock bottom prices, banks and their underwriters can work with clients to find a payment plan that leaves both the bank and the borrower better off.

---

14 Enria et al. (2019)
15 ibid.
16 ECB (2018)
17 (Council of the EU, 2017)

Panetta says new accounting rules can push banks to take a loan that has been designated underperforming and push it into full NPL status, triggering disposal procedures, in ways that do not make sense during a recession. The EBA has tried to address this in its guidance[18], urging banks to consider forbearance measures "only" when they aim to restore sustainable repayment and are thus in the borrower's interests. The guidance's prudential perspective seeks to keep financial institutions from unduly delaying action. But it also tries to discourage banks from running roughshod over borrowers by "taking into account the pressing need to ensure that consumers who have taken out loans are treated fairly at every stage of the loan life cycle."

The private secondary market has the potential to address many of these concerns, by giving banks a place to sell their NPLs to investors with the time and expertise to work with borrowers. When the system works well, the borrower repays more of the loan than might have initially been thought possible, and the investor benefits from higher value than would otherwise be the case.

Asset management corporations (AMC) or "bad banks" traditionally have been used to both clear out the bank balance sheets and give borrowers space to work out restructurings. But tighter state aid rules will affect the availability of this tool going forward. These changes have made it harder to look at strategies that have previously worked for tackling bad loans quickly and systematically in a country facing pervasive economic difficulty.

In the past, authorities have set up an asset-management company, transferred bad loans off the books of troubled banks, and moved forward from there. Under previous state aid rules, it was possible to value the loans at close to their book value when they moved to the AMC. This meant that losses to the affected banks were, if any, small and maneagable. In 2009, the Commission acknowledged[19] that transfer values would inevitably be above market prices but should still be limited to reflect the underlying long-term economic value, or the 'real economic value,' of the assets, based on cash flows and other assumptions. The flexibility inherent in divining this number helped the banks to minimize losses in ways that are no longer permitted under more recent rules.

Ireland, Spain and Slovenia all set up asset management vehicles during the euro crisis that were allowed to acquire bad loans at above current estimates of market price[20].

---

18 EBA (2018)

19 European Commission (2009) Impaired Asset Communication

20 Council of the EU (2017). For a more comprehensive history of bad banks used in various EU countries, see European Commission (2009)

Now the state aid rules are clearer: transfers must be at something at or close to estimated market value, rather than the projected "real economic value" of the asset[21]. In cases of where no market exists, some assets could be valued at pennies on the dollar, which could be very different from how they had been priced on the banks' balance sheets. Wiping out those loans in a hurry could thus create more capital problems for banks already under pressure and subject to corresponding new limits on public-sector capital injections. Since countries have, in the past, accompanied the establishment of asset management companies with capital injections and broader bank restructurings, newer state aid limits can come into play on multiple fronts.

AMCs can be private or state-sponsored, and they can apply to a specific bank or to a type of loan across the industry. State aid may or may not be involved. But as an EU committee[22] noted, "larger magnitude" state-backed entities have been used to kick-start the secondary markets for NPLs. That said, the proviso that state aid rules apply to these entities has taken on increasing importance with the EU's tougher line on all forms of public support for the banking sector, particularly for banks that are still considered viable but might seek precautionary aid. As a result, after the entry into force of the Banking Resolution and Recovery Directive (BRRD) and the Single Resolution Mechanism Regulation (SRMR) taking of Impaired Asset Measures (IAMs) outside resolution, restrictions on state aid limit the amount of aid that can be granted in this context.

The European Commission released an official AMC Blueprint in 2018 that spells out how countries can set up a bad bank with public support while complying with all the new rules. Even before the new restrictions, however, setting up a publicly-backed bad bank was not a simple task. As my colleague Alexander Lehmann wrote[23]: "the difficulties inherent in setting up an AMC and achieving a track record in restructuring should not be underestimated. Countries are well advised to prepare the legal basis for such entities."

Given all of the difficulty in selling off non-performing loans at a loss, it can be tempting to ask whether banks should just hold the loans until maturity. That is a strategy that worked well for the eurosystem, after the Bundesbank was left with collateral from 8.5 billion euros in loans it had extended to the German arm of Lehman Brothers. In keeping with general preferences in Germany to take

---

21 The AMC Blueprint says that transfer pricing must be at estimated market value or be subject to stringent state aid review and restrictions, and that AMCs with a state-aid component should be used only in exceptional circumstances. See EBA (2018) and European Commission (2019).
22 Council of the EU (2017)
23 Lehmann (2017)

advantage of central bank measures rather than sell off assets in a fire sale[24], the Bundesbank itself opted to hold the loans until they had recovered most of their value[25].

This ability to hang on and outperform may be a phenomenon isolated to recent economic trends, says Thomas Wiegand,[26] a managing director at Cerberus Capital Management. "We had a 10 year boom and everything went up. Holding on to an NPL or holding on to any asset was good – if you had sold something in 2015, you should have held it to 2018 and you would have made more money." This is a risk it does not always pay to take. Furthermore, a recovery economy is not the same thing as a recovering physical plant. As Wiegand points out, monetary policy decisions cannot fix roofs. A commercial real estate property that sits vacant and unmaintained, because it is tied up as collateral for a non-performing loan, will deteriorate, hurting both the loan and the surrounding economy. This is not a good use of money for central banks or any other investors, particularly those that have to follow International Financial Reporting Standards (IFRS).

With contemporary bank regulations and accounting standards, the message from the authorities is now clear: get rid of your NPLs as soon as practical. Panetta[27] says banks will want to sell as the accounting value of the loan begins to fall below its actual recovery value – if banks are forced to set aside 100 % of the loan's value as a provision, effectively reducing its book value to zero, they would probably be better off to sell it for whatever they can get under the theory that something is better than nothing.

Another reason not to count on holding assets until they recover is the experience of Japan, which left impaired assets in place for a long time. As Enria[28] says, in that can bring on "a vicious circle of higher funding risks and lack of profitability, and it's very difficult to get out of the hole." Time is clearly a factor in how fast banking sectors and economies can recover from financial crises. The countries that recovered the fastest are those that took the bad loans off bank balance sheets as quickly as they could, even if they then required further disposition in an asset management company.

---

24 See Podlich, Schnabel and Tischer (2017). "The paper does not find any evidence of fire sales in the German banking sector after the Lehman collapse. However, the price reactions point towards a tightening of market liquidity. ... ECB-eligible assets suffer less from tight market liquidity, indicating that unconventional monetary policy measures had a stabilizing effect."
25 Financial Times (2017)
26 Enria et al (2019)
27 ibid.
28 ibid.

Countries around Europe have moved to tackle their bad loans at a staggered pace. Ireland was one of the first to move, followed by Germany, and the Nordic and Benelux countries. The next wave was in central and Eastern Europe, and since 2017 attention has shifted to Southern Europe, in countries like Spain, Italy, Greece and Portugal. Wiegand says transactions were up by 40 % in 2018 in some of these transactions, suggesting the market for NPLs is peaking.

Three factors can help secondary-market buyers create more efficient prices for troubled assets, allowing both a better return for investors and a better sales prices for banks. One is improvements in out-of-court restructuring options. Given the delays that court proceedings can entail, everyone benefits when lenders and borrowers can cut deals in a consensual manner. A second is servicing infrastructure. An NPL portfolio can include thousands of individual borrowers, and working out each of those loans is time-consuming and requires specialized training and a lot of manpower. Companies that provide servicing, either in-house or on a third-party basis, need time to train their staff in ways that take account of best practices from other regions, and they also need an efficient way to get licensed in the jurisdictions where they will be working. The third element is data and documentation. If little is known about a loan, its value will be less than if all of its accrued interest and other components can be accounted for. Likewise, a loan is worth more if all of its accompanying registration documents are at hand and there's a clear process for seeking changes. Wiegand says this sort of paperwork is both essential and rarely readily available. For the system to work properly, banks will need to invest heavily in restructuring units and build their capacity to work with borrowers and investors more efficiently.

Progress is taking place on all of these fronts, and 2018 proved to be a very strong year for bank deleveraging. While non-performing loans remain a problem, they no longer seem to pose a dramatic threat to financial stability. Instead, they remain a political and social issue that will influence confidence in the banking system and in Europe's ability to integrate its financial markets going forward.

All links verified as of 2 Sept 2019

References

Council of the EU (2017). Report of the FSC Subgroup on Non-Performing Loans, from the General Secretariat of the Council to Delegations. (9854/17) May 2017.
Council of the EU (2017a). *Banking: Council sets out action plan for non-performing loans.* July 2017. https://www.consilium.europa.eu/en/press/press-releases/2017/07/11/banking-action-plan-non-performing-loans/

Council of the EU (2019). *"Council adopts reform of capital requirements for banks' non-perform-ing loans."* Press release on final adoption of EU Banking Package including prudential backstop. April 2019. https://www.consilium.europa.eu/en/press/press-releases/2019/04/09/council-adopts-reform-of-capital-requirements-for-banks-non-performing-loans/

Council of the EU and the European Parliament (2019). Text of regulation on minimum loss coverage for non-performing exposures. (PE-CONS 2/19)

EBA (2018). *Final report: guidance on management of non-performing and forborne exposures.* October 2018. https://eba.europa.eu/documents/10180/2425705/EBA+BS+2018+358+Fi-nal+%28Final+report+on+GL+on+NPE_FBE+management%29.pdf/371ff4ba-d7db-4fa9-a3c7-231cb9c2a26a

EBA (2018a). December 2018. *Risk Assessment of the European Banking System.* https://eba.europa.eu/documents/10180/2518651/Risk_Assessment_Report_December_2018.pdf

ECB (2018). Addendum to the ECB Guidance to banks on non- performing loans: supervisory expectations for prudential provisioning of non-performing exposures. March 2018. https://www.bankingsupervision.europa.eu/ecb/pub/pdf/ssm.npl_addendum_201803.en.pdf

ECB, SRB, European Commission (2019). *Monitoring Report on Risk Reduction Indicators, May 2019.* https://www.consilium.europa.eu/media/39698/joint-risk-reduction-monitoring-re-port-may2019.pdf

Enria, A., Ossig, C., Panetta, F., Wiegand, T. and Christie, R., moderator (2019). *NPLs: How and When Do We Solve the Problem, or is it Solving Itself?* Discussion at the conference "EDIS, NPLs, Sovereign Debt and Safe Assets" organised by the Institute for Law and Finance, Frankfurt, 14 June. Video archive at: https://www.ilf-frankfurt.de/seminars/conference-ma-terials/

Euro Area Heads of State and Government (2012). Euro Summit Statement, June 2012. https://www.consilium.europa.eu/media/21400/20120629-euro-area-summit-statement-en.pdf

Euro Area Heads of State and Government (2018). Euro Summit Statement, December 2018 (EURO 503/18). https://www.consilium.europa.eu/en/press/press-releases/2018/12/14/state-ment-of-the-euro-summit-14-december-2018/

European Commission (2009). Communication from the Commission on the Treatment of Im-paired Assets in the Community Banking Sector.

European Commission (2015). Commission Proposal for a European Deposit Insurance Scheme (EDIS). November 2015. https://ec.europa.eu/info/publications/commission-proposal-eur-opean-deposit-insurance-scheme-edis_en

European Commission (2017). "Communication to the European Parliament, the Council, the European Central Bank, the European Economic and Social Committee and the Committee of the Regions on Completing The Banking Union." (COM(2017) 592 final) November 2017. https://ec.europa.eu/finance/docs/law/171011-communication-banking-union_en.pdf

European Commission (2019). Fourth Progress Report on the reduction of non-performing loans and further risk reduction in the Banking Union (COM(2019) 278 final)

European Parliament (2018). *Non-performing loans in the Banking Union: Stocktaking and challenges.* Report from the Economic Governance Support Unit. Authors: M. Magnus, J. Deslandes, and C. Dias. (PE 614.491) October 2018

European Commission (2018a). *AMC Blueprint.* Commission staff working document accompany-ing the communication from the Commission to the European Parliament, the European Council, the Council and the European Central Bank Second Progress Report on the Reduction of Non-Performing Loans in Europe. (SWD(2018) 72 final) https://eur-lex.europa.eu/legal-content/EN/TXT/?uri=SWD:2018:072:FIN

Gelpern, A. and Véron, N. (2019). *"Effective Regime for Non-viable Banks: US Experience and Considerations for EU Reform."* Study prepared at the request of the European Parliament's ECON committee. (PE 624.432) http://www.europarl.europa.eu/RegData/etudes/STUD/2019/624432/IPOL_STU(2019)624432_EN.pdf

Financial Times (2012). *"Bundesbank set to recover Lehman losses."* Article by R. Atkins and E. Hammond, 20 Jan. 2012. https://www.ft.com/content/30d1a26e-42b8-11e1-93ea-00144feab49a

Gros, D. (2015). Completing the Banking Union: Deposit Insurance. Policy contribution, CEPS. https://www.ceps.eu/ceps-publications/completing-banking-union-deposit-insurance/

High Level Working Group on Risk Reduction (2019). *"Considerations on The Further Strengthening of the Banking Union, Including a Common Deposit Insurance System."* Report of the HLWG Chair to the Eurogroup. https://www.consilium.europa.eu/media/39768/190606-hlwg-chair-report.pdf

Lehmann, A. (2017). *"Carving out legacy assets: a successful tool for bank restructuring?"* Policy contribution, Bruegel. https://bruegel.org/wp-content/uploads/2017/03/PC-09-2017-NPL-29317.pdf

Macchiarelli, C., Giacon, R., Georgosouli, A. and Monti, M. (2019). *"Why non-performing loans are still putting the European Banking Union at risk."* LSE European Politics and Policy blog. March 2019. https://blogs.lse.ac.uk/europpblog/2019/03/27/why-non-performing-loans-are-still-putting-the-european-banking-union-at-risk/

Podlich, N., Schnabel, I., and Tischer, J. (2017). *Banks' trading after the Lehman crisis – The role of unconventional monetary policy.* Discussion Paper, Deutsche Bundesbank No 19/2017. https://www.bundesbank.de/resource/blob/704104/3bacc8743cbb502e603-b3ea81fdf77b5/mL/2017-07-03-dkp-19-data.pdf

Schnabel, I. and Véron, N. (2018). *"Breaking the Stalemate on European Deposit Insurance." Peterson Institute for International Economics blog."* March 2018. https://www.piie.com/blogs/realtime-economic-issues-watch/breaking-stalemate-european-deposit-insurance

IV. Sovereign Debt: Is this Really an Obstacle to EDIS and, if so, are Safe Assets the Solution?

Andreas Dombret
A Way to a Viable Level Playing Field

Introduction

Five years ago, the members of the euro area decided to centralise the supervision and resolution of systemically relevant institutions on a European level in order to integrate their systems further and to enhance their resilience. Alongside with substantial changes in financial regulation, the Single Supervisory Mechanism (SSM) and Singe Resolution Mechanism (SRM) have been established and have strengthened the stability of the European financial system. Are we now at the end of the road?

Despite all reform efforts we have seen in the past years, the euro area is still not regarded as crisis proof. This is why the debate about the unresolved issues that pose a potential threat to our financial system is crucial as we need to find a common ground for moving forward. To put it differently, we are not talking about an isolated subject, it is the overall architecture which has to be made ready before a potential next crisis may hit the system.

The general objective of financial regulation is to enable market forces to work in times of distress and downturns as well as in normal times. To achieve this objective, a level playing field is needed. With regard to the issue of sovereign debt and the discussion about a European Deposit Insurance Scheme (EDIS), the euro area finds itself at a breaking point. Establishing the banking union was an essential step to strengthen the financial system and the instalment of its third pillar is definitely a major issue to discuss. But before the euro area can afford to proceed towards further risk sharing, politicians and regulators must ensure that the causes and underlying mechanisms of systemic crises of the past are being contained.

The unresolved issue of Sovereign Debt

As before the crisis, credit institutions are still holding a high level of sovereign debt in their balance sheets – most prominently from their own home state among which many find themselves highly indebted. Not just for the banks affected, this gives cause for concern.

Not too long ago, a feedback loop between the state and domestic banks became apparent in the euro crisis. As public debt started to become unsustainable,

https://doi.org/10.1515/9783110683073-015

banks which were highly exposed to domestic sovereign debt had to be rescued by the sovereign – which in turn put an additional burden on government debt. Finally, we have seen support programs for banks as well as for some governments.

Although the overall debate about the euro crisis is fading, this issue has not been resolved yet and poses a substantial risk for the euro area in particular. Even nowadays one can still observe how the market downgrades banks highly exposed to a sovereign where sound public finances are put at risk. Moreover, the so called sovereign-bank-nexus can work in both directions: highly indebted governments endangering the stability of the domestic banking system and vice versa.

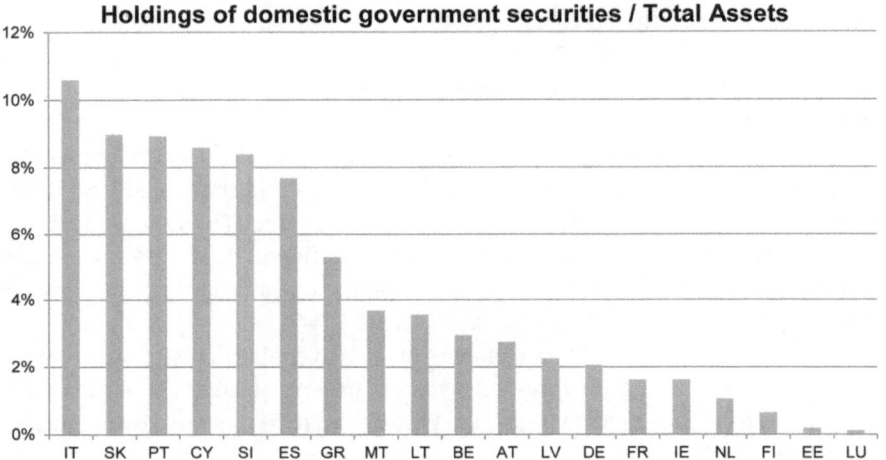

Graph 1: Government debt in banks' balance sheets in the euro area (as of Q1 2019)
Source: Bank of International Settlements

In the aftermath of the crisis, many reforms have contributed to the safety of the financial system. Some of these measures helped to reduce the loop from the one side – a sovereign debt crisis evolving from a shaky domestic banking system – but the potential threat stemming from high amounts of sovereign debt in banks' balance sheets has been left untouched.

The issue of sovereign exposures was reviewed and widely discussed by the Basel Committee. Although its members did not find an agreement with regard to changes of the current regulatory framework, the Basel Committee fortunately presented a thorough regulation proposal in a discussion paper in 2017[1].

---

1 See Basel Discussion Paper "The regulatory treatment of sovereign exposures" (2017) https://www.bis.org/bcbs/publ/d425.htm

The approach outlined in the paper addresses both types of risks stemming from sovereign exposures. On the one hand, exposures to a sovereign entity should be subject to risk weights, depending on the rating of the respective entity or the country risk classification by the OECD, but irrespective of the exposure amount. On the other hand, high amounts to one sovereign entity should be subject to marginal risk weight add-ons, depending on their size relative to the bank's Tier 1 capital.

In this way, both credit and concentration risks would be addressed, leading to higher capital requirements for holding both exposures towards low rated entities and high exposure amounts towards one sovereign, irrespective of its rating.

Table 1: Example of standardised risk weights for sovereign exposures[2]

External rating	AAA to A-	BBB+ to BBB-	Below BBB- and unrated
OECD CRC	0–2	3	4–7 and no classification
Central bank exposures			0 %
Domestic-currency central government exposures	[0–3]%	[4–6]%	[7–9]%
Foreign-currency central government exposures	10 %	50 %	100 %
Other sovereign entities	25 %	50 %	100 %

Source: Basel Discussion Paper

Table 2: Example of marginal risk weight add-on table for sovereign exposures

Exposure to group of connected sovereign counterparties (% of Tier 1 capital)	< 100 %	100–150 %	150–200 %	200–250 %	250–300 %	>300 %
Marginal risk weight add-on	0 %	5 %	6 %	9 %	15 %	30 %

Source: Basel Discussion Paper

---

2 The definition of sovereign entities listed in the left column is described in the discussion paper.

Whereas the members of the Committee could not find a consensus on making any changes to the current treatment, the ideas presented in the paper address the risks stemming from sovereign exposures in the right manner and serve as a blueprint for future regulation.

While contributions from researchers – most notably Nicolas Véron in his paper, published in November 2017[3] – have laid out alternative approaches to the topic, exposures to the domestic sovereign continue to be treated as risk-free. This means that institutions are not required to hold capital for (high) levels of government exposure, denominated in the domestic currency and are not bound to an upper limit (as they are for any other asset class). But, as the crisis has proven, sovereign debt is not risk-free.

Without adequate measures, the danger will persist and there is reasonable concern that the consequences will be even more severe in the next crisis, given that debt levels of many states remain high. The nexus is particularly pronounced in the euro area and this strong interconnection must be addressed.

The Basel Discussion Paper will surely have a future, but Europe needs to move forward on this issue and many proposals to do so are already on the table.

Are Safe Assets the solution?

Some argue that the creation of a safe asset for the euro area would be the tool at hand to address the nexus. In addition to that, many also fear that abolishing the preferential treatment of sovereign bonds might result in a lack of safe assets, as demand for them is already high.

In fact, various models for introducing a safe asset have already been discussed, most prominently the design of so-called "Sovereign Bond Backed Securities" (SBBS) proposed by the European Commission last year[4]. All the models presented share the same idea: bundling European government bonds into one asset and selling it in the form of senior and junior tranches to investors. The desired effect is that institutions' sovereign exposure in the euro area will be more diversified.

The idea, however, has several flaws. While such a model could help to diversify portfolios, it is far from certain that the intended impact to increase the

---

3 See „Sovereign Concentration Charges: A New Regime for Banks' Sovereign Exposures" by Nicolas Véron (2017) https://bruegel.org/2017/11/sovereign-concentration-charges-a-new-regime-for-banks-sovereign- exposures/
4 See „Proposal for a regulation on sovereign bond-backed securities" (2018) https://ec.europa.eu/info/publications/180524-proposal-sbbs_de

availability of safe investment products will actually occur. Several rating agencies already stated that a triple AAA rating for such an asset cannot be guaranteed.

This being said, another simple fact cannot be avoided either: Packaging risks does not make them disappear. Instead, they simply become concentrated in junior tranches, a crucial lesson we learned from the subprime crisis, which puts the desired demand for such a tranche into question.

Finally, introducing such a product does not break the sovereign bank nexus. Quite the contrary, the preferential treatment of government debt would be exacerbated as banks would be even more strongly interconnected to the state's solvency. That is the reason why regulatory initiatives demand that banks should have to back sovereign exposures – even in the shape of bond-backed securities – by sufficient capital in a risk-appropriate manner. That is the reason why it is cited as a condition in the original paper by Markus Brunnermeier and his colleagues[5] in order to provide the basis for a union-wide safe asset. Otherwise, mispricing of sovereign default risk would be even encouraged and pose another risk to financial stability.

Thus, safe assets are neither the answer to break the sovereign-bank-nexus, nor do they lead the way for a European Deposit Insurance Scheme. In fact, it is rather the other way around: breaking the nexus and strengthening the deposit protection in Europe could serve as a prerequisite for a safe asset.

Risk reduction as a prerequisite for EDIS

Legacy risks do pose an obstacle to the introduction of a European Deposit Insurance Scheme. One cannot simply buy insurance for risks that are already in place. For achieving a solid basis for a risk-sharing framework, these risks have to be appropriately contained. Otherwise, risks that have risen in the past would be communitised and incentives to reduce them would shrink accordingly. Speaking of the sovereign-bank-nexus, a high exposure towards the domestic – and especially highly indebted – government increases the ex-ante likelihood of EDIS becoming involved.

But high levels of sovereign debt are not the only pressing issue. While progress on the reduction of non-performing loans (NPL) has been made, more needs to be done since NPL-ratios are still very high in certain countries and must be reduced further. Moreover, national insolvency laws are another issue. Insol-

---

5 See „ESBies: Safety in the Tranches" by Brunnermeier et al. (2016)

vency laws deviate substantially within Europe and so does their efficiency. In order to guarantee a level playing field, a European-wide minimum standard of insolvency mechanisms is needed. In addition to that, the loss absorbing capacity of institutions must be improved. An agreement on this issue has already been reached and banks are required to hold sufficient level of Minimum Requirement for Own Funds and Eligible Liabilities (MREL) instruments by 2024.

Without these measures a viable level playing field cannot be achieved. All of them are factors affecting the overall architecture of our system. Therefore, we should take a look at the fault lines of our current system first, before steps towards further risk-sharing can be made.

Alternatives to a fully-fledged EDIS

Provided that a sufficient level of risk reduction has been achieved, a European Deposit Insurance Scheme can certainly have positive effects. A European fund for deposit protection could reduce the likelihood of bank runs and would improve shock absorbing capacity in the banking system, especially in the event of systemic risks. A fully-fledged EDIS, however, may not be the answer.

Instead, there are alternative designs of a deposit guarantee scheme which should be taken into consideration. In fact, a re-insurance system can be just as effective as a fully-fledged scheme. It can be even more efficient. As the banking systems in Europe still bear national hallmarks, it seems appropriate to design a deposit insurance system in such a way that national risks remain in national ownership.

National funds would thereby serve as a first line of defence while systemic shocks would be addressed by a European backstop. In such a framework, the vast majority of shocks would be caught up nationally, balancing accountability and control. The European backstop could be designed in various ways. It could either consist of a mandatory lending scheme between national funds or of a European fund, becoming involved after the national funds affected have been entirely used up. Such a design would maintain a strong national basis in order to control for risks emerging at the national level and a European wide insurance would serve in case systemic risks arise which overwhelm a single member state.

A way to a viable level playing field

Taking all this into account the question is, at which point a sustainable level playing field would have been achieved. Building on that, what should an adequate deposit protection scheme look like?

Coming back to risk reduction measures, there are gradual steps looking at the intensity of risk reduction. As mentioned, an agreement regarding total loss absorbing capacity has already been reached and the complete build-up of MREL instruments should be a premise for any move towards further risk sharing.

Regarding the issue of insolvency laws the situation is more complex. Since national laws build on each country's own legal philosophy, harmonisation is a difficult task. Yet, if a fully fledged model should be the ultimate goal, investors must face similar conditions in case a counterpart goes bankrupt, requiring a minimum level of insolvency standards all over the euro area.

With regard to non-performing loans many policy measures have addressed the issue and the overall situation in Europe has already improved. Still, more needs to be done and ratios are still too high if deposits are to be protected by a European scheme. In fact, target minimum ratios must be defined. The principle should be: the stronger the reduction of NPL- ratios, the more risk sharing will be feasible.

However, in contrast to NPLs, there is not even a regulatory framework addressing high sovereign exposures. Therefore, regardless of the design of the targeted deposit guarantee scheme, abolishing the preferential treatment of sovereign exposures is a must have. The doom loop is hard to break without extra equity, but it must be broken in order to complete the banking union. For a start, risk weights will surely be small, but will eventually lead the way to a more resilient system.

As a result, one should see the way towards a viable level playing field as a combination of risk reduction measures and risk sharing (i.e. deposit insurance) schemes. In fact, it can be broken into three different "risk reduction packages", each one allowing for another deposit guarantee scheme among the member states. While a regulation of sovereign exposures is an indispensable condition for any of these schemes, there is a variation regarding its intensity. The same holds true for the requirements related to NPLs. In the end, it can be summed up by the following formula: the more risk reduction the euro area can achieve, the more risk sharing via EDIS can be accomplished in the end.

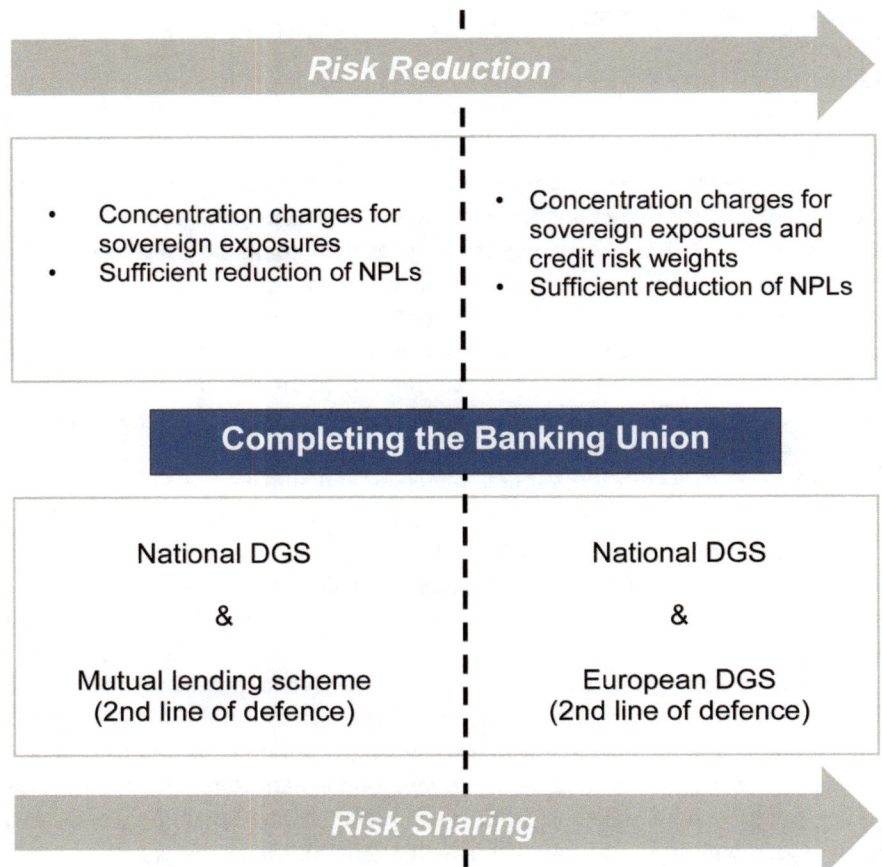

Graph 2: Examples for completing the Banking Union: more risk reduction allows for more risk sharing

Conclusion

Since the crisis, the overarching problem for the euro area has not yet been fully solved: the lack of trust. What is needed is a minimum standard of trust among all member states. Without it, the EU will never be able to achieve a viable level playing field, to break the doom loop, to introduce EDIS or to agree on a safe asset.

Completing the banking union means to address national biases. A lot has been accomplished, but the material risk channels left need to be addressed, especially if we want to accomplish a sustainable framework of risk sharing.

It is crucial that this deadlock be overcome. Cleary, there is urgency on all of these issues, but one should refrain from all too easy solutions. Instead, small and creative steps can help to break this deadlock and to move forward towards a more stable European financial system.

Colin Ellis
Would European "Safe Assets" Be Risk Free?

Abstract: Since the euro crisis subsided following its 2012 peak, policymakers have explored a number of options for making the euro area more resilient to future crises. One of these is to remove explicit linkages between sovereigns and their domestic banks, by creating a new common 'safe asset' for the euro area that banks and other creditors could hold. This paper looks at three different proposals for safe assets to assess whether they could achieve the same credit standards as for the highest rated euro area sovereigns. Unfortunately, this seems very unlikely; and given concerns about the stability of demand for junior assets that would be created under the proposals, it is unclear whether these assets would fare any better in the next euro crisis than peripheral sovereign debt did in the last one.

1. Introduction

As of today, the economic and monetary union (EMU) within the euro area remains a monetary union without full economic, and in particular fiscal, union. As such, this exposes individual sovereigns, banks and creditors to a range of heterogeneous risks across different countries.

One policy response to this heterogeneity would be to pursue full economic and political union. But the political constraints currently appear binding here, despite the single currency ultimately being a political project (Ellis & Oleksiy, 2018). In the absence of full burden-sharing between euro area member states, several proposals have been made to construct less formal mechanisms or support structures to try to shore up the region's resilience to future shocks. Importantly, in the absence of any concrete measures to complete the economic and monetary union by creating a proper fiscal union – including but not limited to automatic fiscal transfers, centralised taxation and spending and the assumption of government debts by a single euro area fiscal authority – the creation of a common safe asset to insulate creditors from heterogeneous risks will necessarily have to be resilient to the institutional fragilities that remain present in the euro area (Ellis, 2018).

The creation of such a European 'safe asset' would supposedly break the doom-loop between sovereigns and banks in the euro area. At the same time,

Note: Please note that this paper reflects the views of the author at the time of writing, and not necessarily any other institutions he is (or has previously been) affiliated with.

https://doi.org/10.1515/9783110683073-016

such an asset should also ideally avoid amplifying heterogeneous credit risks for individual euro area sovereigns.

Despite a concerted lack of interest from many national governments, a number of proposals have been made for the creation of a 'safe' asset, including the creation of Sovereign Bond Backed Securities (SBBS). This paper looks at whether such assets would genuinely prove to be risk free, at least by the standards of the analysis employed by external rating agencies.

2. The role and importance of safe assets in the euro area

The classic definition of a safe asset is that it is one that investors are happy to hold – and even pay a premium for – when economic or financial disruption ensues. These assets typically carry a very low risk of loss across all types of market cycles.

Globally, the most recognised and regularly held safe assets are US government bonds. However, US Treasuries are not the only asset investors accept as safe; German government bonds are also generally seen as safe assets, as are sovereign bonds from other countries. And while the US dominates official reserve holdings, when those reserve holdings are measured as a share of outstanding debt Australia is not far behind the US (Exhibit 1).

Exhibit 1: Reserve currency holdings

	Share of official FX reserves (2017)	FX reserves (held by other countries) as % of general government debt (2017)
United States	62.7	35.4
Euro area	20.1	16.9
Japan	4.9	5.0
United Kingdom	4.5	18.8
Canada	2.0	15.0
Australia	1.8	32.2
China	1.2	2.7
Switzerland	0.2	8.9

Source: Moody's (2018a).

However, the same 'safe asset' status does not hold true for other euro area governments, as reflected both by movements in euro area sovereign yields

(Exhibit 2) and in the credit ratings published by rating agencies (Exhibit 3). In both instances, significant gaps often exist between different euro area member states, primarily reflecting different credit risks.

Ten-year yields, percent

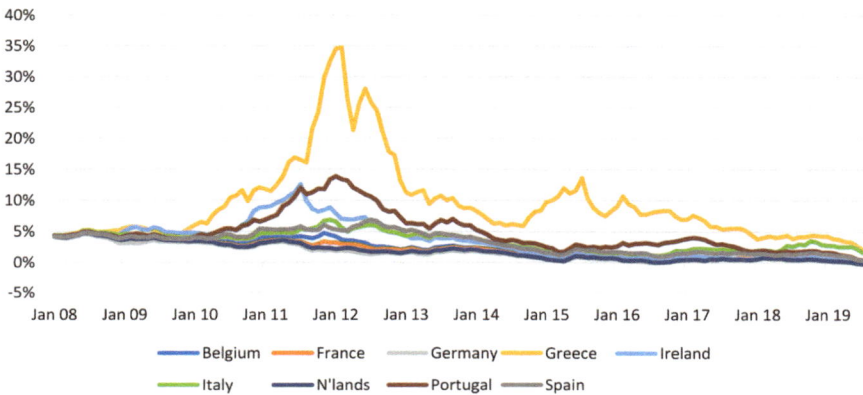

Exhibit 2: Euro area sovereign yields. Ten-year yields, percent
Source: Financial Times.

Exhibit 3: Euro area sovereign ratings

	S&P rating	Moody's rating		S&P rating	Moody's rating
Germany	AAA	Aaa	Ireland	A+	A2
Netherlands	AAA	Aaa	Latvia	A	A3
Luxembourg	AAA	Aaa	Lithuania	A	A3
Finland	AA+	Aa1	Spain	A-	Baa1
Austria	AA+	Aa1	Malta	A-	A2
France	AA	Aa2	Italy	BBB	Baa3
Belgium	AA	Aa3	Portugal	BBB	Baa3
Slovenia	AA-	Baa1	Cyprus	BBB-	Ba2
Estonia	AA-	A1	Greece	B+	B1
Slovakia	A+	A2			

Source: S&P and Moody's; ratings retrieved as of 2 August 2019. Note that ratings refer to issuer ratings.

This is key to the proposals for a common euro safe asset: it would represent a common instrument that investors would always be happy to hold in a downturn, and especially one where contagion risk among euro area member states would likely arise.

A main aim of the safe asset would be to weaken the linkages between banks and sovereign in the euro area. In many countries, domestic sovereign debt represents a significant share of banks' assets, providing a direct channel whereby sovereign credit distress is reflected in banks' own credit metrics. By replacing these sovereign exposures with a common 'safe asset' not tied to the credit standing of any individual euro area sovereign, this channel of contagion from individual sovereigns to their banking sectors would be curtailed. Importantly, this would be expected to happen across all euro area banking systems. By insulating banks from sovereign exposures, the likelihood of banks then requiring sovereign support is reduced, weakening the linkages between sovereigns and banks.

The need to curtail this so-called 'doom loop' is widely accepted by euro area policymakers; for many, it seems to have played a key role in the recent euro area crisis. But at the same time, it is worth noting that others take a different view. For instance, Moody's states that:

> *In our view, it is unlikely that reliance on SBBS will materially alter banks' or sovereigns' exposure to the "doom loop", just as it would have been unlikely to alter the path of the recent crisis.*
>
> *(Moody's, 2019b)*

For the safe asset to play its desired role in inoculating banks from macroeconomic and sovereign risk, the stability of demand for the proposed safe asset is critical. If there is insufficient demand for it to start with – or if demand for the asset falls in a downturn due to investor appetite waning – then it will still leave banks exposed to broader macroeconomic (and sovereign) developments.

One key metric of this is the credit rating that would likely be assigned to the safe asset by rating agencies. Importantly, if the rating for the safe asset was not the highest rating available (AAA for Standard & Poor's, and Aaa for Moody's) then it would not have any claim to be a 'risk free' asset. In fact, in this instance some banking systems – such as Germany, the Netherlands and Luxembourg – would face a reduction in the credit quality of the assets they held if they were only to hold the new non-triple-A common euro area asset, relative to the sovereign debt exposures they currently have.

3. Analysing different 'safe asset' proposals

There have been several different proposals for the creation of a safe asset; but broadly speaking three distinct forms have garnered most discussion. Considering the proposals from Leandro & Zettelmeyer (2018), and also the discussion at the Goethe University Institute of Law and Finance Conference on 14 June 2019, this paper will consider in turn: sovereign bond backed securities; debt issued by a central euro area institution backed by all member states via committed and callable capital; and debt issued by a similar institution, but one that would benefit from seniority relating to its euro area debt holdings relative to other euro area creditors. It should be noted that these three options are by no means an exhaustive list. While ultimately the assignment of a rating would be a matter for the relevant ratings agencies, we can uncover possible rating outcomes from public comments and research, and existing ratings.

3.1 Sovereign Bond Backed Securities

One common proposal for a safe asset is the creation of new securities, backed by a pool of euro area sovereign bonds. The new securities known as Sovereign Bond Backed Securities or SBBS, would be backed by those sovereign bonds and issued in junior and senior tranches, offering a risk-reward decision for investors. The European Systemic Risk Board (ESRB, 2016) proposal for SBBS envisages a 70 % senior tranche, with the junior tranche(s) accounting for the rest.

In and of itself, this represents a fairly simple exercise in structured finance: the pool of assets behind the issuing special purpose vehicle (SPV) would be euro area government bonds, and the aim of the securitisation would be to benefit from diversification among member states and structure to achieve a high rating for the senior tranche. The ESRB believes senior SBBS tranches – sometimes referred to as ESBies – should be "at least as safe as German bunds", which as noted earlier are rated triple-A by both S&P and Moody's. However, it is important to note that any SBBS rating would be a structured finance rating, rather than a fundamental one.

Unfortunately, rating agencies appear to disagree with the ESRB. In its assessment of SBBS, S&P notes that the proposed structure of these securities is similar to standard Collateralized Debt Obligations (CDOs), but with some important differences (S&P, 2017). First, in normal CDOs individual assets only account for a tiny fraction of the total pool, unlike SBBS which would by construction be limited to the (currently 19) members of the euro area. Second, the independence between assets normally striven for in standard CDOs – so that when one asset is impaired, others are unlikely to be or could even offset it – would definitely not be true for SBBS, given the readily evident correlation between euro area sovereigns during the recent euro crisis.

Due to these two factors, S&P has said it would adopt a 'weakest link' approach to rating SBBS. This means that the agency would rank order the underlying sovereigns from the lowest rated (Greece) to the highest (Germany, Netherlands, Luxembourg); and it would then look at where the threshold between the junior and senior tranches fell, and would assign the senior tranche the same rating as the sovereign immediately above that threshold, considering the relative shares of different sovereigns in the underlying asset pool.

Exhibit 4: 'Weakest link' illustration for S&P rating approach

	S&P rating	ECB capital key (%)	Cumulative percentage (rising)
Germany	AAA	26 %	100 %
Netherlands	AAA	6 %	74 %
Luxembourg	AAA	0 %	68 %
Finland	AA+	2 %	67 %
Austria	AA+	3 %	66 %
France	AA	20 %	63 %
Belgium	AA	4 %	42 %
Slovenia	AA-	0 %	39 %
Estonia	AA-	0 %	38 %
Slovakia	A+	1 %	38 %
Ireland	A+	2 %	37 %
Latvia	A	0 %	35 %
Lithuania	A	1 %	35 %
Spain	A-	12 %	34 %
Malta	A-	0 %	22 %
Italy	BBB	17 %	22 %
Portugal	BBB	2 %	5 %
Cyprus	BBB-	0 %	3 %
Greece	B+	2 %	2 %

Source: S&P, ECB and author's calculations.

Exhibit 4 provides a simple illustration here, based on an assumption that the underlying pool of assets from different euro area sovereigns matched the ECB capital key. Given current ratings, S&P would likely rate ESBies as single-A securities. That is because, in the illustration in Exhibit 4, the threshold for the 30 % junior tranche would correspond to Spain, and the sovereigns rated immediately above are Lithuania and Latvia, corresponding to an 'A' rating. However, by reordering Exhibit 4 to put Malta above Spain in the relative rankings, it would also be possible to assign a rating of 'A-'. While this is a higher rating than stated in previous research – reflecting more recent sovereign rating upgrades – it is still a long way from the AAA rating envisaged by the ESRB.

In its published research, Moody's takes a somewhat different approach to considering SBBS. While noting the lack of diversification in the underlying asset pool, and the likelihood of high correlation among member states' sovereign credit assessments, Moody's (2019b) examines the SBBS construct from a full structured finance approach, unlike S&P. In part, this may reflect the fact that it already has methodologies for a variety of CDO structures, including Municipal and Sub-sovereign CDOs.

It is important to note at this point a key difference between S&P and Moody's rating approach. In particular, S&P's main rating scale speaks primarily to the incidence of default – a missed interest payment, a delayed principle payment, or some other action that results in a reduced financial value for creditors. However, it does not normally – and certainly not in the illustration above – speak to the losses that investors would suffer when default occurs.

In contrast, Moody's standard rating scale speaks not only to the incidence or probability of default (PD), but also the losses that creditors face in the event of default. As such, its ratings are closer to an 'expected loss' concept; this is the reason Moody's main rating scale does not have a 'D' rating. For structured finance securities, such as the proposed SBBS, Moody's examines potential losses relative to published idealized loss tables for different rating levels (see Moodys, 2018b). It follows that very small expected losses can correspond to relatively high structured finance ratings.

While details are currently very scarce and it hedges its bets, Moody's analysis of potential ratings for senior SBBS tranches also suggests that a triple-A rating may be unobtainable. In particular, it notes that:

"Given the unique features that distinguish SBBS from typical CDOs the highest achievable rating of a senior SBBS tranche may be different to that of a CDO backed by a diversified portfolio of corporate obligors."

(Moody's, 2019b)

It is worth spelling the implications of this statement. The differences noted by Moody's for SBBS versus conventional CDOs are decidedly negative – concentration and elevated co-movement. As a thought experiment, suppose that we could find a pool of 'normal' assets with the same weighted average rating as euro area governments' debt (using the capital key again for the latter). If the 'normal' CDO were structured so as to achieve a triple-A rating for the senior tranche, the SBBS equivalent would probably be rated lower: that is, not triple-A.

As such, the ratings agencies' judgement of SBBS is that they would not succeed in creating assets that were as safe as German bunds.

There are two important considerations to add to this analysis. First, many structured finance securities benefit not only from seniority of different tranches, but also from 'capital enhancement': literally, the structured finance issuer setting aside a pool of money that is the first mechanism for absorbing any losses that arise. If losses are likely to be small across a diversified portfolio, capital enhancement can result in significant rating uplift for both junior and senior tranches, as they will have to absorb less of any losses that do crystallize. There have been some proposals (see for instance, Leandro & Zettelmayer, 2018) to achieve higher ratings for SBBS via this mechanism, rather than using tranches. While this is possible, it does not seem to have gained significant traction from euro area policymakers. In part, this may reflect the fact that capital enhancement would effectively represent subsidisation of SPV issuance by euro area governments.

The second caveat is more important, and speaks to market demand for these instruments. It is worth noting that there is no technical impediment to stop private sector actors creating SBBS for sale to creditors today. If it wanted to, any appropriately authorised entity could establish an SPV for the purpose of issuing SBBS. The fact that no one has done so speaks very plainly to the lack of demand by private sector investors for these securities. In part, this is likely to reflect the nature of the whole SBBS structure: in particular, while most discussion typically focuses on the senior tranche (ESBies), the fate of the junior trance (EJBies) is critical too. The whole concept of SBBS relies on demand for all tranches, and in particular sustained demand for EJBies in another euro crisis. This remains fundamentally untested. In Moody's view EJBies:

"... would likely fare no better in a future crisis that did lower-rated sovereign debt during the last crisis."

(Moody's, 2019b)

This undermines the whole notion of SBBS, let alone the creation of a 'safe' senior tranche. Unfortunately, this broad issue – the stability of demand for 'junior' securities in the various safe asset proposals – will surface elsewhere as well.

3.2 Issuance by capitalised central body

A second proposal for a 'safe asset' in the euro area relies on a more fundamental credit approach, rather than structured finance mechanics. Euro area governments could establish a new entity (NE), backed by all governments, which would then be able to pursue different options.

One option would be for the NE to purchase a diversified portfolio of euro area sovereign debt at market prices. In this scenario, the credit risk from the underlying sovereigns would be pooled at the NE; and, because it had purchased debt at market prices, the losses it would face when a sovereign defaulted should be smaller than those faced by creditors who bought-and-held the debt at issue. As such, with sufficient capitalisation, the NE could withstand those losses and avoid its own default; but would then likely require recapitalisation in order to maintain its rating if its capital were depleted.

This option seems appealing in terms of creating a safe asset, depending on the form of support that euro area governments offered. A full joint and several guarantee for this entity (or indeed any other) could result in a triple-A rating, if agencies believed that it credibly constituted full credit substitution. Fully automatic triggers for recapitalisation in the event of losses might be able to achieve a similar outcome.

But there are clear downsides to this proposal. First, even if the NE was large enough to buy all existing sovereign debt in the euro area – which would require significant capital from sovereigns – that would not directly address new issuance requirements from sovereigns over time. In principle proceeds from maturing sovereign debt could be used to buy new primary issuance from sovereigns, thereby creating an implicit redistribution mechanism; but it is unclear this would be politically palatable to all euro area governments.

Second, and more important, the purchase of sovereign debt at market prices – implying a discount to par for sovereigns with weaker credit prospects – could be viewed dimly by rating agencies. It is worth noting that the December 2012 buy-back of Greek sovereign debt by the Public Debt Management Agency of Greece (funded by short-term notes issued by the European Financial Stability Fund or EFSF) was deemed as a default – a distressed exchange – by rating agencies. If the NE were to purchase sovereign bonds at prevailing (and significant) market discounts, the same outcome would likely ensue, with associated market fallout and disruption.

This speaks to a very important aspect of ratings that is perhaps not always understood by all euro area policymakers. Typically, credit ratings do not speak to all the obligations of the underlying issuer. If they did, then Greece would have been deemed to have defaulted many more times than the two instances recorded during 2012. That is because every time Greece's official sector obligations (eg to other euro area governments) were restructured, that restructuring process resulted in a reduction in the financial value of the obligations, and hence was a distressed exchange – that is, a default.

Instead, ratings typically speak to the risk that private creditors face; and when the official sector buys back debt at sub-par market prices, that crystallizes credit losses for those private investors. One obvious implication is that, in such an instance of default, the defaulting entity is likely to require direct funding from official sector sources for at least some time, given a lack of willingness from private sector creditors to buy debt at affordable rates for the sovereign.

There are other options that the NE could take. For instance, it could instead issue its own debt and then pass those funds on to euro area governments according to some pre-determined rules or schedule. In this instance, the NE would be more akin to a multilateral bank or fund; and would be not that dissimilar from the existing European Stability Mechanism (ESM), albeit with probably reduced asset risk given the ESM's current lending is concentrated to those countries that were hit hardest by the financial crisis.

At the time of writing, the ESM is rated AAA by Fitch ratings, and Aa1 (with a positive outlook) by Moody's. (Moody's positive outlook is instructive as it reflects the positive outlook currently in place on the French sovereign rating, indicating the strong dependency of the ESM and its rating on the underlying creditworthiness of member states.) If one triple-A is enough, ramping up the ESM could be an option to ensure sufficient safe assets in the euro area.

But here too there are downsides. First, the ESM enjoys such high ratings in part because it is deliberately over-capitalised; so the institution would bear any first losses rather than its creditors. Much like potential capital enhancement for SBBS, this represents implicit subsidisation; meaning that the average cost of issuing €1 of debt via the ESM (for euro area governments) would be higher than €1, in essence with more creditworthy sovereigns subsidising less creditworthy ones.

Second, unless the ESM would undertake to provide all funding for euro area sovereigns – which seems unlikely as noted above due to political constraints – there will remain a gap between the 'safe' euro area funding provided by the ESM, and the 'riskier' funding reflecting the debts issued directly by euro area governments themselves. There are parallels here with the notion that an expanded ESM could issue debt up to some threshold for all governments – for instance, up to 40% of GDP for each country – and then governments themselves would be responsible for issuing remaining debt.

This structure would have echoes of the SBBS proposal, in that there would be a senior 'safe' asset (ESM debt) and a riskier 'junior' debt, such as Italian or

Greek government bonds. Although the transmission mechanisms would be different, it is unlikely that this structure would fare any better in a new euro area crisis, with investors potentially flooding into ESM debt and abandoning bonds issued by riskier sovereigns. It is unlikely this would be a very palatable outcome for euro area governments.

3.3 Issuance by central body with seniority

A third proposal for the creation of a euro are safe asset takes related, but different approach. In this model, the NE would not necessarily be backed by significant volumes of publicly provided capital; but instead by the imposition of seniority, presumably in EU law. In this world, the NE could purchase euro area sovereign debt either at market value (risking defaults, as noted above) or fund governments directly. But instead of relying on a capital cushion to protect it, its seniority relative to other creditors would ensure that it was paid first in the event of a sovereign credit event – potentially even made whole – while private creditors would corresponding bear bigger losses (than if the NE was ranked *parri passu* with them). This seniority could therefore result in a higher rating for debt issued by the NE than the (weighted) average rating of the euro area sovereign debts it purchased.

Instructively, similar machinations were seen during the first Greek default of 2012. Prior to the debt exchange in March 2012, the European Central Bank (ECB) swapped its outstanding stock of Greek government debt – purchased under its Securities Markets Programme (SMP) – for new Greek government bonds that were exempted from the collective action clauses (CACs) imposed on other creditors. This had the effect of subordinating private creditors to the ECB, and thereby increasing private creditors' losses. In fact, Moody's calculates that the recovery rate for private investors on the first 2012 Greek default was just 24 %. That was the lowest recovery rate on a sovereign default since Cote d'Ivoire in 2000.

In principle, it is true that the approach of subordinating other creditors could result in the NE being highly rated. However, at the same time it could also certainly result in the subordinated securities being downgraded as a consequence, given that those subordinated instruments would bear (greater) losses in the event of any default. In the past, rating agencies have sometimes assigned different ratings to different sovereign bonds when losses were not evenly distributed.

As such, subordination of other creditors by the NE could even exacerbate the risk of sovereign default, with all of its associated implications. And investors would certainly demand a higher premium to hold now-subordinated euro area sovereign debt. As with the other two safe asset proposals examined herein, this would therefore again create an effective senior versus junior distinction for financial markets and private investors; and as such would ultimately be unlikely to shield sovereigns from the next euro area crisis.

4. Summary and conclusions

After examining the proposals outlined above, it seems unlikely that it would be possible to create a 'safe euro asset' that would definitely be rated triple-A by multiple rating agencies and would at the same time avoid amplifying credit stresses for weaker sovereigns in the next euro area crisis. For the specific SBBS proposal, a triple-A rating for the senior tranche, matching the rating of the German sovereign, seems very unlikely: instead, the SBBS senior tranche would be viewed by agencies as riskier than German government debt. As such, the 'safe asset' would demonstrably not be risk free from a credit perspective.

Furthermore, it is important to note that all three proposals for a safe asset examined herein effectively result in a *de facto* senior/junior split; and critically, those junior securities would be unlikely to fare any better in the next crisis than lower-rate sovereign debt did in the last crisis. This means that any such safe asset may do very little to shield weaker sovereigns or – given the fact it is impossible to completely sever sovereign-bank linkages – other issuers in those domiciles.

At its heart, this speaks fundamentally to what the various 'safe asset' proposals are trying to do. If the subsidisation principle – either through capital enhancement or capitalisation – is set aside due to its implicit higher cost of issuance, all proposals are essentially trying to repackage, or slice and dice, existing credit risks, rather than actually reduce them.

This is important because it means that any successful 'safe asset' mechanism would necessarily therefore have to represent a(t least an implicit) transfer of risk from weaker euro are sovereigns to stronger ones: a pooling of financial obligations and responsibilities.

If euro area governments were prepared to accept this pooling of financial responsibilities, by far the simplest way to do this from a fundamental credit perspective – and to create a euro area safe asset that would not amplify future crises for weaker sovereigns – would be to move to a proper fiscal union, including but not limited to automatic financial transfers between countries, and joint and several liability for all outstanding debt. This is obviously unpalatable to some euro area governments at it represents assuming responsibility for current, past and future spending by other countries that is unfunded by taxation. But *any* form of safe asset to be constructed will necessarily represent at least a small degree of taking on the burden of other governments' past and future debts. Until this fundamental political issue is resolved, any proposal for a safe asset will risk looking like 'smoke and mirrors' to private sector investors, rather than fundamental change that could start to address the institutional flaws that still pervade the euro area today, seven years after the peak of the crisis. More troublingly, if voters were to increasingly take a similar view then that could amplify risks for the whole political project of economic and monetary union.

References

Ellis, C (2018), "Why the euro crisis is far from over", *Journal of Risk Management in Financial Institutions*, Vol. 11, No. 1.

Ellis, C, and Oleksiy, O (2018), "Cultural Data Mirror International Structural Economic Differences", *World Economics*, Vol. 19, No. 1.

European Systemic Risk Board (ESRB, 2018), *Sovereign bond-backed securities: A feasibility study*, ESRB High-Level Task Force on Safe Assets, Frankfurt.

Leandro, Á, and Zettelmeyer, J (2018), "Safety Without Tranches: Creating a 'real' safe asset for the euro area", Centre for Economic Policy Research (CEPR) *Policy Insight* No. 93, June.

Moody's (2018a), Currency composition of foreign reserves continues to change only gradually, with any major shifts likely years away, published on www.moodys.com, 12 September.

Moody's (2018b), Moody's Idealized Cumulative Expected Default and Loss Rates, published on www.moodys.com, 25 October.

Moody's (2019a), *Sovereign default and recovery rates, 1983-2018*, published on www.moodys.com, 8 April.

Moody's (2019b), *FAQ on Sovereign Bond Backed Securities*, published on www.moodys.com, 17 April.

Standard and Poor's (S&P, 2017), How S&P Global Ratings Would Assess European "Safe" Bonds (ESBies), published on www.standardandpoors.com, 25 April.

Álvaro Leandro and Jeromin Zettelmeyer

Creating a Euro Area Safe Asset without Mutualizing Risk (Much)

Abstract: This chapter surveys three proposals to create "safe assets" for the euro area based on sovereign bonds, in which sovereign risk is limited through diversification and some form of seniority. These assets would be held by banks and other financial institutions, replacing concentrated exposures to their own sovereigns. The most developed idea, to create multi-tranche "Sovereign Bond Backed Securities" (SBBS), of which the senior tranche would constitute a safe asset, has recently received significant criticism. Other ideas include creating a senior, publicly owned financial intermediary that would issue a bond backed by a diversified portfolio of sovereign loans ("E-bonds"); and issuing sovereign bonds in several tranches at the country level while inducing banks to hold a diversified pool of senior sovereign bonds ("multitranche national bond issuance"). We find that none of the competing proposals entirely dominates the others. SBBS do not deserve most of the criticism to which they have been subjected. At the same time, E-bond and multi-tranche national bond issuance have several interesting features—including inducing fiscal discipline, and high resilience to extreme shocks—and warrant further exploration.

Note: This chapter, based on an eponymous article that is forthcoming in the Capital Markets Law Journal, was written while the authors were junior and senior fellow, respectively, at the Peterson Institute for International Economics. The authors are grateful to Olivier Blanchard, Markus Brunnermeier, Lee Buchheit, William Cline, Anna Gelpern, Gabriele Giudice, Mitu Gulati, Patrick Honohan, Patrick Kenadjian, Sam Langfield, José Leandro, Michala Marcussen, Mirzha de Manuel, Jean Pisani-Ferry, Ángel Ubide, Stijn Van Nieuwerburgh, Dimitri Vayanos, Nicolas Véron, Jesús Fernández Villaverde, Jakob von Weizsäcker, an anonymous referee, and seminar participants at the Peterson Institute for International Economics, the European Commission, the IMF, Forum Future Europe, and the Institute for Law and Finance, Frankfurt am Main for helpful conversations and comments and to Cameron H. Fletcher and Madi Sarsenbayev for editorial assistance. The views expressed are those of the authors and do not necessarily represent the views of the IMF.

https://doi.org/10.1515/9783110683073-017

1. Introduction

Policy proposals to create a common public debt security for the euro area have seen a recent resurgence.[1] They respond to two main motivations. First, a financial stability concern. Euro area banks tend to be heavily exposed to their sovereign, while euro area sovereigns are exposed to shocks to their banking sector through both fiscal guarantees (deposit insurance, which remains at the national level) and the impact of banking crises on economic activity. This "doom loop" played a major destabilizing role during the euro crisis, and it mostly remains in place today (Altavilla et al. 2017). The second motivation relates to financial integration, monetary policy, and the external role of the euro. A large, liquid market in euro area debt that does not reflect the sovereign risk of specific member states would help price corporate debt, make it easier for the European Central Bank (ECB) to conduct monetary policy, and increase the attractiveness of the euro as a reserve currency (Monti 2010, Cœuré 2019).

There could be three main approaches to create a euro area safe asset. The first is through collective public guarantees. Euro area sovereigns could jointly issue "Eurobonds," backed by a joint and several guarantee, sharing both proceeds and debt service (De Grauwe and Moesen 2009, Bonnevay 2010). Alternatively, euro area members—or a euro area institution such as the European Stability Mechanism (ESM)—could guarantee portions of the outstanding debt of individual members (Delpla and Weizsäcker 2010, Bini Smaghi and Marcussen 2018).[2] The second involves creating a euro area–level fiscal authority and giving it the right to issue debt, within predefined limits, backed by a dedicated revenue stream (Ubide 2015, Zettelmeyer 2017). The third would create a (senior) financial intermediary, or a regulatory framework for private intermediaries, that would issue debt securities backed by a diversified portfolio of euro area sovereign debt (Monti 2010, Brunnermeier et al. 2011, 2017).[3] The interest collected from these

---

1 See, among others, Brunnermeier et al. (2017), ESRB (2018), European Commission (2018), Leandro and Zettelmeyer (2018a,b, 2019), Giudice et al. (2019).
2 See also Christian Hellwig and Thomas Philippon, "Eurobills, not Eurobonds," *VoxEU*, December 2, 2011, available at https://voxeu.org/article/eurobills-not-euro-bonds (accessed on September 24, 2018).
3 See also Jean-Claude Juncker and Giulio Tremonti, "E-bonds would end the crisis," *Financial Times*, December 5, 2010, available at www.astrid-online.it/static/upload/protected/Junc/Junck-er-Tremonti.pdf (accessed on June 11, 2019), and Thorsten Beck, Wolf Wagner, and Harald Uhlig, "Insulating the financial sector from the European debt crisis: Eurobonds without public guarantees," *VoxEU*, September 2011, available at https://voxeu.org/article/eurobonds-without-public-guarantees-insulating-financial-sector-european-debt-crisis (accessed on September 24, 2018).

debt holdings would be used to service the debt issued by the intermediary or intermediaries.

This paper explains and compare proposals in this third group. It focuses on three proposals.

- The first idea, developed by Brunnermeier et al. (2017), envisages the issuance—by either a public or many private intermediaries—of multitranche debt securities backed by a diversified portfolio of euro area sovereign bonds. The senior tranche of these sovereign bond-backed securities (SBBS), called European Safe Bonds or ESBies, would be sufficiently small, compared to the junior tranches, to make ESBies as safe as a German sovereign bond.
- In the second proposal, referred to as "E-bonds" (Monti 2010), a senior euro area public financial intermediary would lend fixed amounts to each euro area member state as a proportion of its GDP (and possibly the size of its outstanding debt). Seniority could be established through either statute (such as a revision to the ESM treaty) or contract, by subordinating newly issued sovereign bonds to loans from the financial intermediary. The loans would be financed by issuing bonds—"E-bonds"—backed by the diversified portfolio of loans. By setting the maximal amount that the E-bond issuer would lend to each member conservatively, E-bonds could be made arbitrarily safe.
- Third, each member state could issue debt securities in two or more tradable tranches, with the size of the senior tranche relative to the junior tranche(s) equal to the size of the loans of the E-bond issuer relative to the bonds that each member would continue to issue to the market. The senior tranches could subsequently be bundled by private intermediaries (along the lines of the SBBS proposal), who would issue single-tranche securities backed by these portfolios. Alternatively, euro area banks could be required to hold diversified portfolios of the senior tranches directly.

Of the three ideas, only the first has been subject to public debate, including a review by a high-level task force of the European Systemic Risk Board (ESRB 2018). Based on this review, the European Commission submitted a legislative proposal to the European Parliament in May 2018, which was adopted, with modifications, in April 2019 (European Commission 2018, European Parliament 2019).[4] At the same time, the idea has been criticized by some commentators, private sector participants, and euro area governments. Critics have argued that

---

4 See https://oeil.secure.europarl.europa.eu/oeil/popups/ficheprocedure.do?lang=en&reference=2018/0171(COD). The proposed regulation now needs to be considered by the Council before it can become legislation.

the supposed safety of ESBies might turn out to be an illusion if several European countries default at the same time; that there would be little demand for the junior tranches, particularly in a crisis; and that SBBS might sap liquidity from national bond markets, raising sovereign borrowing costs (De Grauwe and Ji 2018, Gabor and Vestergaard 2018).[5]

Conceptually, the three ideas are close cousins. All aim to create "safety" by combining diversification of the underlying sovereign risk with seniority. But the way these ingredients are combined and implemented institutionally differs, giving rise to surprisingly different properties. The legal and practical complications of the three proposals also differ widely.

The remainder of this chapters presents and contrasts the three proposals, drawing on a more technical analysis by Leandro and Zettelmeyer (2019). The main economic properties of each proposal are surveyed first, followed by a description of possible legal and practical complications. A quantitative comparison of the risks of the safe assets that would be generated under each proposal follows. A concluding section distills the takeaways.

---

5 See also Academic Advisory Council to the German Federal Ministry of Finance (2017); Marcello Minenna, "Why ESBies won't solve the euro area's problems," *Financial Times*, April 25, 2017, available at https://ftalphaville.ft.com/2017/04/25/2187829/guest-post-why-esbies-wont-solve-the-euro-areas-problems/ (accessed on September 24, 2018); Standard and Poor's (2017); Grégory Claeys, "Make euro area sovereign bonds safe again," *VoxEU.org*, May 2, 2018, available at https://voxeu.org/article/make-euro-area-sovereign-bonds-safe-again (accessed on September 24, 2018); Ferdinando Giugliano, "Europe's 'Safe Bonds' Are Not So Safe after All," *Bloomberg Commentary*, March 22, 2018, available at https://www.bloomberg.com/view/articles/2018-03-22/europe-s-safe-bonds-are-not-so-safe-after-all (accessed on September 24, 2018); Martin Greive, Andrea Cünnen, Frank Wiebe, and Jan Hildebrand, "Staatliche Schuldenmanager gegen neue Euro-Anleihen," *Handelsblatt*, January 29, 2018; and Wolfgang Münchau, "Eurozone reformers act as if the crisis never happened," *Financial Times*, February 28, 2018, available at https://www.ft.com/content/b55e37f0-1326-11e8-8cb6-b9ccc4c4dbbb (accessed on September 24, 2018). In June 2018 "French German roadmap for the Euro area", the French and German ministries of finance stated that "The Commission proposal for Sovereign Bond Backed Securities (SBBS) has significantly more disadvantages than potential benefits and should not be further pursued" (see https://www.bundesfinanzministerium.de/Content/EN/Standardartikel/Topics/Europe/Articles/2018-06-20-Meseberg-att1.pdf;jsessionid=7A197F85F6BF2D32E1A20A01F7FF3422?__blob=publicationFile&v=3; accessed on September 24, 2018). For a less critical view, see Goldman Sachs (2018).

2. Proposals

A. SBBS/ESBies

Brunnermeier et al. (2011, 2017) proposed the creation of a European Senior (or Safe) Bond based on a combination of diversification and tranching. A financial intermediary would purchase a diversified pool of sovereign bonds at market prices, financed by issuing securities backed by this cover pool ("sovereign bond-backed securities", SBBS) whose payoffs would be the joint payoffs of the bonds in its portfolio. The weight of each country's bonds in the portfolio would be set, by regulation, to correspond to the capital key of the ECB (which in turn reflects the relative size of nominal GDP and population), except that countries with very small debt stocks would be excluded or "underweight," while the remaining countries would be "overweight."[6]

In the version of the proposal adopted by the European Parliament in April 2019, SBBS issuers would be private entities whose sole function would be to issue SBBS in two or more tranches (e.g., senior, mezzanine, and junior or "equity"), purchase the corresponding cover pool, distribute its proceeds among investors, and exercise formal creditor rights in a restructuring event (albeit under instructions; see below). To avoid injecting any risk into the system beyond the underlying sovereign risk, SBBS issuers would be legally separate from the firms that own them and avoid any of the risks associated with market making (cover pool purchases would be based on an order book, avoiding "warehousing risk").

In any given payment period, payments to investors would observe a water-fall structure: the proceeds of the cover pool would first be used to meet the claims of the senior tranche holders, then those of the mezzanine tranche, and finally those of the junior tranche. Any cash flow volatility would thus be passed on to securities holders in line with the contractually prescribed hierarchy of claims. Hence, nonpayment by any sovereign issuer to the SBBS issuer would not constitute a default of any of the SBBS, even if the underlying sovereign bond were in default. Instead, it would trigger a predefined procedure for

---

6 The portfolio weights cannot exactly equal the ECB capital key, because the total volume of the cover pool would in that case be severely constrained by the sovereign debt outstanding in low-debt countries, particularly Estonia, which in 2018 had just €48 million in outstanding central government debt securities (0.2 percent of GDP). Estonia's ECB capital share is 0.28 percent. Hence, if the ECB capital key were to literally apply to the composition of the SBBS cover pool, the maximum SBBS volume would be 48/0.0028 = €17 billion, which is just 0.24 percent of euro area central government debt.

recovery of the underlying debt instrument. The riskiness of the senior tranche would therefore depend on the "thickness" of the subordinated tranches relative to the total SBBS volume (the "subordination level"): The higher the subordination level, the lower the claims of the senior tranche compared to the total claims, and the larger the cushion protecting the senior tranche from sovereign default. Using a default simulation model, Brunnermeier et al. (2017) argue that achieving a five-year expected loss rate as low as that of a German bund (0.5 percent in the adverse calibration of their model) would require a subordination level of about 30 percent. Based on these calculations, both ESRB (2018) and the EU regulation currently under consideration assume that the senior tranche would comprise 70 percent, the junior (equity) tranche at least 5 percent, and the mezzanine tranche the remainder.

How high is the volume of safe assets that could be generated based on the legislative resolution recently passed by the European Parliament (2019)? The resolution allows an absolute maximum deviation of up to 10 percent between the share of each country's central government debt in the cover pool and its share in the ECB capital key. At the same time, it stipulates that countries with illiquid central government debt markets would be excluded from the SBBS cover pool. Assuming that this would apply at least to Estonia, which has almost no sovereign bonds outstanding, it can be shown that the total size of the cover pool would be €920 billion, implying safe assets (senior SBBS tranches) of about €640 billion, just under 6 percent of euro area GDP (see Leandro and Zettelmeyer 2019). Even excluding Estonia, Latvia, Lithuania, and Greece from the cover pool would allow only €950 billion in senior SBBS, about 8 percent of euro area GDP. This is less than half of the euro area sovereign bonds currently held in euro area bank balance sheets (about 17 percent of euro area GDP, according to ECB data).

Generating a sufficiently large volume of senior SBBS to replace sovereign bonds in euro area bank balance sheets—and leave some for other financial institutions, such as insurance companies and pension funds, that currently hold euro area sovereign bonds—would thus require a much more flexible approach to the SBBS portfolio composition than currently stipulated in the legislation proposal. In Leandro and Zettelmeyer (2019), we provide an example in which the SBBS cover pool would be constrained in two ways. First, except for the three countries with the largest debt markets —Italy, Germany, and France— purchases of national bonds must not exceed 50 percent of the bond market (for Italy, Germany, and France the 50 percent limit can be be exceeded, so long as at least €200 billion of tradable debt remain in the market, on the grounds that liquidity as measured by bid-ask spreads appears to be lower for markets with a volume of less than €200 billion, but not more). Second, deviations from the ECB capital key must not exceed the overall deviation under the PSPP as of end-2018 (measured by the root mean squared error, which was about 0.9 percentage points). In other words, we take the deviations observed for the PSPP as a measure of the tolerance of the Eurosystem toward technically motivated deviations from the capital key. Under these assumptions, a much higher volume of senior SBBS could be generated, about €2.5 trillion, or 21 percent of euro area GDP.

Two further properties of SBBS concern their redistributive implications and their potential impact on the sovereign debt market. Unlike proposals to create common euro area safe debt using guarantees by member states, SBBS are designed to avoid any redistribution among the countries included in the cover pool. Any losses due to sovereign defaults or debt restructuring would simply be passed on to the holders of the various SBBS tranches in the prescribed order. Furthermore, since national sovereign bonds would not be subordinated to any of the SBBS tranches (the tranches only establish a seniority ranking among themselves), SBBS should not increase the marginal cost of issuance, except possibly to the extent that they reduce market liquidity by taking a portion of sovereign debt out of the market. The rules governing inclusion in the SBBS cover pool are intended to mitigate this risk. To the extent that SBBS help reduce crisis risks associated with the sovereign exposure of banks, they could of course lower country risk, and hence sovereign borrowing costs. This would be an intended effect and not a source of moral hazard.

Complications
While SBBS are conceptually simple, creating an SBBS market that meets the desired objectives and minimizes the risk of unintended consequences requires a complex structure:

1. To the extent that SBBS intermediaries are private entities, as proposed by the European Commission (2018) and the European Parliament (2019), they must be regulated to ensure that they are indeed robotic entities that do not expose SBBS holders to extra (non-sovereign) risk.
2. To be liquid, SBBS should be as homogeneous as possible both across different SBBS in terms of the country composition of the cover pools and within each SBBS in terms of the characteristics of the underlying bonds. This requires setting a standard for the composition of the SBBS cover pool. It may also require coordination among sovereign issuers to ensure that the requisite bonds are available for purchase.
3. To address the frequently voiced concern that the junior SBBS tranche might not find buyers in a crisis—potentially blocking the entire SBBS production

pipeline[7]—bonds in the SBBS cover pool must receive the same treatment in a debt restructuring as bonds held directly by investors, and countries that lose market access should be excluded from the cover pools of new SBBS.[8] The latter implies that on occasion (namely, following sovereign debt crises) the composition of the SBBS cover pool will differ slightly.

4. SBBS holders must have adequate representation in a sovereign debt restructuring. Technically, the owner of the sovereign debt security is the SBBS issuer; however, since this issuer is simply a conduit for cash flows—it has no "skin in the game"—it has no incentive to negotiate in the way that bond holders usually would, namely, to maximize the recovery value of the debt.

The legislative resolution that was just passed by the European Parliament (2019) seeks to address the first three points, at least to some extent. Point 1 (regulation of intermediaries) is addressed at length in Articles 7 and 8, which set out the obligations of the intermediaries and their investment policies. These articles state that the intermediaries' activities should be limited to issuing and servicing SBBS and require the segregation of their own assets and financial resources from those of the underlying SBBS portfolios. In addition, intermediaries are allowed to invest payments of principal or interest from the underlying sovereign bonds that are due before payments to the holders of SBBS only in cash or other highly liquid assets.

To address point 2, homogeneity of SBBS across issues, the proposal regulates the country weights in the SBBS cover pools (they cannot deviate from the ECB capital key shares by more than 10 percent), while allowing for the exclusion of particular countries from the cover pool under certain circumstances (loss of market access, illiquidity, or when their sovereign bonds are unavailable in the market). It also requires the difference in the maturities of the underlying bonds of a given SBBS issue to be no greater than six months. However, the legislative resolution is silent on the important issue of coordinated issuance of sovereign bonds to ensure the availability of the required bonds. In the absence of coordinated issuance, SBBS issuers would need to purchase some bonds on the second-

---

7 See Academic Advisory Council to the German Federal Ministry of Finance (2017) and Standard and Poor's (2017), among others.

8 These conditions may be not be necessary to ensure that SBBS never lose market access, but together with the condition that SBBS intermediaries do not introduce nonsovereign risk, they are jointly sufficient. To see this, suppose that all bonds in the SBBS cover pool enjoy market access and that the riskiness of the SBBS reflects only the risk of the sovereign bonds in that cover pool. If the SBBS (or any tranche thereof) nonetheless does not have market access, it would be possible to achieve large arbitrage profits by selling euro area sovereign bonds and using the proceeds to purchase an SBBS portfolio at a near-zero price, leading to an identical expected payment stream.

ary market. If this is not feasible at exactly the time when SBBS are issued, these bonds will need to be either bought in advance—injecting "warehousing risk" into the system—or excluded from the cover pool, which would reduce the homogeneity of different SBBS issues.

Point 3, SBBS market access, is addressed by a provision that would require the European Securities and Markets Authority to notify the European Commission when any country loses market access, which would result in the exclusion of that country's bonds from the SBBS' underlying portfolio (Article 4.3a). To prevent discrimination against bonds held by the intermediary in the case of a sovereign debt restructuring, Article 7.4a states that "Member States shall ensure that holdings of sovereign bonds by SPEs [intermediaries] enjoy the same treatment as any other holdings of the same sovereign bond or of other sovereign bonds issued with the same terms."

With respect to the final point, SBBS holder representation in a debt restructuring, the legislative resolution is silent. In effect, any losses that the SBBS cover pool might suffer are taken as a given: the fact that debt restructuring outcomes might influence those losses—and hence that SBBS holders might have an interest in influencing that outcome—is ignored. This makes sense if only a very small portion of the debt is held in SBBS cover pools: in that case, exercising the voting power of the SBBS cover pool would not make a difference, and whether and how SBBS intermediaries vote on a proposed modification of payment terms is irrelevant. However, this also means that the volume of SBBS would be so small as to be irrelevant.

For SBBS to make a difference, a significant fraction of the bond market would need to be held in the cover pool. In that case, the exercise of the associated voting rights would be expected to have an impact on the outcome of a debt restructuring. SBBS intermediaries should therefore be required to vote following instructions that maximize the interests of the SBBS holders collectively. As explained in detail by ESRB (2018), this could be achieved by (1) tasking an independent trustee to provide such instructions (one for each SBBS issue, or perhaps for all SBBS issues whose cover pools contain some debt to be restructured), or (2) requiring the SBBS issuers to follow instructions issued by holders of the "marginal" SBBS tranche, that is, the tranche whose losses are expected to be strictly greater than zero but lower than 100 percent.[9] In the first case (trustees), the regulation would need to lay out requirements for such trustees, and state

---

9 Allowing the holders of other tranches to give instructions may run counter to the collective interest of SBBS holders to maximize total recovery value, because changes in the terms of the debt restructuring may not influence the losses suffered by these holders. For example, if the mezzanine tranche is marginal, then both the junior and senior tranche holders might agree to a

whether there should be one or many trustees. In the second case, the regulation would need to specify a procedure for translating votes from holders of the marginal SBBS tranche into voting instructions to the SBBS issuer, and of course for deciding which SBBS tranche should be considered marginal. (see ESRB 2018 for details). Since the latter will depend on the expected loss given default,[10] this may in turn require some delegation to an independent entity or trustee.

Some of these complications could be avoided by creating a public SBBS intermediary, an option left open by the ESRB, but (implicitly) rejected by the European Commission (2018) and the European Parliament (2019). A public intermediary would obviate the need for regulation, might help coordinate bond issuance, and could perhaps even absorb some warehousing risk (if endowed with some amount of capital). This said, some of the problems that regulation of private intermediaries tries to solve—to ensure that the intermediary does its job and no more than its job, and does not create risks—would continue to exist and would have to be addressed through other means (a clearly defined mandate and governance structure). Furthermore, the need to represent the interests of SBBS holders in a debt restructuring, to resolve conflict of interests across SBBS tranches, and to ensure that bonds held in the SBBS cover pool are treated the same way as bonds held directly by investors would continue to arise. Perhaps more importantly, one of the charms of the SBBS proposal is precisely that although it admits a public intermediary, it does not require it and so can, in principle, be supported by member states that fear that public issuance of euro area safe assets could give rise to implicit guarantees.

B. E-bonds

As in the SBBS approach, an intermediary would hold a portfolio of government debt and issue securities—"E-bonds"—backed by this portfolio (Monti 2010; Leandro and Zettelmeyer 2018a, 2018b, 2019; Giudice et al. 2019). Unlike SBBS, however, E-bonds would be issued as a single tranche. Like ESBies, this would be made safe through a combination of diversification and seniority, but seniority would apply at the level of the intermediary issuing the E-bonds, which would have preferred creditor status. For this reason, the intermediary would need to be

---

restructuring that is deeper than necessary, since the former are wiped out anyway while the latter are repaid in full anyway.

10 The marginal tranche is usually the junior tranche, but in some cases—if debt restructurings affect a large share of the cover pool, and losses given default are high enough—it could be the mezzanine or even the senior tranche.

a public entity. The E-bond intermediary could be equipped with (small) levels of capital to create even safer assets; however, this is not an essential feature. In a barebones design, any losses suffered by the E-bond issuer would be passed on to the holders of E-bonds, just as any losses suffered by SBBS intermediaries would be passed on to SBBS holders.

In principle, the intermediary could fund governments at market interest rates or at some other interest rate. In the first case, it would be purchasing bonds in the primary or secondary markets (as in the SBBS approach); in the latter, it would be originating loans. Because of the intermediary's preferred creditor status, purchases at market prices would lead to large profits over time. If redistributed to sovereigns in proportion to their borrowing (or alternatively, a capital key), this would imply large net transfers from countries with high borrowing spreads to countries with low spreads, since the market prices of high-spread countries reflect far higher risk than is borne by the senior E-bond intermediary (Leandro and Zettelmeyer 2018a). Since higher-spread countries tend to be poorer, this is politically implausible. The E-bond proposal therefore assumes the second possibility, in which the intermediary extends loans at a uniform interest rate that covers its funding and operating costs. The ESM currently operates along similar lines, except that it lends only to crisis countries, whereas the E-bond intermediary would lend to all euro area sovereigns. Because all borrowers would face the same interest rate, this implies expected transfers in the opposite direction, from lower-risk to higher-risk countries. However, as will be shown below, these transfers would be small in magnitude, because the risk that would be redistributed would be low (thanks to the E-bond issuer's preferred creditor status).

The riskiness of E-bonds depends on the riskiness of the loan portfolio held by the E-bond issuer, which in turn depends on the share of each sovereign's debt that it holds. If the share is low, this means that the share of subordinated market debt (the subordination level) is high relative to the volume of senior loans. This implies a high level of protection for the E-bond holders, as the E-bond issuer can lose money only if the country's sovereign bond holders receive nothing at all. Hence, the volume that the E-bond issuer lends to each country will determine both the total volume of E-bonds (equal to the size of the cover pool, since E-bonds are issued in one tranche) and the riskiness of E-bonds, by determining the composition of the cover pool and the subordination levels for each country.

In Leandro and Zettelmeyer (2019), we analyze two options for deciding the level of lending of the E-bond issuer to each euro area sovereign.

- The E-bond issuer could simply lend the same share of GDP to each member, with the GDP share calibrated to achieve the desired safety level. This would lead to a portfolio that is fairly close to the ECB capital key,[11] but it would also imply that for countries whose share of sovereign bonds in GDP is below the limit, sovereign debt markets would disappear entirely. For those countries, there would be no protective cushion of subordinated debt, meaning that any default—even with very small losses given default—would lower the payments to E-bond holders.

- To avoid this problem, the E-bond issuer could observe *two* lending limits: one expressed as a share of GDP and one as a share of total central government debt. These could be set to maximize the total volume of purchases, subject to (1) achieving a desired safety level and (2) not deviating from the ECB capital keys by more than the ECB's PSPP (as discussed in the previous section).

As it turns out, the volumes of E-bonds that can be generated under these two approaches are not all that different. Assuming that the desired safety level is the same as in the SBBS approach (a 0.5 percent five-year expected loss rate, computed using the Brunnermeier et al. (2017) default simulation model), it would range from about €2.2 trillion using the one-limit rule to €2.4 trillion using the two-limit rule. The lending limits on which these volumes are based are 18.7 percent of GDP under the one-limit rule and either 22.8 percent of GDP or 52.5 percent of central government debt under the two-limit rule, whichever is smaller. The fact that the GDP limit is slightly higher in the two-limit rule reflects the presence of the second limit. Ceteris paribus, this reduces the riskiness of the E-bond, since it implies that, for every country, there will be a substantial cushion of subordinated market debt that protects the E-bond issuer from default. To achieve the same overall safety level as in the one-limit case, the GDP-based lending constraint can hence be somewhat relaxed. Whether the GDP constraint or the debt constraint is binding for any given country depends on whether outstanding sovereign debt is higher or lower than 22.8/52.5 = 43.4 percent of GDP. Germany, for example, has only 33 percent of GDP in central government bonds outstanding, so the debt constraint is binding; the intermediary lends debt corresponding to 52.5 percent of the current sovereign debt stock to Germany, which represents 17.4 percent of GDP. Italy's sovereign bonds are about 106 percent of GDP, so the GDP constraint is binding and the intermediary issues loans worth 22.8 percent of Italian GDP, corresponding to 21.5 percent of the sovereign debt stock. As a result, the implicit subordination level, i.e., the share of subordinated bonds in total sovereign debt would be much higher for Italy

---

11 It does not quite correspond to the ECB capital key because the latter is based on population as well as GDP.

(100-21.5 = 78.5 percent) than for Germany (100-52.5 =47.5 percent). Conse-quently, although Italian debt is riskier than German debt, from the perspective of the E-bond issuer lending to Italy might not be riskier than lending to Germany. Whether the E-bond issuer takes any risk at all depends on the maximum assumed losses-given-default for each country. If these are lower than the the subordination level, they would be assumed entirely by the subordinated bond holders, and the E-bond issuer would face no risk. If they are higher than the subordination level, a default would "wipe out" the holdings of the subordinated bond holders, and the E-bond issuer would need to bear the residual loss.

In contrast with the SBBS approach, in which the intermediary receives interest that reflects borrowing risk, the E-bond issuer would charge the same interest to all its sovereign borrowers. Since these are not equally risky, this implies some long-run redistribution among euro area countries. But how much? In Leandro and Zettelmeyer (2019) we show that, under the assumptions of the Brunnermeier et al. (2019) default simulation model and depending on the lending rule used, total expected transfers amount to €7.5-8 billion over five years, or about €1.5 billion per year. In relative terms, this is not high (less than 1 percent of the annual EU budget), reflecting the fact that, due to its seniority, the E-bond issuer does not bear much sovereign risk. As one would expect, redistribution would occur mostly at the expense of Germany and France, who do not contribute to the riskiness of the intermediary but pay a large share of the issuer's funding cost. The beneficiaries are some of the lower rated countries. Interestingly, Italy would be a net contribu-tor, reflecting the fact that the cushion of subordinated Italian debt protecting the E-bond issuer—would turn out to be very high (almost 80 percent). Thus, from the perspective of the E-bond issuer, lending to Italy would be virtually risk-free.

Because E-bonds would give rise to some (albeit modest) redistribution benefitting countries with higher fiscal risks, it is natural to ask whether they would create moral hazard, i.e., weaken fiscal discipline in these countries. The answer is no, because the cost of borrowing from the market would rise as a result of the fact that sovereign bonds are now subordinated to loans from the E-bond issuer. Because E-bond volumes would be capped, the only way to expand borrowing would be to issue more bonds to the market, which would be subordi-nated to the loans from the intermediary. Hence, the marginal cost of borrowing would rise compared to the status quo. The magnitude of this effect can be computed by assuming that yields of subordinated bonds would increase to equalize the expected returns on subordinated and unsubordinated instruments. In Leandro and Zettelmeyer (2019), we show that based on the average loss-given-default (LGD) assumption implicit in the Brunnermeier et al. (2017) default simu-lation model, which range from from from 37 to almost 70 percent, depending on the credit rating of the country as well as default probabilities inferred from market yields observed in April 2019, the cost of borrowing from the market would rise by about 20 and 80 basis points in most countries. The increase tends to be smaller for highly rated countries and (for given credit ratings) for countries with higher subordination levels. Germany is an outlier in one direction, with an expected increase in marginal borrowing costs of only 3 basis points. Greece is an outlier in the other direction, with an expected increase of over 200 basis points.

Importantly, the fact that the marginal borrowing cost goes up does not mean that the overall, or average, borrowing cost rises in each country. On one hand, market borrowing becomes more expensive, but on the other, countries now have access to a low-cost borrowing source, namely, the E-bond issuer. These effects roughly offset each other. They do not *exactly* offset each other only because of the presence of transfers.[12] Thus, the average borrowing cost of Germany and other highly rated borrowers ends up being slightly higher than in the status quo, while the average borrowing cost of Spain, Portugal, Cyprus, and Greece—countries that are the beneficiaries of net transfer—drops slightly. This is easiest to see for Germany: whereas Germany previously borrowed at the bund rate, it now satisfies 52.5 percent of its borrowing needs through lending from the E-bond issuer—on which it still pays the bund rate, since E-bonds are calibrated to be as safe as bunds—and the rest from the market, where borrowing costs are up slightly (by 3 basis points). Germany's overall borrowing costs are thus slightly higher (by just under 1.5 basis points). Since euro area fundamentals are assumed to be unchanged, this higher borrowing cost must be offset by lower borrowing costs elsewhere in the system—namely, among the lower-rated borrowers. Importantly, however, the intended effect of E-bonds is to change the fundamentals of the system, through regulation that would encourage banks to hold them as "safe assets." To the extent that this reduces the doom loop between banks and sovereigns and increases the financial stability of the euro area as a whole, it might reduce borrowing costs even in the highly rated countries.

Complications

The E-bond approach avoids most of the complications of privately issued SBBS, albeit at the expense of creating some new ones. Because there are no private intermediaries, there is no need to create a regulatory structure to supervise them and ensure that they do not create counterparty risk. There is no junior tranche,

---

12 Were it not for the presence of redistribution—and abstracting from any impact of E-bonds on the overall safety of the European financial system—the Modigliani-Miller theorem would hold, which would predict that the overall funding costs of the sovereign should be independent of its capital (financing) structure.

so no regulation is required to ensure it maintains market access. Homogeneity of the E-bond is easy to establish as there is just one issuer. In collaboration with national debt management offices, this entity could match the maturity structure of its loan portfolio with the desired maturity structure of its bond issuance.

The matter of bond holder representation in a sovereign debt restructuring does not disappear entirely but is heavily mitigated by the fact that the "marginal" creditor group almost always consists of bond holders, so debt restructuring negotiations and/or debt exchange offers could proceed as would be the case today (see, for example, Buchheit et al. 2019). The only exception is a situation in which the bond holders would be fully wiped out, in which case the E-bond issuer would become the marginal creditor. Because it would be unsuitable for the E-bond issuer to conduct debt restructuring negotiations on behalf of the E-bond holders—both because the issuer is a public sector entity and because it has no "skin in the game," as any losses are passed on to E-bond holders—a mechanism would be needed through which the E-bond issuer receives instructions from the E-bond holders, along the lines discussed by ESRB for the SBBS approach.

The main new complication, compared to the SBBS approach, is the need to establish the preferred creditor status of the E-bond issuer in a way that is respected both by euro area sovereigns and by the bond holders subordinated to loans of the E-bond issuer. The first condition requires a change in either the ESM Treaty or EU law that would require signatories/member states that borrow from the E-bond issuer to service these loans before making any payments to bond holders. This obligation would be enforced through the same legal channels as other EU treaty obligations. Immunizing sovereigns from legal action by bond holders may require an additional step, namely contractual subordination. This would have the advantage of covering bonds issued both inside and outside the euro area, whereas an approach based only on treaty or domestic statutes would cover only the former.

Contractual subordination means writing into every sovereign bond contract issued by a euro area sovereign, regardless of governing law, a provision that the bond is subordinated to any past and future claims held by the E-bond issuer. This could be achieved through a modification of the pari passu clause, which would state that the bonds rank equally with all other debts of the state *except* obligations arising from international treaties to which the sovereign is a party.[13]

---

13 Language of this type appears in Italy's 2013 Fiscal Agency agreement with Citibank, written in anticipation of a possible issuance of Italian sovereign bonds under New York law, but apparently never used: "The Securities are the direct, unconditional and general and...unsecured obligations of Italy and will rank equally with all other evidences of indebtedness issued in accordance with the Fiscal Agency Agreement and with all other unsecured and unsubordinated

A final question concerns the transition to the new steady state, in which the central government debt stock of each member would consist only of subordinated bonds and loans from the E-bond issuer. The transition phase would begin with passage of the necessary treaty or treaty change. This would lay out the maximum lending volumes for each country and establish formal seniority of the E-bond issuer with respect to all bonds that are issued after the treaty change goes into effect.

Having established the legal framework, one approach would be to immediately begin issuing new debt in the form of loans and subordinated bonds in their steady state proportions (for example, for Spain, this would be €30 of loans for every €70 units of debt under the two-limit rule). If a debt restructuring were to occur during the transition phase—before existing bonds have been fully replaced —nonsubordinated bonds might need to be restructured to ensure that E-bonds receive the same degree of protection as they would in steady state. As long as the existing bonds have not been subordinated legally (via domestic law or treaty), this approach would likely hold up in court (Buchheit 2018). Importantly, however, the sovereign cannot formally commit to pursuing such a strategy, because doing so could be considered tantamount to legal subordination. Hence, the treatment of the existing sovereign bond stock would have to remain unspecified ex ante, creating uncertainty that may raise the cost of borrowing for the E-bond issuer, and hence the cost of lending to each country, beyond what it would be in steady state.[14]

To address this problem, several options could be explored.

The first is to make the E-bond issuer senior, via treaty or treaty change, without including any language that limits this seniority to bonds issued after the treaty change, thereby subordinating the existing debt stock rather than just new debt. This might be consistent with the pari passu clauses of existing bonds— which prohibit formal subordination of the securities by other debt instruments— as long as loans by the E-bond issuer do not constitute debt instruments within

---

general obligations of Italy for money borrowed, except for such obligations as may be preferred by mandatory provisions of international treaties and similar obligations to which Italy is a party." See Gelpern, Anna, 'Italy's Pari Passu Scrubbing' (2013) April 17 <www.creditslips.org/creditslips/2013/04/italys-pari-passu-scrubbing.html> accessed on June 11, 2019.

14 Let J denote the new junior bonds, L the senior loans, and O the outstanding, unsubordinated bonds. The steady state subordination level is given by $s = J/(J+L)$. The subordination level during transition, denoted s_t, may be different, however, depending on the treatment of the outstanding bonds. If outstanding bonds are treated the same as junior bonds—i.e., written off before inflicting losses on loans from the E-bond issuer—then $s_t = (J+O)/(J+L+O)$, which is larger than s as long as $O > 0$. If outstanding bonds are treated the same as senior loans, on the other hand, then $s_t = (J)/(J+L+O)$, which is smaller than s for $O > 0$.

the meaning of these clauses. This would follow the example of IMF loans, which are considered senior without violating the pari passu clauses in government bonds. The caveat is that IMF claims are senior by custom rather than by statute. If the reason why the seniority of the IMF does not conflict with pari passu is that this seniority is not formalized—rather than that IMF loans are not debt obligations in the usual sense but some other kind of claim—then this option will not work. For the reasons explained above (binding euro area sovereigns) it is essential to write the seniority of the E-bond issuer into a treaty signed by euro area members.

A second option is to issue new debt in the form of loans and subordinated bonds in steady state proportions, supported by a legal and institutional structure that ensures that any losses are distributed between old and new debt in proportion to their outstanding volumes. This could look as follows:

1. Each euro area member issues new debt by simultaneously borrowing from the E-bond issuer and issuing to the market with identical maturity, in steady state proportions.
2. Each bundle of new debt issued (and coming due) at the same time is represented by a trustee in a debt restructuring.
3. Trustees are required (by statute or debt contracts) to distribute any proceeds in order of priority (i.e., first to the E-bond issuer and then to the bond holders).
4. The statute (treaty) governing E-bonds commits all euro area governments to offer all trustees the same menu of securities/cash, in the event of a debt restructuring, as to the holders of "old" bonds.

This structure achieves the same degree of protection of the senior sovereign debt tranche (the loan by the E-bond issuer) by ensuring that *in combination*, the new senior and subordinated debt are treated no worse than the outstanding, unsubordinated debt. Hence, the loss that the subordinated bond needs to absorb in order to fully protect the senior debt equals the pro rata losses suffered by the new debt instruments. This implies that the senior debt will be fully protected if and only if the LGD is smaller than the share of the junior debt in the *new* debt, as opposed to its share in the total debt.

If such a structure were to prove infeasible, an alternative approach would be to begin the transition phase by issuing *all* new debt in the form of bonds that are contractually subordinated to (future) loans from the E-bond issuer. Sovereigns would begin to borrow from the E-bond issuer only after the ratio of existing sovereign bonds to new bonds is equal to the steady state ratio between loans and new bonds. For example, for Spain this point would be reached when the existing (nonsubordinated) bonds have been reduced to about 30 percent of the bond stock. At that point, maturing old debt issues would be replaced by loans from the E-bond issuer, while maturing new bonds would be replaced by new bonds and loans from the E-bond issuer in steady state proportions. The disadvantage of this approach is that it would take a long time – more than 10 years – before E-bond "production" could even begin. To accelerate the process once it has started, old bonds could be bought back, financed by loans from the E-bond issuer. To start producing E-bonds immediately, it may be possible to additionally use debt swaps. For example, if the steady subordination level is s (e.g., 70 percent), then s percent of the old bonds could be retired through a voluntary debt exchange offer involving new bonds, and the rest bought back by loans financed by the E-bond issuer.

C. Multitranche Sovereign Bond Issuance, Followed by Pooling

There is a third approach, which is conceptually very close to the E-bond proposal but would not require a public intermediary. Euro area sovereigns would commit to issue bonds in several tranches, in proportions laid out by an EU regulation or an intergovernmental treaty (Wendorff and Mahle 2015). To keep the structure analogous to the E-bond proposal, assume that there would be just two tranches: one senior and the other subordinated to all outstanding senior tranches (i.e., not just the senior tranche of the same bond). Any shortfall in payments would be absorbed by all available junior tranches before any senior tranches take a "hit."

In a second step, senior tranches could be pooled to diversify remaining risk. Depending on the objective, this may or may not require a financial intermediary. If the objective is merely to shield banks from sovereign risk, the pooling could be done by the banks themselves, prodded by appropriate regulation that penalizes deviations from ECB capital key weights. In this minimalist version, there would be no homogeneous, tradable common safe asset. Creating a market in such safe assets—for example, to make the euro more attractive as a reserve currency, or to support euro area monetary policy operations—would require financial interme-diaries to issue bonds backed by identically composed cover pools of senior tranches. As in the SBBS proposal, but unlike the E-bond proposal, this task could be performed by (regulated) private entities. The reason for this is that seniority in this case is not associated with a specific creditor but rather with the debt instrument itself, which, unlike the loans of the E-bond issuer, would be tradable and priced by the market.

As in the E-bond proposal, the volume and safety of the senior instrument would depend on the subordination level, i.e., the volume of junior tranches as a share of the total debt issued. If one assumes that the volume of senior tranches would be limited in the same way as the volume of senior lending by the E-bond issuer discussed in the previous section – that is, either as 18.7 percent of GDP of debt or as the minimum of 22.8 percent of GDP and 52.5 percent of central government debt – the proposal would lead to the same volume of safe assets as in the E-bond proposal.

In the minimalist version of the multitranche bond issuance proposal, banks would buy portfolios of senior tranches in the primary or secondary bond markets, with portfolio weights equal to the shares of each country's senior tranches in relation to all senior tranches. In the version that aims to create a tradable, homogeneous safe asset, competitive financial intermediaries would buy portfolios of the senior sovereign tranche, using the same weights. To maximize the volume of the safe asset, only these intermediaries would be allowed to bid for senior tranches. Because all senior assets would end up in the safe asset cover pools, there would be no secondary market in the senior tranches. To the extent that the volume of safe assets generated in this way exceeds the volume of safe assets that banks and other institutions purchase to hold to maturity, there would, however, be a (liquid) secondary market in the safe asset itself.

With senior debt issuance constrained either by a GDP limit or by both a GDP limit and a debt share, any additional issuance would have to take the form of junior bonds, so marginal borrowing costs in the multitranche bond issuance proposal would rise, relative to the status quo, by the same amounts as in the E-bond proposal. Unlike the E-bonds proposal, however, multitranche debt issuance would not give rise to redistribution. The reason is that the yield of the senior tranche would differ across countries, reflecting differences in risk—unlike the interest rate that countries would pay to the E-bond issuer, which would be the same for all countries. For the same reason, assuming unchanged fundamentals, average debt costs should be unchanged for all issuers compared to the status quo (i.e., one-tranche issuance). That said, the purpose of the proposal (and of the two preceding proposals) is to strengthen euro area fundamentals, by bolstering the financial stability of the euro area and/or raising world demand for euro area debt through the presence of the safe asset. If that is the case, borrowing costs of euro area issuers should decline.

Complications

One consequence of the multitranche bond issuance proposal is that it would lead to smaller markets in tradable sovereign bonds. The yields of these bonds would be higher than those of today's euro area sovereign bonds, and likely more volatile, because they would be subordinated to senior tranches held in banks or safe asset cover pools, and perhaps because they would be less liquid. However, this is no different from E-bonds, and at least in part an intended consequence of the proposal (to raise market discipline while keeping average borrowing costs unchanged). The unintended part is that bond yields could become more sensitive to changes not only in country fundamentals but also in market sentiment. In both the E-bond proposal and the multitranche issuance proposal, it is hence essential that countries have reliable access to official liquidity (e.g., through prequalified access to the ESM).

A further complication that the multitranche issuance proposal shares with the E-bond proposal is the transition problem. The choices and trade-offs are the same as in the E-bond case, with one important exception: because the senior tranches are debt instruments held by the market, rather than loans from a specific public institution, it would likely be impossible to argue that they do not constitute debt instruments within the meaning of the pari passu clauses in currently outstanding bonds. Hence, the possibility of subordinating the existing debt stock seems remote. The two remaining approaches would continue to be feasible, however. In particular, there are at least two ways of engineering the transition without exposing the holders of senior tranches to higher risk than they would face in steady state:

- Create a structure that ensures that losses are shared pro rata between existing bonds and new bonds and are subsequently distributed among the tranches of new bonds in the contractual priority order. With this structure in place, begin issuing all new bonds in several tranches, in their steady state proportions.
- Alternatively, begin by issuing only bonds subordinated to (future) senior bonds, until the share of new (subordinated) bonds in outstanding central government debt is equal to the targeted subordination level. Only then would senior bonds be issued—up to limits specified by statute or in the contracts of junior bonds—replacing old bonds as these mature.

In both cases, the process could be accelerated using debt exchange operations.

Additional complications depend on which variant of the proposal is pursued. In the minimalist version of the proposal, senior tranches would be held by banks directly with no intermediaries to worry about. The version with intermediaries would raise some of the same complications as in the SBBS proposal, but to a lesser extent. The need to regulate intermediaries to ensure that they do not add risk to the system and to ensure the homogeneity of the safe asset carries over to the multitranche issuance proposal. The need to design regulation to ensure market access of the junior SBBS tranche does not carry over, however, since the safe asset would be issued in just one tranche; instead, it is the market access of the national junior bond tranches that must be protected, as described above. Finally, there would be a need to regulate representation of the holders of the safe asset in a debt restructuring, but, as in the E-bond proposal, this is mitigated by the fact that the "marginal" creditors are almost always the junior bond holders. To address extreme defaults in which these would be fully wiped out, the safe bond contract would need to incorporate a mechanism through which the financial intermediaries holding the senior tranches receive instructions from the ultimate bond holders, as discussed in ESRB for the SBBS approach.

3. Safety Comparison

All safe assets discussed in this paper could be constructed to be equally safe in terms of expected losses, namely, with a five-year expected loss rate of 0.5 percent according to the Brunnermeier et al. (2017) default simulation model (adverse calibration). However, the *distribution* of losses would not be the same. One way of illustrating these differences is to compute the loss rates associated with catastrophic "tail events"—i.e., losses that occur with a specific, low probability. Following ESRB (2018), we focus on a standard measure for such tail losses: the value at risk (VaR) at threshold probability p, defined as the maximum loss occurring with at least probability p. Since small losses are more likely than large losses, the VaR declines as the threshold probability increases. The maximum loss rate is given by the VaR at $p = 0$. In the context of this paper, this represents the case where *all* euro area countries default at the highest possible LGD rate assumed in the Brunnermeier et al. (2017) default risk model.

Figure 1 shows VaRs for threshold probabilities between zero and 5 percent for E-bonds/multitranche issuance in the two portfolio variants corresponding to the one-limit and two-limit selection rules, as well as two variants of ESBies: based on the assumptions implicit in the EU legislative resolution (leading to portfolio weights very close to the ECB capital key and a volume of safe assets of below €1 trillion) and based on the more flexible purchase rule discussed in the previous section (implying portfolio weights that are slightly further off the ECB capital key and a volume of safe assets of up to €2.5 trillion). For E-bonds, an additional variant is shown, based on the two-limit rule, which assumes that the intermediary would have some capital (3 percent of its liabilities).

The figure implies that ESBies would be fully protected against risks occurring with probability of about 3–4 percent or higher. They would also be more protected than E-bonds or pools of senior national bonds against tail risks between about 1.7 and 4 percent. This is because ESBies would fully protect against individual or multiple defaults by euro area member states as long as *aggregate* losses do not exceed the size of the subordinated SBBS tranches. Under the worst-case LGD assumptions underlying figure 1, which are taken from Brunnermeier et al. (2017) and range from 40 percent for Germany to 95 percent for Greece, ESBies would still offer full protection if all countries with credit ratings worse than Ireland default—including both Italy and Spain. Once this cushion of junior and mezzanine bonds is depleted, however, holders of ESBies bear the full losses of any further defaults. This explains why the VaR curve for ESBies rises steeply once *p* drops below a critical value. If all euro area countries default, the total loss suffered by the SBBS portfolio (under worst-case LGD assumptions) would be 59 percent in the version based on the European Parliament's legislative resolution and 61 percent in the more flexible version (for the computations, see Leandro and Zettelmeyer 2019). 30 percentage points of this loss would be absorbed by the holders of subordinated tranches. Hence, in the worst case, corresponding to *p* = 0, ESBies would lose (59-30)/70 = 41 percent of their value in the first case, and (61-30)/70 = 44 percent of their value in the second.

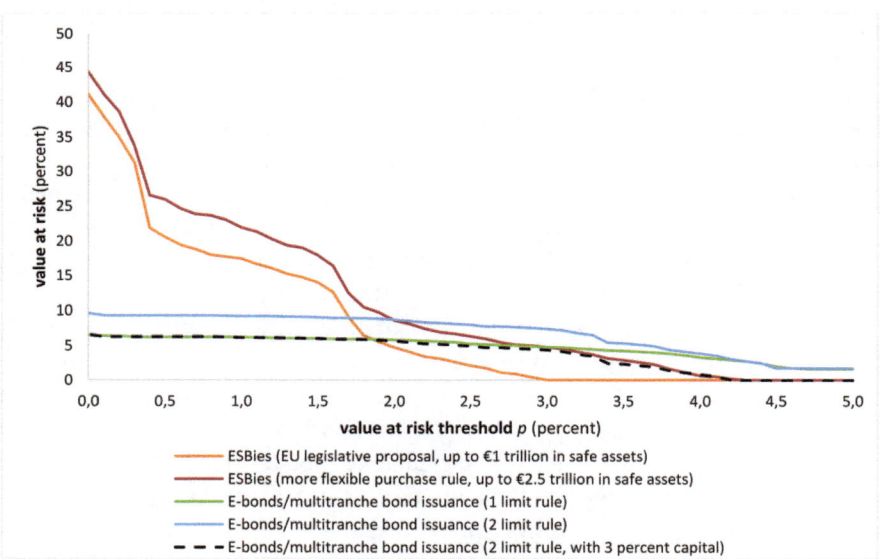

Figure 1: Value at Risk of alternative safe assets at different probability thresholds
Note: The figure shows the Value at Risk (VaR), or maximum loss suffered with probability *p* or lower, for five alternative safe assets. The VaR for E-bonds/multitranche bonds issuance (2-limit rule, with 3 percent capital) is computed by subtracting 3 percentage points from the VaR for E-bonds/multitranche bonds issuance (2-limit rule).
Source: Leandro and Zettelmeyer (2019), based on the adverse calibration of the default simulation model by Brunnermeier et al. (2017).

In contrast, E-bonds and pools of senior national tranches bear losses any time the losses given default of a *single* country exceed the portion of its debt held by subordinated debt holders. However, they continue to offer protection regardless of how many countries default, including full protection for most large borrowers. For example, under the one-limit lending rule, 43.3 percent of German debt takes the form of subordinated bonds, whereas the maximum LGD assumed for Germany is 40 percent. Hence, the highest LGD that the E-bond issuer could pass through to the E-bond holders on account of a German default is zero, as there would be enough subordinated instruments to absorb the blow. For this reason, as the probability threshold goes to zero, the VaRs of national tranching and pooling and E-bonds converge to much lower levels than the VaR of ESBies. The maximal loss, corresponding to a default of all euro area countries, is a surprisingly small number, namely just 6.5 for the one-limit rule and 9.6 percent for the two-limit rule. The reason is that the maximal losses given default corresponding to the senior loans (or tranches) of the large issuers—France, Germany, Belgium, even Italy, on account of its high subordination level—are zero or close to zero, whereas the portfolio weights of countries with higher maximal losses given default are small.

To offer even better protection against severe defaults by large countries or combinations of smaller countries, the E-bond intermediary could be capitalized. Figure 1 shows that 3 percent capitalization would offer the same degree of protection as ESBies for moderate tail risks, along with better protection against extreme risks. The black dashed line represents a downward shift of the VaR for E-bonds (two-limit case) by 3 percentage points. This results in a VaR that initially follows about the same curve as the VaR for ESBies under the more flexible purchase rule, but eventually converges at just 6.6 percent of face value (9.6 percent minus 3 percentage points of capital).

4. Conclusion

This paper evaluates proposals to create a safe asset for the euro area that do not require collective guarantees, nor the creation of a euro area–level fiscal authority which remains politically improbable in the foreseeable future. We compared a proposal to create multitranche, sovereign bond-backed securities (SBBS)—the most senior of which would be the "safe" asset—to two other designs that have received less attention. In the "E-bonds" proposal, a senior, public financial intermediary would lend to all euro area members up to a limit set as a share GDP —or as a share of GDP and a share of the central government debt stock, whichever is smaller—and issue single-tranche securities backed by this portfolio of loans. Alternatively, euro area sovereigns could agree to issue sovereign bonds in several tranches, with a limit on senior issuance set as a share of GDP (or both as share of GDP and a share of the central government debt stock, whichever is smaller). Banks could be required to hold diversified portfolios of these senior tranches. Alternatively, following the SBBS template, regulated private intermediaries could purchase portfolios of senior tranches and issue a homogeneous, single-tranche security backed by these portfolios.

Our comparison does not produce a clear winner. In principle, all three proposals could be designed to generate roughly the same volume of safe assets: about €2.5 trillion, based on central government debt only (while a legislative resolution recently passed by the European Parliament would seem to constrain ESBies to less than €1 trillion, it could be modified to allow larger volumes). Beyond this similarity, the three proposals have different properties that might appeal to some but not to others. SBBS/ESBies and safe assets based on senior national bonds issued to the market would avoid redistribution across countries, while E-bonds would involve some (albeit minor) redistribution, because all sovereigns borrowing from the public intermediary would be charged the same interest rate. E-bonds and multi-tranche bond issuance would provide better protection than ESBies in such worst-case scenarios but would be less effective than ESBies in protecting their holders from deep defaults of individual countries (or a handful of individual countries) in which losses given default exceed the subordination level. SBBS/ESBies would have no impact on the cost of borrowing in sovereign debt markets (except possibly through liquidity effects). In contrast, both E-bonds and multi-tranche bond issuance would raise the marginal cost of borrowing from the market—without, however, increasing the overall cost of borrowing for high-debt countries compared to the status quo, since the higher cost of issuing subordinated instruments would be offset by the lower cost of borrowing through senior instruments.

Among the three proposals, only SBBS have so far received extensive public scrutiny, as well as considerable criticism. Based on the analysis in this paper, much of this criticism appears unwarranted. In particular, the claim that ESBies could not withstand correlated defaults is untrue: while they would suffer higher losses than E-bonds or pools of senior national bonds in a crisis in which most euro area countries (including France and/or Germany) default, they would do well in only slightly less extreme crises, in which most lower-rated countries default. Worries that the junior tranche might not find buyers and that SBBS might sap liquidity from national bond markets can be addressed through regulation: by excluding countries that lose market access from the SBBS cover pool, by prohibiting sovereigns from discriminating against SBBS intermediaries, and by placing limits on the volume of sovereign debt that SBBS issuers can buy.

This said, making ESBies work as intended requires a lot of well-designed regulation—more so than the alternative proposals. Furthermore, the legislative resolution adopted by the European Parliament is still some way off from what would be needed: on one hand, it appears to excessively constrain the volume of SBBS that could be produced; on the other, it fails to regulate the representation of SBBS holders in the event of a debt restructuring. That said, the competitors have their own issues. The E-bond proposal, for example, is predicated on euro area sovereigns respecting the seniority of the E-bond issuer, even when the holders of (subordinated) bonds are their own citizens.

There are several feasible approaches to creating a euro area safe asset. While none is free of drawbacks, the two lesser known ideas analyzed in this paper—E-bonds and multitranche national bond issuance, with GDP-based caps on senior issues—deserve a more thorough examination than they have received so far.

References

Academic Advisory Council to the German Federal Ministry of Finance (Wissenschaftlicher Beirats beim Bundesministerium der Finanzen). 2017. *Ursachengerechte Therapie des Staaten-Banken-Nexus, Letter to German Finance Minister Wolfgang Schäuble* (January 20).

Altavilla, Carlo, Marco Pagano and Saverio Simonelli. 2017. Bank Exposures and Sovereign Stress Transmission. *Review of Finance* 21, no. 6: 2103–39.

Bini Smaghi, Lorenzo and Michala Marcussen. 2018. *Strengthening the Euro Area Architecture: A Proposal for Purple Bonds.* SUERF Policy Note Issue No 35 (May).

Bonnevay, Frédéric. 2010. The argument for a Eurobond: A coordinated strategy for emerging from the crisis. Institut Montaigne Policy Paper (February). Paris.

Brunnermeier, Markus K., Luis Garicano, Philip Lane, Marco Pagano, Ricardo Reis, Tano Santos, David Thesmar, Stijn Van Nieuwerburgh, and Dimitri Vayanos. 2011. *European Safe Bonds (ESBies).* Euro-nomics Group.

Brunnermeier, Markus K., Sam Langfield, Marco Pagano, Ricardo Reis, Stijn Van Nieuwerburgh, and Dimitri Vayanos. 2017. ESBies: Safety in the Tranches. *Economic Policy* 32, no. 90: 175–219.

Buchheit, Lee C. 2018. *The Pari Passu Fallacy – Requiescat in Pace (La Falacia pari-passu – Descanse en paz).* Available at https://papers.ssrn.com/sol3/papers.cfm?abstract_id=3108862 (accessed on June 11, 2019).

Buchheit, Lee, Guillaume Chabert, Chanda DeLong, and Jeromin Zettelmeyer. 2019. *How to Restructure Sovereign Debt: Lessons from Four Decades.* PIIE Working Paper 19-8. Washington: Peterson Institute for International Economics.

Cœuré, Benoît. 2019. *The Euro's Global Role in a Changing World: A Monetary Policy Perspective.* Speech at the Council on Foreign Relations, New York City (February 15). Available at https://www.ecb.europa.eu/press/key/date/2019/html/ecb.sp190215~15c89d887b.en.html (accessed on June 11, 2019).

De Grauwe, Paul, and Wim Moesen. 2009. *Gains for All: A Proposal for a Common Eurobond.* CEPS Policy Brief. Brussels: Centre for European Policy Studies (April 3).

De Grauwe, Paul, and Yuemei Ji. 2018. *How Safe Is a Safe Asset?* CEPS Policy Insight No. 2018-08. Brussels: Centre for European Policy Studies.

Delpla, Jacques, and Jakob von Weizsäcker. 2010. *The Blue Bond Proposal.* Bruegel Policy Brief 2010/03. Brussels: Bruegel.

European Commission. 2018. Proposal for a Regulation of the European Parliament and of the Council on Sovereign Bond-Backed Securities. COM(2018) 339 final. Brussels.

European Parliament. 2019. European Parliament legislative resolution of 16 April 2019 on the proposal for a regulation of the European Parliament and of the Council on sovereign bond-backed securities P8_TA(2019)0373. Brussels.

European Systemic Risk Board (ESRB) High-Level Task Force on Safe Assets. 2018. *Sovereign Bond-Backed Securities: A Feasibility Study.* Frankfurt.

Gabor, Daniela, and Jakob Vestergaard. 2018. Chasing Unicorns: The European Single Safe Asset. *Competition and Change* 22, no. 2: 140–64.

Giudice, Gabriele, Mirzha de Manuel, Zenon Kontolemis, and Daniel Monteiro. 2019. *A European Safe Asset to Complement National Government Bonds.* Draft. Forthcoming working paper.

Goldman Sachs. 2018. Making EMU More Resilient—Assessing the 'Safe Bonds' Proposal. European Economics Analyst (March 14).

Leandro, Álvaro, and Jeromin Zettelmeyer. 2018a. *The Search for a Euro Area Safe Asset.* PIIE Working Paper No. 18-3. Washington: Peterson Institute for International Economics.

Leandro, Álvaro, and Jeromin Zettelmeyer. 2018b. *Safety without Tranches: Creating a "Real" Safe Asset for the Euro Area.* CEPR Policy Insight No. 93 (May). Washington: Center for Economic and Policy Research.

Leandro, Álvaro, and Jeromin Zettelmeyer. 2019. *Creating a Euro Area Safe Asset without Mutualizing Risk (Much).* PIIE Working Paper No. 19-14. Washington: Peterson Institute for International Economics.

Monti, Mario. 2010. *A New Strategy for the Single Market.* Report to the President of the European Commission.

Standard and Poor's. 2017. How S&P Global Ratings would assess European "Safe" Bonds (ESBies). S&P Global Ratings (April 25).

Ubide, Ángel. 2015. *Stability Bonds for the Euro Area.* PIIE Policy Brief 15-19. Washington: Peterson Institute for International Economics.

Wendorff, Karsten, and Alexander Mahle. 2015. Staatsanleihen neu ausgestalten—für eine stabilitätsorientierte Währungsunion. *Wirtschaftsdienst* 95, no. 9.

Zettelmeyer, Jeromin. 2017. A New Fiscal Governance for the Eurozone. In *Quo Vadis? Identity, Policy and the Future of the European Union*, ed. T. Beck and G. Underhill. VoxEU.org eBook.

Isabel Schnabel

The Regulation of Sovereign Exposures in the Context of Broader Euro Area Reforms

1. Euro area sovereign bonds are no safe assets

In the early years of the European Monetary Union, sovereign bonds in the euro area were treated by capital markets largely as safe assets, as reflected in low sovereign bond spreads (see Figure 1). In most of the 2000s, a country like Greece could finance itself almost at the same conditions as Germany. With hindsight it is clear that markets did not properly reflect the existing risks, possibly counting on bail-outs of weak countries by other member states or simply underestimating the risks.

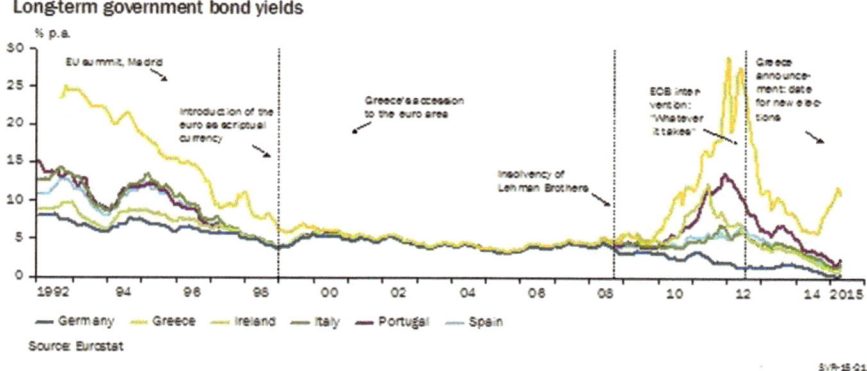

Figure 1: Evolution of long-term government bond yields.
Source: German Council of Economic Experts (2015), Chart 2.

This changed abruptly when the global financial crisis began. Sovereign bond yields started to diverge and skyrocketed in the euro area crisis. Draghi's courageous "Whatever it takes" speech and the announcement of the OMT (outright monetary transactions) program calmed down markets in a significant and suc

Note: This paper was prepared for the conference "EDIS, NPLs, Sovereign Debt and Safe Assets" on June 14, 2019 at the University of Frankfurt. This paper should not be reported as representing the views of the European Central Bank (ECB). The views expressed are those of the author and do not necessarily reflect those of the ECB.

https://doi.org/10.1515/9783110683073-018

cessful way. But the ghost of sovereign risks was out of the bottle, and OMT did not turn member states' sovereign bonds into safe assets.

One fundamental reason for the bonds' riskiness is that they are issued in a currency that the central bank in the respective country cannot control. In essence, this is similar to a country issuing bonds in a foreign currency. Moreover, the promise to buy sovereign debt under OMT is limited for legal and political reasons, and is bound to tight conditions, in particular a macroeconomic adjustment program at the European Stability Mechanism (ESM). Moreover, the events in Greece had shown that sovereign default was indeed possible within the euro area. Hence, it is anything but surprising that sovereign bond spreads remained elevated after the euro area crisis.

In the crisis, banks in the crisis countries massively bought domestic sovereign debt, using the liquidity provided by the central bank (ESRB, 2015). This "carry trade" (Acharya and Steffen, 2015) was attractive due to high yields on the one hand, and privileged regulation of sovereign exposures on the other. While this behavior likely had a stabilizing effect on sovereign bond markets (Visco, 2016; Tabellini, 2018), it further reinforced the sovereign-bank nexus, which had already been fostered by the large-scale taxpayer-funded bank bail-outs. It also exposed banks to credit and concentration risk, while at the same time making sovereign debt restructuring costlier, as this could not be done without risking a banking crisis.

2. Sovereign-bank nexus still matters

As a legacy from that time, banks' sovereign exposures remain high in many countries (see Figure 2). But sovereign exposures are a much broader phenomenon. While the level of sovereign exposures differs substantially across the euro area, banks in all countries show a home bias in sovereign exposures (see the dark blue bars in Figure 2). In fact, the exposures towards the domestic sovereign in all considered countries are well above the 25 percent large exposure limit (relative to own funds), which applies to non-sovereign exposures in banking regulation. Also banks in Germany, a country which did not experience a crisis in the sovereign debt market but rather served as a safe haven, display high sovereign exposures, with a strong concentration in domestic debt.

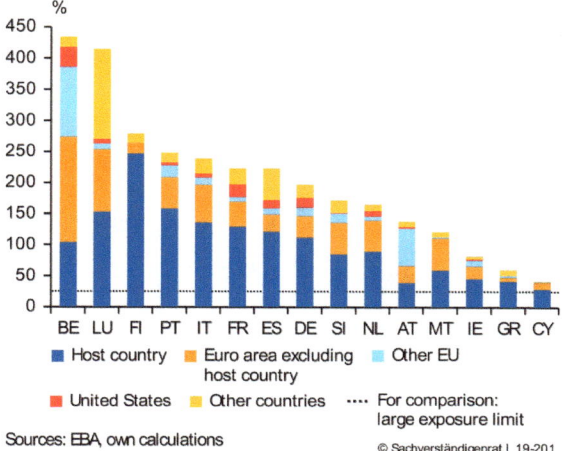

Ratio of banks' sovereign exposures to own funds by country and country groups

Sources: EBA, own calculations

© Sachverständigenrat | 19-201

Figure 2: Ratio of banks' sovereign exposures to own funds.
Source: German Council of Economic Experts (2018), Chart 66 (updated).

The share of domestic exposures has even increased in recent years in some member states, such as Portugal, France and Spain (see Figure 3). Hence, little progress has been made in reducing the link between sovereigns and banks through direct exposures.

The sovereign-bank nexus remains one of the central vulnerabilities of the euro area. Banks are connected to their sovereigns through various channels, direct and indirect, as illustrated in Figure 4.

Banks' domestic sovereign exposures *directly* expose banks to sovereign risk. Vice versa, the sovereign is exposed to bank risks through implicit and explicit government guarantees, be it through taxpayer-funded bail-outs or through national deposit insurance. The credibility of these guarantees in turn hinges on the sovereign's fiscal strength.

In addition, there are *indirect* linkages through the domestic economy. Banks are affected in many ways by the country's economic policy. A sovereign debt problem would depress the domestic economy and therefore banks. Vice versa, a crisis in the domestic banking sector negatively affects lending and the domestic economy, in turn leading to lower tax revenues and larger public expenditures. How strong these indirect effects are hinges on the structure of the financial system. An integrated European banking market where domestic firms have access to banks from all over Europe would be more resilient to domestic disturbances, just as the domestic economy would be less dependent on domestic banks. A

Ratio of exposures to its host country to own funds

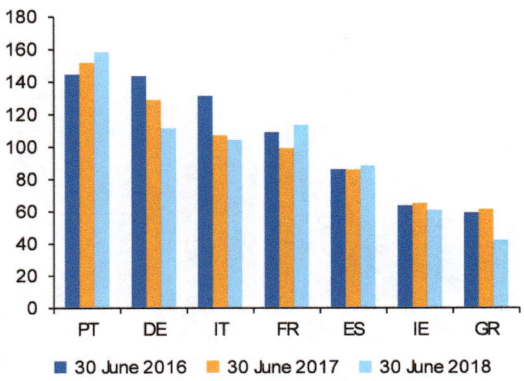

Sources: EBA, own calculations

© Sachverständigenrat | 19-202

Figure 3: Ratio of exposures to domestic sovereign over own funds.
Source: German Council of Economic Experts (2018), Chart 67 (left panel, updated).

well-developed capital market could help to diversify firms' funding sources and would therefore further reduce the dependence of the domestic economy on domestic banks.

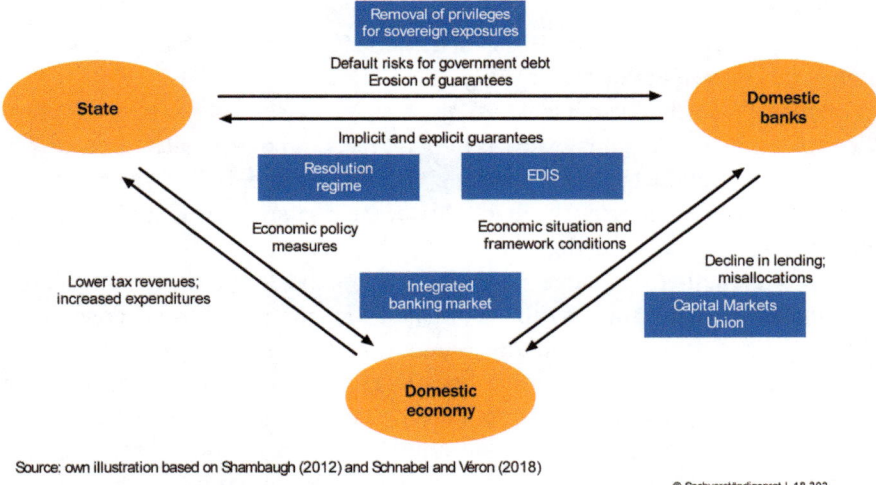

Source: own illustration based on Shambaugh (2012) and Schnabel and Véron (2018)

© Sachverständigenrat | 18-303

Figure 4: The sovereign-bank nexus.
Source: German Council of Economic Experts (2018), Chart 65.

For these reasons, one central goal of euro area reform is mitigating the sovereign-bank nexus (see Bénassy-Quéré et al., 2018). This includes the removal of privileges for sovereign exposures, a more credible resolution regime, the introduction of a European Deposit Insurance Scheme (EDIS), the integration of banking and capital markets, as well as the development of a truly European capital market, as envisaged in Capital Markets Union.

3. Determinants of the sovereign-bank nexus

The events in Italy in 2018 surrounding the formation of a new, populist government and the budget negotiations with the European Commission illustrate the sovereign-bank nexus in action. In May 2018, sovereign bond spreads increased sharply in several member states, and at the same time banks' CDS spreads showed a similar development (Figure 5).

The graph also shows that, while Italian CDS spreads remained elevated due to continuing uncertainty in Italy, other member states' spreads started to decouple from Italy (Figure 5, left panel). Moreover, there is no simple one-to-one relationship between sovereigns and banks. For example, German banks also experienced sharp spikes in CDS spreads (right panel) although there were no rising risk premia in sovereign bond markets.

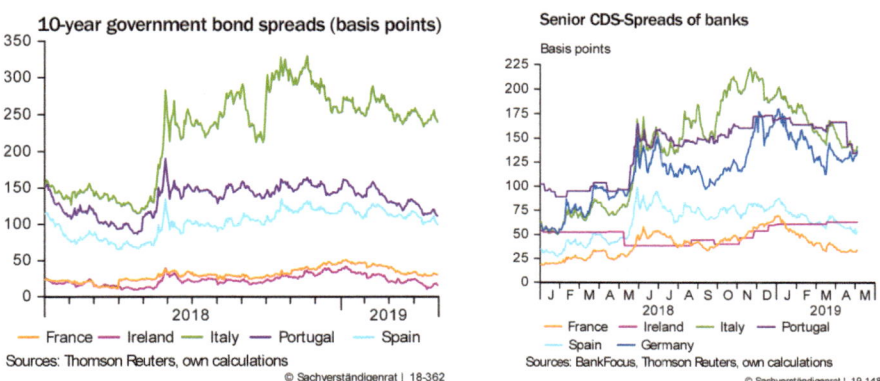

Figure 5: CDS spreads of sovereigns and banks in response to political events in Italy.
Source: German Council of Economic Experts (2018), Chart 64 (top panels, updated).

When having a closer look at the size of the spread increase in May 2018, one can see a clear relationship to debt-to-GDP ratios for government bond yields, and to tier 1 capital ratios for banks' CDS spreads (see Figure 6). This seems to suggest that the vulnerability of states and banks to spillovers depends on the states' and the banks' strength.

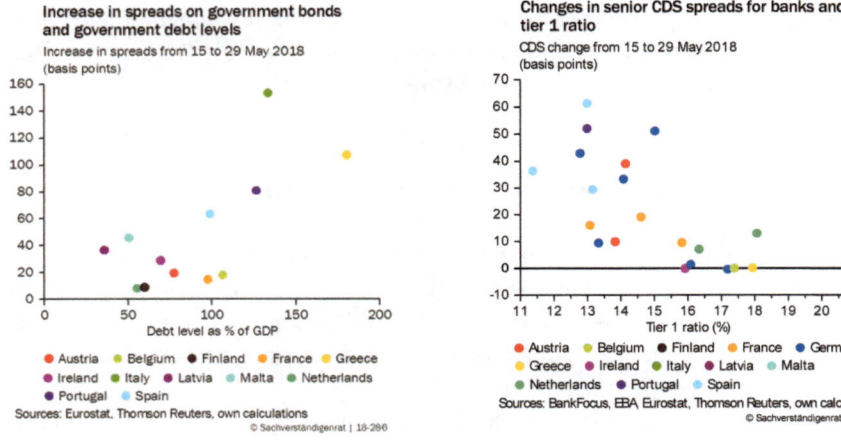

Figure 6: Relationship between spread increases and fundamental factors.
Source: German Council of Economic Experts (2018), Chart 64 (bottom panels, updated).

A similar finding emerges from a more sophisticated analysis analyzing the determinants of the sovereign-bank nexus, as measured by the elasticity of sovereign CDS spreads to bank CDS spreads. Figure 7 (medium and right panel) shows that there is a positive relationship between the strength of the sovereign-bank nexus and countries' debt-to-GDP ratios, and a negative one with banks' tier 1 capital ratios. This suggests that a strengthening of states – through a reduction in public debt relative to GDP – and banks – through higher bank capital – would contribute to mitigating the sovereign-bank nexus.

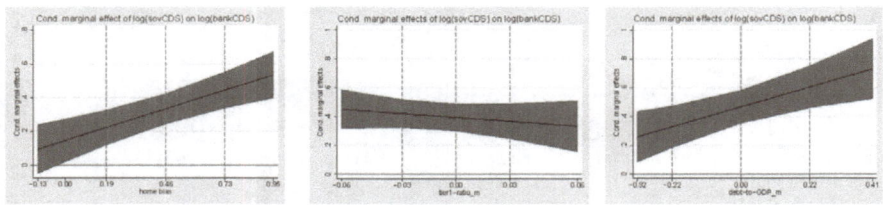

Figure 7: Determinants of the sovereign bank nexus.
Source: Schnabel and Schüwer (2016).

A third factor that came out strongly in this analysis is banks' home bias, defined as the deviation of the share of domestic sovereign bonds in the overall bond portfolio relative to a well-diversified portfolio based on GDP shares. This suggests that a removal of regulatory privileges for sovereign exposures in bank regulation is another important avenue to mitigate the sovereign-bank nexus.

4. How to regulate sovereign exposures

There have been numerous proposals how sovereign exposures could be regulated. One of the most prominent proposals is that of sovereign concentration charges by Véron (2017). According to this proposal, capital requirements should be introduced for sovereign exposures, but these should be linked to concentration in an increasing fashion rather than to credit risk. Such a proposal can be thought of as a "soft" large exposure limit, which avoids undesirable cliff effects. A calibration of this proposal using the parametrization suggested by Véron shows moderate effects on tier 1 capital ratios even when using a static approach that does not take into account banks' reshuffling their sovereign bond portfolios (blue bars in Figure 8).

Change of tier 1 ratio in basis points

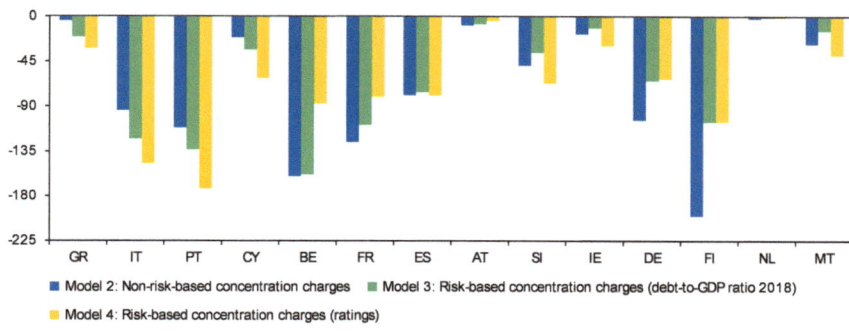

Sources: EBA, Eurostat, Standard & Poor's, own calculations

Figure 8: Calibration of different proposals for removing regulatory privileges for sovereign exposures.
Source: Rutkowski and Schnabel (2019).

However, the proposal by Véron does not take account of the differences in the creditworthiness across countries. It thus maintains the fiction of the old regulation that all countries have the same default risk, while acknowledging that this risk is not zero and may have adverse effects on banks.

A more consistent approach would take differences in creditworthiness into account as well, leading to risk-based concentration charges. One way to do this is by using countries' credit ratings. However, this is unattractive due to cliff effects when rating changes occur. A continuous calibration could be linked to the deviation of the debt-to-GDP ratio from the Maastricht ratio of 60 percent (Rutkowski and Schnabel, 2019). Figure 8 shows calibrations for both models. The major difference to the model by Véron is a stronger effect on more highly indebted countries like Greece, Italy, Portugal and Cyprus, and a milder effect on countries like Finland and Germany.[1]

5. Relationship to other euro area reforms

A regulation of sovereign exposures would contribute to a more stable euro architecture by increasing market discipline and removing distortions in sovereign bond prices. It would increase the resilience of banks by reducing concentration risk and by raising banks' loss absorption capacities through higher capital buffers. It would also facilitate sovereign debt restructuring by mitigating the link between banks and sovereigns.

However, it could go along with destabilizing effects, especially in highly indebted states. This explains why many countries are so strongly opposed to this type of proposals. In order to mitigate destabilizing effects, additional stabilizing measures ("more risk-sharing") may be needed, as argued in the "7 + 7 report" on euro area reform (Bénassy-Quéré et al., 2018). Potential candidates are a European Deposit Insurance Scheme (EDIS), the introduction of safe assets, and a fiscal stabilization mechanism.

5.1 European deposit insurance

A European deposit insurance scheme (EDIS), the proposed third pillar of the European Banking Union, is another instrument to mitigate the sovereign-bank nexus, and its introduction is closely linked to the removal of regulatory privileges for sovereign exposures. It would hardly be advisable to introduce EDIS without at the same time removing regulatory privileges of sovereign exposures because this could set incentives to invest even more in domestic sovereign debt. Thereby, sovereign risks could be shifted to the European level through EDIS. Therefore, an appropriate regulatory treatment of sovereign exposures is needed to shield EDIS from sovereign risks. In turn, EDIS could act as an important stabilizing measure.

---

1 For a discussion of other issues, like procyclicality of risk-based concentration charges and transition requirements, see Rutkowski and Schnabel (2019).

5.2 Safe assets

Introducing a European "safe asset" would be another way to mitigate the sovereign-bank nexus because it would provide banks with an instrument they can invest in, thereby reducing credit and concentration risk at the same time. This is one important advantage of a safe asset, as stressed by Alogoskoufis and Langfield (2018). Another one is that it may stabilize capital flows in crisis times. Hence, there is again a complementarity with the regulation of sovereign exposures.

But "safe assets" have to be designed in an incentive-compatible and credible way, otherwise they may even exacerbate the sovereign-bank nexus. They could lead to an overborrowing of sovereigns due to moral hazard, a lack of market discipline and reduced speed of reforms, and a destabilization of capital flows if safety is questionable.

5.3 Fiscal stabilization tools

A regulatory treatment of sovereign exposures would decrease the stabilizing role of banks for sovereign debt markets. This could be compensated for by introducing macroeconomic stabilization instruments, such as a European unemployment reinsurance. It is important to design such a mechanism in an incentive-compatible way to avoid undesirable incentive effects and permanent transfers. Important features would be a reinsurance principle, ex-ante conditionality, and experience ratings. A well-designed fiscal stabilization tool could provide important additional risk sharing in the euro area, while limiting moral hazard.

6. The way forward

The euro area is still not stable. In spite of far-reaching reforms, more has to be done. Mitigating the sovereign-bank nexus should take center stage in future reforms. The nexus creates high risks for the euro area as a whole, which overcompensate potential benefits from a national perspective. But there is a tension between market discipline and financial stability because higher market discipline may endanger financial stability in crisis times. Therefore, measures enabling greater market discipline should be accompanied by measures providing for more stabilization (Bénassy-Quéré et al., 2018). This article has pointed out some complementarities with other policy measures. In designing new measures, or packages of measures, a balance has to struck between elements raising market discipline and those providing for more stabilization. Basing such packages on economic, rather than just political reasoning may help to remove red lines and clear the way towards a more stable future of the euro area.

References

Acharya, Viral V., and Sascha Steffen (2015): "The 'greatest' carry trade ever? Understanding eurozone bank risks," *Journal of Financial Economics*, 115, 215–236.

Alogoskoufis, Spyros, and Sam Langfield (2018): "Regulating the doom loop," European Systemic Risk Board Working Paper No. 74, Frankfurt.

Bénassy-Quéré, Agnès, Markus Brunnermeier, Henrik Enderlein, Emmanuel Farhi, Marcel Fratzscher, Clemens Fuest, Pierre-Olivier Gourinchas, Philippe Martin, Jean Pisani-Ferry, Hélène Rey, Isabel Schnabel, Nicolas Véron, Beatrice Weder di Mauro, and Jeromin Zettelmeyer (2018), "Reconciling risk sharing with market discipline: A constructive approach to Eurozone reform", CEPR Policy Insight No. 91.

ESRB (2015): ESRB Report on the Regulatory Treatment of Sovereign Exposures. European Systemic Risk Board, Frankfurt.

German Council of Economic Experts (2015): "Consequences of the Greek Crisis for a More Stable Euro Area," Special Report, Wiesbaden.

German Council of Economic Experts (2018): "Advancing Banking and Capital Markets Union More Decisively," in Annual Report 2018/2019, Chapter 5, Wiesbaden.

Rutkowski, Felix, and Isabel Schnabel (2019): "Risk-Based Concentration Charges as a Way to Mitigate the Sovereign-Bank Nexus," unpublished working paper.

Schnabel, Isabel, and Ulrich Schüwer (2016): „What Drives the Relationship between Bank and Sovereign Credit Risk?", German Council of Economic Experts Working Paper No. 07/2016, Wiesbaden.

Schnabel, Isabel, and Nicolas Véron (2018): "Breaking the stalemate on European deposit insurance," VoxEU Column, 6 April 2018, https://voxeu.org/article/breaking-stalemate-european-deposit-insurance.

Shambaugh, Jay C. (2012): "The euro's three crises," *Brookings Papers on Economic Activity*, 43 (1), 157–231.

Tabellini, Guido (2018): "Risk sharing and market discipline: finding the right mix," VoxEU Column 16 July 2018, https://voxeu.org/article/risk-sharing-and-market-discipline-finding-right-mix.

Véron, Nicolas (2017): "Sovereign concentration charges: a new regime for banks' sovereign exposures," Study provided at the request of the Economic and Monetary Affairs Committee, PE 602.111, European Parliament, Brussels.

Visco, Ignazio (2016): "Banks' sovereign exposures and the feedback loop between banks and their sovereigns," Speech, Euro50 Group – The Future of European Government Bonds Markets, Rome, 2 May 2016.

Patrick Kenadjian

What do Sovereign Debt and "Safe Assets" Have to do With EDIS?

Introduction

This article concerns itself with the issues discussed in the fourth panel of the EDIS, NPLs, Sovereign Debt and Safe Assets Conference held on June 14, 2019 at the Institute for Law and Finance of Goethe University in Frankfurt am Main (the Conference), entitled "Sovereign Debt: Is this Really an Obstacle to EDIS and, if so, are Safe Assets the Solution?" The short answer is yes, sovereign debt is an obstacle, primarily because it is a political issue which the discussions at the Conference made clear would have to be resolved before progress could be expected on a European Deposit Insurance Scheme (EDIS). And no, "safe assets" are not the solution, because, in the absence of some form of mutualization, which is politically unfeasible for the moment, current proposals are too complex, too uncertain and will take too long to implement. Happily, there is another solution which is less complex and both faster and easier to implement, sovereign concentration charges, as described by Nicolas Véron in his contribution to this volume.

But let us start at the beginning. The European Union's banking union project (the Banking Union) was launched in June 2012 at the height of the Eurozone crisis, with the Member State governments desperately searching for a way out of what was labeled first as a "vicious circle" and then as a "doom loop" between sovereign governments and their banks, where a crisis originating in one area weakened the other, which in turn further weakened the first. The examples were clearly at hand, a major banking sector problem, as in Ireland could (and did) cause fiscal distress for the sovereign and, conversely, a sovereign debt crisis could (and did) result in financial distress for the sovereign's banks, as in Greece.

The solution to break the loop was deemed to involve three parts, or pillars, the centralization of bank supervision under the auspices of the European Central Bank (the ECB), the creation of a central authority for overseeing the resolution of banks in financial distress, and a common deposit insurance system for Euro area banks. It was thought that the three pillars together would work against the fragmentation and centrifugal forces experienced in the Eurozone crisis. Banks would be subject to uniform supervision, uniform rules would govern their failure and resolution, and the protection of their deposits would no longer be dependent on the financial resources of the state in which the bank was organized or operated.

https://doi.org/10.1515/9783110683073-019

The linkages and the ways to break them can be envisioned as follows (with my thanks to Isabel Schnabel on whose work it is based):

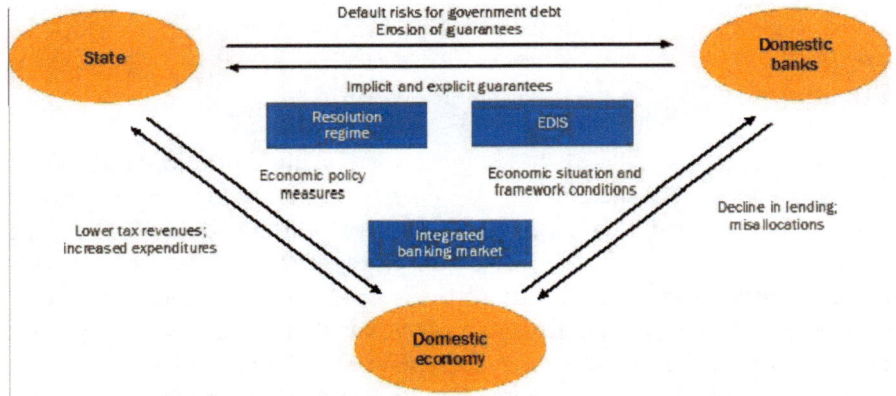

Source: own illustration based on Schnable article in this volume

As noted in the introduction to this volume, the first two pillars have been largely implemented, whereas the third, deposit insurance, remains stalled. So, why is this the case and what can be done to promote forward movement was the central question addressed by the Conference?

The problem as presented

The initial, and perfectly reasonable, objection to implementing EDIS as the third leg of the Banking Union was that there should first be a reduction of risk, especially related to legacy assets such as non-performing loans (NPLs) before any move towards mutualization of the deposit insurance systems could be agreed to. Mutualization being the "third rail" of European Union politics especially, but not exclusively, in Germany, this objection was both obvious and entirely understandable.

But as the NPL situation is being gradually worked through, another issue has more recently gained prominence, that of domestic sovereign debt concentration in the portfolios of some Eurozone banks, often in the same countries where excessive NPLs were initially flagged as the main problem. A cynical view of this would be that it is yet another excuse to delay and ultimately block EDIS, part of the continuing North South divide within the Euro area. On closer reflection, however, the concern is perfectly understandable. The object of the European Banking Union was to break the "doom loop" between banks and their sovereigns, so that it is surely legitimate to ask whether the banks in jurisdictions where the sovereign's debt is less solid should be allowed to accumulate as much of that debt as they please, free from the discipline provided for other investments under the Basel rules on capital adequacy by capital charges and concentration limits, thus doubling down on their vulnerability to their sovereign's financial strength or weakness, and still benefit from the protections of EDIS for their deposits, which will no doubt have been used in part to fund such purchases.

Eurozone banks' domestic sovereign debt exposure is well in excess of their Tier 1 capital. In his excellent 2017 study on the matter, Nicolas Véron estimates that a typical Eurozone bank's median domestic sovereign exposure amounts to 135% of its Tier 1 capital. (Véron, 2017). The percentages Nicolas cites vary from country to country, from a low of 21% for Finnish banks to a high of 209% for Belgian banks. In the case of countries which fared the worst during the Eurozone crisis, the percentages are 60% for Greece, 79% for Ireland, 155% for Portugal and 171% for Italy, as of June 30, 2016. In her contribution to this volume, Isabel Schnabel notes that the concentrations are well above the 25% of Tier 1 capital which the Basel rules on capital adequacy apply to other large exposures (more on this below), apply even to German banks and has even increased in recent years in some Member States, such as Portugal, France and Spain. She also notes a clear relationship of debt-to-GDP ratios for government bond yields and to Tier 1 capital ratios for banks' CDS spreads. So the question seems a legitimate one to ask.

Having asked that question, the issue is how to resolve it. The freedom of Eurozone banks to accumulate as much of their domestic sovereign debt as they please depends on two regulatory decisions the European Union made in its implementation of the Basel rules on capital adequacy. The first, and most serious, was to decide that the zero risk weight for sovereign debt issued in the sovereign's own currency held by its banks would apply within the European Monetary Union (EMU) to any Member State sovereign debt issued in euros. This decision arguably disregarded the original reasoning behind the sovereign debt zero risk weight, which was that a sovereign issuing debt in its own currency could always issue more of that currency to cover the servicing and reimbursement of that debt. So, it is fine for Japan issuing in yen, the United States issuing in dollars or the United Kingdom issuing in pounds sterling. Those sovereigns control their currency. The logic is more questionable for Member States of the EMU issuing in euros. They do not control that currency; under the European treaties the ECB does. In that sense, Italy issuing in euros is closer to the situation of an emerging market issuer issuing in dollars than to Japan issuing in yen. The second decision was to exempt sovereign debt from the normal asset concentration rules under the Basel system, which normally limit exposures to any issuer or group of issuers to 25 % of the financial institution's capital and, instead, to impose no limitations at all. There was no fallacy in reasoning here, merely the recognition that sovereigns rely on their domestic financial institutions to buy their obligations to ensure their continued access to the market and thus their ability to finance and refinance themselves at a reasonable cost. It is also the case that under the liquidity requirements of Basel III financial institutions need to hold increasing amounts of liquid assets, among them principally sovereign paper, when available.

This leads to the question of whether, if we were to reduce the amount of domestic sovereign debt a financial institution may hold, in order to get to EDIS – and as Anita van den Ende of the Netherlands Ministry of Finance mentioned at the conference, the current Dutch government's coalition agreement stipulates that they will not agree to EDIS until the sovereign debt problem is resolved through the assignment of appropriate risk weightings to government bonds on banks' balance sheets – can we accomplish that simply by imposing risk weights or exposure limits on the banks' holdings of sovereign debt? Or do we need to create a new instrument, a "safe asset" that would provide a substitute low risk weighted and liquid asset for the financial institutions to hold and be a substitute source of demand for the debt the sovereign can no longer rely on its banks to buy and hold unlimited amounts of? The problem may be most acute for some of the sovereigns since the banks who have to diversify their sovereign holdings will have the choice of 18 other sovereigns within the Euro area whose debt they may hold instead of their own sovereign's debt, some of which debt may be looking for a good home since those sovereigns' own banks may need to cut back on their own holdings. The sovereign, on the other hand, especially if its credit rating is lower than the average of the EU19, may have trouble finding a substitute good home for its debt. Within reason there will usually be investors willing to buy riskier debt in exchange for a higher coupon rate, but not necessarily to continue to hold it, especially in a crisis.

How to manufacture safe assets

Hence, the idea of manufacturing "safe assets" out of sovereign debt issued by EMU sovereigns, which would be designed to be both liquid and highly rated. Because of the political problems with mutualization within the Euro area, the simplest solution, issuing debt backed by the full faith and credit of all EMU Member States, is off the table. Hence, proposals have focused on structured products. While several variations have been proposed, almost all center on having an entity, which could be a public sector authority or one or more private actors, accumulate sovereign debt in a portfolio and then issue debt representing interests in that portfolio, tranched according to seniority, with there being at least two tranches, a senior one representing 70 % of the principal amount of securities issued by the vehicle and one or more junior tranches. The senior tranche would represent a senior claim to the payments from the debt held in the portfolio, and would receive 100 % of the payments on the debt held up to the amount necessary to meet its obligations to investors. The junior tranche(s) would absorb 100 % of any losses due to defaults on debt in the portfolio and the relative size of the senior and junior tranches would be set so that the senior tranche should be unaffected by, say partial defaults by Greece, Portugal or Ireland and haircuts on Italian and Spanish debt, and the tranche should be highly rated. (Brunnermeier 2011). For a more up to date description of such Sovereign Bond Backed Securities, or SBBS, _see_ ESRB 2018, which envisages a 70 % senior tranche and a portfolio makeup weighted according to the ECB's capital key.

The idea takes inspiration from the structures used to design "private label" asset backed securities (ABSs) prior to the financial crisis, only using better assets this time. It is clever but the problems with it are hardly trivial. Jeromin Zettelmeyer and Alvaro Leandro, in their contribution to this volume, dissect them in exquisite detail, so I will limit myself here to a few broader observations. To start with, there is the fact that the solution is based on a structured product approach, which will have a certain degree of structural complexity and an unfortunate kinship with the kinds of structured products which triggered the last Great Financial Crisis. In a future crisis they risk starting to look just as dodgy as the last set did and thus lose both liquidity and market value even if the senior tranches bear no actual credit losses. The senior tranches of many private label ABSs actually suffered minimal credit losses in the crisis but nonetheless declined precipitously in market value when investors decided to dump them all at once. History may not repeat itself with SBBS because the reason investors bailed out of private label ABSs during the financial crisis was primarily because, with hundreds of assets in each portfolio, no one could figure out quickly what all the assets were, let alone what they were worth. For SBBS the portfolio should be easier to analyse since it will be made up of securities of at most 19 different sovereigns, though with different maturities and potentially various other characteristics. But in a crisis, cool, rational analysis may not win out over panic and the herd instinct. And this relative simplicity brings with it another problem we will consider in a moment. Beyond that there are practical problems of execution in accumulating the portfolios from sovereign debt management offices each working on different issuance schedules keyed to refinancing existing maturities on terms and conditions which may not be uniform across Member States and which are issued under different home country laws, so that even if the words on the debt instruments are the same, their legal consequences may be different. After Brexit, a possible solution to legal diversity, issuing under English law, which was used for the Greek restructured bonds, is likely to be unworkable. In any event there will be costs involved in accumulating and administering these portfolios, which will have to be covered by someone, and finally there is the issue of how they will be rated.

There has been an assumption that the senior tranches of SBBS (ESBies) will be highly rated, and of course that rating is essential for the success of the product. The 2018 ESRB study refers to them as intended to be "at least as safe as German bunds" which are rated triple-A by both Standard & Poor's and Moody's. Unfortunately, when the rating agencies actually looked at the proposed structures what they saw was a lack of diversification (at most 19 issuers compared to hundreds in a conventional collateralized debt obligation (CDO) structure), coupled with a serious degree of correlation ("elevated co-movement") among the issuers, as demonstrated during the Eurozone crisis. Standard & Poor's noted in its analysis of ESBies that it lowered its ratings on nine Eurozone sovereigns simultaneously on January 13, 2012, at the height of the crisis. This has led them to conclude that they would not be likely to rate the product triple-A.

Colin Ellis of the University of Birmingham provides an excellent analysis of the rating methodologies in his contribution to this volume. While the two major credit rating agencies approach the rating of ESBies somewhat differently, their conclusion is the same: as currently proposed, *i.e.* without further credit enhancement in the form of guarantees or over-collateralization, ESBies are not likely to be rated as highly as German bunds. In fact Standard & Poor's, using a "weakest link" approach, indicates a single A rating. (Standard and Poor's 2017).

This is even putting to one side the question of what these assets would do for the liquidity and thus the pricing of the balance of a sovereign's debt that do not find their way into these assets – and of course there would have to be a limit to how much these vehicles purchase, for the reasons Zettelmeyer and Leandro discuss. They also note that most of the "safe bond" proposals would require a significant time to be put together and come to market. So, all in all, while "safe assets" present a fascinating intellectual exercise and the European Commission is busy at work proposing changes to its structured product rules to facilitate the issuance of such assets (without which, as structured products, under current regulation they would attract additional capital charges and discounts relative to those which the underlying sovereign debt would attract), I would not place great hopes on them to solve the sovereign debt obstacle to EDIS in the short, or even medium, term.

In a separate paper Zettelmeyer and Leandro have proposed an alternative approach to safe assets not involving tranching, which is very ingenious, but suffers from two problems, depending on which two possible structures you choose. The first is simple over-collateralization (the "Capitalisation" approach): you include more bonds in the portfolio than the face value of the safe asset you sell to the public. That makes the structure safer but also more expensive, as the excess collateral is a dead weight cost. And the amount is very large. To support €2.6 trillion in financing, the authors estimate that an amount equivalent to 6-7 % of Euro area GDP would be required. And that could be seen as a pure subsidy to the issuers whose debt is being purchased. The second (the "E-bonds" approach) is to have the entity which constructs the portfolio and sells the safe asset to the public be a preferred creditor vis-à-vis the sovereign issuers whose debt they buy. That has the effect of subordinating the balance of the debt of those sovereign issuers and thus presumably increasing their costs of issuance. (Leandro and Zettelmeyer 2018). The calculations involved are somewhat complicated, but the authors assume that, for example 77.5 % of Italy's debt would be held by the market as would 69.5 % of Spain's debt, all subordinated. Thanks to this subordination, the portion of the debt held in the portfolio should escape any losses on default. And still, the authors admit, the E-bonds are not entirely protected from a series of small crises, because they suffer losses any time a default occurs by a country which exceeds the proportion of debt held by the market outside of the E-bonds.

So, as a practical matter I believe that leaves us with either risk weighting or limitations on concentrations if we think that sovereign debt overweighting in Euro area bank portfolios is a real problem. Of the two alternatives I think, as a practical matter that risk weighting is not likely to be endorsed any time soon at the Basel Committee level where we know that Japan among others is opposed. Of course, the EU could decide to solve its own problem internally. As Raghuram Rajan points out in his recent book, this is a peculiarly European problem, which the Europeans could – in his mind should – solve by themselves. (Rajan 2019). As I noted above, this is indeed a problem of the EU's own making and one it could solve by amending its capital requirements regulation, but I am skeptical that there is much appetite in Brussels to do this for fear of disadvantaging European banks in international competition. So I think that leaves us with the question of how to limit the current level of concentration without doing excessive harm to either the banks or the sovereigns.

What is the problem again?

But first, I would like to step back a moment and reflect on the extent to which the over weighing of domestic sovereign debt in EMU bank portfolios is a serious problem for financial stability or as a prudential matter which requires a radical solution. We all understand that during the Euro crisis there was a clear correlation between credit default swap ("CDS") spreads of banks and sovereign in the Eurozone. It grew from 0.1 to 0.8 between 2007 and 2013. (Fratzcher 2015). Fratzcher and his co-authors conclude that there was two-way causality between shocks to sovereign risk and bank risk, with the former being more important in explaining bank risk than vice-versa. Thus there seems to be a well-established and academically documented feedback loop at work between banks and their sovereigns. The authors conclude that an increase in sovereign CDS spreads by 100 basis points correlates with an increase in bank spreads by 38 basis points on average and the effect in the other direction is a rise in sovereign risk by 28 basis points for every 100 point deterioration in bank risk. So we know that, at least during a financial crisis, we can expect that the cost of bank financing will increase when financing costs of its sovereign increases. We also understand the contagion mechanism that is likely to underlie this correlation. As sovereign risk increases, its bond prices fall and the banks that hold them incur portfolio losses. In addition, the value of these bonds as collateral for borrowing by the banks in refinancing operations such as repos, which banks are using more and more as unsecured inter-bank lending has deceased. An older link between sovereign and bank ratings, the ceilings which rating agencies used to impose, according to which private entities could not be rated higher than their sovereigns, which was still in effect at the time of the Euro crisis, has since disappeared.

And yet it is worth remembering that the actual instances in which the doom loop functioned in this direction, *i.e.* when banks have been brought down because of their over-exposure to their sovereign are in the minority. There were "debt programs" in three countries, Greece, Ireland and Portugal. Spain escaped a formal program through direct help for its banks and Italy, though wounded, did not need either a "bail-out" or a debt program. In one case, Greece, it was clearly the state's deficits which brought down its banks. When it restructured, its banks became insolvent. In Ireland and Spain it was the banks' problems which almost brought down the state, in the case of Ireland when it guaranteed their debts and in Spain when it became clear it could not rescue its banks. Cyprus' banks were brought down by their holdings of Greek bonds. Italy and Portugal's problems were primarily due to slow growth, although in Portugal's case, the problems at its two largest banks certainly contributed to its need to a program.

So, a rather mixed record, with Greece the clearest case for the proposition that over concentration in domestic sovereign bonds brought down its banks. Of course, Greece was an outlier during the crisis, as the only sovereign which had to restructure its debt with private sector involvement (PSI) and that to an extreme extent with haircuts of over 50 % (and up to 76 % on some bonds) and it was the

French and the German banks that were initially over exposed to Greece. They were bought out of their positions by the Eurosystem of central banks, thus shifting a problem of private sector banks into a public sector problem, which was ultimately "solved" by exempting the Eurosystem central banks from having to participate in the March 2012 restructuring, allowing them instead to exchange their existing Greek government bonds for new bonds at par which, by reducing the amount of publicly held bonds to be exchanged, increased the haircut on the exchange and thus the effect on the banks' balance sheets. (Minenna 2019).

Nonetheless, a sober examination of the current situation of Italian banks by an Italian economist based on a careful analysis of the cost of five year CDS protection for Italian sovereign debt, the spread of ten year Italian sovereign debt over German Bunds and the movement of spreads for Italian bank deposits and repos concludes that "redenomination risk has not disappeared" and that the doom loop is "alive and well." (Codogno 2019) So while history presents us with a rather mixed bag, with overall fewer instances of the doom loop moving from the state to the banks, there is still enough evidence in the other direction that it would be foolish to dismiss the chance of a return. But how should we go about preventing it and at what cost?

In their excellent contribution to this volume, Anita van den Ende and her colleagues from the Dutch Ministry of Finance, do a first rate job of presenting the problem and analysing the economic consequences of changing the EU's prudential treatment of sovereign exposures, by applying the risk weights from the "standard approach" in the EU's Capital Requirements Regulation (CRR) and the risk weights (marginal risk weight add-ons) discussed in a December 2017 discussion document from the Basel Committee on Bank Supervision (BCBS). (Basel Committee 2017).

Simply applying the standardized approach would result in an average decrease in Tier 1 capital of 100 basis points, with banks in countries like Greece, Belgium and Italy losing closer to 200 basis points. When applying the BCBS approach, including concentration charges the numbers are larger: on average the banks would need to increase Tier 1 capital by 1.80 % to maintain current Tier 1 ratios, but with somewhat surprising regional effects, including 2.39 % basis points for German banks, compared to 2.15 % for Italian banks, 2.38 % for French banks, 4.79 % for Belgian banks, but only 0.81 % for Dutch banks. They also note that the marginal impact is larger for smaller banks with assets under €200 million, than for larger banks.

These numbers are far from trivial and the not unexpected fact that it is the smaller banks that would have to bear the largest burden of a change in prudential regime should also be a cause for concern for the adoption of such an approach. The approach also suffers from the focus on a single element of the sovereign-bank nexus, the sovereign exposure channel, while ignoring the safety net channel discussed below and other reasons why banks choose or are forced to hold sovereign debt. These other factors are considered in detail in a 2018 IMF study (Dell'Ariccia 2018), which Anita and her colleagues cite. The IMF authors do find a link between the size of a bank's sovereign debt holdings and the impact on its financial stability in case of a sovereign debt crisis, but note that a crucial reason banks hold sovereign debt is to meet their liquidity requirements which, as noted above, Basel III has formalized through the introduction of liquidity requirements. The IMF authors emphasize that regulatory changes should not be undertaken, focusing just on one aspect of a problem, without consideration of the whole picture.

The IMF authors draw our attention to the "safety net" channel, noting that in the Eurozone crisis CDS spreads rose most for banks whose sovereigns' financial strength was called into question. While the authors focus on this development in the context of potential bail-outs, it seems to me that the same concern should apply to the insurance of bank deposits. From the point of view of the retail depositor, the safety net means first and foremost deposit insurance. And here we return to EDIS, the purpose of which is to decouple the safety of bank deposits from the financial strength of the bank's sovereign. Thus, if it is possible that a significant source of vulnerability of a bank to its sovereign is not primarily through the bank's holdings of that sovereign's debt obligations, but rather through the fear that in case of difficulty the sovereign will not be able to provide sufficient support to its banks to fend off liquidity or solvency problems, then no amount of balance sheet cleanup or portfolio diversification will disentangle this connection, and only the establishment of EDIS, which would definitely free domestic banks from reliance on their sovereign's support will work, so we should understand that simply requiring banks to cut back on their sovereign bank holdings without also providing EDIS will not solve our problem.

An additional piece of the puzzle may be found in a recent study by Gabrielli and Labonne for the Federal Reserve bank of Boston, which, *inter alia*, analyzed the home country risk premia for Spanish, Italian and French banks during the Euro crisis and found that before the ECB's August 2012 announcement of its outright Monetary Transactions (OMT) program in the famous "whatever it takes" speech in London, their banks paid a risk premium attributable to their home country on the order of 0.4 %, which turned negative after the announcement of OMT. (Gabrieli 2018). No purchases were made under OMT, so no changes occurred in the banks' portfolios, but the announcement that the ECB was ready to stand behind the weaker sovereigns by buying their obligations, sufficed to rectify market perception of the banks involved.

Two German researchers, Falko Fecht and Patrick Weber have come to similar conclusions by examining the effect of the introduction of blanket deposit guarantees for German banks on October 5, 2008 on the levels of deposit of two similarly situated groups of local banks, cooperative banks and savings banks, which had similar business models and separate deposit guarantee systems. In fact the authors say the main difference between the two sets of banks is that the savings banks are partly owned by municipalities and thus their deposits are considered to benefit from a quasi-government guarantee. Prior to October 5, the researchers establish a correlation between Google searches for terms like "deposit insurance", which they use as a proxy for high anxiety among depositors, and withdrawals of deposits from cooperative banks, but not from savings banks. In fact, deposits at savings banks increased. This effect disappeared after the October 5 announcement. They conclude that heterogeneity in the backing and credibility of deposit insurance schemes led to the reallocation of deposits among banking sectors, with potentially destabilizing effects, and that this shows that there is clearly a role for EDIS to play in mitigating this effect. (Fecht 2019). The authors explain the importance of using German banks for their study because it allowed them to exclude another source of concern about bank deposits during the Eurozone crisis in other countries, which was "redenomination risk", the fear that the country would leave the EMU and that its banks' obligations would be redenominated into a new currency subject to sharp devaluation. This was obviously not a concern anyone had about Germany. Hence they could isolate the effect of adding a national deposit guarantee to sectoral insurance funds on bank stability and conclude that adding EDIS to national insurance schemes might well have a similar effect. Their conclusions could lead us to ask whether we are talking about putting the cart before the horse when we require a reduction of sovereign debt holdings as a pre-requisite for EDIS.

Concentration charges as the simplest and swiftest solution

However, if we continue to think we have a problem that needs solving, I think that Nicolas Véron's November 2017 study on sovereign concentration charges for the European Parliament provided at the request of the Economic and Monetary Affairs Committee of the Parliament, gives an interesting framework for thinking about a solution. Nicolas advocates a system which, rather than relying on risk weights or an inflexible cap on concentration, would impose a sliding scale of concentration charges on concentrations (overweighting) of sovereign obligations in excess of the normal Basel threshold of 25 %, an approach quite similar to the marginal risk weight add-on considered in the BCBS 2017 paper cited above by Anita and her co-authors. Nicolas, however, would add an additional margin to allow for temporary inventories of sovereign debt that result from market making activities, for a total exempt holding of 33 % of Tier 1 capital, subject to appropriate transitional arrangements. The surcharges would start at 15 % for exposures between 33 and 50 %, 30 % up to 100 % and 50 % up to 200 % and then become truly prohibitive above 200 %, designed to allow the banks to weather at least one major sovereign debt restructuring and potentially more, without their capital being wiped out. The calibration depends on the historical experience with large sovereign debt restructurings which have involved haircuts (forced losses on exchange of existing bonds for new ones) of up to 30 to 50 %. If this system were adopted, Nicolas estimates the banks would need to diversify into five to six sovereigns to avoid any concentration charges and would incur only negligible charges if they diversified into only three to five sovereigns.

Nicolas estimates the disruption to the banks is likely to be relatively minimal. At the 33 % level he sees French banks, for example, needing to shed €250 billion in French government bonds but, as a result of similar divestitures by other Eurozone banks, having almost €600 billion of other Eurozone sovereign obligations to choose from. German banks would have to shed and reinvest €242 billion and Italian banks €145 billion. At the 100 % level, the numbers decline to €120, €155 and €75 billion. Dutch banks would only need to shed less than €15 billion at the 33 % level and nothing at the 100 % level. The effects on German banks are interesting and applying the system across the board would require them to shed €155 to €242 billion of triple-A rated German government bonds for something less valuable and one can imagine their expressing some reluctance at being required to do so. The different effects reflect the degrees of sovereign debt exposure by banks in the various countries, with German banks holding domestic sovereign debt amounting to a weighted average of 151 % of their Tier 1 capital, well above the Eurozone median holding of 135 % and not that far behind Italian banks at 171 %, but significantly above French and Spanish banks at 114 % and 102 %, respectively and Dutch banks at 46 %. All amounts and percentages are based on June 30, 2016 data and it is possible that current data would yield a larger or a smaller need to shift portfolios. A recent Deutsche Bank research note estimates that a large exposure rule at 25 % could drive a €1 trillion sovereign rebalance. (Deutsche Bank 2019). Press analysis of ECB data indicates that Eurozone banks bought a net €1 billion of their domestic governments' debt in the 12 months to January 2019. (Financial Times 2019).

A serious advantage of Nicolas' proposal is that it can be implemented by the European Union without needing to wait for an international consensus at the Basel Committee, by simply amending its Capital Requirements Regulation ("CRR") and having the changes enforced by the Single Supervisory Mechanism, subject to appropriate transitional arrangements, which Nicolas suggests could be between five and ten years, starting with the highest level or bucket of concentration and grandfathering existing stocks of sovereign exposure. The transitional provisions are important to avoiding a "cliff effect" upon implementation. Implementing concentration charges would not need to put a stop to attempts to create Eurozone "safe assets" which may serve other useful purposes, such as providing a "risk free" Euro denominated asset in which investors from around the world would invest, thus bolstering the position of the Euro as an international reserve currency. But it could be implemented without waiting for us to be able to solve the problems noted above that the current proposals for such assets bring with them. It simply focuses on the core of the problem, concentration, and provides a direct solution to it. How much concentration it eliminates will depend on the degree of calibration chosen, as well as the timetable for implementation. Both can be adjusted, depending on how serious and urgent the concentration problem is deemed to be.

In her contribution to this volume, Isabel Schnabel misses in Nicolas' proposal any differentiation among Member States based on their credit worthiness. She recognizes that using credit ratings would lead to undesirable "cliff effects" upon a change in ratings and ponders the desirability of a continuous calibration based on the deviation of a country's debt from the 60% Maastricht Treaty ratio, although she recognizes this would have drastic effects on countries like Greece, Italy, Portugal and Cyprus. While I can follow her logic, it is clearly premised on the idea that the 60% ratio is both reasonable and immutable. Without wishing to relitigate the sad story of the application or lack thereof of Articles 104c(2) and 126 (2) of the Treaty on the Functioning of the European Union (TFEU), nor the rather peculiar origin story of the ratios, I think serious doubts can be allowed on both counts. Currently more than two-thirds of the Member States are not in compliance with the Protocol which sets forth the 3% deficit and 60% debt-to-GDP ratios, including, as of 2016, such paragons of fiscal virtue as the Netherlands, Finland, Germany and Austria, as well as the more usual suspects of Greece, Italy, Portugal, Belgium, Spain and France. Add to that the history of excessive deficit procedures under the Protocol, which are perhaps more an illustration of the inability of the EU to function when it tries to substitute rigid rules for economic realities than an evidence of its functioning. I think it would be inadvisable to double down on the Protocol numbers, for which there appears to be little or no theoretical or empirical economic basis, but only historical political happenstance, by making them the basis of further restrictions. Put simply, the 60% and 3% limits were products of another, pre-financial crisis, economic era, where growth was on the order of 3% and most Member States more or less met the percentages. Since then, growth assumptions have changed and if one wants to apply the Domar Model, which links debt limits to fiscal deficit ratios divided by real growth plus inflation rates, one could come up with a debt limit closer to 100% based on a 3% deficit cap.

Of course, for Nicolas' solution to be adopted, the Member States will have to agree that the proposal is good for them as well as for their banks. One can imagine that Member States with the highest credit ratings might pause before endorsing a proposal which could require their banks to diversify away from their triple-A rated debt into less highly rated debt. Will they really see this as contributing to their banks' financial stability? This would affect primarily Germany, since in the case of the two other triple-A rated Member States, the Netherlands and Luxembourg, their banks are, according to Nicolas' data, under rather than over-exposed to their sovereign debt.

The second consideration for sovereigns is, as noted above, whether they can live without the home bias of their domestic financial institutions. The transition period and the proposal to grandfather existing debt, if adopted, should go a long way towards making the proposal palatable to the sovereigns, especially if it allows them to unblock the process of adopting EDIS. It should also be noted that, despite the home bias we have been discussing, in no case analysed by Nicolas did domestic banks, as of June 2016 hold more than 30 % of their sovereign's debt, with Italy and Germany coming closest while Spanish banks held a little over 20 % and Portuguese banks a little over 15 %, so the degree of dependence of sovereigns on their domestic banks is not that high and the concentration charge may well affect the debt of other sovereigns they hold.

Conclusion

In conclusion, while I recognize the financial stability, prudential and political issues surrounding the overweighting of home country sovereign debt in the portfolios of Euro area banks, I am not convinced they warrant as radical a solution as a hard cap or resorting to risk weights. Therefore, Nicolas' solution, being less radical and more targeted, strikes me as a good compromise. Safe assets, while intellectually challenging and potentially useful for other purposes, such as enhancing the role of the euro as a reserve currency, present too many unresolved problems to be implemented in a reasonable time frame. Sovereign risk weights present political problems which also make them unlikely to allow us to move forward on EDIS any time soon. In contrast, concentration charges have the advantage of being the least intrusive solution which can be implemented with the greatest speed and least disruption to allow us to move forward with EDIS. It goes without saying that the two could and should be moved forward in parallel and that, as soon as agreement is reached on the shape and calibration of concentration charges, the next steps of EDIS could be implemented.

References

Basel Committee (2017), The Regulatory Treatment of Sovereign Exposures, discussion paper, Basel Committee on Banking Supervision, December 2017.

Brunnermeier (2011) Marcus Brunnermeier, Luis Garciano, Philip R. Lane, Marco Pagano, Ricardo Reis, Tano Santos, Stijn van Nieuwerburgh and Dimitri Vayanos, European Safe Bonds (ESBies), September 2011.

Codogno (2019), Lorenzo Codogno, Fiscal rules and fiscal capacity, High Level Policy Dialogue, School of Transnational Governance, European University Institute, September 2019.

Dell'Ariccia (2018), Giovanni Dell'Ariccia, Caio Ferreira, Nigel Jenkinson, Luc Laeven, Alberto Martin, Camelia Minoiu, Alex Popov, Managing the bank-sovereign nexus, IMF Monetary and Capital Markets and Research Department No. 18/16, International Monetary Fund, 2018.

Deutsche Bank (2019), How to fix European banking … and why it matters, Deutsche Bank Research, 13 March 2019.

ESRB (2018), Sovereign bond-backed securities: A feasibility study, European Systemic Risk Board High-Level Task Force on Safe Assets, 2018.

Fecht (2019), Fear, deposit insurance schemes, and deposit reallocation in the German banking systems, F. Fecht, S. Thum and P. Weber, Bundesbank Discussion Paper No. 12/2019, Deutsche Bundesbank, 2019.

Financial Times (2019), Eurozone banks buy sovereign bonds, reviving "doom loop" fears, Financial Times, 7 March 2019.

Fratzcher (2015), Marcel Fratzcher and Malte Rieth, Monetary Policy, Bank Bailouts and the Sovereign bank Risk Nexus in the Euro area, European Economy Discussion Paper 009, September 2015.

Gabrieli (2018), Gabrieli, S. and Labonne, C. Bad Sovereign or Band Balance Sheets, Euro Interbank Market Fragmentation and Monetary Policy, Federal Reserve Bank of Boston Working Paper No. 18-3 (2018).

Leandro and Zettelmeyer (2018), Alvaro Leandro and Jeromin Zettelmeyer, Safety without Tranches, creating a "real" safe asset for the euro area, Center for Economic Policy Research Policy Insight No. 93, June 2018.

Minenna (2019), Marcello Minenna, The New Eurozone Risk Morphology, available at SSRN, February 25, 2019.

Rajan (2019), The Third Pillar, The revival of community in a polarized world. Raghuram Rajan, William Collins, 2019.

Standard and Poor's (2017), How S&P Global Ratings would Assess European "Safe" Bonds (ESBies), Standard and Poor's 2017.

Véron (2017), Nicolas Véron, Sovereign Concentration Changes: A New Regime for Sovereign Exposures, European Parliament, November 2017.

Nicolas Véron

The Key to Completing the Banking Union: Sovereign Concentration Charges

The aim of completing the banking union and breaking the bank-sovereign vicious circle meets a broad rhetorical and analytical consensus in the European financial and economic policy debate. The "imperative to break the vicious circle between banks and sovereigns" has been reaffirmed by euro area leaders on multiple occasions since their seminal summit declaration of 29 June 2012. Most economists, economic historians and political scientists now concur that the bank-sovereign vicious circle – variously dubbed "doom loop", deadly embrace, *Teufelskreis* and similar nicknames – was an essential driver of the euro area crisis and that breaking it is a core component of any agenda to make the euro area resilient to future shocks (e.g. Benassy-Quéré & coauthors, 2018; Farhi and Tirole, 2016; Howarth and Quaglia, 2016; Tooze, 2018). While the expression "completing the banking union" is inherently more ambiguous, it is more often than not used as synonymous to breaking the bank-sovereign vicious circle – and rightly so, since that was the unequivocally stated aim of the leader's declaration of 29 June 2012 which is universally viewed as the starting point of the banking union project.

This is largely, however, where the consensus ends – for now. Towards the end of the Second Barroso Commission in 2013-2014, the European Union was able to adopt an impressive package of banking union and banking-union-related legislation: some of it directly flowing from the June-2012 summit and its aftermath, namely the Single Supervisory Mechanism (SSM) Regulation ((EU) 1024/2013) and Single Resolution Mechanism Regulation (SRMR, (EU) 806/2014); and the rest initially proposed earlier but adapted during the legislative process to fit the banking union project, namely the Capital Requirements Regulation and fourth Directive (CRR and CRD4, respectively (EU) 575/2013 and 2013/36/EU), the Deposit Guarantee Scheme Directive (DGSD, 2014/49/EU) and the Bank Recovery and Resolution Directive (BRRD, 2014/59/EU). By contrast, however, the Juncker Commission has marked a period of legislative pause. Amendments to CRR, CRD, SRMR and BRRD have been adopted, not least to transpose parts of the Basel III accord, but none marks a significant change in the framework set by the 2013-2014 legislation. A major proposal, published in late 2015 by the European Commission and establishing a European Deposit Insurance Scheme (EDIS, COM/2015/586), has failed to make progress through the legislative machinery – and the Commission has appeared to water down its own proposal in a communication on banking union two years later (COM/2017/592). Meanwhile, much of the

https://doi.org/10.1515/9783110683073-020

discussion in the Council and the public space has unfolded around analytically ill-defined categories of "risk reduction" and "risk sharing" with, at least until recently (see below), a sense of general deadlock.

To be sure, the last five years have not been wasted time for the banking union project – far from it. It has been a time of implementation and collective learning, marked by a number of milestones. These include the comprehensive assessment of the euro area's main banks and subsequent assumption of licensing and supervisory authority by the ECB on 4 November 2014; the establishment of the Single Resolution Board (SRB) and its assumption of resolution authority under the SRMR on 1 January 2016, with the ongoing build-up of its single resolution fund (SRF) that reached €33 billion as of mid-2019;[1] the first case of a bank's resolution by the SRB under BRRD, of Banco Popular Español in June 2017; and the decision in 2018 to "backstop" the SRF by the European Stability Mechanism (ESM) by 2024 at the latest, thus operationalizing a political commitment made in late 2013.

Even so, the bank-sovereign vicious circle is still there. It is even debatable how much it has been eroded by the banking union reforms. The late spring of 2018 was a sharp reminder of its persistence, with immediate spillovers to the Italian banking sector from an increase of Italian sovereign spreads following the formation of a government coalition perceived as euro-inimical. Thus, almost everyone agrees that the banking union project, understood as breaking the bank-sovereign vicious circle, remains seriously unfinished. The question is how to find a plausible way to complete it.

The bottleneck of concentrated sovereign exposures

A standard and apt depiction of the bank-sovereign vicious circle goes like this: contagion from banking sector weakness to sovereign credit weakness, or vice versa, can be (and generally is) both direct and indirect. The direct channels are, from banks to sovereigns, the various guarantees that governments provide to the domestic banking sector, either explicit (deposit insurance) or implicit (loosely referred to as "bailout" when the guarantee materialized); and, from sovereigns to banks, sovereign exposures (i.e. loans to sovereigns and sovereign bonds held by the bank as assets), and the fact that the erosion of guarantees resulting in a decline in sovereign credit also makes the banks look weaker. The indirect channels are through the domestic economy, which suffers from either banking sector fragility or

---

1 SRB website, at https://srb.europa.eu/en/node/804.

sovereign financial weakness, and whose deterioration in turn has negative impact on the banking sector and on the government. These multiple channels are summarized in the following chart (which to the author's knowledge was first drawn in a similar form by Olivier Blanchard and his colleagues in internal documents of the International Monetary Fund in the summer of 2011, sadly left unpublished).

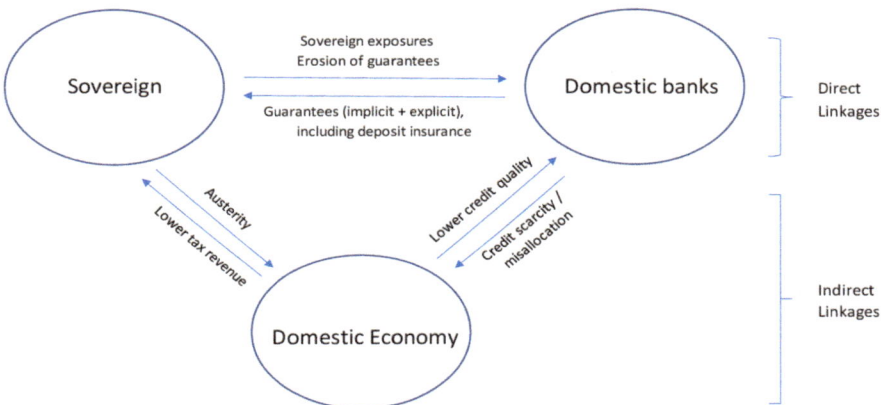

In principle, breaking the bank-sovereign vicious circle entails breaking all six arrows displayed in the chart. The lower (indirect) four are best addressed through cross-border integration of the banking sector inside the euro area, meaning both the emergence of banks that have significant operations in several euro area countries, and the ability for such banks to manage their capital and liquidity in a seamlessly integrated manner throughout the euro area without being hampered by "ring-fencing" imposed by national authorities, e.g. specific capital or liquidity requirements on a subsidiary in a given member state (such barriers to euro-area-wide capital and liquidity management are often referred to in the policy debate as "home-host issues"). The upper (direct) arrows can be broken by actions to lower or eliminate both the sovereign exposures and the national guarantees. Since experience teaches that a developed banking system requires public guarantees, even though these should be kept as limited as possible, the latter aim means equalizing these guarantees and pooling them at the euro-area (or banking-union[2]) level. Since banks need to keep sovereign

---

2 This chapter does not discuss the specific challenges that may exist in EU member states that may choose to be in the banking union without adopting the euro as their currency, through the "close cooperation" process set in Article 7 of the SSM Regulation.

exposures, not least to comply with regulatory liquidity requirements, the former aim means diversification of those exposures away from being concentrated in a single member state.

In sum, a policy program to complete the banking union / break the bank-sovereign vicious circle has to include components along three directions:

- Diversification of euro-area sovereign exposures of euro-area banks;[3]
- Equalization and pooling at the euro-area / banking-union level of explicit and implicit public guarantees;
- Removal of barriers to cross-border integration inside the euro area, including the phasing out of current national ring-fencing practices and instruments.[4]

The second component of "guarantee-pooling" is complex and multifaceted, and this chapter is not the place to develop it. Suffice to say that EDIS, in a form that makes the deposit guarantee unambiguously identical for all deposits up to the mandatory threshold (currently €100,000) no matter where in the euro area they are held, is a necessary but not sufficient part of it. Additional reforms should include the clarification of the regime for non-viable banks, which currently suffers from ambiguity about the dividing line between what BRRD calls "resolution" (harmonized in EU law) and "national insolvency proceedings" (not harmonized, and opening the possibility of significant state aid as happened with two Italian banks based in the Veneto region in June 2017). Crisis-time intervention instruments, such as liquidity guarantees and precautionary recapitalizations as well as emergency liquidity assistance, should also be available at the euro-area level (with due safeguards) in order to credibly dismantle them at the national level and thus remove their contribution to bank-sovereign vicious circle.

All three components are relevant, and indeed essential, to any serious project to complete the banking union. Such an effort is made harder, however, by the fact that these components are dependent on each other, but in a way that is not symmetrical: namely, the second component is a prerequisite for the third, and the first is a prerequisite for the second. These linkages are not yet universally accepted, despite being easy to understand. It is thus worth detailing them briefly.

- <u>Removing ring-fencing requires the pooling of guarantees.</u> As long as member states offer guarantees, whether deposit insurance or any other prospect

---

3 Sovereign exposures outside of the euro area do not contribute to the bank-sovereign vicious circle, nor do the euro-area exposures of non-euro-area banks.

4 This component also includes the recognition in capital regulation of the risk-mitigation benefits of cross-border integration in the euro area: see on this e.g. Jokivuolle and Virén (2019).

of using public funds to address future bank crisis situations, they will impose national ring-fencing requirements under the corresponding mandate (s) and the imperative of defending financial stability. In other words, ring-fencing will persist unless the euro-area level is convincingly equipped to protect financial stability even in a major banking crisis, which is not currently the case.

– Pooling guarantees requires the diversification of sovereign exposures. The pooling of guarantees, including deposit insurance, at the euro area represents a major act of risk sharing and must be unambiguously directed at protecting the stability of the banking system, not assistance to national governments. As long as banks can act as a channel of preferential funding of sovereign (or sub-sovereign) borrowers, as is currently the case, there will be an understandable reluctance to provide this euro-area umbrella with the distributional implications it may entail. Thus, a necessary condition for guarantee-pooling is the removal of the possibility that governments may lean on "domestic" banks so that they give them credit even when other lenders or investors would not.

The implications are rather simple and stark. In theory, these reforms could be made in sequence – sovereign exposures first, then guarantees (including EDIS), then home-host, in that order as each reform unlocks the next one. In practice, however, this is unrealistic because diverging member states' preferences are not likely to allow, say, an agreement on sovereign concentration charges without EDIS. As a consequence, the only way to break through the thicket of intertwined interests at stake is a "grand bargain" or package approach, in which all three dimensions would be unlocked in a single cycle of political decision-making – even as the respective technical aspects are distinct, and would presumably be treated in separate EU legislative acts. A simultaneous discussion of sovereign exposures, EDIS, other guarantee-pooling matters under a predictable regime for non-viable banks, and home-host issues, is thus the only way to achieve satisfactory results, in spite of the considerable complexity this approach entails. This need for a comprehensive approach appears to be at least tacitly acknowledged by euro area negotiators (Eurogroup, 2019).

Sovereign concentration charges

As the previous section makes clear, dealing with the challenge of concentrated sovereign exposures is the key to the rest of the agenda to complete the banking union. This section details the issue and the case for sovereign concentration charges as an appropriate policy response, based on the more extensive analysis provided in Véron (2017).[5]

To provide the right policy response, it is important to start from the right diagnosis. The problem at hand is the concentration of euro-area banks' sovereign euro-area exposures, typically with an overwhelming share of these in the country where the bank is headquartered, or home country. This "home bias", measured as home-country to total euro-area sovereign exposures, was as high as 75 percent in median over a sample of 63 banks reporting to the European Banking Authority (EBA) in mid-2016, and does not appear to have decreased significantly since then. There is no ostensible reason for it, as EU banking regulation makes no difference between the home country and other member states in terms of regulatory treatment. As a consequence, the drivers of that concentration are not a matter of broad consensus, even as studies (e.g. Altavilla and coauthors, 2017) suggest moral suasion from home-country authorities play a role. Irrespective of causality, the concentration of sovereign exposures obviously participates in the perpetuation of the bank-sovereign vicious circle.

The overall amounts of euro-area banks' sovereign exposures, by contrast, do not appear excessive – what reform should aim at is their diversification within the euro area, not their overall reduction. Also and importantly, the problem at hand, from the perspective of completing the banking union, is not that EU sovereign exposures receive a credit risk-weighting of zero ("zero risk-weighting") in risk-weighted capital calculations under the EU capital requirements legislation – this may be viewed by some as a problem, but it is in any case a separate one, that is not specific to the euro area. The zero-risk-weighting of domestic sovereign exposures in domestic currency is part of the global Basel capital framework, and it is apt in the euro area that all sovereign bonds are covered by this provision, at least as long as no pan-euro-area sovereign-like "Eurobonds" exist – i.e., for the foreseeable future. In other words, the challenge to complete the banking union is to address sovereign concentration risk in the euro area, not sovereign credit risk as such.

The concept of sovereign concentration charges (occasionally referred to in the past as "marginal risk-weight add-ons") has emerged in the mid-2010s as a

---

5 The author views his analysis of 2017 as still entirely relevant to the ongoing debate, with one minor correction: unlike in Véron (2017), promotional banks (e.g. BNG in the Netherlands) should be entirely exempted from sovereign concentration charges, since their *raison d'être* is to lend to domestic sovereign or sub-sovereign entities. This exemption, however, should not apply to public banks that compete in other market segments, such as Germany's *Landesbanken* and *Sparkassen*.

way to address this challenge through a targeted twist in capital regulation:[6] euro-area sovereign exposures would remain zero risk-weighted, but only if they do not exceed a certain threshold of concentration ("exemption threshold"). Exposures to a given euro-area country above that threshold, multiplied by a coefficient ("sovereign concentration charge") that rises with concentration, would be added to the denominator of capital calculations (namely, risk-weighted assets) and thus result in additional capital requirements. A version of this mechanism appears to have been included in the final report of a high-level group on sovereign exposures to the EU Economic and Financial Committee that was (unfortunately) left unpublished in June 2016 and was referred to at the time in public pronouncements (Enria, Farkas and Overby, 2016; Dutch Presidency of the Council, 2016). It was echoed in a document released at the global level by the Basel Committee on Banking Supervision in late 2017, which however fails to distinguish the specific case of the euro area from other jurisdictions that have a national currency.[7]

While the principle of sovereign concentration charges is straightforward, its implementation would require a number of policy choices, mainly in terms of calibration and transitional arrangements, that are discussed at length in Véron (2107), and only sketched here.

The calibration should be at least sufficient to disincentivize exposures that would be so large that a single (or perhaps two simultaneous) sovereign credit event(s) would entirely wipe out a bank's regulatory capital. Since haircuts in a sovereign debt restructuring can be as high as 50 percent, this suggests that the calibration should make an exposure ratio (measured as the ratio of a bank's exposure to a given sovereign and its sub-sovereign entities to its Tier-1 capital, the usual benchmark for characterizing large exposures) of above 100 percent unattractive, and be dissuasive for exposure ratios above 200 percent. Véron (2017) correspondingly suggests an exemption threshold at 33 percent – i.e. sovereign exposures to a single euro-area member state of less than 33 percent of a bank's Tier-1 capital are not charged at all, and those between 33 and 100 percent of Tier-1 are charged only mildly.

As for transitional arrangements, the charges should be phased-in gradually over an extended period, and all pre-existing exposures at the time of first

---

6 Given the structural nature of the effort to reduce sovereign home bias, it is indispensable that this change in the capital regulatory approach be introduced through general and binding rules, known as "pillar one" in the prudential jargon (with reference to the architecture of the Basel Accords), and not in a case-by-case manner under supervisory discretion ("pillar two").

7 This flaw was highlighted in the author's public comment to the Basel Committee, available at https://www.bis.org/bcbs/publ/comments/d425/nicolasveron.pdf.

implementation could be "grandfathered" (i.e. exempted from the application of sovereign concentration charges) to minimize the risk of sell-offs. The entry into force of the reform should also be preceded by widespread public consultation and information, not least to clarify the fact that sovereign concentration charges do not entail an end to the zero risk-weighting of sovereign exposures as long as these are properly diversified. This feature also implies that euro-area banks would suffer no competitive disadvantage relative to their non-euro-area peers, thus preserving an international level playing field. Existing precedents, for example in the area of taxation, suggest that a well-handled transition would happen without triggering any undesired market developments.

Even so, there is no denying that the introduction of sovereign concentration charges would increase market discipline in sovereign debt markets – indeed, this is part of the reform's purpose. Earlier responsiveness of prices and spreads to a deterioration of perceived debt sustainability would improve the incentives on public policymakers. But in order not to be destabilizing, greater market discipline for sovereign issuers needs to be complemented by a stronger euro-area-wide safety net on the euro-area banking sector. As already argued above, this is why the pooling of guarantees, starting with a single European deposit insurance scheme, should be introduced in the same policy package as sovereign concentration charges.

Prospects for reform

There have been a number of false starts in the discussion over completing the banking union in the past five years, which have led some observers to grow increasingly cynical about the possibility of achieving results. Radical pessimism appears unwarranted, however. While politically difficult, a policy package as exposed above is within reach during the term of the new European Commission.

The report of June 2019 (Eurogroup, 2019) lays an apt basis for that discussion, as it correctly suggests a discussion of the steady state before consideration of transitional arrangements, and lists most of the relevant issues to be included. As for the market environment, the reduction in non-performing loans over recent years, and the current levels of sovereign debt spreads that do not compromise individual member states' debt sustainability, should assuage concerns that have been expressed in the past under the codeword of "risk reduction". These current conditions should also reassure any doubters that sovereign concentration charges, with a careful calibration and appropriate transitional arrangements, can be introduced without any market disruption if they are part of a broader policy package that includes the pooling of guarantees. On the day she was elected, the new President of the European Commission pledged that she will "focus on completing the banking union" (von der Leyen, 2019). In May 2019, a leaked internal document of the European Commission suggested that sovereign concentration charges were being actively considered for near-term reform.[8]

Policymakers in the euro area now share a broad understanding that their collective framework needs reform to offer an acceptable degree of resilience in the face of probable future internal or external shocks – in other words, just perpetuating the status quo would be reckless. At the same time, the political conditions, including public acceptance, do not appear to be currently met for radical moves towards a fully-fledged fiscal union in the euro area, including the introduction of Eurobonds or other robust designs of a common "safe asset", which would arguably require amending the EU Treaties. Completing the banking union would greatly enhance the euro area's resilience, and also lay the basis for a greater international role of the euro, without the need for major steps towards fiscal union or for any change in the treaties. It should be the main political priority for euro area economic and financial reform in the years ahead.

References

Altavilla, Carlo, Marco Pagano, and Saverio Simonelli (2017), "Bank Exposures and Sovereign Stress Transmission", *Review of Finance* 2017:1-37, Oxford University Press. Available at https://papers.ssrn.com/sol3/papers.cfm?abstract_id=2848937.

BCBS (2017), "The Regulatory Treatment of Sovereign Exposures", discussion paper, Basel Committee on Banking Supervision, December. Available at https://www.bis.org/bcbs/publ/d425.htm.

Bénassy-Quéré, Agnès, Markus Brunnermeier, Henrik Enderlein, Emmanuel Farhi, Marcel Fratzscher, Clemens Fuest, Pierre-Olivier Gourinchas, Philippe Martin, Jean Pisani-Ferry, Hélène Rey, Isabel Schnabel, Nicolas Véron, Beatrice Weder di Mauro and Jeromin Zettelmeyer (2018), "Reconciling risk sharing with market discipline: A constructive approach to euro area reform", CEPR Policy Insight No. 91, London: Centre for European Policy Reform, January. Available at https://cepr.org/active/publications/policy_insights/viewpi.php?pino=91.

Dutch Presidency of the Council (2016), "Strengthening the banking union and the regulatory treatment of banks' sovereign exposures", Presidency note for the Informal ECOFIN, 22 April. Available at https://www.rijksoverheid.nl/binaries/rijksoverheid/documenten/kamerstukken/2016/04/14/bijlage-8-presidency-paper-strengthening-the-banking-union/bijlage-8-presidency-paper-%E2%80%93-strengthening-the-banking-union.pdf.

---

8 See Huw Jones, "Exclusive: Europe prepares raft of post-Brexit banking reforms", *Reuters*, 15 May 2019, available at https://uk.reuters.com/article/uk-eu-banks-exclusive/exclusive-europe-prepares-raft-of-post-brexit-banking-reforms-idUKKCN1SL19F.

Enria, Andrea, Adam Farkas, and Lars Jul Overby (2016), "Sovereign Risk: Black Swans and White Elephants", *European Economy*, July 8. Available at http://european-economy.eu/2016-1/sovereign-risk-black-swans-and-white-elephants/.

Eurogroup (2019), "Considerations on the Further Strengthening of the Banking Union, including a Common Deposit Insurance System", June. Available at https://www.consilium.europa.eu/media/39768/190606-hlwg-chair-report.pdf.

Farhi, Emmanuel, and Jean Tirole (2016), "Deadly Embrace: Sovereign and Financial Balance Sheet Doom Loops", NBER Working Paper 21843, National Bureau of Economic Research, January (revised November). Available at https://www.nber.org/papers/w21843.

Howarth, David, and Lucia Quaglia (2016), *The Political Economy of European Banking Union*, Oxford University Press.

Jokivuolle, Esa, and Matti Virén (2019). "Loan portfolio diversification in the euro area, capital requirements, and the European Banking Union", SUERF Policy Note 87, July. Available at https://www.suerf.org/docx/f_c6969ae30d99f73951cb976b88a457af_6655_suerf.pdf.

von der Leyen, Ursula (2019), "A Union that strives for more: My agenda for Europe", Political guidelines for the next European Commission 2019-2014, Brussels, July. Available at https://www.europarl.europa.eu/resources/library/media/20190716RES57231/20190716RES57231.pdf.

Tooze, Adam (2018), Crashed: How a Decade of Financial Crises Changed the World, Allen Lane.

Véron, Nicolas (2017), "Sovereign Concentration Charges: A New Regime for Sovereign Exposures", European Parliament, November. Available at https://www.europarl.europa.eu/thinktank/en/document.html?reference=IPOL_STU%282017%29602111.

V. Structure of EDIS

Dominique Laboureix

The Role of Deposit Insurance in Promoting Financial Stability and Protecting the Ordinary Saver's Money

Deposit Insurance is a critical part of the financial safety net, ensuring that depositors can have full confidence that their deposits will be safe if their bank fails. Following the crisis of 2008 a series of reforms were introduced in Europe, as part of a coordinated international response. It was decided that the taxpayer should no longer be first in line to foot the bill for a failing bank. The concept of bank resolution was born.

This means that for major banks, the authorities have the powers to address the failure of a bank through application of resolution tools. Furthermore, following the experience of the financial crisis, it became clear that further integration was needed for the euro area countries. As such the first two pillars of the Banking Union, the Single Supervisory Mechanism and Single Resolution Mechanism, were established, shifting responsibility for supervision and resolution to the European level. Under the Single Resolution Mechanism centralised decision-making power in respect of resolution has been entrusted to the Single Resolution Board (the "SRB").

However, under the European approach, resolution is the exception, with the starting assumption being that such firms would be placed in insolvency, just as any other business would go into insolvency in case of failure. As such, the effective management of deposit insurance continues to be key to the management of bank failures. Depositors must have confidence that the authorities will be able to manage the failure of a bank, either through application of resolution tools or, for smaller banks, through a rapid pay-out of covered deposits.

A lack of confidence in the deposit insurance system can lead to contagion across the financial system. If depositors believe that the authorities will not effectively protect covered deposits, then depositors may become incentivised to withdraw their deposits, increasing the risk of bank runs. This risk can only be addressed through the development of an operationally effective Deposit Guarantee Scheme (DGS), right across the Banking Union.

In the financial crisis, Member States significantly enhanced the protection provided to depositors, in particular through the DGS directive of 2009, which required all Member States to increase coverage to a harmonised level of

https://doi.org/10.1515/9783110683073-021

€100,000[1]. However, for some Member States, Covered Deposits are now equal to multiples of the Member States' GDP[2]. This could undermine confidence in the effectiveness of the guarantee, especially given the experience of the crisis where some Member States, such as Ireland, Portugal, Spain or Greece, had difficulty in borrowing on the international markets. While DGSs remain at the national level, these can be thrown into disarray in a time of crisis. Once the ordinary saver loses trust in the DGS, a bank run is on the cards.

This is why completion of the Banking Union, through development of a European level for deposit insurance would enhance the confidence of depositors. The use of funds, managed at the Banking Union level, to manage bank failures would strengthen the DGSs of all Member States, ensuring that even in a crisis DGSs would continue to perform their function effectively. The ordinary depositor could have confidence that his or her savings are protected and backed by a fund built up at the Banking Union level. Even if there were a potential failure of some banks in several countries, a system of protection at the Banking Union level would be able to provide confidence.

Design considerations

Building a Deposit Insurance Fund at the Banking Union level

When considering how a deposit insurer for the Banking Union could be designed, it is critical that the chosen approach would enable the effective management of bank failures. As noted above, it is only through enabling the effective management of bank failures that confidence in the financial system, and broader financial stability, will be maintained.

In the first place, building up an ex-ante fund at the Banking Union level will be important to build depositors' confidence that a failure could be managed effectively. Building a central fund will also allow for mutualisation of risk across Member States, increasing the overall stability of the system by risk pooling. A Banking Union DGS, with the capacity to raise funds from banks operating in all Member States in the Banking Union, would be able to cope with the failure of a greater number of banks. Looking to the American example of the FDIC, we can already see the benefits of having a strong central fund, which enables the authorities to manage the failure of a firm effectively.

---

1 Further enhancements to the DGS Directive were later agreed in 2014.
2 https://ec.europa.eu/epsc/sites/epsc/files/5p_note_edis.pdf

Risk-based contributions, collected from all banks in the Banking Union, would be the means of building such a fund. By applying risk-based contributions at the bank level, the system would ensure that banks which expose the deposit insurance to the greatest level of risk must also make the largest relative contributions. This reduces the risk of moral hazard, and also addresses the concern that there would be risk transfers between Member States. Effectively and appropriately priced risk-based contributions, levied at the bank level, would ensure that if a Member State had a particularly risky banking sector then those banks would pay proportionately more towards the central fund – both before and after a bank failure.

Clearly, the eventual design is for legislators to agree, but the SRB would highlight the importance of creating a simple approach that the SRB can implement, and which is predictable for the banks. Without transparency around the calculation methodology, the possible incentive benefits of the risk indicators used to calculate contributions might not be realised.

Managing a Banking Union deposit insurance scheme

We currently have both a single supervisor and a resolution authority at the level of the Banking Union. By contrast, we still have 29 different DGSs operating across the 19 Member States in the Banking Union. Having a DGS at the Banking Union level would improve interactions, in terms of having one authority with which to communicate. A single Banking Union authority with responsibility for Deposit Insurance at the Banking Union level may also reduce some concerns about moral hazard.

The design should be transparent and simple, so that citizens can understand the scheme and therefore have increased confidence in their deposit insurance. The design of a European scheme to protect depositors should account for this by being relatively simple as well as being quick and easy to access if required, thus providing confidence. At the end of the day, a DGS will not fulfil its role if it does not inspire confidence among the general public in a time of crisis.

An important aspect of this is ensuring that the authorities can react rapidly, through providing for effective, quick and transparent decision-making. The Single Resolution Mechanism Regulation (the "SRMR") provides an example of governance which accounts for the need for rapid action. A Banking Union-level DGS could be usefully integrated into the SRB's decision-making fora. This would be helpful, insofar as it would ensure that the resolution authority and deposit insurer are fully aligned. At the same time, it is important for SRB governance to be as efficient as possible.

Enhancing the European DGS framework

This paper has concentrated on the management of failure through pay-out to covered depositors. However, it should be recalled that other "alternative measures" are also available to DGSs for the management of bank failures. These already exist at the national level in a number of EU Member States, and we view these as potentially offering significant benefits in terms of enhanced efficiency.

In the US context, the Federal Deposit Insurance Corporation (the "FDIC") typically uses "purchase and assumption" style transactions to manage bank failures. Purchase and assumption agreements provide for the transfer of relevant books to an acquiring institution, with the process managed directly by the FDIC under an administrative procedure. The FDIC has broad powers, and is able to act directly as an administrator. Importantly, purchase and assumption transactions have proven to be both more cost-efficient and less disruptive for depositors than a liquidation.

A similar approach in the Banking Union, by providing DGSs with the possibility to apply an administrative procedure to manage a "purchase and assumption" style transaction would enable the more effective management of small and medium sized bank failures. Management of these procedures by a centralised authority would ensure the application of consistent standards, and thereby further reduce the risk of moral hazard.

Another important, broader consideration relates to the insolvency system more generally. Currently the SRB faces 19 different insolvency systems. This would also be an important challenge for a deposit insurer for the Banking Union as well. Cross-border banks, for which failure would be managed by insolvency, rather than through application of resolution tools, could be particularly challenging. Harmonised insolvency rules for banks, or more precisely, a harmonised banking liquidation regime, would therefore contribute to the functioning of a European protection scheme for depositors.

Ensuring that bank insolvencies can be managed effectively is of direct importance for a European deposit insurer, given that losses would only be borne by the central fund to the extent that insufficient returns are realised from the estate of the failed bank.

Interactions with the resolution framework

Introduction of a Banking Union DGS would support resolution planning, given that it could enable a more consistent approach across the Banking Union.

Currently, if there were a cross-border bank failure, then the resolution authority would have to engage with multiple DGSs throughout resolution planning.

Furthermore, a more efficient DGS, with a high level of funding, could potentially address the failures of larger banks than might be feasible under the current approach. This avoids the risk that banks could be unable to enter insolvency solely because of the limitations of a particular Member State's DGS, and supports the general principle that resolution is only an exception to the general rule.

The creation of a central deposit insurance fund at the Banking Union level could also have benefits if the SRB determined that the use of DGS funds would be necessary under the resolution scheme to ensure that depositors continue to have access to their funds (in line with article 79 of the SRMR). In this case, a single DGS with which to coordinate would have clear benefits from a planning perspective, and the increased size of the DGS could also enhance the DGS' capacity to support the SRB's resolution action.

Sequencing

Beyond the question of how the end-state Banking Union DGS should be designed, there is also the important question of how it should be introduced. In this context, sequencing has been an important topic for discussion. It is important to begin to make progress, possibly by first addressing liquidity.

Under an approach focussing on liquidity, the Banking Union DGS would only provide liquidity support to national DGSs. This would be designed to ensure that European DGSs would always have a sufficient level of funding to meet the liquidity needs for a given bank failure. Any losses that would materialise following the liquidation of a bank would be borne at the national level, with fees levied on the relevant national banking sector, rather than from all banks in the Banking Union.

At the same time, and as noted above, it is important to avoid complexity, so that depositors can fully understand the protection provided, and therefore develop confidence in the overall system. For sequencing, this would hold true across all stages of the implementation of Banking Union deposit insurance. The different steps towards the final steady state should all enhance the protection received by depositors. In particular, care should be taken to avoid introducing new complexities in the transitional arrangements, which depositors might view as reducing the overall quality of the deposit insurance.

Furthermore, the approach selected should clearly lead towards the eventual Banking Union system. In particular, for any form of Banking Union DGS, it will be important to begin collecting funds, and to create a central authority at the Banking Union level with responsibility for management of those funds and the broader deposit insurance system. This will both enhance confidence in the current Deposit Guarantee systems, while also enabling a more logical progression towards the final Banking Union deposit insurance system.

By contrast, a different possible design of a Banking Union DGS could be mandatory lending. Under such an approach, liquidity would be ensured by making intra-DGS lending mandatory in case of need. However, because this would not create a central authority or a central fund, it would be unclear how this would connect to the steady state scheme to guarantee and protect deposits. Furthermore, such an approach, because it would not develop a central fund, would not bring the enhancements to confidence that development of a central fund might bring.

Conclusion

The development of a deposit insurer at the Banking Union level must be focussed on ensuring that bank failures can be managed effectively, so that depositors can have full confidence in the financial safety net. Only by ensuring that the practical aspects of the deposit insurance system work effectively, will further benefits to financial stability be realised. Focussing on practical aspects will also help in avoiding overly political topics, and instead enable progress on technical features relating to the eventual design of the Banking Union DGS.

With regards to the next steps, it is important to make progress, possibly through first addressing liquidity. At the same time, the practical approach recommended for the design of the end state of European deposit insurance should also be applied to the transitional phases. It should be ensured that the sequencing of a Banking Union DGS leads to a consistently higher standard of deposit insurance for citizens.

After the last financial crisis in 2008, Europe took a decision to ensure that the ordinary taxpayer would be protected in case of any future shocks to the banking system. While we have made great progress in setting up a single fund that could intervene in the case of resolution, we have so far failed to put in place a deposit guarantee system for the Banking Union to complete the protection of ordinary people's savings.

If we believe that by pooling our resources together we are stronger, as the founders of the European Coal and Steel Community believed back in 1952, we should favour a system that would make our European financial system much more resilient when the next shock hits.

Nicoletta Mascher

Designing a European Deposit Insurance Scheme for Euro Area Banking Union

The last financial crisis triggered major reforms in the institutional infrastructure of the European Union and prompted joint efforts to preserve the single currency and secure financial stability. The 2012 vision of a euro area banking union (BU) has been largely implemented; the system has developed its safety net with a more harmonised supervisory approach, a single rulebook, a pan-European authority to conduct supervision of the largest banks and ensure high standards of national supervisory approaches, as well as a single resolution fund. As a result of the adopted measures, European banks have become safer, with larger capital and liquidity buffers. Meanwhile the reform momentum has weakened[1].

The architecture underpinning the BU in the euro area remains incomplete. Regulatory divergences across countries, loopholes in supervisory risk coverage, complexity of rules and a multitude of actors involved leave the framework vulnerable to new emerging crises. Furthermore, the absence of a common deposit insurance scheme impinges on the confidence of depositors and the credibility of the safety net, the lack of which will continue to play a major role in determining the magnitude of external support needed to buttress stability of the system in future crisis situations.

The establishment of a European Deposit Insurance Scheme (EDIS) would be a fundamental step to consolidate progress achieved and support a more efficient, stable and prosperous banking sector in the euro area. Despite improved profit indicators, euro area banks continue to underperform

---

1 Compare e.g. IMF (2018), *Euro Area Policies*, FSAP, July 2018, IMF Country Report No. 18/226; or CEPR (2018), Reconciling risk sharing with market discipline: A constructive approach to euro area reform, Policy Insight No. 91.

Note: I would like to thank my colleagues F. Vancompernolle and O. Francova for their invaluable assistance in preparing this article.
Disclaimer: The views expressed in this note are those of the author and do not necessarily represent those of the European Stability Mechanism (ESM) or institutions for which the author worked in the past, or their policy.

https://doi.org/10.1515/9783110683073-022

other sectors[2] as well as their non-European competitors[3]; an average 6.2% (Chart D) return on equity as of end-2018 compares to 12.6% recorded in 2007. In terms of asset quality, as measured by non-performing loans (NPLs)[4] to gross loans (Chart C), there is a large disparity of results across banks and between countries. Nonetheless, euro area banks have made significant progress in reducing NPLs from their crisis peaks (8.8%[5]) and the pace of decline has picked up in the last few quarters. With a 4.1%[6] NPL ratio, euro area banks have achieved the European Banking Authority's (EBA) target ratio, paving the way for a more constructive dialogue on risk sharing in the banking union.

A well-designed and credible common deposit insurance scheme can actually incorporate the right incentives to further foster risk discipline and efficiency. In addition, an identical level of depositor protection across the euro area, backed by a single prefunded arrangement, will decrease, if not eliminate, the risk of bank runs under distressed market conditions. Euro area depositors and banks would benefit from EDIS as the costs of financial and debt crises will fall. EDIS would also weaken the link between banks and their national sovereigns by disentangling deposit protection from available national public resources; it would therefore eliminate the need for ring-fencing by host countries, thus promoting financial integration, cross-border consolidation and a more efficient allocation of capital and liquidity. Ultimately, EDIS would boost confidence and benefit the entire euro area also in terms of growth potential.

---

2 Cau, E., Joyce, M., Wilkinson, S., Chandrasekaran, M., K., Goel, A., Manners, Ch., Fall, O., De Santivanes, F. G., Yang, J., (2019), *Banks-Playing catch –up*. Barclays, European Equity Strategy, Equity Research, 17 July 2019.
3 According to IMF calculations on a sample of 431 publicly-traded banks, European banks appear to be more leveraged and have bigger problems with loan ratios than US banks. Xu, T. T., Hu, K., Das, U., S., (2019), *Bank Profitability and Financial Stability*, IMF Working Paper WP /19/5, p. 23.
4 The term NPLs is used in this contribution as a shorthand term. However, in technical terms it means non-performing exposures (NPEs), following the EU definition (as defined in Commission Implementing Regulation (EU) 2015/227, later amended by Commission Implementing Regulation (EU) 2015/1278).
5 ESM own calculations on SNL Financial for a large sample of euro area banks, (2013Q4), see Chart C.
6 ECB Consolidated Banking Data. Gross non-performing loans and advances as % of total gross loans and advances for domestic banking groups and stand-alone banks (2018Q3).

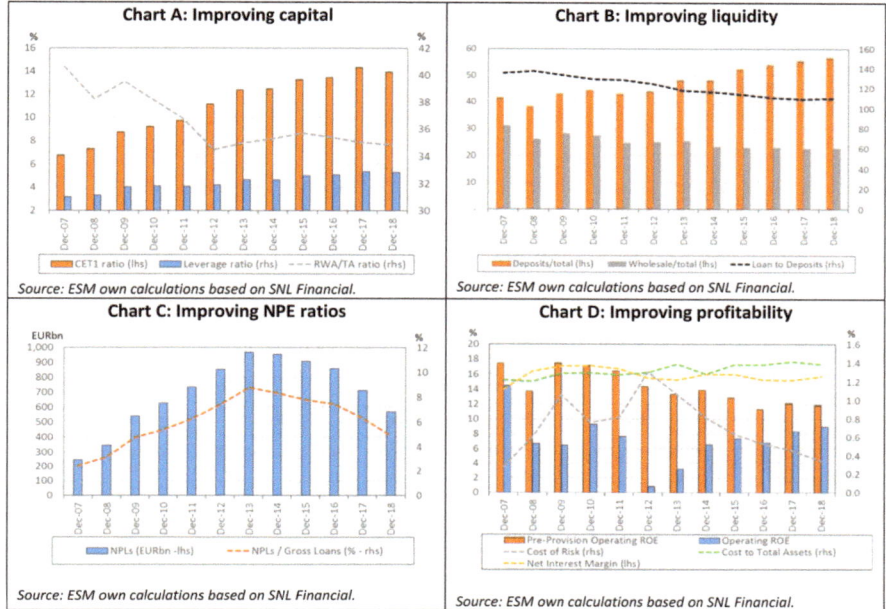

Chart A: Improving capital — Source: ESM own calculations based on SNL Financial.

Chart B: Improving liquidity — Source: ESM own calculations based on SNL Financial.

Chart C: Improving NPE ratios — Source: ESM own calculations based on SNL Financial.

Chart D: Improving profitability — Source: ESM own calculations based on SNL Financial.

To promote a policy debate on EDIS, a stepwise approach can help address the remaining loopholes in the banking union, strike the right balance between risk sharing goals and risk reduction targets and build consensus across euro area member states. To this end, we outline a four-step roadmap for tackling the remaining gaps in the supervisory and resolution framework (the first two BU pillars[7]), overcoming crisis legacies and ensuring substantial progress on EDIS implementation. Our argument unfolds in three chapters. The first summarises why EDIS would make a difference in the banking union set-up and what desirable properties EDIS would have. The second elaborates on additional pieces of the banking union puzzle that determine progress on EDIS. The third details a roadmap that would balance risk reduction and risk sharing initiatives. In conclusion, we highlight that complexity of the institutional framework coupled with a historical transition in banking business models and risk profiles warrant a flexible and dynamic approach for the banking union to remain relevant.

---

7 The banking union consists of three pillars: a) single supervisory framework, b) single resolution, c) still pending common European Deposit Insurance Scheme (EDIS). It is supported by a single rulebook.

1. THE ARCHITECTURE OF A COMMON DEPOSIT INSURANCE FOR THE EURO AREA

Why the euro area needs EDIS

The financial crisis brought to the fore the risk related to the lack of common European solutions. The financial turmoil made it evident that different national schemes and uncoordinated actions across the euro area are not only insufficient to weather major financial crises, but they can also permanently distort competition and increase fragmentation in the internal market. The eroding confidence of depositors and impaired credibility of the safety net played a major role in the unprecedented magnitude of public interventions to preserve financial stability. Savers, withdrawing their deposits from distressed banks, amplified the pressure on them and put further strain on already weakened sovereigns. The ring-fencing measures enacted by euro area cross-border groups in response to the crisis and the related provisions in the regulatory framework continue to affect the functioning of the market for banking services in Europe after more than 10 years.

Under the current national Deposit Guarantee Scheme (DGS) system, the level of deposit protection in each country still depends on national resources and the sovereign's ability to ensure orderly liquidation procedures. The lack of confidence among the general public and market participants that the scheme will hold in situations when the national banking system is put under stress leaves the system vulnerable to bank runs and contagion effects. The 2014 Deposit Guarantee Schemes Directive (DGSD)[8] has unified minimum deposit coverage in the European Union and set some harmonised criteria on scope, eligibility, financing model, target levels and repayment time. It also covers cooperation modalities between the national guarantee schemes, including mutual lending. Despite some harmonisation, a number of differences persist between DGSs given the different starting points, speeds of transition to the target level, target discretions, alternative use of the funds and complementary funding arrangements which can involve temporary state financing. Further heterogeneity across the board relates to specific categories of banks and their affiliation to voluntary schemes or institutional protection schemes (IPSs).

A strong and common safety net securing euro area banks is even more needed given the specificities of the euro area; however, a long lead time may be necessary. The role of euro area banks in the overall economy is much

---

8 Directive 2014/49/EU of the European Parliament and of the Council of 16 April 2014 on deposit guarantee schemes (DGSD)

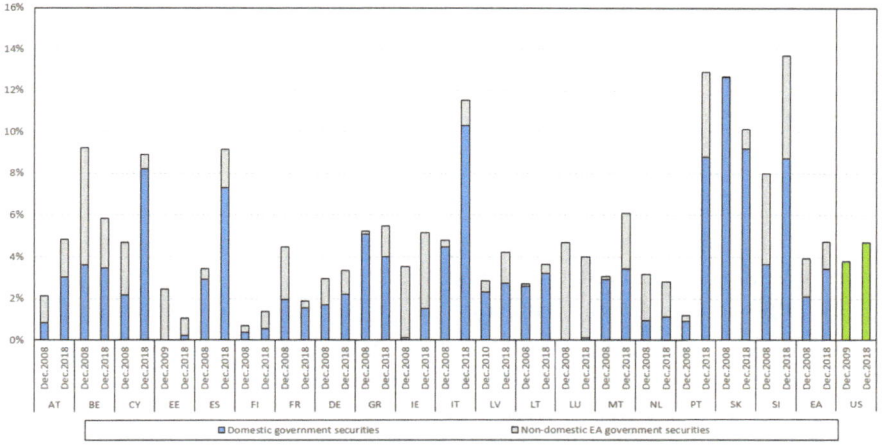

Chart E: *MFIs' government debt securities as % of total assets*

Source: ECB Statistical Datawarehouse: Monetary and Financial Institutions (excl. ESCB), Federal Reserve: All Commercial Banks.
Note: Euro area: The numerator and the denominator takes data from the aggregated balance sheet of the MFI sector at accounting values. Assets and liabilities are presented at aggregated level for the euro area as a whole and euro area Member States. **US:** the numerator includes US Treasury securities held by all commercial banks in the US. The denominator is the total assets of all commercial banks.

higher than in other jurisdictions.[9] Banks remain key financing providers for small and medium size enterprises. In addition, euro area households entrust banks with around 40 % of their assets as deposits.[10] Any disruptions in the banking sector can have a far-reaching impact on the euro area economy. Such a setting reinforces the need for efficient solutions safeguarding bank stability in distress. In spite of that, progress on EDIS is hindered mainly by differences in the risks faced by banks due to the composition of their balance sheets, legacy problems and concerns about the sovereign-financial nexus. Since 2008, banks have strengthened their capital buffers, but a sharp increase in sovereign yields could result in significant losses for those with larger bond holdings (Chart E). Uneven levels of NPLs across the euro area represent another hurdle for EDIS implementation. On average, banks have significantly reduced NPLs from peak levels of 8.8 % of gross loans in the midst of crisis. However, in seven euro area countries, the NPL ratio still exceeds the 5 % threshold, above which, according to EBA guidelines, banks should establish specific operational and governance

---

9 The Voice of Savings and Retail Banking Institute (2015), *Financial Systems in Europe and in the US: Structural Differences Where Banks Remain the Main Source of Finance For Companies.* September 2015. Research paper.
10 Lagarde, Ch., (2019), *The Euro Area: Creating a Stronger Economic Ecosystem*, IMF, 2019.

arrangements to ensure risk reduction[11]. These features require not only well-calibrated solutions but also a gradual approach to their implementation.

Which EDIS for the euro area?

Various proposals for EDIS design have been discussed. Similarly to the original proposal by the European Commission, most proposals foresee a gradual introduction in several stages[12]. The proposals range from simple mechanisms for providing liquidity support to national schemes to a fully-fledged single fund which will provide for loss mutualisation. In the status quo under the DGS directive, national deposit guarantee funds would continue to build up their resources to at least 0.8 % of covered deposits by 2024.

Under the initially envisaged fully-fledged EDIS proposed by the European Commission in 2015, EDIS would eventually fully insure eligible deposits up to the established threshold. According to an increasing participation share in subsequent stages, EDIS would cover not only liquidity shortfalls in the insolvency procedure but also residual losses after recovery from the insolvency estate. To alleviate national concerns, the revised Commission proposal in 2017[13] envisaged a more gradual introduction of the insurance scheme, which would be limited to liquidity needs in the first re-insurance phase. Secondly, to address concerns related to legacy risks and moral hazard, the Commission proposed not to move automatically to the co-insurance phase, making it contingent on a set of conditions.

The more recently discussed mandatory lending model suggests keeping the available funds either entirely in national deposit guarantee schemes (DGS), or partially, in national compartments of a central fund. National compartments or national DGS would be subject to loan agreements in case of national shortfalls. The hybrid model is an in-between option which entails a split between the supranational fund and funds remaining with the national DGS[14]. The models also differ in the way contributions are calculated:

---

11 EBA Guidelines on management of non-performing and forborne exposures
12 See e.g. European Commission (2015), Proposal for a Regulation of the European Commission and the European Parliament and of the Council amending Regulation (EU) 806/2014 in order to establish a European Deposit Insurance Scheme; or Schnabel, I., Véron, N., (2018), *Breaking the Stalemate on European Deposit Insurance*. Peterson Institute for International Economics.
13 European Commission (2017), *Communication from the Commission on completing the Banking Union*, Brussels, 11.10.2017 COM(2017) 592 final
14 EU Council (2018), *Bulgarian Presidency Progress report on Banking Union*. July 2018, p. 10.

loss mutualisation will follow when banks' risks are parametrised against euro area averages, while national compartments are fed on the basis of national risk averages. The combination of calculation methods and target levels can significantly alter the insurance scheme and risk of unwarranted cross-subsidisation effects (see below).

Each model creates different confidence effects, while the economic rationale for a fully mutualised scheme is definitely strong. The re-insurance and the hybrid model would hold funds at centralised level. These funds would be readily available in case of a liquidity shortfall. Therefore, this solution seems more robust in case of a pay-out event, compared to the mandatory lending mechanism. However, implementation and operational costs might be lower without establishing a central fund as foreseen in two sub-options of the mandatory lending model. This could have different implications if there is the intention to move later to a phase of full loss sharing. There are very valid economic reasons for that; a study published by the ECB demonstrates the benefit of full mutualisation of losses in the steady state with a fully pre-funded arrangement at the envisaged 0.8 % level of eligible deposits[15].

A fully mutualised EDIS is most likely to provide the best insurance properties, which is crucial from a financial stability perspective. When more resources can be mobilised, larger shocks can be contained and better absorbed with limited impact on bank creditors. The design with a high level of joint depositor protection and full loss coverage is the most compatible with the long-run objective of a truly integrated banking sector and appears as the most appropriate long-term solution benefitting financial stability. All alternative approaches, like re-insurance, co-insurance or other hybrid solutions could be viable intermediate steps while progressing on the other banking union dossiers and allowing for further risk reduction. In order to achieve a high level of risk mutualisation associated with the third stage of EDIS, some structural features of the insurance scheme can help build consensus and overcome fears of cross-subsidisation and moral hazard. Besides the transitional arrangements, the contribution system and the scope of interventions are key architectural components, as discussed below.

Cross-subsidisation fears remain a main hurdle. In choosing the right architectural features of the scheme, it is important to consider whether more vulnerable countries might systematically contribute less than they would benefit from EDIS. This so-called cross-subsidisation effect will depend on the EDIS

---

15 ECB Occasional Paper Series; *Completing the Banking Union with a European Deposit Insurance Scheme: who is afraid of cross-subsidisation?* April 2018.

architecture, its phasing-in and on risk-based calibration of contributions. Cross-subsidisation is a desirable outcome of the insurance arrangement if it helps to absorb major shocks. However, it is less palatable if it increases the risk of moral hazard and causes a permanent transfer of resources from some countries to other countries. In this respect, the debate could benefit from further and more updated research, covering scenarios for different transitional arrangements and factoring progress in risk reduction and the build-up of loss absorption capacity. To make the results of these studies more compelling, close cooperation among all institutions would be an asset, as well as a deeper involvement of the industry in the development of the project.

Achieving a high level of risk mutualisation associated with the third stage of EDIS is possible only in the long term when the concerns of participating countries are addressed. The use of a sequenced approach when phasing in EDIS can help disentangle interwoven links, define a credible path and avoid missteps. Missing pieces of the banking union need to be added while widening the mutualisation scope in a gradual manner together with a continuous implementation of risk reduction measures and further harmonisation and strengthening of supervisory practices and law. Priority could be given to the elements of the BU that have a direct impact on the risk of EDIS pay-outs; while carefully considering linkages, spill-overs and preparing, at each stage, the necessary conditions that can make the next step acceptable.

The Eurogroup High-Level Working Group has actually mapped out all the missing pieces and developed a sequenced packaging framework.[16] This framework can further evolve so that elements of risk reduction and risk sharing are reconciled. The phase-in of EDIS is associated with the gradual implementation of additional measures acting as incentives for further risk reduction. The definition of risk-based bank contributions to EDIS plays a key role here.

Another important structural aspect is related to the range of possible uses of the common fund in the transitional phases and in the steady state. It should be defined whether EDIS will be used also for alternative interventions. It could, for example allow for financing the transfer of assets and liabilities or deposit books in the context of insolvency proceedings or even for alternative measures to prevent the failure of a credit institution as per article 11 of the Directive on Deposit Guarantee Schemes, namely those tools envisaged under the national schemes to preserve the sound part of a business and depositors' access

---

16 Eurogroup (June 2019), *Consideration on the Further Strengthening of the Banking Union, Including a Common Deposit Insurance System – Report of the HLWG Chair.*

to their savings. These alternative measures, like the FDIC "Purchase and Assumption" deals[17], can be more effective in minimising the cost of a crisis, maximising the recovery rate in case of insolvency and preserving essential functions. If these measures are not administered under the same regime, national deposit insurance schemes will likely maintain their own reserves for these interventions, in addition to EDIS and the Single Resolution Fund (SRF). And the sovereign-bank nexus, which a pan-European insurance should help to loosen, would re-emerge.

How to calibrate contributions to EDIS?

To provide the right incentives, EDIS should be considered as any other insurance and bank contributions should take into account risk-based components specific to each bank's risks. A riskier bank would contribute more to cover its deposits similar to the FDIC approach which includes the CAMEL scoring system for banks (Capital adequacy, Asset quality, Management, Earnings, and Liquidity) and selected financial indicators. Those indicators should also dynamically reflect risk reduction measures. This type of structure could help dissipate concerns about the risk of free riding and indirect support to countries, which are affected by high levels of public debt. A good and balanced calibration system can embed the right incentives for banks to operate under a less risky business model.

    Consistency with the resolution framework, prudential requirements and supervisory judgement is key to avoiding the double counting of risks but also flaws or gaps in the selected approach. For example, in the treatment of large groups, which may resort to resolution more easily, the calibration could envisage a corrective factor for the likely limited reliance on EDIS and higher MREL requirements. At the same time, it could also encompass an indicator of interconnectedness to factor in a potential knock-on effect of a large group failure on the whole sector. Risk sensitivity could be enhanced with a strong link to the supervisory assessment and the institution's risk appetite. Furthermore, calibration can encompass individual risk reduction objectives, in line with the bank-specific supervisory judgement, including, for instance, NPL reduction targets. This way the system could internalise the risk specificities of each bank, embedding the

---

17 So called P&A is a resolution transaction in which a healthy institution purchases some or all of the assets (outstanding loans) of a failed bank and assumes some or all of the liabilities (deposits). FDIC (2019), *Resolutions Handbook*, chapter 4.

forward-looking and qualitative component of the supervisory judgement, and hence catering for new, emerging risks. Thus, it could even become a vehicle to enhance risk discipline. If well designed, the methodology would also be able to capture institution-specific risks related to an overexposure to the domestic sovereign, without introducing exogenous country-based correction factors.

Current EBA guidelines[18] **could be used as a basis for discussions on the risk calibration.** These guidelines use risk factors which are consistent with the supervisory approach; they allow for flexible calibration to reflect the prudential assessment and country specificities; however, looking forward there may be a need for stricter and more uniform rules. The use of risk indicators or parameters that are not part of the supervisory toolkit should be clearly justified and cautiously introduced where necessary. The 2014 DGS Directive already spells out criteria to cater for unintended pro-cyclical effects. At the same time, the system should avoid indefinite extensions of the timeline for achieving given targets due to prolonged downturns.

A good methodology would benefit from a clear design; this would increase transparency and facilitate the next steps. The Commission suggested anchoring the method for calculating contributions in a delegated act specific to the initial phase and a second methodology calculation specific to the subsequent stages of EDIS.[19] Defining the calculation method for the two phases beforehand and making it transparent from the beginning could help to set clear expectations on the conditions to move to the subsequent steps. This would give time to the industry to adapt and provide reassurance to member states that legacies of the crisis are being effectively addressed, the resilience of the banking sector has further increased and that residual risk will be adequately covered and fairly priced.

2. BANKING UNION REFORMS AND CONDITIONS FOR A SUCCESSFUL IMPLEMENTATION OF EDIS

To implement EDIS, a good system of incentives is needed to make risk mutualisation agreeable to all countries. In the aftermath of the financial crisis, the policy debate was dominated by efforts to achieve a balance between so-called risk reduction and risk sharing to make agreement on further coopera-

---

18 EBA (2015), *EBA Guidelines on methods for calculating contributions to DGSs.*

19 European Commission (2015), *Proposal for a Regulation of the European Commission and the European Parliament and of the Council amending Regulation (EU) 806/2014 in order to establish a European Deposit Insurance Scheme*, Article 74a-74d, Official Journal of the European Union.

tion palatable to all member states. The fourth European Commission risk reduction report confirms[20] that related indicators point to a decreasing level of risk in the banking industry. As highlighted above, further risk sharing through an appropriate calibration of EDIS represents an opportunity to provide additional incentives for risk reduction. Contrarily, delaying the process while waiting for further risk reduction could increase uncertainty if not accompanied by clear and credible risk reduction targets.

The currently weakening economic outlook and rising external risks call for stepping up efforts to identify shared solutions that would address the remaining vulnerabilities. The experience gained over the last period of economic growth highlights that EDIS represents only one of the necessary reforms. The reinforcement of the existing banking union pillars remains a priority, while achieving further risk reduction also involves progress on several legislative files, the gradual phase-out of Options and National Discretions (ONDs) and the full implementation of Basel III. Related to that, the euro area needs to address different channels of persisting links between banks and their national sovereigns. In the longer term, more decisive measures could include the extension of existing capital and liquidity waivers, which would make it easier for banks to benefit from the single market[21]. Making cross-border operations less costly will facilitate cross-border consolidation and allow for stronger financial integration; however, this will inevitably increase risks of contagion if the necessary safeguards are not properly implemented and fine-tuned.

Among all necessary measures, the development of bank resolution and liquidation frameworks ranks first due to its direct connection to EDIS. The

---

20 European Commission (2019), *Communication from the Commission Fourth Progress Report on the reduction of non-performing loans and further risk reduction in the Banking Union.* Brussels, 12.6.2019 COM(2019) 278 final.

21 Article 7 and 8 of the CRR define conditions for the application of capital and liquidity waivers within banking groups. The regulation is based on the authority at Member state level. More precisely, cross border capital waivers can only be applied to the parent entity at solo level. Where both the subsidiary and the parent credit institution are authorised and supervised in the same Member State, prudential requirements may be waived for subsidiaries of credit institutions, as well as parent credit institutions, following a case-by-case assessment (Article 7,1 and 2). For liquidity, Article 8 provides for a full or partial waiver to the individual application of liquidity requirements, provided supervision is carried out on the basis of a single liquidity sub-group (SLSG) and conditions set out therein are fulfilled. Thus, liquidity cross-border waivers may be granted according to level 1 legislation. However, additional safeguards make the application of these rule quite restrictive; ONDs and other articles of the CRR come into play when considering such application: credit risk weights and large exposures limits can actually prevent the parent from granting committed credit line to the subsidiary in the amount needed.

harmonisation of national bank insolvency regimes, full harmonisation of creditor hierarchy, but also transparent and clear rules on precautionary recapitalisation and state aid are essential elements for improving the credibility of the system and enabling all parties involved to take the first small step forward. Transparent rules for precautionary recapitalisation would allow for taking corrective measures at an early stage and reducing challenges related to enforcement of regulation and coordination across different authorities. In addition, the clarification of rules for state aid and criteria for the flexible use of burden sharing could enhance trust between the member states and EU institutions and allow for more predictable outcomes of the euro area bank resolution regime. The alignment of insolvency regimes is considered a priority by most countries as only ensuring the same treatment of creditors across the board can create the conditions for achieving comparable recovery rates in insolvency, all other things being equal. As a result, access to the European deposit protection scheme would be uniform across the euro area and the risk of cross-subsidisation would be reduced.

The close link between banks and their domestic sovereigns continues to hinder euro area financial stability. The strong bias that banks have in buying sovereign bonds of their home country reinforces the link between sovereigns and banks. A strong sovereign – bank nexus can amplify the impact of financial crises on the real economy and leave banks dependent on their home sovereign. Proposals to tackle this issue range from limited technical changes to bank accounting (mandatory mark-to-market valuation), to far-reaching sovereign exposure limits and sovereign concentration thresholds. Such measures, if not calibrated properly and phased in over time, could have negative repercussions on bond markets, pose an excessive strain on more vulnerable sovereign issuers, and lead to strong pro-cyclical and cliff effects. In this respect, the Basel Committee determined in December 2017 that there is no international consensus to recommend introducing risk weights or risk limits on sovereign exposures on a global scale.

The most straightforward solution could be the introduction of charges based on domestic sovereign exposures, in the form of higher contributions to EDIS. This option would not affect banks' capital requirements and would encourage diversification of riskier portfolios to non-home country euro area sovereigns. Hence, this option could be combined with technical policy actions including more far-reaching ones, such as the introduction of safe assets in the long term. Credit risk charges on sovereign exposures, however, could feasibly kick in only as ultima ratio in the steady state when EDIS is a fully-mutualised fund and the risk of moral hazard is higher. In the intermediate phase, non-risk based concentration charges on sovereign portfolios could be more suitable to calibrate contributions and smoothen the transition to the final stage. At the same time, the relevant supervisor can play a more prominent role in enhancing risk discipline, including bank-specific action on additional capital requirements in case of high sovereign risk. In addition, supervisory stress tests can encompass more severe scenarios to better reflect risks from sovereign holdings (see paragraph above: *How to calibrate contributions to EDIS?*).

3. ROADMAP TO FINE-TUNING THE BANKING UNION – CONNECTING THE DOTS

Implementing EDIS is not a standalone challenge. As mentioned in previous chapters, a sustainable banking union requires reforms beyond the simple implementation of EDIS. This chapter aims to depict a possible way forward considering the implication of reforms to foster a safer, more profitable and integrated euro area banking industry.

The proposed concept takes into account the political and economic reality and calls for a staged approach for reconciling risk reduction and risk sharing. In the outlined roadmap, the different stages of EDIS are linked to the implementation of measures that could increase the resilience of banking union. The stepwise approach relates to the 2017 Communication by the European Commission[22] and further develops the report of the High Level Working Group chairman submitted to the June 2019 Eurogroup. The roadmap takes into account economic linkages and acknowledge that further risk reduction could actually help to advance the transition from a first phase of EDIS towards a fully-fledged European scheme. In addition, the proposed EDIS architecture includes incentives for enhancing risk reduction in the banking industry.

The BU roadmap also foresees progress in complementary areas. In all subsequent stages, work will continue to ensure convergence of national rules, the discontinuation of unwarranted national discretions and further development of the single rulebook. The implementation of the risk reduction package approved in May 2019, finalisation of transposition of Basel III into the EU framework, and the implementation of an Anti-Money Laundering package will require further efforts. Finally, once the fully mutualised EDIS is in place, cross-border banking groups could be enabled to allocate capital and liquidity more freely and efficiently, relaxing current conditions on capital and liquidity requirements at individual level ("home-host issue"). This in turn will favour investment diversification and reduce the home-bias in banks' investment decisions.

---

22 Eurogroup (June 2019), *Consideration on the Further Strengthening of the Banking Union, Including a Common Deposit Insurance System – Report of the HLWG Chair.*

Step 0: "Setting the stage" (until 2020)

- A preparatory phase would allow the member states and the EU institutions to discuss and agree upon the design of EDIS and in parallel, implement the recently approved risk-reduction legislation.[23] It would also provide scope for reinforcing the second pillar of the banking union.
- Quantitative impact studies, coordinated across EU institutions and with adequate involvement of the banking industry, could underpin a sound calibration of contributions and foster policy debate. So far, there has been only a limited number of comprehensive studies and scenario analyses on the implementation of EDIS. If undertaken at an early stage, these studies can enable transitional arrangements to phase EDIS in.
- In the preparatory phase, agreement should be reached on a method to calculate EDIS contributions taking into account the degree of mutualisation in all subsequent stages. To ensure legal certainty, it would be desirable to frontload the methodology and the planned roll-out in all three stages from the beginning, together with details of the Regulation on EDIS. This could also provide enough time for banks to adapt.
- Progress on EDIS would go hand in hand with further development in the oversight capabilities over the financial sector: the agenda could include harmonisation of the single rulebook, supervisory practices and scope of risk/activity coverage, and stronger coordination across authorities (AML Action Plan and Shadow Banking).
- On the resolution framework, identified shortcomings and inconsistencies can be overcome to ensure credibility of the system. Loopholes to be fixed include burden sharing rules and ranking of creditors, while the toolbox for resolution might need to be expanded. Further work is envisaged on bank insolvency proceedings (possibly via a directive) and liquidity in resolution.
- NPL workout and MREL build-up will continue and risk reduction may facilitate an early introduction of the common backstop to the SRF.

Step 1 "Initiating the European backstop and insurance schemes": The remaining preparatory technical work necessary for the design of a common backstop to the Single Resolution Fund (SRF) and EDIS are completed (2021–2023)

- An assessment of risk reduction, scheduled for 2020 to inform decision about the possible early introduction of the common backstop, also represents an

---

23 Official Journal of the European Union (2019), *Risk reduction package*. Official Journal of the European Union. L 150, Volume 62, 7 June 2019.

opportunity to progress on EDIS.[24] Positive results of the risk reduction assessment could allow not only for progress on the common backstop to the SRF but also for entry into the first phase of EDIS. In parallel, additional steps towards a complete banking union could gradually phase in.

– At this stage, a limited degree of risk sharing is counterbalanced by a lower risk level and a more risk-sensitive contribution to EDIS. For phase 1 of EDIS (re-insurance), the calculation methodology would incorporate incentives for adequate risk reduction, including adherence targets to bank-specific NPL strategies and a strong link to the supervisory assessment and the institution's risk appetite. EDIS would provide liquidity in case of need, while losses would be covered nationally. A clear risk-based approach in defining the conditions for participation in the European insurance scheme can provide reassurance to the member states that legacies of the crisis are being effectively addressed, resilience of the banking sector has further increased and that residual mutualised risk will be adequately covered and fairly priced. As EDIS does not imply a high degree of risk sharing in step 1, bank contributions do not need to be adjusted for sovereign risk.

– At this stage, enhancing the banking union's regulatory strength, supervisory scope and interinstitutional coordination could mitigate concerns about a higher degree of risk sharing in the future. New rules for burden-sharing and creditor hierarchy in bank liquidation and resolution would be implemented. This would ensure the highest possible level of legal certainty before launching the full mutualisation of safety nets.

Step 2 "Deepening the European Deposit Insurance Scheme": Before moving to full mutualisation, the treatment of sovereign exposures in bank balance sheets needs to be addressed (2024-2027)

– This step would be marked by phasing in further risk mutualisation through loss coverage by EDIS. The higher level of risk sharing through EDIS could be offset by the fact that at this stage, bank contributions to EDIS will account for excessive sovereign exposures via concentration parameters but without sovereign rating differentiation. The latter is considered here as a last resort corrective measure for excessive sovereign exposures that have not been resolved before entering the final stage.

– The legislation mitigating the negative links between banks and governments needs to start phasing in before the introduction of fully-mutualised EDIS.

---

24 EU Council (December 2018), *Terms of reference of the common backstop to the Single Resolution Fund*, 4 December 2018, Council of the European Union.

Also, to provide adequate time for banks to adjust, the measures could start slowly, phasing in towards the end of the second step in 2027. If the system of risk calibration has been well crafted and all the conditions to move to the second stage are met, transition could progress smoothly without further large-scale supervisory exercises[25]. Additional scrutiny of the health of the banking sector could even send a negative signal and undermine the role of the supervisory authorities.

- The measures to be in place before entering the final stage of EDIS need to provide reassurance concerning the stability and consistency of the overall framework. Action will be warranted to start phasing out ONDs persisting in national legislation, including those in national prudential provisions. The degree of certainty could be reinforced by a sound and robust AML framework. Finally, the ESM backstop to the SRF shall be in place, in the event it had not been introduced earlier.
- At this stage, discussions about the home-host balance can be resumed and a roadmap set in place before the final stage.

Step 3 "Moving to a complete Banking Union": Member states could approve the implementation of phase 3 of EDIS, which foresees full mutualisation, implementation of a scheme to diversify sovereign exposures and the introduction of more lenient conditions for capital and liquidity waivers (by end 2027)

- After taking stock of previous progress, stage 3 of EDIS, which entails the full mutualisation of deposit insurance, can start. A fully mutualised insurance scheme would reinforce the banking union framework and could complement the fully mutualised SRF when confidence into the banking sector is fully restored.
- The last stage of EDIS would be introduced, if minimum funding requirements of EDIS are met (0.80 % of covered deposits) and all the required qualitative risk reduction measures agreed in the June 2016 "Council Conclusions Roadmap to Complete the Banking Union" are implemented.
- The calculation of contributions to EDIS would take into account not only NPLs, MREL and level 3 asset euro area benchmarks, but potentially also the sovereign risk factor for excessive holdings of domestic sovereign bonds, in addition to the risk-free concentration factors introduced before.

---

25 A new Asset Quality Review to check health conditions of all participating banks was envisaged in the EC proposal as a necessary prerequisite for moving to the final stage.

Summary scheme

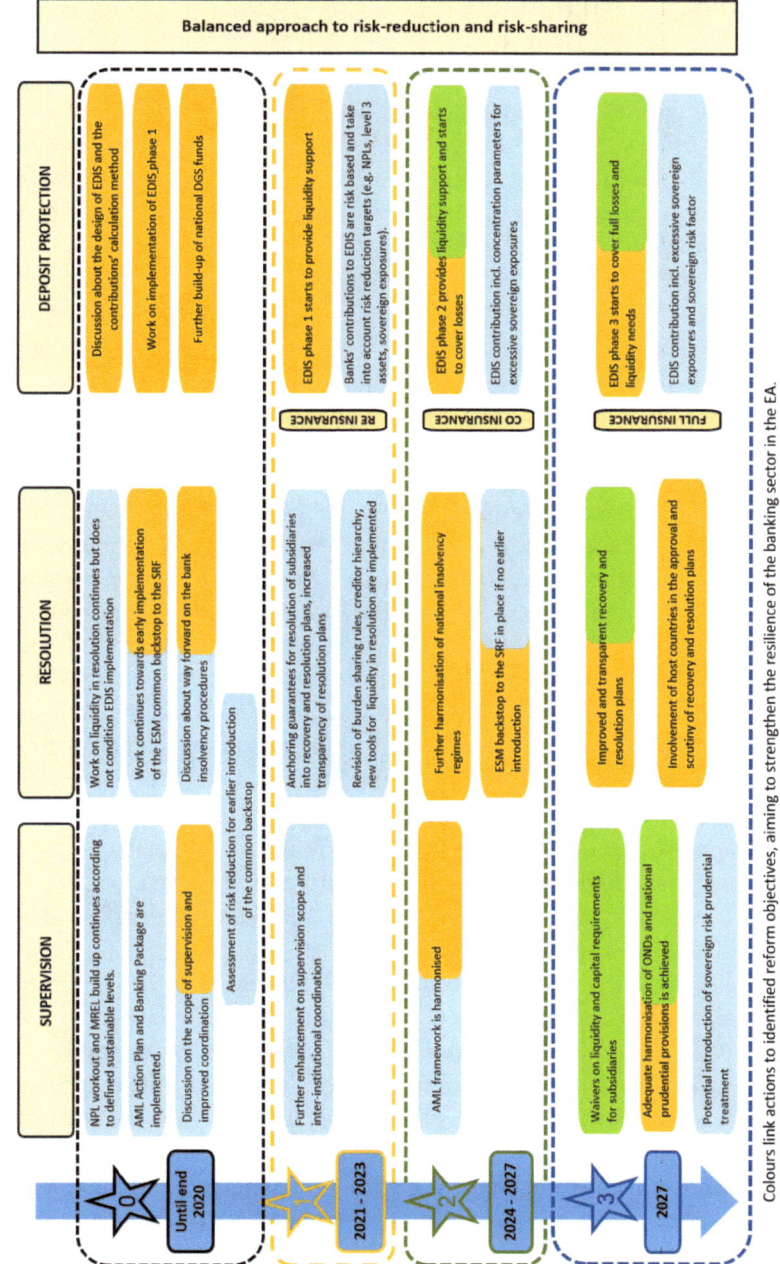

Balanced approach to risk-reduction and risk-sharing

DEPOSIT PROTECTION

- Discussion about the design of EDIS and the contributions' calculation method
- Work on implementation of EDIS phase 1
- Further build-up of national DGS funds

RE INSURANCE
- EDIS phase 1 starts to provide liquidity support
- Banks' contributions to EDIS are risk based and take into account risk reduction targets (e.g. NPLs, level 3 assets, sovereign exposures).

CO INSURANCE
- EDIS phase 2 provides liquidity support and starts to cover losses
- EDIS contribution incl. concentration parameters for excessive sovereign exposures

FULL INSURANCE
- EDIS phase 3 starts to cover full losses and liquidity needs
- EDIS contribution incl. excessive sovereign exposures and sovereign risk factor

RESOLUTION

- Work on liquidity in resolution continues but does not condition EDIS implementation
- Work continues towards early implementation of the ESM common backstop to the SRF
- Discussion about way forward on the bank insolvency procedures

- Anchoring guarantees for resolution of subsidiaries into recovery and resolution plans, increased transparency of resolution plans
- Revision of burden sharing rules, creditor hierarchy; new tools for liquidity in resolution are implemented

- Further harmonisation of national insolvency regimes
- ESM backstop to the SRF in place if no earlier introduction

- Improved and transparent recovery and resolution plans
- Involvement of host countries in the approval and scrutiny of recovery and resolution plans

SUPERVISION

- NPL workout and MREL build up continues according to defined sustainable levels.
- AML Action Plan and Banking Package are implemented.
- Discussion on the scope of supervision and improved coordination

Assessment of risk reduction for earlier introduction of the common backstop

- Further enhancement on supervision scope and inter-institutional coordination

- AML framework is harmonised

- Waivers on liquidity and capital requirements for subsidiaries
- Adequate harmonisation of ONDs and national prudential provisions is achieved
- Potential introduction of sovereign risk prudential treatment

⊙ 0 Until end 2020

☆ 1 2021 - 2023

☆ 2 2024 - 2027

☆ 3 2027

Colours link actions to identified reform objectives, aiming to strengthen the resilience of the banking sector in the EA.

Safety
Integration
Profitability

4. Conclusions: What follows after EDIS?

The banking union's three pillars can evolve together and strengthen each other to foster confidence and promote stability. This contribution strives to demonstrate that opposing views can be overcome if all players are ambitious enough in pursuing a long-term objective: a fully integrated market for banking services where resources can be freely and efficiently allocated. Following a gradual phase-in of pre-defined sequences, the euro area could agree on the further removal of barriers across jurisdictions, which would enable banks to benefit from the full potential of a truly integrated market environment.

Discussions on the right balance between the free movement of capital and liquidity and national control of subsidiaries and intra-group transfers can be settled more easily, once the euro area moves to a common deposit insurance scheme. This requires that capital and liquidity regulations apply to banking groups as a whole, rather than being ring-fenced at national level. An amendment to the Capital Requirement Regulation (CRR) addressing the home-host balance issue could be introduced following the entry into stage 3 of EDIS implying full mutualisation. An improved and transparent recovery and resolution framework, coupled with a fully mutualised deposit insurance scheme should provide sufficient reassurance that subsidiaries in host countries are well protected. From a governance perspective, host countries need to be adequately involved in the approval and scrutiny of recovery and resolution plans. Additional safeguards may be sought in the macroprudential toolkit; host countries could retain their powers to make proposals for macroprudential buffers, potentially applicable at solo level in a selective way, to cater for specific concern about the financial stability of a member state. Finally, the MREL and capital requirements need to be set consistently within the group structure and according to the resolution strategy, while allowing for a flexible application of MREL targets to reflect the size and risk of every single bank.

Implementing EDIS is not an ultimate goal, but only another intermediate step. The banking industry plays a key role as a financing provider and guardian of households' savings in the euro area. In the absence of fully developed capital markets, it performs tasks crucial for future growth of the euro area economy. It is of utmost importance to define adequate safety nets, capable of fending off contagion and sustaining the needs of the economy even under distress. A common European deposit insurance scheme represents an additional layer of protection against potential risks; its implementation also provides an opportunity to fine-tune the regulatory framework. Looking forward, BU robustness and its suitability to support a safe, profitable and integrated banking industry will depend on rules and criteria evolving in response to market conditions. Euro area

banking regulation will require repeated upgrades while adapting to new challenges arising from global competition, technology and pressures from alternative service providers.

References with hyperlinks

[1.] Carmassi, J., Dobkowits, S., Evrard, J., Parisis, L., Silva, A., Wedow, M., (2018) *Completing
the Banking Union with a European Deposit Insurance Scheme: who is afraid of cross-
subsidisation?*, ECB Working Paper April 2018, ECB Occasional Paper Series No. 208/ April
2018. [on-line]. Available at: https://www.ecb.europa.eu/pub/pdf/scpops/ecb.op208.en.
pdf

[2.] Cau, E., Joyce, M., Wilkinson, S., Chandrasekaran, M., K., Goel, A., Manners, Ch., Fall, O., De
Santivanes, F. G., Yang, J., (2019), *Banks-Playing catch –up. Barclays*, European Equity
Strategy, equity Research, 17 July 2019. [on-line]

[3.] CEPR (2018), *Reconciling risk sharing with market discipline: A constructive approach to
euro area reform*, CEPR Policy Insight No. 91. [on-line]. Available at: https://www.delorsin-
stitut.de/2015/wp-content/uploads/2018/01/20180117_Reconciling-risk-sharing-and-mar-
ket-discipline_Enderlein-et-al.pdf

[4.] EBA (2015), *EBA Guidelines on methods for calculating contributions to DGSs*, [on-line].
Available at: https://eba.europa.eu/documents/10180/1089322/EBA-GL-2015-10_GL+on
+Calculation+of+Contributions+DGS.pdf/92da0adb-3e16-480f-8720-94f744ea7a44

[5.] ECB Consolidated Banking Data: http://sdw.ecb.europa.eu/

[6.] EU Council (2018), *Bulgarian Presidency Progress report on Banking Union*. Brussels, 12
June 2018 (OR. en) 9819/18. [on-line]. Available at: http://data.consilium.europa.eu/doc/
document/ST-9819-2018-INIT/en/pdf

[7.] EU Council (December 2018), *Terms of reference of the common backstop to the Single
Resolution Fund*, 4 December 2018, Council of the European Union. [on-line]. Available at:
https://www.consilium.europa.eu/media/37268/tor-backstop_041218_final_clean.pdf

[8.] Eurogroup (June 2019), Consideration on the Further Strengthening of the Banking Union,
Including a Common Deposit Insurance System – Report of the HLWG Chair. Council of the
EU, June 2019, [on-line]. Available at: https://www.consilium.europa.eu/media/39768/
190606-hlwg-chair-report.pdf

[9.] European Commission (2015), Proposal for a Regulation of the European Commission and
the European Parliament and of the Council amending Regulation (EU) 806/2014 in order to
establish a European Deposit Insurance Scheme, [on-line]. Official Journal of the European
Union. 2019. Available at: https://eur-lex.europa.eu/legal-content/EN/TXT/?uri=CE-
LEX:52015PC0586

[10.] European Commission (2017), *Communication from the Commission on completing the
Banking Union*, Brussels, 11.10.2017 COM(2017) 592 final, [on-line]. Available at: https://ec.
europa.eu/finance/docs/law/171011-communication-banking-union_en.pdf

[11.] European Commission (2018). *Survey on access to finance*. [on-line]. Available at: https://
ec.europa.eu/growth/access-to-finance/data-surveys_en

[12.] European Commission (2019), Communication from the Commission Fourth Progress Report
on the reduction of non-performing loans and further risk reduction in the Banking Union.

Brussels, 12.6.2019 COM(2019) 278 final. [on-line]. Available at: https://ec.europa.eu/finance/docs/policy/190612-non-performing-loans-communication_en.pdf

[13.] FDIC (2019), *Resolutions Handbook*, chapter 4. [on-line]. Available at: https://www.fdic.gov/bank/historical/reshandbook/index.html

[14.] IMF (2018), *Euro Area Policies, FSAP*. July 2018, IMF Country Report No. 18/226. [on-line]. Available at: https://www.imf.org/~/media/Files/Publications/CR/2018/cr18226.ashx

[15.] Lagarde, Ch., (2019), *The Euro Area: Creating a Stronger Economic Ecosystem*, IMF, 2019. [on-line]. Available at: https://www.imf.org/en/News/Articles/2019/03/28/sp032819-the-euro-area-creating-a-stronger-economic-ecosystem

[16.] Official Journal of the EU (2014), Directive 2014/49/EU of the European Parliament and of the Council of 16 April 2014 on deposit guarantee schemes, OJ L 173, 12.6.2014, p. 149–178. [on-line]. Available at: https://eur-lex.europa.eu/legal-content/EN/TXT/?uri=CELEX%3A32014L0049

[17.] Official Journal of the EU (2015), Commission Implementing Regulation (EU) 2015/1278 of 9 July 2015 amending Implementing Regulation (EU) No 680/2014 laying down implementing technical standards with regard to supervisory reporting of institutions as regards instructions, templates and definitions, L205/1. [on-line]. Available: https://eur-lex.europa.eu/legal-content/En/TXT/PDF/?uri=OJ:JOL_2015_205_R_0001

[18.] Official Journal of the EU (2015), Commission Implementing Regulation (EU) 2015/227 of 9 January 2015 amending Implementing Regulation (EU) No 680/2014 laying down implementing technical standards with regard to supervisory reporting of institutions according to Regulation (EU) No 575/2013 of the European Parliament and of the Council Text with EEA relevance, Official Journal L 48, 20.2.2015, [on-line]. Available at: https://eur-lex.europa.eu/legal-content/GA/TXT/?uri=CELEX:32015R0227

[19.] Official Journal of the European Union (2019), *Risk Reduction Package*. Official Journal of the EU L 150. Volume 62, 7 June 2019. [on-line]. Available at: https://eur-lex.europa.eu/legal-content/EN/TXT/PDF/?uri=OJ:L:2019:150:FULL&from=EN

[20.] Schnabel, I., Véron, N., (2018), *Breaking the Stalemate on European Deposit Insurance*, Peterson Institute for International Economics. 2018. [on-line]. Available at: https://www.piie.com/blogs/realtime-economic-issues-watch/breaking-stalemate-european-deposit-insurance

[21.] SNL Financial

[22.] The Voice of Savings and Retail Banking Institute (2015), *Financial Systems in Europe and in the US: Structural Differences Where Banks Remain the Main Source of Finance For Companies*. September 2015. Research paper. [on-line]. Available at: https://www.wsbi-esbg.org/SiteCollectionDocuments/Financial%20systems%20in%20Europe%20and%20in%20the%20US.FINAL.pdf

[23.] Xu, T. T., Hu, K., Das, U., S., (2019), *Bank Profitability and Financial Stability*, IMF Working Paper WP /19/5, [on-line]. Available at: https://www.imf.org/en/Publications/WP/Issues/2019/01/11/Bank-Profitability-and-Financial-Stability-46470

Arthur J. Murton
A Look at the FDIC Through the Lens of Deposit Insurance

Introduction

The U.S. system for deposit insurance evolved over a long period of time into the fully federal system that exists today. The federal system of deposit insurance was first preceded by a number of state-run systems, and then coexisted for decades alongside other state systems (including some state-chartered privately run systems), but essentially all of those state systems had disappeared by the end of the first post-war banking crisis.

In addition to being a deposit insurer, the Federal Deposit Insurance Corporation (FDIC) is a bank supervisor or, depending on the type of institution, back-up supervisor. The FDIC also is a resolution authority with resolution powers that allow for flexible responses depending on the nature of the crisis confronted while rapidly returning assets to the private sector.

Reforms to the federal system that have given rise to the FDIC's authorities over time have been part of the longstanding debate about the trade-off between financial stability and moral hazard. Some of these reforms have reduced regulatory discretion and other reforms have broadened the powers of the FDIC as deposit insurer. In sum, these reforms have sought to strike a fine balance to optimize incentives and outcomes.

The brief history provided here should make it clear that the arrangements underpinning the FDIC's authorities have changed over the years in important ways. Looking back at this history, there are several observations about the U.S. system as it stands today that some may consider apropos of current discussions in the European Union of its proposed European Deposit Insurance Scheme (EDIS):

- The FDIC has found its capacities as deposit insurer and resolution authority to be complementary.
- A single resolution (or insolvency) regime for insured depository institutions (IDIs) under the FDIC's authority has proven effective.

Note: This article contains my personal views, which may not reflect those of the Federal Deposit Insurance Corporation. I would also like to thank Joanne Fungaroli and Lee Davison of the FDIC for very helpful review of and improvements to this paper.

https://doi.org/10.1515/9783110683073-023

- The U.S. system of deposit insurance has allowed for more than one deposit insurer to varying degrees over time.[1]
- The geographic distribution of losses differed significantly between the two banking crises that occurred in the United States over the past four decades.

This article further discusses aspects of this history, experience and lessons learned, first by providing a high-level description of the current U.S. system of deposit insurance and a brief history of the FDIC, and then by discussing how this system works in practice in four areas: deposit insurance coverage, the Deposit Insurance Fund (DIF), risk-based pricing of deposit insurance, and the resolution of failed banks.

I. Overview of the Current FDIC System

The FDIC insures 5,362 commercial banks and savings associations (Insured Depository Institutions, or IDIs).[2] These IDIs have just over $18 trillion in assets, and almost $13 trillion in deposits – of which an estimated $7.7 trillion is insured. The industry has an equity capital base of $2 trillion, or 11.4 percent of assets. The industry earned $237 billion in 2018, for a return on assets of 1.28 percent. IDIs are present throughout the United States and vary greatly by size and business models.

Certain aspects of the FDIC's statutory framework bear highlighting for this overview. The FDIC's deposit insurance limit is $250,000, which sounds simple but in reality is quite complex under applicable coverage rules. The FDIC is

---

1 Of the deposit taking institutions in the United States today, the FDIC is the deposit insurer of those representing more than 90 % of their total assets, with the one other deposit insurance system – managed by the National Credit Union Administration (NCUA) – insuring deposits in credit unions, which represent the rest. U.S. law requires all institutions taking deposits in the United States to participate in one of these deposit insurance systems, except for the U.S. branches of foreign banks that were not grandfathered in as IDIs when the law changed in 1991 to otherwise exclude those branches from participating. For decades after being established in 1933, the FDIC coexisted as a deposit insurer of commercial banks, alongside the Federal Savings and Loan Insurance Corporation (FSLIC) (which was created in 1934 to insure the deposits of thrift institutions) and other deposit insurance systems that operated at the state level for both banks and thrifts. FSLIC and all but one of these state systems did not survive the U.S. banking and thrift crises of the 1980s.
2 The figures in this paragraph are as of March 31, 2019, as further described in the FDIC's Quarterly Banking Profile, First Quarter 2019 (available at: https://www.fdic.gov/bank/analytical/qbp/2019mar/qbp.pdf).

governed by a five-member board of directors and a Chairman who is appointed for a five-year term. De novo banks must receive FDIC approval for deposit insurance and the FDIC can remove deposit insurance from existing IDIs. The FDIC has an ex ante fund and assessment authority that requires a risk-based pricing system, but otherwise gives the FDIC Board broad discretion in how banks pay for deposit insurance. The FDIC has receivership authority which essentially provides a uniform insolvency regime for all IDIs. The creditor hierarchy places domestic deposits above general creditors; this is known as depositor preference (further discussed below in Text Box 1). Finally, the FDIC not only is the primary federal supervisor of IDIs that are state-chartered banks and savings institutions that are not members of the Federal Reserve System, but also has backup examination authority for all other IDIs. Insights gained through the supervisory process positions the FDIC, if necessary, to intervene to protect the DIF.

II. Brief History

II.1 Creation of the FDIC and Decades of Stability

The FDIC was created in 1933 in the midst of the Great Depression. After the stock market crash of 1929, an estimated 9000 banks suspended operation in the United States and President Roosevelt declared a banking holiday immediately upon taking office in March of 1933. Three months later, the United States Congress (Congress) passed the Banking Act of 1933 which created the FDIC. This was not without controversy, as the president, senior legislators, and the American Bankers' Association initially opposed the creation of federal deposit insurance. The concerns expressed then were similar to concerns voiced in the current EDIS discussion: the system would be too expensive, subsidize poorly run banks, and lead to excessive risk-taking. However, popular demand for safe bank deposits won out over these concerns.

Deposit insurance had a history in the United States prior to the creation of the FDIC. At the state level, fourteen U.S. states had put in place deposit insurance arrangements over the previous one hundred years, but all of these had ceased operations by 1933. In addition to the state efforts, there had been numerous legislative proposals for federal deposit insurance between 1886 and 1933.

The creation of the FDIC helped to stabilize the banking system. While bank failures continued during the rest of the Great Depression, they numbered annually in the dozens, rather than thousands. Beginning in the early 1940s and for the next three decades, annual bank failures were in the single digits. This was due not only to the post-war U.S. economic expansion, but also to government measures to limit competition among banks. These included: prohibition on interest on demand deposits, ceilings on interest rates on other deposits, geographic restrictions on branching, and restrictions on the activities of banks.

During this period, the FDIC was not the only deposit insurer in the United States. The Federal Savings and Loan Insurance Corporation (FSLIC), which was created in 1934, insured the deposits of thrift institutions (as opposed to commercial banks) and other deposit insurance systems operated at the state level for both banks and thrifts.

II.2 Crisis of the 1980s and Developments Thereafter

The U.S. deposit insurance crisis of the 1980s and early 1990s comprised two crises: one in the savings and loan industry and one in the commercial banking industry. The crises led to a number of changes in deposit insurance in the U.S.

Savings and loans institutions (S&Ls) were regulated and supervised at the federal level by the Federal Home Loan Bank Board (FHLBB) and their deposits were insured by the FSLIC, which was a FHLBB subsidiary. Generally speaking, this was a mono-line industry offering savings accounts and issuing home mortgages. As such, it was an industry greatly exposed to a particular macroeconomic risk: a severe spike in interest rates.

This spike materialized in the early 1980s as the central bank sought to bring inflation under control. High interest rates raised funding costs above the yield on long-term fixed-rate mortgages, creating negative earnings for much of the industry. The losses rendered much of the industry insolvent and the resulting failures threatened to drain the resources of the FSLIC. The regulatory policy responses to this situation were poor: forbearance, lax accounting, artificial capital instruments, and an ill-advised expansion of powers. It is widely accepted that these measures allowed the losses to balloon and ultimately outstrip the resources of the FSLIC and the industry, thus requiring taxpayers to bear costs exceeding $100 billion. The FSLIC was abolished and the Resolution Trust Corporation, initially administered by the FDIC, was created to resolve the insolvent institutions. The FDIC assumed the responsibility for insuring the deposits of the surviving industry.

The crisis in the commercial banking industry was of a different nature from that of the S&Ls. Commercial banks held fewer long-term fixed-rate assets and were thus not as vulnerable to a spike in interest rates. Instead, the problems were driven by a series of regional recessions accompanied by boom-and-bust markets in farmland, energy, and commercial real estate. During this crisis, more than 1600 banks failed and the FDIC deposit insurance fund was depleted.

The demise of the FSLIC and the severe problems faced by the FDIC led to calls for reform of the deposit insurance system. The concerns centered on the way deposit insurance was funded and the exercise of regulatory discretion.

The amount banks paid for deposit insurance was set by statute at one-twelfth of one percent of deposits per year. This "flat-rate" system had two implications. First, the FDIC had no authority to manage the fund balance; for example, the FDIC could not build up the fund during good times nor replenish it to protect taxpayers. Second, the rate that banks paid did not vary by risk and thus risky banks were charged no more than safe banks. This was viewed as both unfair and creating incentives for excessive risk-taking.

The concern about regulatory discretion was twofold. As banks experience problems, supervisors can require corrective actions to avoid failure such as raising capital, limiting certain activities, and replacing management. The view at the time was that supervisors of both S&Ls and commercial banks were not forceful enough in requiring these corrective actions, which led to more and costlier failures.

There were also concerns about the way the FDIC exercised its discretion when resolving failed banks. At that time, the FDIC had considerable leeway when a bank failed to protect not only insured depositors, but also uninsured depositors and other creditors. When Continental Illinois, the seventh largest U.S. bank was on the brink of failure, the FDIC used this discretion to protect all depositors and creditors. In the period immediately before that event the FDIC limited protection to insured depositors only when small IDIs failed. This disparate treatment was widely viewed as unfair, and, after Continental, the FDIC then started to use its discretion also to protect all depositors in most small IDI failures. While this addressed the fairness question, it heightened concerns about moral hazard and lack of depositor discipline.

In 1991, Congress enacted the FDIC Improvement Act (FDICIA) to address concerns about funding and regulatory discretion. It abolished the flat-rate funding system and required the FDIC to levy assessments on IDIs as necessary to maintain the DIF at or above a target level and to put in place risk-based pricing of deposit insurance premiums. To address regulatory discretion, FDICIA established (1) Prompt Corrective Action (PCA), which requires supervisors to force corrective measures as a bank's condition deteriorates, and (2) the Least-Cost Test, which constrained the FDIC's ability to provide protection beyond insured depositors.

During this time, the state-chartered privately operated deposit insurance systems faced severe problems as well. By the end of the crisis, all but one had failed or gone out of existence, and the one that exists to this day functions only as a supplement to FDIC deposit insurance.

Text Box 1:
National Depositor Preference Amendment of 1993

Congress, in 1993, adopted the National Depositor Preference Amendment (NDPA), which established a uniform order for distributing a failed IDI's assets and created a preference for depositors in that distribution priority. Before the NDPA, the order of distribution of the assets of a failed IDI in the United States was determined according to the law of the jurisdiction that chartered the institution, whether under the Federal law applicable to a federally chartered bank or under the relevant state law applicable to a state-chartered bank. Approximately thirty state law distribution schemes existed at that time, some specifying depositor preference to differing degrees and others mandating pro rata distributions.

Congress adopted the NDPA as part of its budget reconciliation process, rather than as the result of a meaningful policy deliberation. Nonetheless, the FDIC has found this priority scheme to be helpful in resolution. The NDPA, by giving deposit claims preference, 1) made it easier to determine the value of uninsured deposits and to isolate general creditor claims; 2) facilitated bids for uninsured deposits since an acquirer does not need to bid for the claims of general unsecured creditors; and 3) allowed the claims of unsecured creditors to serve as loss-absorbing capacity, thereby reducing losses to the DIF.

The crisis subsided in the early 1990s. The number of IDI failures, which peaked in 1989 at 206, fell from 124 in 1991 to six in 1995. The DIF recovered from a negative balance of $7 billion in 1991 to $36 billion in 1996, when it reached the statutory target at that time of 1.25 percent of insured deposits. The replenishment of the DIF was due in large part to the near tripling of deposit insurance premiums during this period from 8.3 basis points of domestic deposits to a minimum of 23 basis points.

Once the DIF reached its target level, the banking industry argued that, after several years of paying historically high premiums, IDIs should not be required to build the fund significantly beyond the target level. In 1996, Congress prohibited the FDIC from requiring IDIs that were well-managed and well-capitalized to pay into the DIF. For the next ten years, while IDIs experienced year after year of record profitability, virtually no premiums were assessed to build the DIF.

Just prior to the financial crisis of 2008, Congress removed the restriction on assessments in response to arguments made by both the FDIC and the industry that the system was flawed for two reasons. First, it did not make sense to charge virtually no premiums during long periods of strong profits and then charge very steep premiums during intense crisis periods when earnings and capital were weak. Second, new IDIs were able to enter the system and existing IDIs were able to grow rapidly, without proportional contributions to the DIF.

As it turned out, after Congress relaxed the law there was little time to build the DIF before the onset of the crisis. The DIF was once again depleted – a negative balance of $20 billion in 2010 – and IDIs were once again required to pay high premiums when they were least able to afford them.

Looking back, the FDIC's experience across this recent history has shown that losses from bank failures across crises shifted among geographic regions. As shown by the charts below, regions of the United States that experienced the most significant concentrations of bank failures contributing to losses to the DIF in the late 1980s to early 1990s were significantly different from the regions with that experience during the most recent financial crisis.

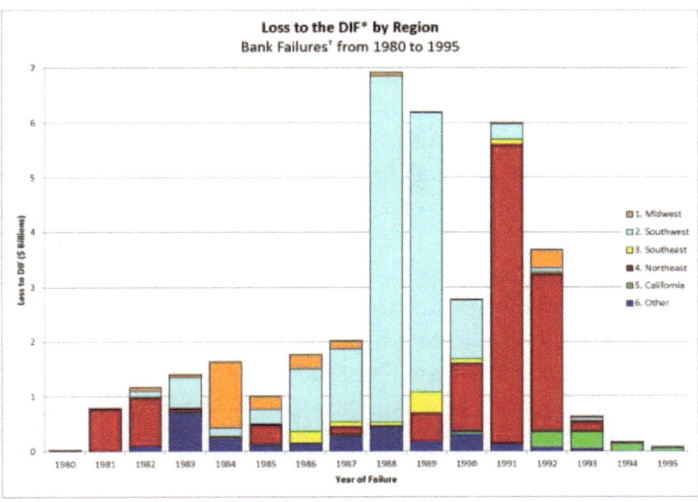

*Estimated losses as of November 30, 2017.
†Transactions include failures and open bank assistance transactions. FSLIC and RTC failures are excluded.

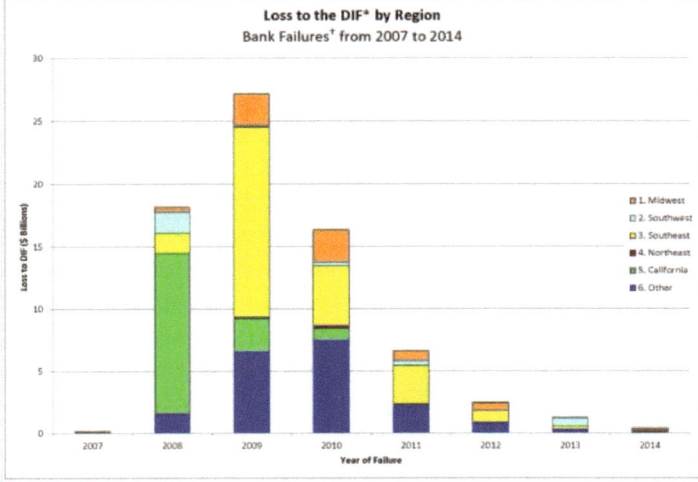

*Estimated losses as of November 30, 2017. Estimated losses include those attributable to the Temporary Liquidity Guarantee Program (TLGP).
†Transactions include failures and open bank assistance transactions.

314 — Arthur J. Murton

Not only did the regions hit hardest differ across crises, but the underlying causes of those crises and the magnitude of the losses to the DIF across crises also differed.

III. Deposit Insurance in Practice in the United States

III.1 Deposit Insurance Coverage

The FDIC's deposit insurance limit is $250,000, which sounds simple but in reality is quite complex under the coverage rules. The complexity arises from several features of the system, some statutory and some regulatory. The first is the construct of multiple ownership categories. This allows an individual to have separate fully-insured accounts at the same IDI, so long as the accounts are held in separate ownership capacities. These account types include, among others: single, joint with family members, and trust. The treatment of a trust account depends on whether it is revocable or irrevocable. Another complicating feature is "pass-through" coverage in which an account that is for the benefit of multiple parties receives coverage as if each of those parties had an account.

The presence and interplay of these and other features has three implications. First, it is possible to insure deposits in amounts well beyond the stated limit of $250,000. Second, the rules are difficult for the public and bankers to understand; as a result, the FDIC devotes considerable resources to clarifying these. Finally, the complexity presents significant operational challenges when resolving a failed IDI in order to provide insured depositors with timely access to their funds.

III.2 Deposit Insurance Fund (DIF) Sources and Uses

The FDIC is funded by quarterly assessments on IDIs and maintains an ex ante deposit insurance fund, known as the DIF. The statutory minimum target for the DIF is 1.35 percent of insured deposits,[3] which was reached in fall 2018. The fund balance as of March 31, 2019 was $105 billion. The assessment base is essentially the total liabilities of IDIs and the risk-based pricing system brought in approximately $9.5 billion in assessment revenue in the 2018 calendar year. Other

---

3 The Dodd-Frank Wall Street Reform and Consumer Protection Act of 2010 increased the required minimum reserve ratio to this level.

sources of funding to the DIF include interest earned on investments of funds and dividends from receiverships through recoveries from the liquidation of failed IDI assets, which amounted to approximately $1.6 billion and $3.3 billion, respectively, in the 2018 calendar year.

The FDIC may raise additional funding for the DIF not only by increasing regular assessments, but also by imposing special assessments or collecting prepaid assessments, which were options that the FDIC deployed in 2009. In June 2009, the FDIC announced a special assessment on IDIs of $5.5 billion in order to maintain a positive DIF balance, but which reduced industry earnings and capital when IDIs were under stress and losing money. In December 2009, the FDIC required banks to prepay just over three years of estimated deposit insurance assessments, or $45.7 billion, to strengthen the DIF's liquidity. The novel and unprecedented use of prepaid assessments met the FDIC's liquidity needs without reducing the capital of the industry, since IDIs accounted for the prepaid assessment as a prepaid expense (an asset), which did not affect earnings and which occurred at a time when most IDIs were highly liquid. Certain IDIs were exempt from the prepaid assessment if the FDIC determined that the prepayment would adversely affect an institution's safety and soundness or cause undue harm to the institution.

The FDIC also has statutory borrowing authorities that it can exercise to meet additional DIF liquidity needs through borrowing from the U.S. Treasury's Federal Financing Bank, from the Federal Home Loan Banks, or from IDIs themselves. This borrowing is subject to a "maximum obligation limitation." While somewhat complex, in the simplest terms, this allows the FDIC to borrow at least 90 percent of the fair market value of the assets available for repayment.

The DIF may be used to pay out insured depositors when an IDI fails, to provide the liquidity needed for the FDIC, as receiver, to pay administrative expenses in order to resolve a failed IDI, and to absorb losses pari passu with holders of uninsured deposit claims to the extent that recoveries from the liquidation of a failed IDI's assets are insufficient to repay this class of claims in full. As a tool to preserve liquidity and to minimize losses at a time when financial markets are turbulent and asset values are highly uncertain, the FDIC also has the ability to give assurances or guarantees, in lieu of making cash outlays, as part of the transaction terms with third parties acquiring all or parts of failed IDIs.

III.3 Risk-based Pricing

IDIs pay for deposit insurance under a risk-based system, which is designed – not surprisingly – to charge riskier banks more than safer banks. The purpose of a risk-based approach is two-fold: to mitigate moral hazard by improving incentives and to provide a more equitable system.

IDIs pay assessments quarterly and the amount that an IDI pays is the product of a risk-based rate and its assessment base (essentially its liabilities). To determine the risk-based rates, the FDIC uses two approaches, one for IDIs under $10 billion in assets and another for larger IDIs. Both approaches use as inputs supervisory ratings and publicly available financial characteristics of the IDIs. The supervisory ratings are known as CAMELS ratings, an acronym which stands for Capital, Asset quality, Management, Earnings, Liquidity, and Sensitivity (to market risk).

For IDIs under $10 billion in assets, the rate is determined by a formula with the following characteristics of the IDI: CAMELS, capital ratio, non-performing loans (NPLs), owned real estate, loan mix, net income, brokered deposits, and recent growth rate. The choice of these characteristics and the weights attached to them were derived from empirical analysis of the probability of bank failure.

For IDIs over $10 billion in assets, the rate is determined by a "scorecard" approach based on expert judgment of supervisors and bank analysts subject to empirical back-testing. The FDIC chose a different approach for larger IDIs for several reasons: larger IDIs tend to be more complex; data on failures for larger IDIs was much more limited; and the scorecard approach more closely resembled the way market participants would analyze these firms. The scorecard uses CAMELS and financial ratios to score the probability of failure and the severity of loss in failure.

Because larger IDIs are more complex and subject to greater scrutiny by both supervisors and market participants, the large-bank approach allows for discretionary adjustments to the rates produced by the scorecard. These adjustments are infrequent, may raise or lower the rate, and are subject to appeal by the IDI.

IV. Resolution of Failed IDIs

IV.1 Recent FDIC Experience

Since 2008, the FDIC has served as receiver for over 525 failed IDIs, nearly all of which were small community banks. Approximately 95 percent of resolutions conducted by the FDIC since that time involved the sale of the IDI's franchise and assets to an open institution, generally involving a single acquirer assuming nearly all of the failed IDI's liabilities. This transaction, termed a purchase and assumption or "P&A" transaction, is often both the easiest for the FDIC to execute and the least disruptive. P&A transactions require lead time to identify potential buyers and to allow them to conduct due diligence of the failing IDI.

In the vast majority of the 525 failures the acquiring institutions assumed all of the deposits – including uninsured deposits – of the failed IDI. In the typical failure of an IDI that is a community bank[4] , an all-deposit transaction is possible under the least-cost test because the amount of uninsured funding is quite small and an all-deposit transfer helps to preserve the franchise value of the IDI.

In short, the typical FDIC resolution event of the crisis was the failure of a community bank in which the FDIC had enough lead time to market the franchise and conduct an auction. The typical outcome was a purchase and assumption transaction in which all deposits were transferred and thus in which depositors suffered no loss.

IV.2 The Resolution Process

The FDIC works with the other federal banking regulators and the state banking regulators to supervise the safety and soundness of IDIs. Each appropriate federal banking agency (which may include the FDIC) and the FDIC (acting in its capacity as deposit insurer) take prompt corrective action when IDIs fall below required capital standards. Such actions can include, among others, requirements that the IDI be recapitalized or cease and desist from certain activities.

If the corrective actions do not prevent the IDI from becoming nonviable, the regulators take the steps to close the IDI. Closing an IDI consists of the revocation of its charter by the chartering authority (applicable federal or state regulator), and appointment of the FDIC as receiver to pay deposit insurance and liquidate the failed IDI's receivership estate.

The primary causes of an IDI's failure are balance sheet insolvency (assets insufficient to meet obligations or critically undercapitalized) or cash flow insolvency (inability to meet obligations as they become due). Although less frequently invoked, there are nonetheless several other causes that could give rise to placing an IDI in receivership – for example, loss of insured status, violation of law, or unsafe and unsound banking practices.

The FDIC serves in two capacities in IDI resolutions: Insurer for deposits according to coverage rules and receiver for the failed IDI. Each receivership is a

---

4 For more information, see the FDIC's Community Bank Study, available at: https://www.fdic.gov/regulations/resources/cbi/study.html.

separate legal entity and the FDIC, as receiver, steps into the shoes of the failed IDI, determines all claims against the failed IDI, takes the actions necessary to liquidate and wind-up the failed IDI's affairs, and otherwise manages the receivership's operations.

Generally, placing an IDI into receivership imposes a temporary 90-day stay on contractual actions (breach, termination, security enforcement, etc.) against the IDI without the consent of the FDIC, as receiver. With respect to the failed IDI's qualified financial contracts (QFCs) with a counterparty (or its affiliates), a counterparty can terminate any such QFCs that the FDIC, as receiver, does not transfer on an all-or-nothing basis to another financial institution during the first business day after the appointment of the receiver.

IV.3 Resolution Strategy and Transaction Types

In developing its strategy to resolve a failing IDI, the FDIC will evaluate the mix of assets and liabilities of the failing IDI, the market conditions expected at the time of closing, the availability of bidders, and the least cost test.

In doing so, the FDIC may determine, for example, that offering to sell a mix of the failed IDI's assets and deposits would generate higher bids than in a deposit-only or other transaction. A prospective acquiring institution may find such a mix attractive in order to acquire earning assets that offset deposits as part of the transaction. Compared to available alternatives, a transaction offering such a mix may allow the FDIC to draw less DIF liquidity at closing and may allow for the rapid return to the private sector of the failed IDI's assets. This in turn reduces the number of FDIC staff that would be needed post-closing to manage the liquidation of those assets.

So long as the transaction satisfies the least cost test, the FDIC as receiver can use a Purchase and Assumption Agreement (P&A) for that transaction to transfer any combination of assets and liabilities to the acquiring institution that submitted the winning bid. Under the least cost test, the FDIC by law must select the resolution alternative that results in the lowest cost to the DIF. The FDIC determines this by comparing all bids using the same set of assumptions for the value of assets, liabilities and claims.

P&As can take multiple forms and can include several options:

- *Whole Bank or Modified Whole Bank:* Transfers almost all assets to the acquirer at book value. Because assets are purchased "as is," acquirers generally bid a discount for those assets. For a modified whole bank transaction, some pre-identified distressed assets are excluded. Depending on prevailing market conditions, the transaction may include "loss-share" (further

described below), pursuant to which the FDIC provides coverage to the acquirer on agreed terms and conditions for losses on hard-to-value assets.
- *Optional Loan Pools:* Loans are grouped into homogenous pools which are offered separately from the deposits with reserve prices. Bidders bid on the deposits and/or certain loan pools.
- *Clean Bank:* Only insured deposits, cash and cash equivalents are transferred to the acquirer.
- *Insured Deposits Only:* Only insured deposits are transferred to an agent institution. The agent institution is paid the dollar amount of deposits assumed minus the premium paid to obtain deposit relationships and branch locations.

The use of loss-share depends on market conditions, generally in order to reduce cost in times of uncertain asset values. This approach provides risk sharing for the DIF with private sector banks (P&A with loss-share) or with capital market investors (securitization LLCs). It also leverages private sector expertise to manage and sell assets that are subject to loss-share. The acquirer has skin in the game and significant upside potential. Most importantly, loss-share encourages buyers and increases competition in a market otherwise offering only cash buyers seeking fire sale pricing.

A payout of insured deposits generally occurs only if, at closing, there is no acquirer for at least the failed IDI's insured deposits. In such a case, the FDIC would then pay out insured deposits to depositors and liquidate the assets of the failed IDI to pay creditors. The FDIC may establish a Deposit Insurance National Bank (DINB), generally for a short term, to facilitate payment of insured deposit amounts. Uninsured deposit liabilities represent claims against the receivership estate that would be paid following the claims process from the proceeds of liquidating the failed IDI's assets.

A bridge bank also is available as a temporary arrangement when the FDIC, as receiver, needs more flexibility to consider resolution strategies and the optimal means to exit from receivership. It gives the FDIC, as receiver, time to evaluate and stabilize the institution and to prepare it for sale. It also gives prospective acquirers more time to assess the institution, while making deposits and banking services available to customers. A single bridge institution can handle multiple depository institution failures. In forming a bridge institution, the FDIC, as receiver, may transfer most of a failed IDI's assets and liabilities to a newly-chartered financial institution controlled by the FDIC. The FDIC has several years thereafter (two years plus up to three one year extensions) to resolve the institution placed in the bridge institution.

IV.4 Closing Process

The FDIC has well-established processes that it uses as it prepares to close a failing IDI. The FDIC forms a "closing team" to plan and execute the resolution. Approximately 17 functional managers are selected and the closing team can consist of 30 to 150 staff, depending on the size and complexity of the IDI. When the FDIC is appointed receiver, it takes possession of the premises of the failed IDI and all of its records, normally at the close of business on a Friday. The closing team and employees of the failed institution then work on-site over the weekend to settle the affairs of the failed institution and transfer its assets to the acquiring institution or bridge bank.

The acquiring institution or bridge bank usually resumes normal operations on the next business day. Customers of the failed institution automatically become customers of the acquiring institution or bridge bank and have complete access to their funds.

Conclusion

The FDIC, acting in its several capacities, has a suite of tools and powers to supervise and to work jointly with other regulators to supervise IDIs, to evaluate and price the risks that IDIs pose to the DIF, to set assessment rates and collect deposit insurance assessments, to otherwise manage the DIF, and to resolve IDIs so as to maximize recoveries at the least cost to the DIF and to ensure undisrupted access to insured deposits.

As part of its on-going activities, which now also include responsibilities for resolution planning involving large and complex financial institutions, the FDIC works closely with other domestic authorities and with foreign authorities, such as foreign deposit insurers, bank supervisors, resolution authorities and central banks, to address global financial issues of importance to the United States, including its deposit insurance system, banking sector, and financial stability.

Anita van den Ende, Charles Nysten and Nikki Kersten

Decoupling Risks: The Rationale for Improving the Regulatory Treatment of Sovereign Exposures and an Impact-Analysis of the Basel Committee Discussion Document

1. Introduction

The process towards a European banking union started in 2012 when the euro area leaders stated their intent "to break the vicious circle between banks and sovereigns".[1] Important steps have been taken regarding the banking union and in strengthening the resilience and resolvability of banks, including centralizing supervision within the Single Supervisory Mechanism (SSM) and creating a Single Resolution Mechanism (SRM). Yet, the so-called bank-sovereign nexus has not been sufficiently addressed, as the current prudential framework does not adequately reflect the risks of sovereign exposures. This results in concentrated sovereign exposures with a significant home bias, which makes the financial system more vulnerable to shocks and goes against the idea of integrated European financial markets. The lack of incentive to diversify and provision for risk is particularly problematic in a banking union where risks are shared between financial institutions and ultimately Member States. In paragraph 2 of this article we discuss the rationale for a change of the regulatory treatment of sovereign exposures (RTSE) in a European context.

In paragraph 3 and 4 we provide an empirical assessment of the impact of changing the prudential treatment of sovereign exposures, using data from the EBA 2018 Transparency Exercise from 128 EU27 banks. We show the impact on EU27 banks of the standard approach from the Capital Requirements Regulation (CRR) as well as the impact of the calibration put forward in the discussion document of the Basel Committee on Banking Supervision (BCBS) in December 2017.[2] We aim to provide a more empirical perspective and shed light on the

---

1 Euro Area Summit Statement, 29th of June 2012. Link: https://www.consilium.europa.eu/media/21400/20120629-euro-area-summit-statement-en.pdf
2 Basel Committee on Banking Supervision (2017). 'Discussion paper the regulatory treatment of sovereign exposures' Link: https://www.bis.org/bcbs/publ/d425.pdf

---

Note: The article is written in a personal capacity.

https://doi.org/10.1515/9783110683073-024

impact on EU27 banks in order to bring the discussion on RTSE forward, as it creates a factual basis on which to base future policy. The calibrations we used in this article – either the Standard Approach or the calibration from the Basel discussion document – do not represent the Dutch position regarding the desirable calibration of RTSE. We consider the calibration a point to be further reviewed.

2. Completing the banking union: breaking the bank-sovereign vicious circle

2.1. Addressing the contagion channel between sovereigns and banks

Figure 1 provides a graphic illustration of the most important contagion channels in the bank-sovereign nexus. The banking union has for good reasons focused on limiting the contagion channel from banks to the sovereign. The most obvious channels through which banks can affect the sovereign are explicit and implicit guarantees. Given the size of banks and their importance to the wider economy as credit providers, banks were for a long time considered too-big-to-fail. This has rightfully been curtailed through strengthened prudential rules, centralized supervision and a resolution framework. However, risks also flow from the sovereign to banks. This contagion channel necessitates further attention, as in the regulatory framework for banks (CRR/CRD-IV) sovereign risk is not addressed. The standardized approach from the CRR allows banks to assign a zero risk-weight to sovereign exposures funded in the domestic currency. Banks that use the internal ratings-based (IRB) approach may apply the standardized approach for these exposures. Sovereign exposures are also exempted from the large exposure rules in the banking book.[3] This means that banks can run up these exposures to a very high level without having to hold capital for it.

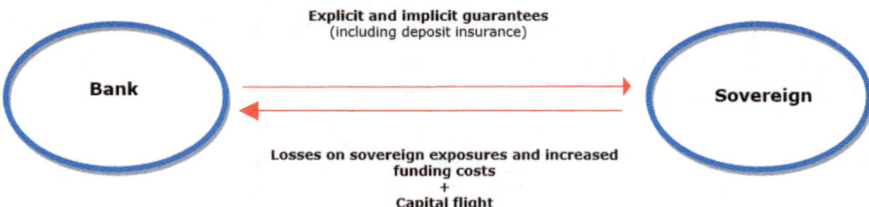

Figure 1: Contagion channels in the bank-sovereign nexus

---

3 See article 114(4) and article 400 of Regulation (EU) 575/2013.

Empirical evidence clearly shows that sovereign exposures are not risk-free. There has been a long history of sovereign distress periods in different regions. Sovereign debt crises have often coincided with banking or currency crises and are generally associated with significant loss of economic output.[4] The average haircut on sovereign holdings in case of a restructuring has been 50 % over the period 1998-2010.[5] Sovereign risk not only presents itself in the situation of a default of a sovereign; it is a continuous concern for the profitability, solvency and liquidity of a bank.

The first channel through which sovereign risk can affect banks is through losses on direct exposures of banks, such as sovereign bonds, loans or credit-default swaps (CDS). A second channel for sovereign risk to manifest itself is through the funding channel.[6] The two can negatively reinforce each other. Losses on sovereign exposures held in the trading book or losses on divestments of sovereign exposures directly affect solvency and profitability of a bank. In addition, changes in the market valuation of sovereign exposures can also hit banks in their funding position. In particular, when sovereign exposures are relatively large compared to eligible capital, a downgrade of the sovereign will increase the risk premium demanded by creditors of a bank. These higher funding costs translate into lower future profitability, which further undermines the ability to attract capital and funding. In addition, a decline in the value of sovereign collateral could require further collateralization of transactions by a bank. If the availability of high-quality (sovereign) collateral on a bank's balance sheet becomes scarce or is no longer accepted, the bank can no longer attract short-term funding which jeopardizes its liquidity position.

2.2. The need for reforming RTSE in the banking union

Risk of financial instability from sovereign exposures for banks' solvency, liquidity and profitability become more pronounced when banks have concentrated exposures to lower rated sovereigns. The banking union makes these risks more

---

4 For a discussion see Basel Committee on Banking Supervision (2017). 'Discussion paper the regulatory treatment of sovereign exposures' (see page 5-8). Link: https://www.bis.org/bcbs/publ/d425.pdf
5 Dell'Aricca et al. (2018). 'Managing the bank-sovereign nexus'. IMF Monetary and Capital Markets Department and Research Department (No. 18/16).
6 ESRB (2015). ESRB report on the regulatory treatment of sovereign exposures (see page 59). Link: https://www.esrb.europa.eu/pub/pdf/other/esrbreportregulatorytreatmentsovereignexposures032015.en.pdf

acute given the potential for destabilizing capital flows within a common currency area. An increase in sovereign risk on a bank's balance sheet incentivizes creditors to withhold funding and invest their money elsewhere (capital flight), especially when the bank has a concentrated exposure to the sovereign. Such outflows are pro-cyclical and most likely to occur when banks or sovereigns are already in a vulnerable situation. For other types of exposures, these risks are managed through the regulatory framework by risk-weights (based on the rating) and concentration limits (based on sovereign exposure relative to eligible capital). For sovereign exposures this is not the case.

While the introduction of EDIS can partially prevent the outflow of covered deposits, it does not prevent other (non-covered) creditors from demanding higher risk premiums or withdrawing their funding. As such, the issue of sovereign risk is still highly relevant in the context of EDIS. Moreover, the introduction of an EDIS would reinforce moral hazard if the prudential treatment of sovereign exposures is not addressed first, since it would introduce more risk sharing within the EU banking system. If sovereign risk is not addressed in the regulatory framework, banks have no prudential incentive to monitor or provision for sovereign risk. Since banks are not required to hold capital for sovereign exposures, this could incentivize banks to hold riskier sovereign exposures, while deposits are at the same time collectively insured under an EDIS. EDIS would thus facilitate moral hazard by individual banks to the detriment of the overall stability of the EU banking sector. Therefore, banks need to be required to provision for sovereign risk and need to be incentivized to diversify their exposures, before an EDIS is introduced. This will contribute to overall financial stability in the banking union.

During the European sovereign debt crisis, banks were largely responsible for (re)financing the government debt of their home sovereign. This resulted in an increase in the sovereign exposure. In itself this can be viewed as something positive, as the sovereign retains its creditworthiness and the exposure to government debt by the bank is limited vis-à-vis its capital. A build up sovereign exposure, however, has risks and cannot mask a structural deterioration of the credit quality of the sovereign. If this does occur, a bank with a large exposure that is insufficiently diversified will be at risk if the sovereign runs into problems.

Reforming RTSE is thus necessary to act as a counterbalance to avoid excessive build-up of government debt and provide for sufficient provisioning of capital to withstand shocks. A more risk-sensitive approach would have the added benefit of avoiding that public debt crowds out private debt on balance sheets. Given the current divergence in the associated costs of capital between public and private debt, there are clear incentives to invest in public over private debt. This can lead to a pro-cyclical tightening of credit to the private sector relative to the public sector. Furthermore, banks with already large exposures are incentivized to 'double down' and increase their exposures to the sovereign further, as the fate of the sovereign and the bank become more intertwined.

3. Approaches to address sovereign risk

In this paragraph we discuss two possible approaches to capture sovereign risk: (1) the standardized approach of the CRR and (2) the proposals made in the December 2017 discussion document from the BCBS. In paragraph 4 we show the impact of these approaches on the average Tier-1 capital positions of banks in a particular Member State. We chose to analyze the impact of the standardized approach since it is the approach to sovereign exposures that is currently in use for sovereign exposure which are not denominated in the currency of the home sovereign. We chose to analyze the options put forward in the BCBS discussion document, as the 2016 Roadmap for the Completion of the Banking Union states that the Council will consider next steps on RTSE following up on the work of the Basel Committee. In that light the BCBS discussion document could be expected to play a role in the future European policy discussion.

3.1 The standardized approach from the CRR

In the standardized approach, exposures are risk-weighted on the basis of credit ratings as illustrated in table 1. However, within the EU, banks have the discretion to apply a 0 % risk-weight to their sovereign exposures denominated in the domestic currency. The impact analysis in paragraph 4 shows the impact of the risk-weights from the standardized approach when applied to all sovereign exposures.

In the large exposure framework exposures to entities are capped at 25 % of capital. As we will show in paragraph 4, domestic sovereign exposures of banks exceed 25 % of Tier-1 capital by a wide margin. Hence, if the large exposures framework would fully apply to sovereign exposures, the concentrated holdings of debt would have to be diversified substantially. In the trading book individual exposures are allowed to be higher than the 25 % limit, though incrementally increasing capital charges are applied. The impact of the trading book concentration charges is not included in our impact analysis, since we do not have information on the distribution between the trading and the banking book, which we would need to calculate the concentration charges in the trading book. Methodologically, we would however have preferred to also include the large exposure framework to address concentrations.

Table 1: CRRRisk-weights for sovereign exposures in the standardized approach

Credit Step / External rating	AAA to AA-	A+ to A-	BBB+ to BBB-	BB+ to B-	Below B-	Unrated
Risk-weight	0 %	20 %	50 %	100 %	150 %	100 %

3.2 The BCBS discussion document

In the BCBS discussion document, credit risk is also addressed based on credit ratings by using the risk-weight of table 2. However, the risk-weights are lower than in the standardized approach and the rating categories are broader. For our calculations we use the upper bound risk-weight from the BCBS discussion document. In the annex, the impact of all the separate elements of the BCBS discussion document can be found. In addition to the risk-weight, the BCBS discussion document also introduces marginal risk-weight add-ons to mitigate concentration risk (table 3). This approach of concentration charges is different from the hard limit in the current large exposure framework. It introduces the possibility to price concentration risk on a marginal basis. Escalating marginal charges provide an incentive to diversify and thereby price in concentration risk. In our calculations, the concentration limit is applied on a consolidated level. We combine the risk-weight and the concentration charge. This combined approach is similar to the current regulatory framework in the CRR for non-sovereign exposures: risk-weights are combined with the large exposure limit in the banking book which functions as a backstop.

Table 2: BCBS risk-weights for sovereign exposures

External rating	AAA to A-	BBB+ to BBB-	Below BBB- or unrated
Domestic-currency central government exposures	0-3 %	4-6 %	7-9 %

Table 3: BCBS proposed marginal risk-weight add-on for sovereign exposures

Exposure to sovereign counterparty (% of Tier 1 capital)	< 100 %	100-150 %	150-200 %	200-250 %	250-300 %	> 300 %
Marginal risk-weight add-on	0 %	5 %	6 %	9 %	15 %	30 %

4. Results

4.1 Home bias of sovereign exposures

European banks have large exposures to the home sovereign. Table 4 shows that the (weighted) average exposure to the home sovereign of EU banks is equal to 91 % of Tier-1 capital. It also shows that the (weighted) average exposure to the home sovereign equals 47 % of the total exposure to all sovereigns.

Table 4 and all subsequent calculations in this article are based upon the consolidated bank-level data from the EBA 2018 transparency exercise.[7] This database is composed of 128 EU banks using end-2017 data on a group consolidated basis.[8] Member States that do not have banks headquartered in their territory are not in the EBA dataset.[9] The dataset includes direct sovereign exposures, such as central, regional or local governments' bonds and loans. From the 128 EU banks in the EBA dataset, 10 banks did not provide data on their

---

7 https://eba.europa.eu/risk-analysis-and-data/eu-wide-transparency-exercise/2018/results
8 For all banks data on capital and sovereign exposures from 31-12-2017 is used. For 5 banks data from 30-06-2018 is used as no data from 31-12-2017 was available. This concerns: 1) Deutscher Apotheker & Ärztebank; 2) Landeskreditbank Baden-Württemberg Forderbank; 3) Münchener Hypothekbank; 4) Banque et caisse d'epargne de l'état Luxembourg; 5; Nederlandse Waterschapsbank
9 This concerns Lithuania, Latvia and Slovakia.

sovereign exposures or capital and are therefore not incorporated in the dataset.[10] We also excluded 9 public sector promotional banks which do not hold 'covered deposits'.[11] This leaves us with 109 banks.

Table 4: Home bias as a % of Tier-1 capital (EBA, YE 2017 data)[12]

Member State	Number of banks in sample	Unweighted average domestic sovereign exposure ratio (% Tier-1 capital)	Weighted average domestic sovereign exposure ratio (% Tier-1 capital)	Weighted domestic sovereign exposure as % of total sovereign exposure
Eurozone MS				
AT	6	54 %	53 %	29 %
BE	6	95 %	122 %	27 %
CY	2	69 %	45 %	73 %

---

10 This concerns the following banks 1) Promontoria Sacher Holding (AT); 2) Raiffeisen-holding Niederösterreich-Wien registrierte Genossenschaft mit beschränkter Haftung (AT); 3) VTB Bank (AT); 4) Cooperative Bank (CYP); 5) Banco Mare Nostrum (ES); 6) Permanent TSB Holdings (IER); 7) JP Morgan Bank Luxembourg (LUX); 8) State Street Luxembourg (LUX); 9) ABLV Bank (LV); 10) Commbank Europa (MLT).

11 Public sector promotional banks are credit institutions of which a central, regional or local government directly or indirectly guarantees at least 90 % of the balance sheet. We added an additional requirement that the bank also does not take 'covered deposits'. If a bank takes covered deposits we consider it proper that a bank does take into account sovereign risk. Deposits are vulnerable to large and sudden capital flight and banks which rely on public guarantees would be particularly compromised. These criteria are based upon the current state-of-play in the negotiations of the banking package with regard to the leverage ratio. As public sector bank are dependent on the home sovereign by design and created to meet public policy objectives a different treatment of these institutions is warranted. The following institutions are therefore excluded from the dataset: 1) Kuntarahoitus Oyj (FIN), 2) BPIFrance (FRA), 3) SFIL (FRA), 4) Landeskreditbank Baden-Württemberg Forderbank (GER), 5) Landwirtschaftliche Rentenbank (GER), 6) NRW.Bank(GER), 7) BNG (NLD), 8) NWB (NLD) and 9) Kommuninvest (SWE).

12 Notes: (1) The weighted average in column 3 is calculated by dividing the home sovereign exposure of banks in a MS by total Tier-1 capital; (2) the home bias is calculated by dividing the home sovereign exposure by the total sovereign exposure of those banks; (3) Some institutions have not provided a complete breakdown of their sovereign exposures. The EBA template allows this when at least 90 % of sovereign exposures is to their 'home Member State' (see point 18 of guidelines). In calculating the sovereign exposure ratio we have used this figure of 90 % and assumed an equal distribution of the remaining 10 % among all the other EU Member States. This approach could lead to a lower concentration as 90 % is the minimum threshold and exposures could therefore be higher.

Table 4: (continued)

Member State	Number of banks in sample	Unweighted average domestic sovereign exposure ratio (% Tier-1 capital)	Weighted average domestic sovereign exposure ratio (% Tier-1 capital)	Weighted domestic sovereign exposure as % of total sovereign exposure
DE	17	175 %	123 %	53 %
EE	1	0 %	0 %	0 %
ES	12	180 %	127 %	55 %
FI	1	14 %	14 %	26 %
FR	7	214 %	122 %	56 %
GR	4	70 %	66 %	70 %
IE	4	33 %	46 %	46 %
IT	11	169 %	138 %	58 %
LU	3	28 %	44 %	33 %
MT	2	48 %	67 %	50 %
NL	4	37 %	34 %	27 %
PT	5	149 %	135 %	62 %
SI	3	101 %	98 %	52 %
Non-Euro MS				
DK	4	26 %	25 %	28 %
GB	6	53 %	43 %	27 %
HU	1	218 %	218 %	77 %
BG	1	37 %	37 %	53 %
PL	2	172 %	155 %	90 %
RO	1	227 %	227 %	90 %
SE	6	52 %	31 %	40 %
Total (weighted average)	109	118 %	90 %	47 %

4.2 Impact of implementing the standardized approach and BCBS options on EU banks

We have applied the prudential treatment outlined in paragraph 3 to the banks in the dataset. Table 5 provides an overview of the weighted average impact at the level of the Member State. The impact is presented as the impact on the banks' Tier-1 ratio, measured in percentage of the risk-weighted assets (RWA).[13]

The **second column** of table 5 shows the current weighted average Tier-1 ratio per Member State. On average this ratio is 16,00 % in the EU. Subsequently the **third column** shows the impact of applying the current calibration of the standardized approach. The standardized approach is shown as this framework currently applies to exposures not funded in the domestic currency. On average, the Tier-1 ratio would decrease by 100 basis points (from 16,00 % to 15,00 %). Since the standardized approach contains escalating risk-weights depending on the rating of the sovereign, the impact is most pronounced for banks with exposures to lower rated sovereigns. The limitation of the standardized approach is that it does not take into account concentration risk as sovereign exposures are exempted from the large exposure framework (see paragraph 3.1).

The **fourth column** shows the average combined impact of the BCBS risk-weight and the concentration charge and the **fifth column** shows the marginal impact in basis points. We consider a combination of both the BCBS risk-weight and a concentration charge similar to the current approach in the CRR that includes a risk-weight and a large exposure rule. The average marginal impact of the risk-weight and concentration charge is 28,3 basis points (from 16.00 % to 15.72 %).

The **final column** shows the average impact on the Tier-1 capital; it shows the required increase in Tier-1 capital for the current Tier-1 ratio to remain constant. On average the Tier-1 capital of EU banks would have to increase by 1.80 % for the Tier 1 ratio to remain constant. Additionally, we have looked at whether the impact would be higher for smaller banks (assets < €200 billion) or larger banks (assets > €200 billion) and found that the smaller banks on average experience a higher impact. The marginal impact is 35.5 basis points for smaller banks, compared to 26.6 basis points for larger banks. More detail on the impact of the options put forward in the BCBS discussion document can be found in the Annex.

---

13 For calculation purposes all exposures to sovereigns are treated as exposures funded in the domestic currency even where this concerns a third country to which the preferential treatment does not apply. We used ratings from S&P from August 2018.

Table 5: Impact ofstandardized approach or BCBS-options on EU banks(EBA, YE 2017 data)

	Capital ratio (T1/RWA)			Marginal impact on capital ratio (basis points)	T1 Capital change (%)
	Current Tier-1 ratio	Standardized approach	BCBS UB + Conc. charge	BCBS UB + Conc. charge	BCBS UB + Conc. Charge
Eurozone MS					
AT	14.05 %	13.20 %	13.89 %	-15.6	1.12 %
BE	19.26 %	17.25 %	18.38 %	-88.0	4.79 %
CY	13.49 %	12.54 %	13.39 %	-9.7	0.72 %
DE	16,13 %	15.42 %	15.75 %	-37.7	2.39 %
EE	14.02 %	13.95 %	14.01 %	-1.1	0.08 %
ES	13.05 %	11.74 %	12.83 %	-22.0	1.71 %
FI	20.26 %	20.06 %	20.19 %	-7.5	0.37 %
FR	14.97 %	14.45 %	14.62 %	-34.8	2.38 %
GR	17.03 %	14.89 %	16.79 %	-23.9	1.43 %
IE	19.89 %	19.09 %	19.75 %	-14.9	0.76 %
IT	14.44 %	12.72 %	14.13 %	-30.4	2.15 %
LU	18.01 %	17.23 %	17.84 %	-16.8	0.94 %
MT	15.86 %	15.29 %	15.74 %	-11.5	0.73 %
NL	17.70 %	17.27 %	17.56 %	-14.3	0.81 %
PT	13.74 %	12.00 %	13.46 %	-28.1	2.09 %
SI	18.34 %	16.82 %	18.10 %	-24.7	1.36 %
Non-Euro MS					
DK	20.11 %	19.98 %	20.00 %	-11.3	0.56 %
GB	17.76 %	16.88 %	17.56 %	-20.0	1.14 %
HU	15.21 %	12.24 %	14.65 %	-56.0	3.82 %
BG	15.87 %	15.17 %	15.78 %	-9.5	0.60 %
PL	16.34 %	14.39 %	15.98 %	-35.6	2.22 %
RO	18.37 %	15.02 %	17.63 %	-73.6	4.17 %
SE	23.65 %	23.58 %	23.51 %	-13.6	0.58 %
Total	16.00 %	15.00 %	15.72 %	-28.3	1.80 %

The calculations in this article illustrate the potential impact on banks' capital, in case of an improved regulatory treatment of sovereign exposure. The results of our analysis, in terms of the absolute impact on the Tier-1 ratio of banks, should be qualified in a number of ways. First, the calculations do not take into account any capital that banks may already hold for their sovereign exposures, as this information is not public and only accessible by the supervisor. The impact of the analysis could thus be overstated if the bank already holds capital for sovereign exposures on the basis of its internal model or on behest of its supervisor. The Basel Committee assessed that for a sample of 142 internationally active banks, the internal model on average required a risk weight of 6.5 %. This highlights the added value of doing a similar exercise by the SSM on the basis of more complete information. Second, the results are presented as weighted averages for Member States but the impact for individual banks can differ. We choose for this way of presentation because it gives a clear summary of the impact without focusing on individual banks. We weighted the impact by calculating the total capital and risk-weighted assets for all banks headquartered in an individual Member State. This approach is not without disadvantages, as outliers can drive the results. Generally, one can say that Member States with a higher share of smaller banks vis-à-vis the total size of the banking sector are more likely to have on average a higher impact. Third, it should be noted that in some Member States banks already have on average higher Tier-1 ratios and would thus be in a better position to absorb additional requirements. Fourth, the dataset only includes direct exposures on a consolidated bank level. We can thus not indicate what the impact would be on local subsidiaries, as we lack the supervisory data. Lastly, the impact of reforming RTSE on the functioning of sovereign bond markets is an open empirical question that is also a function of the calibration. On the one hand, the institution of a capital requirement would make sovereign bonds less privileged versus other financial instruments. On the other hand, regulation in line with the standard approach or BCBS discussion document would stimulate diversification, which could increase demand from investors outside the home Member State. An appropriate transition period could be considered to ensure a smooth transition.

5. Conclusion

This article argues that the dimension of sovereign risk is insufficiently addressed in the current regulatory framework, and therefore an appropriate weighting of credit- and concentration risk is desirable in its own right. However, it is particularly salient in the banking union where common arrangements for addressing and sharing risk are created, such as supervision and resolution, and where capital is mobile in a common regulatory area. For new elements of risk sharing – such as an EDIS – to be viable, the treatment of sovereign risk needs to be addressed. By reforming RTSE, banks are stimulated to diversify and hold adequate capital for sovereign holdings, which will make them less vulnerable to instances of sovereign distress. An incentive to diversify sovereign holdings should also mitigate any impact on the functioning of sovereign debt markets. We consider reforming RTSE a vital element in the overall framework for a more stable currency union and more financial stability in the EU. The Roadmap for Completion of the Banking Union from 2016 also recognizes that further steps have to be taken to reduce the risks within the financial sector. However, action on RTSE has not been forthcoming while other legislative proposals, for example on EDIS, have been put forward and are discussed.

With this article we contribute to the debate on RTSE by demonstrating that changing the prudential treatment of sovereign exposures is a desirable, necessary and feasible policy option. The combined effect of the upper bound BCBS risk-weight and concentration charge would not be more than several tens of basis points for the majority of Member States. For three of the EU Member States the combined impact is 40 basis points or higher. This calculated impact is also likely to be an overestimation, as discussed in paragraph 4.2. Whether the BCBS options provide for sufficient risk-reduction is a point that merits further attention.

Annex

Table 6: Impact of standardized approach or BCBS options on EU banks

	Capital ratio (T1/RWA)						Marginal impact on capital ratio (basis points)	T1 Capital change (%)
	Current ratio	Standardized approach	BCBS lower bound (LB)	BCBS upper bound (UB)	BCBS Conc. charge	BCBS UB + Conc. charge	BCBS UB + Conc. charge	BCBS UB + Conc. Charge
Eurozone MS								
AT	14.05 %	13.20 %	13.99 %	13.90 %	14.05 %	13.89 %	-15.6	1.12 %
BE	19.26 %	17.25 %	19.11 %	18.66 %	18.95 %	18.38 %	-88.0	4.79 %
CY	13.49 %	12.54 %	13.42 %	13.39 %	13.49 %	13.39 %	-9.7	0.72 %
DE	16.13 %	15.42 %	16.08 %	15.91 %	15.96 %	15.75 %	-37.7	2.39 %
EE	14.02 %	13.95 %	14.02 %	14.01 %	14.02 %	14.01 %	-1.1	0.08 %
ES	13.05 %	11.74 %	12.97 %	12.87 %	13.00 %	12.83 %	-22.0	1.71 %
FI	20.26 %	20.06 %	20.25 %	20.19 %	20.26 %	20.19 %	-7.5	0.37 %
FR	14.97 %	14.45 %	14.94 %	14.80 %	14.79 %	14.62 %	-34.8	2.38 %
GR	17.03 %	14.89 %	16.86 %	16.80 %	17.01 %	16.79 %	-23.9	1.43 %
IE	19.89 %	19.09 %	19.86 %	19.75 %	19.89 %	19.75 %	-14.9	0.76 %
IT	14.44 %	12.72 %	14.29 %	14.18 %	14.38 %	14.13 %	-30.4	2.15 %
LU	18.01 %	17.23 %	17.96 %	17.84 %	18.01 %	17.84 %	-16.8	0.94 %
MT	15.86 %	15.29 %	15.84 %	15.74 %	15.86 %	15.74 %	-11.5	0.73 %
NL	17.70 %	17.27 %	17.67 %	17.56 %	17.70 %	17.56 %	-14.3	0.81 %
PT	13.74 %	12.00 %	13.59 %	13.51 %	13.69 %	13.46 %	-28.1	2.09 %
SI	18.34 %	16.82 %	20.10 %	18.10 %	18.34 %	18.10 %	-24.7	1.36 %
Non-Euro MS								
DK	20.11 %	19.98 %	20.10 %	20.00 %	20.11 %	20.00 %	-11.3	0.56 %
GB	17.76 %	16.88 %	17.71 %	17.57 %	17.76 %	17.56 %	-20.0	1.14 %
HU	15.21 %	12.40 %	14.93 %	14.81 %	15.05 %	14.65 %	-56.0	3.82 %

Table 6: (continued)

	Current ratio	Standardized approach	BCBS lower bound (LB)	BCBS upper bound (UB)	BCBS Conc. charge	BCBS UB + Conc. charge	BCBS UB + Conc. charge	BCBS UB + Conc. Charge
	Capital ratio (T1/RWA)						Marginal impact on capital ratio (basis points)	T1 Capital change (%)
BG	15.87 %	15.17 %	15.82 %	15.78 %	15.87 %	15.78 %	-9.5	0.60 %
PL	16.34 %	14.39 %	17.48 %	16.07 %	16.25 %	15.98 %	-35.6	2.22 %
RO	18.37 %	15.02 %	16.17 %	17.88 %	18.10 %	17.63 %	-73.6	4.17 %
SE	23.65 %	23.58 %	23.64 %	23.51 %	23.64 %	23.51 %	-13.6	0.58 %
Total	**16.00 %**	**15.00 %**	**15.93 %**	**15.80 %**	**15.92 %**	**15.72 %**	**-28.3**	**1.80 %**

Klaus Adam, Thiess Büttner, Joachim Hennrichs, Jan P. Krahnen and Jörg Rocholl

Rethinking Europe's Deposit Guarantee Scheme

The debate on a European deposit guarantee should not be limited to discussing whether or not to have it, but also how to design it.[1]

Today's debate on a European deposit guarantee scheme one-sidedly emphasizes the dangers of further mutualization of risks. Wisely designed, however, a European deposit insurance can help containing the costs associated with risk mutualization, potentially even reducing risk.

Today, all EU countries are required to create a scheme that is capable of safeguarding bank deposits up to an amount of 100,000 euros per customer and bank. Hitherto, deposit insurance has been organized on a national basis: If there is a financial crisis in one country, the domestic deposit guarantee will intervene. If the funding requirements exceed fund liquidity, the respective country's government may be forced to provide further funds.

Creating a European deposit guarantee has been on the European policy agenda for several years. Already in 2015, the five Presidents of the European Commission, Eurogroup, Euro Summit, European Parliament and European Central Bank (ECB), in their first joint report, called for a Europe-wide deposit guarantee scheme as an important step towards completing the Economic and Monetary Union.

In Germany, this claim largely met resistance, or was rejected outright. Critics have emphasized in particular that a European deposit guarantee scheme would contribute to the mutualization of bank liabilities in the euro area. The criticism is that southern European countries could, for example, access the guarantee funds set up in Germany to protect savers.

However, although the ultimate liability for a deposit insurance promise *de-jure* currently lies with institutions within the country of domicile, there is an *implicit* risk-sharing effective between individual countries in the Monetary Union. This problem became apparent, for example, during the Greek financial crisis in 2011. At that time, Eurozone governments provided Greece with financial

---

1 This text has been published in the Frankfurter Allgemeine Zeitung (FAZ) on October 16. 2019 (in German). Andreas Dombret and Patrick Kennadjian, the editors, have invited us to include an English version of the original text in their book, as it adds to its content. Please note that our concept of a European deposit re-insurance scheme has been published first-time in the FAZ and had not been presented or discussed on the conference to which this book is devoted to.

https://doi.org/10.1515/9783110683073-025

assistance. This happened despite the explicit no-bailout clause in the EU treaty. The rescue was motivated by substantial amounts of Greek government debt on the balance sheet of some major banks domiciled in "donor" countries. A default, so it was believed, would jeopardize the solvency of these banks and may have turned out to be even more expensive than a direct rescue of the borrower country, Greece.

These events have shown in an exemplary way that, at the national level, stability of public finances and of banks are linked with the potential to aggravate a financial crisis. In the case of major dislocations, state funds will be needed in order to stabilize banks, and/or the deposit scheme. Since this requires the mobilization of significant resources in the short term, market participants may consequently have doubts about the sustainability of the state's fiscal policy. As a consequence, prices of government bonds issued by this country will drop, causing losses in bank trading books and increasing the pressure on financial institutions. This self-reinforcing, vicious cycle can also have a destabilizing effect on countries with seemingly sound fiscal policies so that financial assistance is needed.

Meanwhile, the European Stability Mechanism (ESM) has come into existence, which is a special intergovernmental mutual fund providing liquidity with conditions to states in the event of a crisis. This is an improvement compared to the situation in 2011, as today an intervention can be based on clear rules and conditions. However, this fund is backed by the member countries jointly, such that the risk-sharing continues through the ESM. Moreover, in the event of a crisis, it may also be questioned whether the available funds do really suffice.

Note that risks are transferred among countries not only through financial assistance by the ESM but also through interventions by the ECB. While a direct risk-sharing among countries within the European System of Central Banks (ESCB) via Emergency Liquidity Assistance (ELA) credit lines has been ruled out in principle, the programs relying on buying government bonds and other securities do, in fact, share the risk of sovereign defaults.

Thus, despite national responsibility for deposit insurance, there is an implicit sharing of risk in the current system, leading to a redistribution of losses among participating countries in a financial crisis. This is particularly problematic from a regulatory point of view. To the extent that investors, national financial regulators, and governments can assume that existing risks will be redistributed to the disadvantage of other countries in a crisis, the willingness to effectively prevent and reduce those very risks decreases. Thus, implicit risk sharing will ultimately undermine the efficiency and performance of the European financial system.

A European deposit guarantee scheme can replace the existing implicit risk-sharing with an explicit contractual commitment. Properly designed, it would reduce the risk tolerance of banks and national guarantee institutions before a loss occurs. Moreover, the liability promise of a deposit re-insurance scheme could be formulated as a conditional promise, depending upon some restrictions pertaining to a bank's exposures. Also, the premium that an insured bank would pay, can be sensitive to those risk characteristics. In fact, it can be made fair, i.e. risk-adequate, by actuarial standards. A European deposit guarantee could then influence the banks' risk behavior and reduce actual loss expectation.

Against the background of significant variation in the composition of bank portfolios across countries, e.g. the share of own national government bonds in total bank debt, or the volume of non-performing loans, the importance of charging risk-adequate premiums is evident. Modern methods of risk measurement allow premiums to be set according to an individual, case-specific risk profile. As a result, a high default risk translates into an equally high deposit insurance premium.

Just like life insurers who cover people with different mortality probabilities without necessarily causing a redistributional side-effect, a proper European deposit insurance would be based on the expected default risk and the associated loss given default, thus averting redistribution effects.

Of course, determinants of bank default risk are to some extent under the control of policy makers. Examples include national insolvency laws or a country's fiscal stance. For that reason, the risk-adequate premiums will need to be country-specific, depending on loan portfolio composition, and on government holdings on bank balance sheets.

Nevertheless, based on past experience, it will be difficult to assess country-specific risks beyond doubt. Especially in economically difficult times, the danger of a political intervention affecting premium setting for deposit insurance has to be taken seriously. A European deposit guarantee, therefore, has to hard-wire risk-adequate premium setting in their statutes. This also includes a monitoring role vis-à-vis national deposit insurers, and a harmonization of their risk models.

So what should such a European scheme ideally look like? Given the institutional structure of the European Union, it should follow a subsidiarity principle in line with established regulatory policy ideas and align liability and decision-making. That is why we are proposing a European deposit *re*-insurance, rather than a plain-vanilla, all-encompassing deposit insurance. It would complement rather than replace the existing national guarantee schemes. The national systems continue to secure deposits in domestic banks only.

The European deposit reinsurance would be a second stage of protection at the European level, based on the insurance principle, analogous to reinsurance in property insurance. It covers the claims of individual national deposit insurance schemes from a defined amount of damage up to a defined maximum amount, say from 50.000 to 100.000 Euro – which is the maximum statutorily guaranteed deposit. Importantly, the European reinsurance should perform a monitoring function vis-à-vis national deposit insurers, encompassing the necessary information and intervention rights.

The proposed two layered deposit insurance scheme allows it to compensate for differences in the risk levels between national deposit insurers (layer one) by an adequate pricing of the reinsurance services on layer two. Deposit reinsurance, through its premium scheme, provides clear incentives for risk reduction on the part of the national deposit insurers. The European deposit reinsurance will be more effective, if a strong role as supervisor is assigned to it from the beginning. This will allow the reinsurance entity to oversee risk management practice, including risk measurement and premium setting at the national level. It will be relevant here, like in other parts of the European supervisory regime, to minimize the possibility of national politicians to intervene in the process, once its rules are properly laid out.

Ultimately, within the framework of European deposit reinsurance, each banking institution could decide for itself whether it wants to participate in the reinsurance system despite possibly high premiums or whether it wants to reduce positions with a higher risk and only enter the system at a later date. To be effective, the choices made by banks have to be disclosed to bank clients, allowing them to transfer accounts from banks with lower insurance standards to competing institutions offering higher standards.

A properly designed European deposit reinsurance system is therefore by no means another step towards increased mutualization of risks. On the contrary, it can serve to even reduce the existing implicit risk-sharing. From an economic perspective, this weighs more heavily than the fact of a legally agreed liability within the framework of reinsurance. By actively limiting risks, an appropriately structured European deposit reinsurance system can increase the stability and efficiency of the European financial system in a way that is redistribution-neutral. Obviously, our re-insurance scheme proposal presupposes the willingness of European governments to allow for a reflection of country-specific risks in deposit insurance premiums – and thus to deviate from the existing regulatory practice of classifying government bonds as being risk-free by definition.

German Federal Ministry of Finance – non-paper
Position paper on the goals of the banking union

What do we want?

We want a banking union that guarantees financial stability, protects the tax-payer and allows for the greatest possible degree of European market integration while also addressing the risks inherent in a more closely integrated banking union.

Deepening market integration in the area of banking services makes for a European single market that is stronger overall, which in turn lays the foundation for greater prosperity in all Member States. Improving the conditions for the use of capital and liquidity by cross-border banks helps overcome market fragmentation where it still exists. This makes a key contribution to boosting the profitability of European banks and to reducing competitive disadvantages at the international level.

From a macro-economic perspective, overcoming the existing market fragmentation has two advantages: on the one hand, European companies and consumers gain access to financing and other banking services that are better, more efficient and cheaper. This increases Europe's growth potential. On the other hand, an increase in cross-border investments and business activities would mitigate the risks of the sovereign-bank nexus and would result in improved, Europe-wide responsiveness to economic cycles. In the Anglo-American sphere, this question is being discussed as part of a debate on private risk sharing.

Both of the above-named effects were seen in the U.S. when the banking market there was completed from the 1980s and 90s onwards. The possibility of reducing Europe's competitive disadvantage compared to the U.S. clearly illustrates the importance of completing the European banking union.

Finalising the overarching structure of the banking union also requires a European deposit insurance scheme. It is necessary to first reduce and then continuously review the risks, which also determine the likelihood of recourse to the European deposit insurance scheme. This requires a consistent, effective supervisory regime and crisis management, which should be based on harmonised bank insolvency legislation and on the further development of a European resolution regime, which should serve as the foundation for a deeper integration of cross-border EU banking groups. We also need adequate regulation for sover-

Note: Written by a team of German Federal Ministry of Finance officials, including Levin Holle.

https://doi.org/10.1515/9783110683073-026

eign bonds. Finally, we should keep working consistently to reduce non-performing loans on bank balance sheets.

However, a complete banking union also opens up arbitrage opportunities, which risks placing a particularly heavy burden on the Member States, which make a big contribution to integration. The Member States, as business locations, diverge not only in terms of deposit insurance, but also, for example, in terms of tax law, which provides for different corporate tax bases in the EU and for differences in the treatment of the deductibility of contributions to the Single Resolution Fund (bank levies).

Such differences would enable some Member States not only to profit from the solidarity of all Member States via a European deposit insurance scheme, but also to use more advantageous tax rules to position themselves as attractive locations for banks – at the expense of other Member States. A banking union that is based on the fair balance of interests must also eliminate such arbitrage opportunities.

What needs to be done?

1. A more efficient supervisory regime and crisis management

The existing regime whereby the Single Resolution Board (SRB) generally functions as the central resolution authority only (a) for significant institutions and (b) to safeguard the public interest has already proven that it works in practice. However, the notion of a European single resolution scheme is undermined in cases where resolution is not found to be in the public interest and where national funds are then used to support small banks or in cases where banks and creditors benefit more from national insolvency proceedings than from a bail-in. It is here that the U. S. model provides a good example of the ways in which supervisory and resolution regimes can be strengthened and improved. The strength of the Federal Deposit Insurance Corporation (FDIC) results in no small part from the fact that it can draw on a foundation of largely harmonised insolvency and resolution legislation as well as the fact that it has sufficient powers to take action in a timely, decisive fashion (preventing forbearance) and to ensure that banks that are not viable are wound down.

a) Supervision and resolution of banks:

Instruments which have so far been available only for the resolution of systemically important banks (e.g. for the transfer of the deposit-taking business or for the establishment of a bridge bank) should also be made available to smaller banks that are not systemically important. The SRB should be involved where there is a risk of distortions of competition on the single market. In light of the Federal Constitutional Court's recent judgements, it might also be feasible to give the SRB the power to assume responsibility for direct supervision as a pre-emptive measure.

At the same time, it must be ensured that the European Single Resolution Fund (SRF) and Common Backstop cannot be accessed by institutions that have no systemic importance. Rather, the least cost principle must apply: in individual cases where financing resolution measures costs less than compensation payments to depositors, there needs to be the possibility of financing resolution measures for such institutions by using the funds intended for the deposit insurance scheme. The SRB could be assigned responsibility for taking the decision as to whether, based on cost-effectiveness considerations, alternative funds should be used for depositor compensation.

b) European legislation on bank insolvency:
There is very little harmonisation within the EU regarding the main national insolvency rules that apply to banks. So far, only the resolution of systemically important banks has been harmonised; for big banks, resolution has been centralised via the SRB. Smaller banks are generally liquidated in national insolvency proceedings. In contrast, systemically important banks are not liquidated in resolution proceedings. Rather, the goal is to continue the systemically important business via a recapitalisation that is primarily funded by the bank's owners and private financiers.

The lack of harmonisation in this area complicates the resolution of banks with cross-border operations. This becomes particularly problematic when banks and creditors are better placed in proceedings under national insolvency legislation than they would be with a resolution in accordance with the Bank Recovery and Resolution Directive. When this happens, national insolvency legislation undercuts the provisions that are tailored to fit the specific set of interests at play when a bank is wound down.

What is more, the SRB also needs to take into account 19 different national insolvency regimes when performing a resolution due to the no-creditor-worse-off principle, which stipulates that no creditor may incur greater losses as a result of a resolution than they would have in national insolvency proceedings. This is complex, increases legal and compensation risks and results in groups of creditors receiving different treatment despite being fundamentally the same.

For this reason, we need a single European set of laws on bank insolvency.

c) Deeper integration of EU banking groups:

Host countries, i.e. countries whose banking sectors are dominated by the subsidiaries of foreign banks, fear that a crisis in the parent company could result in a liquidity drain and thus impact the host country's real economy. In order to protect themselves in case the subsidiary (which is resident in the host country) fails, these countries advocate maintaining the status quo, whereby capital and liquidity requirements as well as the minimum requirements for own funds and eligible liabilities (MREL) must be met on an individual basis for the event of a resolution, and where limits on large exposures also apply within the same group ("ringfencing").

Home countries, i.e. Member States where the parent companies are resident, believe that such national ringfencing requirements prevent the parent companies from efficiently managing their capital and liquidity. Home countries therefore strive for the fully flexible deployment of capital and liquidity within cross-border corporations by having provisions whereby only the group as a whole would be obliged to meet the capital and liquidity requirements and MREL. If market integration is to progress, we need to strike an appropriate balance between the interests of both the host and home countries.

The German banking sector has its own set of specificities. It continues to be characterised by a large number of small banks with a regional outlook. However, the share of foreign subsidiaries in the German banking sector has been rising steadily (and is likely to continue to do so). At 5 %, this share is roughly twice as high as the total liabilities of German banks' foreign subsidiaries in all EU Member States. To build business models that are sustainable in the long term, German banks will need to further expand in other EU countries. A stronger banking union will also facilitate this.

A forward-looking solution needs to take into account host countries' interests while also achieving the greatest possible degree of integration. One approach would be to combine a maximum of flexibility for a group-wide deployment of funds within the European banking union with comprehensive safeguards for the host countries in the event of a crisis. In ordinary times, capital and liquidity could be allocated flexibly within the group throughout the European banking union. Only in the event of a crisis would capital and liquidity be made available to the subsidiaries in the host countries, regardless of where they were previously held in the group. This would occur via a case-by-case decision based on a waterfall payment scheme within the group that would be set out by a legal text. Such provisions would provide the ECB and the SRB with guidelines on how available funds should be distributed within the group in the event of a crisis, which could also be of decisive importance for the distribution of SRF funds.

Where necessary, special provisions for banks under company law should also be harmonised so as to complement or adjust to the supervisory changes. Such a harmonisation would remove any barriers that might currently exist under company law and that could hinder the free flow of liquidity within the ordinary course of business or hamper the cross-border distribution of funds by the ECB/ SRB in the event of a crisis.

One option would be to create a European legal form for banks or to further develop the European Company (SE), all the while respecting participation rights.

2. Further reduction of risks

a) "Safe portfolio"/regulatory treatment of sovereign bonds:

The financial crisis and the sovereign debt crisis showed that sovereign bonds are not a risk-free investment. Currently, however, banks do not need to assign an appropriate risk-based valuation to sovereign debt that they hold (zero-risk weighting); neither do regulatory restrictions on concentration exist (limits on large exposures). Banks therefore hold large amounts of sovereign bonds on their balance sheets without the corresponding risk provisioning. In addition, banks mainly hold sovereign bonds issued by their home country ("home bias"). During a crisis, this sovereign-bank nexus presents a large risk to financial stability in the monetary union.

The introduction of risk-based concentration charges would create incentives to reduce home bias and spread risks with regard to sovereign bonds. In this case, banks would also have to make provisions for risks arising from sovereign debt.

This type of model would be based on the introduction of base risk weighting for different qualities of loans, measured using ratings, for example. This would include a certain allowance for sovereign debt, which would be exempt of the capital, requirements irrespective of the rating (e.g. up to a concentration of 33% of the Tier 1 capital of the individual bank). This type of exemption for a "base concentration" would reflect the need for banks to maintain, due to regulatory requirements and for refinancing purposes within the central bank system, a certain quantity of safe, liquid assets, which generally consist of sovereign bonds.

The size of the degree of concentration of sovereign debt issued by a single country on banks' balance sheets could then be addressed using a concentration factor, which would increase with increasing concentration. Multiplying the concentration factor by the base risk weighting would give the risk-based concentration charges, based on the rating and the degree of concentration. Hence, the lower the quality of the loan and the higher the concentration of the liabilities from individual countries or borrower units on the bank's balance sheets, the higher the applicable risk-based concentration charge would be.

This type of model can be calibrated in such a way that it would not involve excessively large additional capital requirements for Eurozone banks in comparison with the status quo. Nevertheless, in this case there would already be an incentive for banks to more intensively diversify their sovereign bonds portfolios and hence function better as a buffer in crisis situations. In addition, challenges resulting from the transition could be mitigated by having an appropriate phase-in period (5 to 7 years).

In this way, banks in all countries would build up a "safe portfolio" of sovereign bonds over time. This would also help countries with weaker credit ratings.

b) Reduction of non-performing loans:

The reduction of non-performing loans (NPLs) on banks' balance sheets that was agreed as part of the banking package must be implemented consistently. An NPL ratio of 5 % gross / 2.5 % net should be reached in all Member States.

c) Money laundering:

In addition to the systematic implementation of the Anti-Money Laundering Action Plan, measures should also be taken – based on a thorough "post mortem" analysis of the most recent cases – to further improve the combating of money laundering and terrorist financing across the EU.

3. European deposit insurance scheme

Ultimately, a European deposit insurance scheme will also become realistic within the framework of a stronger overall banking union architecture. The aim of such a scheme is to stabilise the financial system by counteracting bank runs caused by depositors losing confidence in the capacity of the national banking system. In the course of deeper market integration, the varying capacities of the national deposit guarantee schemes (NDGSs) could be balanced out within a European reinsurance scheme. To this end – once the target level set out in the EU Deposit Guarantee Schemes Directive has been achieved, and on the basis of an intergovernmental agreement – resources would be accumulated in a European deposit insurance fund in addition to the NDGS resources. The European deposit insurance fund, which would have national compartments and be administered by the SRB, could provide liquidity to the NDGSs when needed, in the form of repayable loans. Furthermore, it must also be ensured that the target level for the NDGSs and also the contributions from banks continue to be increased in line with the overall level of deposits, in order to counteract an exponential attraction of deposits at the cost of other banking sectors.

In order to ensure that NDGSs in Member States with small banking sectors (which therefore have limited possibilities for repaying liquidity loans) can also access sufficient resources, a reinsurance model could also be considered during the steady state of the banking union (in other words in a second phase, once all the other elements of the banking union have been implemented). The reinsurance model could involve, in addition to liquidity provision, a – limited – loss-bearing component. In this way, more resources could be provided to the NDGS than in the case of a model which involves a complete repayment of the loan.

In order to avoid creating the wrong incentives (shifting of liability to the European level), national responsibility must however continue to be a central element. Hence it would only be possible to call on the European reinsurance scheme once national resources had been exhausted[1]. The European contribution would also be capped; a need for resources that exceeded this contribution would have to be covered by the Member State in question.

If the Member State did not have sufficient capacity, then the European Stability Mechanism (ESM) could also support the Member State with normal programme resources, on the basis of a case-specific decision and with suitable requirements (conditionality), as is standard practice in such cases.

4. Prevention of arbitrage

Key factors leading to distortion of competition among Member States can be found in the area of tax law. Hence, the common corporate tax base (CCTB) represents an important step in the fight against profit shifting within the EU, which is aimed exclusively at minimising tax payments. For this reason, Germany, working together with France, is pushing for the CCTB, so that Europe will have fair conditions for the taxation of companies. In particular, the CCTB would create a level playing field within the EU and therefore also enhance the competitiveness of the European single market as a whole. In addition, Germany and France are also pushing for a minimum effective tax. This is an attempt to end the race to the bottom in the area of tax rates, which is detrimental to Member States'

---

1 The German deposit guarantee schemes could fulfil this requirement by means of an equalisation mechanism among each other.

budgets. This type of minimum tax would also lead to more tax equity with regard to the differences between the traditional and digital economies.

Outside of this discussion, further progress with the banking union cannot be allowed to lead to a situation where competition-distorting tax arrangements, especially for profit-shifting purposes, continue to be promoted. This involves arbitrage possibilities with regard to tax rates as well as tax bases. For this reason, we absolutely need uniform taxation of banks within the EU.

In the intergovernmental agreement on the Single Resolution Fund, the Member States expressed their wish to achieve a level playing field with regard to the tax treatment of bank levies. This should now be implemented.

Next steps

1. There is already a Commission proposal on EDIS that has been discussed in detail. In the areas of crisis management (home/host) and sovereign bond regulation, more technical work is needed:
- Expert groups have been tasked with writing up in-depth analyses by December 2019. Their reports will contain:
  a) proposals to (i) fine-tune and strengthen the supervisory regime and crisis management, and (ii) create a single market for banking services, including safeguards for hosts (this includes special company law rules for banks, if necessary as an accompaniment to adjustments in supervisory law).
  b) calibration models for the adequate regulation of sovereign bonds.
     The Commission should then propose rules based on these in-depth expert reports.
- The Commission should also propose bank insolvency legislation that can then be discussed in the Council. This needs to happen soon.
- The Commission could also submit a new proposal for a European deposit reinsurance scheme.

2. The Commission should propose legislation ensuring the uniform taxation of banks. In addition, we expect the Council to engage in deliberations on a common corporate tax base (CCTB) and a minimum tax. These deliberations must be results-oriented and aimed at advancing international negotiations, and they should lead to well-designed Commission proposals.
- Furthermore, member states should make voluntary commitments to standardise their tax treatment of bank levies.